# A History of Drink and the English, 1500–2000

This book is an introduction to the history of alcoholic drink in England from the end of the Middle Ages to the present day. Treating the subject thematically, it covers who drank, what they drank, how much, who produced and sold drink, the places where it was enjoyed and the meanings which drinking had for people. It also looks at the varied opposition to drinking and the ways in which it has been regulated and policed.

As a social and cultural history, it examines the place of drink in society and how social developments have affected its history and what it meant to individuals and groups as a cultural practice. Covering an extended period in time, this book takes in the important changes brought about by the Reformation and the processes of industrialization and urbanization. This volume also focuses on drink in relation to class and gender and the importance of global developments, along with the significance of regional and local difference. Whilst a work of history, it draws upon the insights of a range of other disciplines which have together advanced our understanding of alcohol. The focus is England, but it acknowledges the importance of comparison with the experience of other countries in furthering our understanding of England's particular experience.

This book argues for the centrality of drink in English society throughout the period under consideration, whilst emphasizing the ways in which its use, abuse and how they have been experienced and perceived have changed at different historical moments. It is the first scholarly work which covers the history of drink in England in all its aspects over such an extended period of time. Written in a lively and approachable style, this book is suitable for those who study social and cultural history, as well as those with an interest in the history of drink in England.

**Paul Jennings** is a lecturer in History at the University of Bradford, UK. He has a special interest in the history of drink and drinking places, on which he has taught, written and broadcast for thirty years.

# Perspectives in Economic and Social History
Series editors: Andrew August
                Jari Eloranta

1  **Migrants and Urban Change**
   Newcomers to Antwerp, 1760–1860
   *Anne Winter*

2  **Female Entrepreneurs in Nineteenth-Century Russia**
   *Galina Ulianova*

3  **Barriers to Competition**
   The Evolution of the Debate
   *Ana Rosado Cubero*

4  **Rural Unwed Mothers**
   An American experience, 1870–1950
   *Mazie Hough*

5  **English Catholics and the Education of the Poor, 1847–1902**
   *Eric G. Tenbus*

6  **The World of Carolus Clusius**
   Natural history in the making, 1550–1610
   *Florike Egmond*

7  **The Determinants of Entrepreneurship**
   Leadership, culture, institutions
   *Edited by José L. García-Ruiz and Pier Angelo Toninelli*

8  **London Clerical Workers, 1880–1914**
   Development of the labour market
   *Michael Heller*

9  **The Decline of Jute**
   Managing industrial change
   *Jim Tomlinson, Carlo Morelli and Valerie Wright*

10 **Mining and the State in Brazilian Development**
   *Gail D. Triner*

11 **Global Trade and Commercial Networks**
   Eighteenth-century diamond merchants
   *Tijl Vanneste*

12 **The Clothing Trade in Provincial England, 1800–1850**
   *Alison Toplis*

13 **Sex in Japan's Globalization, 1870–1930**
   Prostitutes, emigration and nation building
   *Bill Mihalopoulos*

14 **Financing India's Imperial Railways, 1875–1914**
   *Stuart Sweeney*

15 **Energy, Trade and Finance in Asia**
   A political and economic analysis
   *Justin Dargin and Tai Wei Lim*

16 **Violence and Racism in Football**
   Politics and cultural conflict in British society, 1968–1998
   *Brett Bebber*

17  **The Economies of Latin America**
    New cliometric data
    *Edited by César Yáñez and Albert Carreras*

18  **Meat, Commerce and the City**
    The London food market, 1800–1855
    *Robyn S. Metcalfe*

19  **Merchant Colonies in the Early Modern Period**
    *Edited by Victor N. Zakharov, Gelina Harlaftis and Olga Katsiardi-Hering*

20  **Markets and Growth in Early Modern Europe**
    *Victoria N. Bateman*

21  **Welfare and Old Age in Europe and North America**
    The development of social insurance
    *Edited by Bernard Harris*

22  **Female Economic Strategies in the Modern World**
    *Edited by Beatrice Moring*

23  **Crime and Community in Reformation Scotland**
    Negotiating power in a burgh society
    *J. R. D. Falconer*

24  **Policing Prostitution, 1856–1886**
    Deviance, surveillance and morality
    *Catherine Lee*

25  **Narratives of Drunkenness**
    Belgium, 1830–1914
    *An Vleugels*

26  **Respectability and the London Poor, 1780–1870**
    The value of virtue
    *Lynn MacKay*

27  **Residential Institutions in Britain, 1725–1970**
    Inmates and environments
    *Edited by Jane Hamlett, Lesley Hoskins and Rebecca Preston*

28  **Conflict, Commerce and Franco-Scottish Relations, 1560–1713**
    *Siobhan Talbott*

29  **Drink in the Eighteenth and Nineteenth Centuries**
    *Edited by Susanne Schmid and Barbara Schmidt-Haberkamp*

30  **Merchants and Profit in the Age of Commerce, 1680–1830**
    *Edited by Pierre Gervais, Yannick Lemarchand and Dominique Margairaz*

31  **Jewish Immigrants in London, 1880–1939**
    *Susan L. Tananbaum*

32  **Commercial Networks and European Cities, 1400–1800**
    *Edited by Andrea Caracausi and Christof Jeggle*

33  **A Global Conceptual History of Asia, 1860–1940**
    *Edited by Hagen Schulz-Forberg*

34  **Consuls and the Institutions of Global Capitalism, 1783–1914**
    *Ferry de Goey*

35  **Merchant Communities in Asia, 1600–1980**
    *Lin Yu-ju and Madeleine Zelin*

36  **Insanity and the Lunatic Asylum in the Nineteenth Century**
    *Edited by Thomas Knowles and Serena Trowbridge*

37  **Philanthropy and the Funding of the Church of England, 1856–1914**
    *Sarah Flew*

38  **Merchants and Trading in the Sixteenth Century**
    The golden age of Antwerp
    *Jeroen Puttevils*

39 **Early Modern Trading Networks in Europe**
Cooperation and the case of Simon Ruiz
*Ana Sofia Ribeiro*

40 **Prostitution and Social Control in Eighteenth-Century Ports**
*Marion Pluskota*

41 **Labour and Living Standards in Pre-Colonial West Africa**
The case of the gold coast
*Klas Rönnbäck*

42 **Development Economics in the Twenty-First Century**
*Edited by Davide Gualerzi and Claudia Sunna*

43 **Sanitation in Urban Britain, 1560–1700**
*Leona Jayne Skelton*

44 **A History of Drink and the English, 1500–2000**
*Paul Jennings*

**Forthcoming**

**Franco Modigliani and Keynesian Economics**
Theory, facts and policy
*Antonella Rancan*

**Rural–Urban Relationships in the Nineteenth Century**
Uneasy neighbours?
*Edited by Mary Hammond and Barry Sloan*

**Merchants and Trade Networks in the Atlantic and the Mediterranean, 1550–1800**
Connectors of commercial maritime systems
*Edited by Manuel Herrero Sánchez and Klemens Kaps*

**Workers, Unions and Payment in Kind**
The fight for real wages in Britain, 1820–1986
*Christopher Frank*

**A History of Professional Economists and Policymaking in the United States**
Irrelevant genius
*Jonathan S. Franklin*

# A History of Drink and the English, 1500–2000

Paul Jennings

Routledge
Taylor & Francis Group
LONDON AND NEW YORK

First published 2016
by Routledge
2 Park Square, Milton Park, Abingdon, Oxon OX14 4RN

and by Routledge
711 Third Avenue, New York, NY 10017

First issued in paperback 2017

*Routledge is an imprint of the Taylor & Francis Group, an informa business*

© 2016 Paul Jennings

The right of Paul Jennings to be identified as author of this work has been asserted in accordance with sections 77 and 78 of the Copyright, Designs and Patent Act 1988.

All rights reserved. No part of this book may be reprinted or reproduced or utilised in any form or by any electronic, mechanical, or other means, now known or hereafter invented, including photocopying and recording, or in any information storage or retrieval system, without permission in writing from the publishers.

*Trademark notice*: Product or corporate names may be trademarks or registered trademarks, and are used only for identification and explanation without intent to infringe.

*British Library Cataloguing in Publication Data*
A catalogue record for this book is available from the British Library

*Library of Congress Cataloging in Publication Data*
Jennings, Paul, 1954- author.
A history of drink and the English, 1500–2000 / Paul Jennings.
    pages cm
    1. Drinking of alcoholic beverages–Great Britain–History.
    2. Bars (Drinking establishments)–Great Britain–History.
    3. Alcoholic beverage industry–Great Britain–History. I. Title.
    GT2883.G7J45 2016
    394.1'30941–dc23
    2015031287

ISBN 13: 978-1-138-09010-1 (pbk)
ISBN 13: 978-1-8489-3555-6 (hbk)

Typeset in Times New Roman
by Sunrise Setting Ltd, Paignton, UK

**For Albert and Frank**

# Contents

*List of figures*   x
*Preface and acknowledgements*   xi

   Introduction   1
1  Drinking   8
2  Producers and sellers   38
3  Places and spaces   70
4  Meanings   99
5  Drunks   122
6  Anti-drink   147
7  Regulation   184
   Conclusions   211

*Index*   215

# Figures

| | | |
|---|---|---|
| 2.1 | England's premier brewing centre | 53 |
| 2.2 | Arthur and Sarah Gray and staff, with neighbouring shopkeeper to the right, at the Black Swan Tavern, Thornton Road, Bradford, c. 1915 | 54 |
| 3.1 | Schema of pub interiors, clockwise from top left: fully licensed mid-Victorian pub; early beerhouse; late-century urban pub; inter-war improved house | 79 |
| 3.2 | Pub interior, Bolton, 1938, photographed by Humphrey Spender, showing the gin-palace style and the presence of women | 85 |
| 4.1 | A drink after work, the George, Great George Street, Leeds, 1954, photographed by Marc Riboud for *Picture Post* | 111 |
| 5.1 | Out of it: young man in Newton Abbot, Devon, 2014; still from the documentary film *A Royal Hangover*, directed by Arthur Cauty | 135 |
| 6.1 | The drunkard as animal: Thomas Heywood's *Philocothonista* | 148 |
| 6.2 | *Gin Lane* by William Hogarth, 1751 | 152 |
| 6.3 | Children against drink outside Sunbridge Road Mission, Bradford, 1906 | 159 |

# Preface and acknowledgements

More than thirty years ago I began to research the history of the pub in the industrial city of Bradford, West Yorkshire. Two things quickly became apparent. The first was that I required knowledge of many related subjects: the histories of the brewing industry, of leisure pursuits generally, of consumption habits, of the system of licensing and of policing, to name only a few. The second was that the history of this then largely taken-for-granted institution was rooted in, and reflected, the broader economic, social, cultural and political history of England. It could therefore only be properly understood in that context. Thirty years on this book now draws upon all this work to offer an introduction to the wider history of drink from the early modern period to the turn of the millennium. In addition to my own researches it has necessarily benefited from the work of many scholars, all I trust properly acknowledged in the notes and to all of whom I owe a debt of gratitude. I would like to acknowledge also the work of the following groups. In the UK the Brewery History Society was founded in 1972 and publishes *Brewery History*, a journal with a subject matter much broader than its title suggests and covering many countries. I have been pleased to serve on its editorial board for several years now. In the US the Alcohol and Temperance History Group was founded in 1979 and published the *Social History of Alcohol Review*, later broadened to become the *Social History of Alcohol and Drugs: An Interdisciplinary Journal* as the group became the Alcohol and Drugs History Society. The society's conference in London in 2013 afforded a fruitful opportunity to hear and discuss drinking and other drug matters with many scholars from several disciplines and countries. More recently in the UK, the Drinking Studies Network, originally the Warwick Drinking Studies Network, has similarly offered occasions for stimulating exchanges. Finally, I enjoyed and benefited from discussions with students on the Drink and Society course which I taught within the former School of Lifelong Education and Development at the University of Bradford. Their positive response to its treatment of the subject supported my adoption of a thematic approach in this book.

Over the years I have benefited from the help of many archivists and librarians, all of whom I have acknowledged in earlier work, but for this book in particular I would like to thank staff at the J. B. Priestley Library of the University of Bradford, the Brotherton Library of the University of Leeds, Cambridge University Library, the Senate House Library, University of London and the Library of the

London School of Economics and Political Science. I would like to thank Andrew August for his original approach to me for a book proposal as I began work on the project. For generously reading and commenting upon various parts of the book I am grateful to John Ackroyd, David Beckingham, David Fahey, John Greenaway, James Kneale, Donna Melia, Dave Russell, George Sheeran, Deborah Toner, Andrew Whittingham and Henry Yeomans. Of course, only I am responsible for any errors or shortcomings it contains. I would like, above all, to thank my mum, Felicity, Albert and Frank for their love and support.

# Introduction

The English have always had a reputation for drinking. As Shakespeare's Iago explains the source of a drinking song he has just performed:

> I learn'd it in England, where indeed they are most potent in potting: your Dane, your German, and your swag-bellied Hollander, – drink, ho! – are nothing to your English.[1]

A century later, Daniel Defoe noted the excessive drinking of the Dutch and the Germans before going on to observe:

> but I believe I may venture to challenge all the world to show the like quantity of beer, and ale, and wine, and cider, and brandy, arrack, and geneva, and other strong waters, consumed in so narrow a compass of land, or among an equal number of people, as is now in this country of England.[2]

And at the height of the moral panic over so called binge drinking at the beginning of a new millennium, Labour's health spokesman Frank Dobson could express a widely held belief in asserting that the English 'have been binge drinkers since time immemorial'.[3] Foreigners have shared that opinion. The French Renaissance writer Rabelais could use the phrase 'as drunk as an Englishman', expecting his readers to understand the reference.[4] The Swiss César de Saussure, visiting in the 1720s, noted, amongst several observations on drinking, that 'On the whole the people of this country are very fond of liquors, which are said to be necessary because of the thickness and dampness of the atmosphere'.[5] This opinion of the national drinking habit has persisted. In a 2014 British Council survey of over 5,000 18–34 year olds from several countries (Brazil, China, India, Germany and the US) the option most frequently chosen for British people's worst characteristic was drinking too much, an opinion which the British shared.[6]

The English have not, of course, been alone in being viewed in this way. Shakespeare's words had such force precisely because the Danes, the Dutch and the Germans did have such a reputation,[7] and such reputations also persisted. Towards the close of the nineteenth century, according to alcohol specialist Norman Kerr, it was Belgium, Denmark and Russia which exhibited 'the greatest proportional extent of inebriety'.[8] In truth, many countries have consumed more alcohol than the English. The French in the mid 1860s drank annually some fifteen gallons per head more of their national drink of wine than the English consumed of their beer and well over twice as much spirits. And whilst the English drank little wine, the French also drank half as much beer.[9] In the early 1990s, over the whole of Europe, total per capita consumption of alcohol was greater than that of the United Kingdom in thirteen other countries.[10] But levels of consumption are not necessarily linked to drunkenness. The drinking cultures of southern European countries, where wine is a part of everyday life, frequently accompanies meals and overt intoxication is rare, has been held to contrast with northern beer or spirit cultures, where drinking is for special contexts, is more sporadic and often involves getting drunk.[11] Indeed, it was partly in an effort to shift English drinking culture to this allegedly more civilized continental form that major changes to licensing were introduced in legislation in 2003.

It is to get to grips with representations and realities such as these that this book offers an introduction to the history of alcoholic drinks in England over some five centuries from the sixteenth to the turn of the millennium. In so doing, it rests upon a number of key assertions. The first is the central importance of alcohol in human societies. It has been, as Gina Hames expressed it in her global survey, 'omnipresent in human history'.[12] Of course, not all societies have consumed it – the Muslim world is the obvious example – but most have.[13] Nor has alcohol been the only substance used by humans to alter their consciousness. For David Courtwright, the 'psychoactive revolution', in which 'People everywhere have acquired progressively more, and more potent, means of altering their ordinary working consciousness' is 'One of the signal events of world history'.[14] Angus Bancroft, similarly, has looked at the whole range of psychoactive substances, from coffee to heroin.[15] This book recognizes that range, but its focus is alcohol, as for Ian Hornsey, examining its role in the long evolution of human society, it is the 'best known and most widely used means of altering human consciousness'.[16] For the Royal College of Psychiatrists, reporting in 1986, it was simply 'our favourite drug'.[17]

The second is the ambivalence of alcohol: 'the ambiguous molecule', as one study termed it.[18] Throughout history, its consumption has been viewed both positively and negatively. Or as Mariana Valverde put it, 'alcohol has in fact been considered simultaneously as socially problematic and socially acceptable in a multitude of ways'.[19] In the study of drink it has, however, been the negative, both for the individual and for society, which has tended to be the main focus of attention. This is no doubt necessarily the case for those interested in medicine or the law, for example. But in the historical study of drink, too, the early focus on the nineteenth-century temperance movement, or the fascination which the so called Gin Craze of the early eighteenth century has exerted, tended to emphasize drink's darker side. Influenced by anthropology, in particular, however, attention has also been paid by historians to 'constructive drinking', in which it is a pleasurable activity, full of meaning for those enjoying it, and one therefore not to be treated solely as a problem.[20] This book is concerned both with the positive and the negative dimensions of drink. Drinking had many positive meanings for people, from the everyday sociability of the alehouse or pub to the celebration of life's rituals and triumphs. Its production and sale have been hugely significant economic activities. Drinking places have played important economic and social roles well beyond that of simply a meeting place to drink. And yet there are undoubtedly negative consequences, both for the individual and society, of heavy drinking and drunkenness. Very many people have therefore condemned and opposed it, and societies have sought in various ways to regulate its use and even, as most famously in the case of the United States, to prohibit its production and sale altogether.

The third is that the history of drink reflects broader economic, social, cultural and political developments in society and it can only be properly understood by analysing their interplay. This book therefore follows the lead of a number of scholars of drink. It can, as Susanna Barrows and Robin Room evocatively put it, introducing the outcomes of a 1984 conference on the social history of alcohol, 'serve as a revealing stain on the slide in the historian's microscope, highlighting the structures and relations of a society and the processes of stasis and change'.[21] Similarly, Finnish alcohol researcher Pekka Sulkunen observed how 'we can look through the window not only from society to alcohol but also from alcohol to society'.[22] The study of drink thus offers insights into the wider society; and to understand its history in turn requires that a society be comprehended in all its aspects. Craig Heron, in his study of that of Canada, described his aim as 'to untangle the specific economic, social, cultural and political strands woven through our particular approaches to pleasurable experience'.[23] This book shares the historical vision which that aim expresses.

It is a work of history, then: one which addresses the fundamental task of understanding ourselves in time and explores basic questions of continuity and change. But it is a work which has sought to learn from the insights of scholars from other disciplines who have looked at alcohol. Indeed, many students of drink have asserted the necessity of so doing. For Barrows and Room, for example, the collection of papers they introduced was 'Purposefully eclectic and interdisciplinary'.[24] Across a whole range of disciplines, including sociology, law, anthropology, criminology, literature, media studies, economics, geography, psychology, medicine and health sciences, a vast amount of work has indeed been done to further our understanding of the ambiguous molecule. This, however, should not be taken to suggest that the subject here is to be covered in all its aspects; I have neither the space nor the presumption. Scientific and medical aspects, for example, are not explored, although where relevant their social or political consequences are discussed.

Two final assertions are the importance of a global context and the significance of regional and local variation. The first has two aspects. As will be seen from the beginning of this study, with the importance of wine imports into medieval England, through to its close in 2000 with the dominant market position of a global drinks industry, and in many other ways – in the international cooperation of temperance organizations, for example – the history of drink has always had a global dimension. The other aspect is the value of comparison with the experiences of other countries. Although the subject has that global dimension, the drink histories of particular countries are products of their own unique contexts; but by looking comparatively at the interplay in particular countries of the economic, social, cultural and political, we can gain greater insight into their individual experiences. Developments and concerns experienced by many countries – the massive changes wrought by industrialization and urbanization, for example, or the antagonism which women's drinking has provoked – were played out in differing ways in particular cases.[25] There are, fortunately, now many studies of the history of drink at various periods in particular countries.[26]

A similar point may be made about the second assertion: the significance of regional and local variation, which several studies have also noted.[27] Key aspects of our subject – patterns of consumption, levels of prosecution for drunkenness or the strength and vigour of temperance feeling, to give just three of myriad examples – all differed between regions and localities. Similarly, national developments, such as the legal framework of regulation which developed for the public sale of alcohol, were played out differently according to local circumstances. Of course, a work such as this cannot possibly explore its subject in all the detail which a fully comparative approach, both internationally and locally, would require. It is important to note nonetheless that its approach has been shaped by an acknowledgement of their significance.

A few words must be said about the chosen chronology. Every historian faces the problem of periodization. My chosen starting point of 1500 does not imply any great turning point in the history of drink. In brewing, for example, Judith Bennett argued that 1350 was a truer watershed than 1500.[28] Similarly, drink and drinking places had been regulated for centuries before the introduction of a national system of licensing in 1552. But one has in the end to start somewhere and doing so at 1500 will certainly not preclude comment on earlier developments where relevant. As a starting point it also has the merits of including the Reformation and its effects and acknowledging the more long-term origins in the early modern period of the processes of industrialization and urbanization.[29] As to an end date, whilst one has to be wary of coming too close to the present to preclude achieving the necessary perspective, a general history of drink such as this has to include some consideration of the great changes of the post-war world. And, in the specific case of regulation, the ending of 450 years of magistrates' control of licensing in 2005 seemed an appropriate point at which to close.

The book is divided into seven chapters, each of which covers the whole period under consideration. Each offers answers to a range of key questions about the history of drink. The basic ones of what was drunk, how much, by whom and how this has changed over time form the subject matter of Chapter 1. Chapter 2 looks at the producers and sellers of alcoholic drink. Chapter 3 considers the places in which men and women drank and how they functioned as spaces – that is, what people did in them and how they interacted with each other. Chapter 4 examines the varied meanings of drinking for individuals and groups. Chapter 5 then focuses on one meaning in particular: intoxication. Drunkenness was one consequence of drinking which particularly excited condemnation. The final two chapters accordingly examine first that hostility, but also a much broader range of anti-drink sentiment and campaigning, and second the complex history of regulation, its administration and enforcement.

## Notes

1 *Othello*: II.iii.71–4.
2 D. Defoe, *The Complete English Tradesman* (New York: Burt Franklin, 1970), vol. 2, p. 223.
3 In 2005, quoted in H. Yeomans, *Alcohol and Moral Regulation: Public attitudes, spirited measures and Victorian hangovers* (Bristol: Policy Press, 2014), p. 179.
4 F. Rabelais, *The Histories of Gargantua and Pantagruel* (Harmondsworth: Penguin, 1955), p. 72.
5 Madame Van Muyden (ed.), *A Foreign View of England in 1725–1729: The Letters of Monsieur César de Saussure to his family* (London: Caliban Books, 1995), p. 103.
6 *As Others See Us: Culture, attraction and soft power* (London: British Council, 2014), pp. 20–1, at www.britishcouncil.org/organisation/policy-insight-research/research/as-others-see-us [accessed 12 November 2015].
7 A. L. Martin, *Alcohol, Violence and Disorder in Traditional Europe* (Kirksville, MO: Truman State University Press, 2009), p. 72.
8 A. Vleugels, *Narratives of Drunkenness: Belgium 1830–1914* (London: Pickering & Chatto, 2013), p. 33.
9 Based on W. S. Haine, *The World of the Paris Café: Sociability among the French working class, 1789–1914* (Baltimore, MD: Johns Hopkins University Press, 1996), p. 91; G. B. Wilson, *Alcohol and the Nation: A contribution to the study of the liquor problem in the United Kingdom from 1800 to 1935* (London: Nicholson and Watson, 1940), p. 335; T. R. Gourvish and R. G. Wilson, *The British Brewing Industry 1830–1980* (Cambridge: Cambridge University Press, 1994), p. 30.
10 M. Plant, *Women and Alcohol: Contemporary and historical perspectives* (London: Free Association Books, 1997), p. 4.
11 R. Room, 'Intoxication and bad behaviour: understanding cultural differences in the link', *Social Science & Medicine*, 53:2 (2001), pp. 189–98, on p. 6.
12 G. Hames, *Alcohol in World History* (London: Routledge, 2012), p. 134.
13 For the Muslim world see R. Phillips, *Alcohol: A history* (Chapel Hill, NC: University of North Carolina Press, 2014), pp. 58–64.
14 D. T. Courtwright, *Forces of Habit: Drugs and the making of the modern world* (London: Harvard University Press, 2001), p. 2.
15 A. Bancroft, *Drugs, Intoxication and Society* (Cambridge: Polity Press, 2009), p. x.
16 I. S. Hornsey, *Alcohol and Its Role in the Evolution of Human Society* (Cambridge: Royal Society of Chemistry, 2012), p. 550.
17 Royal College of Psychiatrists, *Alcohol: Our favourite drug* (London: Tavistock Publications, 1986).
18 G. Edwards, *Alcohol: The ambiguous molecule* (Harmondsworth: Penguin, 2000).
19 M. Valverde, *Diseases of the Will: Alcohol and the dilemmas of freedom* (Cambridge: Cambridge University Press, 1998), p. 9.
20 M. Douglas, 'A distinct anthropological perspective', in M. Douglas (ed.), *Constructive Drinking: Perspectives on drink from anthropology* (Cambridge: Cambridge University Press, 1987), pp. 3–15, on pp. 3–4.
21 S. Barrows and R. Room, 'Introduction', in S. Barrows and R. Room (eds), *Drinking: Behavior and belief in modern history* (Berkeley and Los Angeles, CA: University of California Press, 1991), pp. 1–25, on p. 1.

22 P. Sulkunen, 'Images and realities of alcohol', *Addiction*, 93:9 (1998), pp. 1305–12, on p. 1308.
23 C. Heron, *Booze: A distilled history* (Toronto: Between the Lines, 2003), p. 2.
24 Barrows and Room, 'Introduction', p. 1.
25 For this point see I. Tyrrell, 'Tasks and achievements of alcohol and temperance historiography', in J. S. Blocker and C. K. Warsh (eds), *The Changing Face of Drink: Substance, imagery and behaviour* (Ottawa: Histoire sociale/Social History, 1997), pp. 381–401.
26 For the constituent parts of the UK see A. Cooke, *A History of Drinking: The Scottish pub since 1700* (Edinburgh: Edinburgh University Press, 2015); E. Malcolm, *'Ireland Sober, Ireland Free': Drink and temperance in nineteenth-century Ireland* (Dublin: Gill and Macmillan, 1986); W. R. Lambert, *Drink and Sobriety in Victorian Wales c. 1820-c. 1895* (Cardiff: University of Wales Press, 1983). There are far too many studies of other countries to cite here but see, for example, T. Brennan, *Public Drinking and Popular Culture in Eighteenth-century Paris* (Princeton, NJ: Princeton University Press, 1988), J. S. Roberts, *Drink, Temperance and the Working Class in Nineteenth-century Germany* (London: George Allen & Unwin, 1984); W. J. Rorabaugh, *The Alcoholic Republic: An American tradition* (Oxford: Oxford University Press, 1979) in addition to other works which I cite.
27 For example, B. Kümin and B. A. Tlusty, 'The world of the tavern: An introduction', in B. Kümin and B. A. Tlusty (eds), *The World of the Tavern: Public houses in early modern Europe* (Aldershot: Ashgate, 2002), pp. 3–11, on p. 9. In addition to works cited elsewhere, for a detailed local study see, for example, R. Donovan, 'Drink in Victorian Norwich', in four parts in *Brewery History*, 130 (2009), pp. 18–64, 132 (2009), pp. 67–133, 134 (2010), pp. 87–139 and 137 (2010), pp. 73–165.
28 J. M. Bennett, *Ale, Beer and Brewsters in England: Women's work in a changing world, 1300–1600* (Oxford: Oxford University Press, 1996), p. 6.
29 K. Wrightson, *Earthly Necessities: Economic lives in early modern Britain 1470–1750* (London: Penguin, 2002), p. 22. For a view of the similarities between the centuries before and after 1500 see C. Dyer, *An Age of Transition? Economy and Society in England in the Later Middle Ages* (Oxford: Clarendon Press, 2005), pp. 4 and 7.

## Bibliography

Bancroft, A., *Drugs, Intoxication and Society* (Cambridge: Polity Press, 2009).
Barrows, S. and Room, R., 'Introduction', in S. Barrows and R. Room (eds), *Drinking: Behavior and belief in modern history* (Berkeley and Los Angeles, CA: University of California Press, 1991), pp. 1–25.
Bennett, J. M., *Ale, Beer and Brewsters in England: Women's work in a changing world, 1300–1600* (Oxford: Oxford University Press, 1996).
Brennan, T., *Public Drinking and Popular Culture in Eighteenth-century Paris* (Princeton, NJ: Princeton University Press, 1988).
Cooke, A., *A History of Drinking: The Scottish pub since 1700* (Edinburgh: Edinburgh University Press, 2015).
Courtwright, D. T., *Forces of Habit: Drugs and the making of the modern world* (London: Harvard University Press, 2001).
Donovan, R., 'Drink in Victorian Norwich', *Brewery History*, 130 (2009), pp. 18–64, 132 (2009), pp. 67–133, 134 (2010), pp. 87–139 and 137 (2010), pp. 73–165.
Douglas, M., 'A distinct anthropological perspective', in M. Douglas (ed.), *Constructive Drinking: Perspectives on drink from anthropology* (Cambridge: Cambridge University Press, 1987), pp. 3–15.

Dyer, C., *An Age of Transition? Economy and Society in England in the Later Middle Ages* (Oxford: Clarendon Press, 2005).

Edwards, G., *Alcohol: The ambiguous molecule* (Harmondsworth: Penguin, 2000).

Gourvish, T. R. and Wilson, R. G., *The British Brewing Industry 1830–1980* (Cambridge: Cambridge University Press, 1994).

Haine, W. S., *The World of the Paris Café: Sociability among the French working class, 1789–1914* (Baltimore, MD: Johns Hopkins University Press, 1996).

Hames, G., *Alcohol in World History* (London: Routledge, 2012).

Heron, C., *Booze: A distilled history* (Toronto: Between the Lines, 2003).

Hornsey, I. S., *Alcohol and its role in the evolution of human society* (Cambridge: Royal Society of Chemistry, 2012).

Kümin, B. and Tlusty, B. A., 'The world of the tavern: An introduction', in B. Kümin and B. A. Tlusty (eds), *The World of the Tavern: Public houses in early modern Europe* (Aldershot: Ashgate, 2002), pp. 3–11.

Lambert, W. R., *Drink and Sobriety in Victorian Wales c. 1820-c. 1895* Cardiff: University of Wales Press, 1983).

Malcolm, E., *'Ireland Sober, Ireland Free': Drink and temperance in nineteenth-century Ireland* (Dublin: Gill and Macmillan, 1986).

Martin, A. L., *Alcohol, Violence and Disorder in Traditional Europe* (Kirksville, MO: Truman State University Press, 2009).

Phillips, R., *Alcohol: A history* (Chapel Hill, NC: University of North Carolina Press, 2014).

Plant, M., *Women and Alcohol: Contemporary and historical perspectives* (London: Free Association Books, 1997).

Roberts, J. S., *Drink, Temperance and the Working Class in Nineteenth-century Germany* (London: George Allen & Unwin, 1984).

Room, R., 'Intoxication and bad behaviour: Understanding cultural differences in the link', *Social Science & Medicine*, 53:2 (2001), pp. 189–98.

Rorabaugh, W. J., *The Alcoholic Republic: An American tradition* (Oxford: Oxford University Press, 1979).

Sulkunen, P., 'Images and realities of alcohol', *Addiction*, 93:9 (1998), pp. 1305–12.

Tyrrell, I., 'Tasks and achievements of alcohol and temperance historiography', in J. S. Blocker and C. K. Warsh (eds), *The Changing Face of Drink: Substance, imagery and behaviour* (Ottawa: Histoire sociale/Social History, 1997), pp. 381–401.

Valverde, M., *Diseases of the Will: Alcohol and the dilemmas of freedom* (Cambridge: Cambridge University Press, 1998).

Vleugels, A., *Narratives of Drunkenness: Belgium 1830–1914* (London: Pickering & Chatto, 2013).

Wilson, G. B., *Alcohol and the Nation: A contribution to the study of the liquor problem in the United Kingdom from 1800 to 1935* (London: Nicholson and Watson, 1940).

Wrightson, K., *Earthly Necessities: Economic lives in early modern Britain 1470–1750* (London: Penguin, 2002).

Yeomans, H., *Alcohol and Moral Regulation: Public attitudes, spirited measures and Victorian hangovers* (Bristol: Policy Press, 2014).

# 1   Drinking

**Questions, sources and explanations**

We begin with some basic, essential questions: how much was drunk, what types of drink, by whom and how have these changed over time? They are simply stated, yet they present a challenge of considerable magnitude to the historian. That challenge arises in particular from the nature of the sources and the profusion and complexity of explanatory variables. Each merits some brief introductory remarks.

The sources from which to make an estimate of total drink consumption simply do not exist for the first two hundred years covered by this history. There are figures for the amount of wine imported into the country, but wine, it can be stated with confidence, formed only a fraction of total consumption. Those figures exist because wine imports were taxed, with the corollary, of course, that they exclude amounts not taxed, a point which applies to many of the statistics of drink available to the historian. Looking at the whole range of drinks, this applied at various times to smuggled imports of wines and spirits, to illicit distilling and to legitimate private brewing. Estimates of consumption, which are actually derived from statistics of production, must therefore take some account of their uncertain coverage.[1] Further, whilst from them we can make estimates of either total or per capita consumption, what of drinking by individuals? Here again the evidence poses problems. There are many examples from the medieval period onwards of the allowance of drink for groups such as soldiers and sailors, members of religious institutions, inmates of hospitals and poor houses and workers, for example, at harvest time. The amounts given, however, might be notional or ideal, rather than those actually enjoyed.[2] The ability to question modern drinkers directly might seem to obviate such difficulties, except that here too there are problems. Those questioned tend to underestimate their consumption, either deliberately due to guilt or embarrassment or, as it is termed, the 'social desirability phenomenon'. More prosaically, they might simply not be able to remember.[3]

Actual amounts drunk are one thing, but what of the alcohol content of those drinks? The fact that this has varied considerably over time complicates further any analysis of long-term trends in drinking. In the first place, it is simply not always clear just how strong a particular drink was in the past. In the second, for much of this history a significant proportion of ale or beer was brewed weaker for women, children and servants. Conversely, the later seventeenth and early eighteenth centuries were years of growing popularity of stronger beers and distilled spirits. In the later nineteenth and through the twentieth century, in contrast, the strength of beer declined. But then the later twentieth century was again a period when the popularity of wine in particular, which was of course stronger than beer, grew markedly. The alcohol content of what was consumed is something we will also need to take into account.

Turning now to explanations for the trends we might identify, we are confronted with a seemingly limitless array of variables, arising from drink's centrality in society across the centuries. George Wilson, in his pioneering 1940 study of the subject, sought to address that complexity by grouping the influences on consumption, broadly speaking, into three kinds: the increase or decrease of opportunity, social changes and educational and moral causes. These three in turn were divided into respectively three, eight and six components. Even this is deceptively simple. Wilson was particularly concerned with those influences which were working to *decrease* consumption (from his temperance point of view the preferred direction) in the period 1800 to 1935. Thus his 'social changes', for example, comprised 'counter-attractions' to the pub and drink and 'competitive luxuries' like tobacco and gambling. Nevertheless, his analysis did acknowledge the question's complexity in its attention to the varied influences of demographic, economic, social, cultural, political and legal changes.[4] His grouping of influences was used in turn by two nutritionists in the mid 1970s, a time, in contrast to Wilson's, of rising consumption, in an ambitious attempt to chart its history over three centuries.[5]

More recently, a number of historians and scholars from other disciplines have offered syntheses of long-term trends. In so doing, periods of revolutionary change have been identified. Peter Clark, the pioneering historian of the English alehouse, argued that 'medieval and early modern Europe witnessed two great revolutions in drinking taste': the first was the shift from ale to beer over the twelfth to sixteenth centuries, the second the rise of spirit-drinking, which had spread by the eighteenth century to most parts of Europe as well as the New World.[6] Revolution, too, was the view of social historian John Burnett, who surveyed the histories of a range of drinks. He argued for 'two great periods of transformation'. The 'first drinks revolution' occurred between the mid seventeenth and mid eighteenth centuries, as the choice in both alcoholic and non-alcoholic drinks broadened with the spread of spirits, tea, coffee and chocolate. The second, from the 1960s onwards, was characterized particularly by a trend towards cold drinks and the Europeanization of UK drinking habits, as consumption of lager, wine, cider, coffee and soft drinks all rose.[7]

Continuity, in contrast, has been stressed by other synthesizers. Historical geographer James Kneale pointed to what he saw as a long decline of alcohol consumption, starting in the late seventeenth century, but posited, like Burnett, a 'significant shift' from the 1960s. Similarly, historians of the early modern period Phil Withington and Angela McShane emphasized 'the essential continuity of modern drinking practices over time', but like Kneale saw the recent past as a major discontinuity, particularly in relation to consumption by women. They, however, also noted within that essential continuity fluctuations over time.

These in turn were stressed by cultural historian James Nicholls.[8] And for economic historian John Chartres, there was a pattern of cyclical peaks: the second quarter of the eighteenth century, the 1860s to the 1900s and, again, the late twentieth century, each temporarily reversing the long-term decline.[9]

Analyses, then, have recognized issues of continuity and change, but have sought to comprehend them within defined historical periods. This seems a sensible approach and one which will be followed here. Some changes were protracted, such as the changeover from ale to beer in the medieval and early modern periods, or the long decline of consumption from around 1700. Others, in contrast, like the surge in spirit consumption in the early eighteenth century, or the overall growth, and changes in the pattern of, drinking in the later twentieth century occurred over comparatively short periods of time. My first period is the late medieval and early modern down to the mid seventeenth century, one of high overall consumption, a move from ale to beer and fluctuating levels of wine-drinking. My second covers some two centuries from the later seventeenth to the later nineteenth, which did indeed see a long-term decline of consumption, but with significant fluctuations within that, and a diversification of drinking choice, both alcoholic and non-alcoholic. The third posits a marked downward trend in consumption, beginning in the last third of the nineteenth century and lasting until the immediate post-Second World War years. Fourth, in common with other analyses, are the major changes in levels and patterns of consumption of the later twentieth century. The emphasis in this chapter will be on the relationship of consumption to economic change and living standards. Succeeding chapters elaborate the important influences on consumption patterns of production and retail, the social context of drinking, the cultural importance of drink and the impact of the ways in which drinking has been contested and regulated.

## Medieval and early modern

For late fourteenth- and fifteenth-century England the following pattern of drink consumption may be suggested. First, the whole population, of both sexes and all ages, drank. Second, total consumption rose from already high levels. Third, there began the shift in consumption from ale to hopped beer. Fourth, wine-drinking declined. I shall take each point in turn. As Judith Bennett succinctly put it, 'most people drank most of the time' and what they drank was ale. It formed a basic element of the diet of men, women and children, providing within that limited diet an important source of energy and nutrition. Non-alcoholic alternatives were 'unhealthy, unsuitable, or unavailable'. The most obvious was water, but supplies might be polluted, a situation which worsened, and indeed persisted, for centuries. Milk was made into cheese and butter rather than drunk. Wine was too expensive for the majority of the population.[10] There was cider and perry, important in parts of the south and west, where mead (from honey) and piment (spiced wine) were drunk too.[11]

Consumption levels were high. The allowances of groups such as soldiers and sailors, monks and servants indicate as much as a gallon of ale each per day, although, as was noted above, this may not always have represented actual consumption. The records of Norwich Cathedral priory, for example, show that two kinds of ale were brewed (at other religious houses there were as many as four different kinds), a superior one for the brethren and one of secondary quality for the servants and workers, for whom the individual allowance was a gallon a day. The most vulnerable in society also received their due ration. At the hospital of St John the Baptist, Chester, 'for the sustentation of poor and silly persons', the daily allowance for each inmate in the early fourteenth century was half a gallon of ale.[12]

Whether the poorest in medieval society drank ale regularly is subject to some dispute. For Bennett, whilst the very poor sometimes had to content themselves with water, ale was drunk by most peasants and labourers, even if weaker and in smaller amounts. Clark and Christopher Dyer, the latter a historian of living standards in the later Middle Ages, have argued in contrast that whilst the better-off drank ale regularly, poorer villagers and labourers, due to its high price in relation to earnings, might have to drink water, whey or buttermilk instead and ale only as circumstances permitted.[13] Where there is general agreement is on rising consumption following the Black Death, although this may actually have accelerated changes already under way. The reduced number of consumers resulting from the pestilence, lower grain prices and greater price stability produced a rise in per capita consumption as overall living standards rose.[14] Harvest workers in Sedgeford, Norfolk, in the thirteenth century had been each allowed up to three pints of strong ale daily, or four to five of thinner; prior to the Black Death this may have risen to five pints of strong ale; and by the early fifteenth century it was up to six pints of best ale or a gallon of thinner.[15] In Suffolk by the early fifteenth century the members of the manorial household of Dame Alice de Bryene consumed each on average between three and four pints per meal, or, again, about a gallon a day.[16]

Accompanying this rise in consumption was the beginning of a shift from ale to beer. Ale was made from water and barley malt (although sometimes wheat, oats and millet or a mixture of barley and oats, known as dredge, were used), with the addition of spices after fermentation for taste and for purposes of preservation. The resulting drink was of variable quality, thick (rather like soup) and soon deteriorated.[17] Beer, made from the addition of hops to fermented malt and water, was more stable, palatable, drew more alcoholic content from less grain, lasted longer and could be moved around more easily.[18] It was being imported from continental Europe certainly by the fourteenth century: for example, from the Low Countries into Yarmouth and from northern Germany into Hythe, the port of Colchester, by the 1390s. By the middle of the next century that port was dealing with hops, rather than the finished product, indicating local production.[19] The change was facilitated by immigrants from the Low Countries and Germany, who brought with them both their preference for beer and skill in brewing it. By the mid fifteenth century some 16,000, mostly Dutch, were working in England.[20]

Beer-drinking then spread throughout the country, but it was a slow and 'highly complex' process, as Clark characterized it, based in its intrinsic qualities, which made it more economical to make, especially as the price of raw materials rose in the sixteenth century, and its relative cheapness, which was more attractive when real wages began to decline. But consumer preference was also important, for a clearer, lighter and more palatable drink, although this was counter-balanced, it has been suggested, by local belief in ale's greater wholesomeness and English suspicion of a foreign product.[21] Certainly, beer's ascendancy was not to be complete until the late seventeenth century.

Wine consumption in this period was much reduced from its earlier eminence, when the wines of Gascony, for which England was the biggest single market, were of 'immense importance' to the country's trade. In the early fourteenth century imports exceeded 20,000 tons annually, with every port in the country engaged in the trade.[22] It was Gascon wine, it has been suggested, rather than colder weather, which led to the decline of native English viticulture, formerly a significant source.[23] But the Hundred Years War from 1337 was to prove disastrous. Wine was 'never again as cheap or abundant' and by the late fifteenth century the volume of trade was not more than half that of the good years.[24] But it was always a luxury item, whose enjoyment was restricted chiefly to the wealthy. Now, as they experienced financial difficulties, the aristocracy were cutting back on consumption, either by reducing daily allowances or, as was the case with the gentry, dropping out of regular wine-drinking altogether. A shift in taste in the fifteenth century towards the sweeter wines of the Mediterranean, like malmsey or rumney, reinforces this conclusion, as they too were expensive and could only be purchased in small volumes.[25]

At the close of the fifteenth century, then, high levels of consumption of ale and beer were based in their centrality to the diet of the English people and sustained by rising real wages. The succeeding century, in contrast, saw them decline in economic 'hard times' for labouring people.[26] This would lend support to A. Lynn Martin's view, based on data of individual consumption, that although some examples still reveal levels comparable with earlier years, the early modern period witnessed an overall decline.[27] On the other hand, whilst poverty did become a growing problem, the second half of the sixteenth and first half of the seventeenth centuries were decades of growing overall material prosperity. Between 1566 and 1641 the national income of England and Wales more than doubled and since the 1530s had possibly quadrupled. Towns expanded and the urban population grew both absolutely and proportionately. The 'middle sort of people', comprising prosperous manufacturers, independent tradesmen, those in commerce, law and other professional services, as well as substantial commercial farmers, did well.[28] There was thus an expanding market for food and drink. The growth of commercial brewing and the expansion of the retail sector in drink (to be examined in Chapter 2) support this view of growth.

Drink remained an essential item of diet, with no diversification as yet into alternative beverages, and consumption levels were still high. The household of the Essex cleric William Harrison, who claimed himself a 'poor man' on £40 a year in the late sixteenth century, shared three hogsheads (216 gallons) of beer in a typical brew. That same cleric, in his much quoted *Description of England*, testified to the growing prosperity of those middling and upper sections of society with his elaboration of the great variety of wine now drunk in the country. He identified around eighty-six types, including French, Italian, Grecian, Spanish and Canarian wines, and asserted that from 20,000 to 30,000 tons and upwards was then imported.[29] Foreign visitors noted this too, like the Venetian envoy to London in 1554, observing that the English 'consume a great quantity of wine, which is brought from Candia [Crete], Spain, the Rhine and from France, this last being prized more than the rest'. Based upon such testimony André Simon, in his classic work on the wine trade, argued for a 'very flourishing' trade in Elizabeth's reign.[30] Later historians have been more cautious. W. B. Stephens provides for Henry VIII's reign an annual average import of some 10,000 tons, representing no advance upon the close of the previous century, and still half the medieval peak. In the late sixteenth century the most important remained French wine at around 8,000 tons. But there was then in the early seventeenth century a very considerable increase, doubling to 20,000 tons by 1623 and averaging some 37,700 tons annually in the period 1637 to 1641, or a more than doubling of consumption.[31] This was, as Phil Withington has characterized it, a 'dynamic market' for alcohol (and tobacco) driven, as suggested here, by the consumption of the more affluent.[32]

## Later seventeenth to later nineteenth centuries

For our earlier period the best use has been made of the available evidence to chart changes in drinking patterns. But from the late seventeenth century we have for the first time statistics from which it is possible to suggest aggregate consumption. As has been indicated, these are not without difficulties. Wilson, in his detailed examination of them, found the records of beer production prior to 1800 'very unsatisfactory' due to the prevalence of private, untaxed brewing. As for production which did pay tax, Peter Mathias, in his history of the eighteenth-century brewing industry, took the view that 'the returns are probably less fallible than those of some other excised commodities, and more reliable as a guide to actual production over a series of years than most other eighteenth-century statistics'.[33] These cover brewing by common (wholesale) brewers and brewing victuallers – that is, publicans on their premises – and comprise figures for both strong and small beer. The latter was the weaker brew for women, children and servants, whose alcohol content has been estimated at 2 per cent,[34] and which accounted for nearly two-fifths of all beer brewed for sale. Based upon a population estimate of some five million for 1700, this suggests a weekly per capita consumption at this time of nearly five and a half pints.[35] To this needs to be added some estimate of private brewing. One was made by the contemporary statistician Gregory King for 1695 and including it more than doubles per capita consumption to 11.8 pints per week.[36] Finally, brewer H. A. Monckton based his estimates of private brewing upon the assumptions of (unnamed) experts. Using these figures produces a total of over 15 pints a week.[37] This corresponds to a contemporary estimate of a quart per head per day and is compatible with another modern estimate, this time for London, of per capita consumption of strong beer alone of just under ten pints a week.[38] This beer was indeed strong, perhaps as much as 10 to 12 per cent alcohol.[39]

As per capita figures, however, they take no account of the age structure of the population at this time or of differences between men and women. Children formed a much greater share of the total than in modern times and although they drank small beer it is reasonable to assume this was not in the same quantities as adults. Individual adult consumption could therefore be much higher. Servants at Arbury, Warwickshire, in the 1670s each averaged about six pints daily, probably eight for the men and four for the women, although, again, this was mostly small beer.[40] The men in the London print shop observed by Benjamin Franklin in the 1720s drank six pints of strong beer at work every day.[41] The coal heavers, the men who unloaded coal from ships on the Thames, were said to sustain their heavy work with a gallon of beer a day.[42]

By this time, this was universally beer brewed with hops. Already by the late sixteenth century William Harrison was noting how ale had become an 'old and sick men's drink'.[43] Nevertheless, it survived in more northerly parts of the country to the late seventeenth century. Roger Lowe, an apprentice shopkeeper in Lancashire, makes reference to it in his diary in the 1660s and 1670s, including to 'bragged', made from fermenting honey and ale together.[44] But what was termed ale would by this time also appear to have been brewed with hops, as the author of the 1703 *Guide to Gentlemen and Farmers for Brewing the Finest Malt Liquor* put it, 'All good Ale is now made with some small mixture of Hops, tho' not in so great Quantity as Strong beer, design'd for longer keeping'. Maturation was a defining factor of such beer and one brown beer, brewed in London, acquired the nickname 'porter's ale' or 'porter's beer' from the 1720s due to its popularity with those essential and ubiquitous workers. Porter then became, over the succeeding century, a key staple drink.[45]

There was now a growing variety of beers. This was already evident from the early seventeenth century, but increased after the Restoration with the expansion of inland trade. The beers of a number of brewing centres like Dorchester, Norwich, Derby, Hull, Nottingham and, most famously, Burton were being transported to London, from where within a decade of the navigation of the Trent from 1712 over a thousand barrels a year were shipped to the capital. It was expensive at 7s 6d for a dozen bottles, but the total amount is clearly indicative of a ready market.[46] Provincial Englishmen also enjoyed greater choice: Nicholas Blundell, of a Lancashire gentry family, received two hampers of bottles filled with 'Bristol' beer in August 1702.[47] Cider too was exported from its heartlands in the West Country, and by the 1680s Lechlade in Gloucestershire, on the newly navigable upper reaches of the Thames, was a centre for its shipment to the capital. By the early eighteenth century, Defoe was reporting 20,000 hogsheads imported there annually.[48]

Clearly such consumption was being fuelled in particular by the continued growth in the number of the 'middle sort of people'. This was true also of wine. An examination of surviving account books of members of the gentry, London merchants and professional men, covering the second half of the seventeenth and first half of the eighteenth centuries, shows wine to have been an essential item of their consumption.[49] It was an important indicator of wealth and status, as for Pepys, for example, whose wine cellar was a sign of his success in life.[50] In fact, with the exception of the 1680s, wine imports were about half the levels of the early seventeenth century.[51] This was mostly still from France – 62 per cent of London imports in 1675, and 72 per cent a decade later – and mostly claret, 'the leading wine of Restoration England', and indeed of Pepys's cellar, with the bulk of the rest Spanish.[52] The popularity of luxury claret with the wealthy survived the general decline of French wines during the long years of war between the two countries. Queen Anne's steward purchased nearly 28,000 bottles of Haut Brion and Margaux, a taste shared by her royal successors and their leading Whig supporters, none more so than Sir Robert Walpole himself, whose annual wine budget in 1733 was a staggering £1,150, over a third of which, around 234 bottles a month, was claret.[53]

In general consumption, however, port was the principal beneficiary of the wartime embargo on French wine. The transition was facilitated by the Methuen Treaty (actually three treaties) of 1703 with Portugal, which in return for the removal of restrictions on English cloth imposed a third less duty than on French wines. Its relative cost, availability and strength, probably 14 to 17 per cent alcohol by volume and often laced with brandy, ensured that port became the everyday wine for taverns and the middling sort. From less than one half in 1714, from the 1730s and for the rest of the century Portugal supplied 70 per cent of the country's total wine imports.[54] By the 1780s, at any one time there were in Oporto forty or more active British wine firms, – as its historian describes it, 'a golden age for Portuguese wines'.[55]

With both beer and wine there was a shift in taste to stronger drink. Defoe noted this trend at the time: as he put it, 'the Stream of the Nation's Palate runs, I say, for stronger and dearer Liquors'. It was true most of all of the growth in the taste for 'strong waters' – distilled spirits.[56] There is evidence for the spread of the trade from the late sixteenth century and by the early years of the seventeenth it was well-established as a consumer good; but the home market remained small until that century's last quarter. It was mostly imported, primarily brandy from France. Brandy was also used to make punch, with water, lemons, sugar and nutmeg (the five ingredients of its Hindi name), which enjoyed a vogue amongst the better-off from the mid seventeenth century.[57] With the collapse of the brandy trade following the government's wartime embargo, although smuggling continued, home-produced spirit, in effect gin, became the 'principal dynamic element in the home market for drink'.[58] The amount of British spirits excised for sale rose from an annual average of just over half a million gallons in 1684–9 to almost one and a half million in 1700–9 and rose thereafter, although not continuously, to reach a peak in the 1740s of over seven million gallons, with a peak of 8.2 million in 1743. The estimated share of the drinks market taken by spirits increased from 5 per cent in 1700 to 21.9 per cent in 1745.[59] Any estimate from these figures of per capita consumption is hazardous in the extreme, given that not all production would have been taxed and the highly uneven geography of consumption. For what it is worth, a very rough calculation for the peak 1740s' average, assuming that Londoners were the main consumers (although not the only consumers, as Chapter 2 will indicate) and taking a figure for the number of those aged fifteen and over of around 400,000, gives an astonishing adult per capita consumption in the capital of 2.7 pints of gin a week.[60]

What explains this extraordinary growth? On the supply side, the domestic distilling trade was opened up through the removal of the monopoly of the Distillers Company of London. The demand thereby created for malted grain would have the desired effect of aiding agricultural interests then affected by low prices and giving a needed boost to the government's coffers in time of war.[61] Gin was also cheap at a time when strong beer had become more expensive with the doubling of excise duty in 1710.[62] In a further deliberate boost to the trade, its retail sale was also unrestricted for almost thirty years.[63] On the demand side, the early eighteenth century saw a substantial rise in the real incomes of wage earners and even more so of the middling sort. The good harvests of the 1730s and 1740s, and consequent low food prices, were boons to distillers and drinkers alike.[64] Gin then was a novel luxury, at a time which historians have identified as the early years of a consumer revolution, when the desire for new tastes found expression in tea, coffee and chocolate, as well as spirits, but one which was within the financial reach of the poor.[65] For them, however, it has been argued the luxury of spirits was enjoyed in the context of 'fundamentally uncertain conditions of life and employment', in which it made more sense to indulge in 'meaningful expenditure' than pointless attempts at long-term accumulation.[66] It was particularly drunk by working women with improved disposable income, in the capital at least, and with its purchase facilitated by its accessibility.[67]

In the late seventeenth and the first half of the eighteenth centuries, then, overall alcohol consumption was high. This was exaggerated by the shifts to stronger beers and wines and spirits. Although, as shown above, it is very difficult to compare with earlier periods, for some historians these years represent a rising trend or plateau of consumption.[68] From this point, however, the picture is more clearly one of long-term decline. But before examining subsequent trends in the consumption of the great staple drink – beer – I will chart the stories of gin and wine.

The high levels of gin consumption were 'reversed dramatically' from the middle of the century, returning to their 1700 level, as a result of a combination of influences. After several failed attempts, effective fiscal controls were finally imposed and the sale of gin was restricted to licensed publicans, measures which were facilitated by the support of the brewing lobby and the larger distillers. In several years thereafter, at times of grain shortage, the government introduced restrictions on distilling itself. Further, and crucially in Clark's view, more effective competition from porter, due to better marketing and a fall in its real price, also shifted consumption away from gin.[69] It also declined relative to another spirit, West Indies rum, whose market share rose from 3 per cent in 1730–9 to 21.6 per cent in 1760–9. Rum, together with arrack, a spirit distilled from a variety of sources, including rice or dates, was also used as an alternative to brandy for punch.[70] From the mid 1780s consumption of gin rose again with a reduction in duty, but more particularly because of developments in its retail sale, with the growth of a new generation of gin shops, as will be examined in the next chapter. Another reduction in spirit duty in 1825 saw a further rise, but this can be attributed to a diversion of production from illegal to legal channels rather than representing any real increase. Consumption then fluctuated at this higher level until the mid 1870s. The output of British spirits did not again reach its early-eighteenth-century peak until the late 1830s, but the much greater population meant that per capita consumption was then around half a gallon per year, well below that of the earlier period.[71]

Total wine consumption was stagnant or falling over much of the eighteenth century, although smuggling and adulteration, with anything from river water, spirits, sugars and the juices of indigenous berries, meant that actual consumption was understated.[72] But later in the century, port's popularity extended from the middling ranks to the elite, as its quality improved and it appealed to emerging ideals of English masculinity. This was the period of renowned drinkers of port like the playwright Sheridan or prime minister Pitt: the former drinking two to three bottles at a time at one London tavern after the success of *The School for Scandal*, the latter purchasing in a single year over 5,000 bottles of wine, nearly half of which was port.[73] But its consumption was not restricted to the elite; it was widely available. Around a third of publicans, just over 11,000, took out a separate wine licence in 1800, rising to nearly 26,000 by 1860, or around 40 per cent of fully licensed premises.[74] Nevertheless, whilst aggregate consumption did increase between the end of the eighteenth century and the 1850s, per capita fell by half.[75]

This remained the overall picture of wine consumption for the remainder of the century and beyond, but within that two developments should be noted. The first was the growth in the popularity of sherry, although as 'sack' it had been drunk from the sixteenth century. Imports grew rapidly from the 1820s. By the 1840s it was being consumed in equal amounts to port and by the 1850s had overtaken it. This popularity, it has been argued, was based in a shift in middle-class taste towards a drink associated more with respectability and refinement, with which to complement the more aggressive, masculine connotations of port. It was also linked to women and to the ideal of domesticity. Sherry was the preferred wine of the royal personifications of these ideals: Victoria and Albert.[76] The second was the revival of a taste for lighter wines, a result of a number of complementary influences. First was their promotion as being of better quality, and therefore more conducive to good health, and more temperate and civilized than the stronger, often adulterated, port. Cyrus Redding, characterized as 'the first great wine writer', in his *A History and Description of Modern Wines*, first published in 1833, put forward such arguments to a middle-class audience and rated French wines the best in the world. Second were the arguments for a freer trade in wine, which would improve competition and thus quality; and, it was hoped by some, a lower price would increase consumption, including amongst the respectable working classes. Such arguments were aired before a parliamentary select committee in 1852, but no consensus of opinion was reached and no immediate action was forthcoming. It was Gladstone as Chancellor of the Exchequer who took the arguments forward by reducing duties but favouring lower strength wines, and in his Refreshment Houses and Wine Licences Act of 1860 he opened up the wine trade by permitting shopkeepers to sell to the off trade and providing for the sale of wine at 'places open for public refreshment, resort and entertainment' which sold food.[77] The results of all these measures were, however, limited. Take-up of the new licences was relatively low within the overall total of drinking places.[78] Total consumption of wine did rise and, within that, lighter French wines benefited, but it was short-lived. Per capita consumption halved between the 1870s and the eve of the First World War. Port and sherry continued to account for more than half of British wine imports, although sherry's reputation did suffer from the failure of producers to protect its name. Take-up of the new refreshment-house licences was low. Gladstone's efforts to broaden wine's appeal were not successful; it remained largely a drink of the middle and upper classes.[79]

Beer remained the main drink of the mass of the population, but here too the picture is one of declining consumption from the early eighteenth century. The figures for taxed production of strong and small beer suggest that annual per capita consumption over the century or so from the 1720s to the 1830s halved from a barrel to half a barrel, a little under three pints a week. This, however, excludes private brewing. Figures based on the malt tax, which take account of that, produce an average for that latter decade of over five pints a week. But this is much less than the suggested fifteen-and-more pints of the beginning of the eighteenth century.[80]

How can we seek to explain this fall in beer consumption? To some extent, as has been suggested, it was offset by a shift in taste towards stronger beers, but it is still a substantial fall. One reason was the decline of private brewing. Using Monckton's estimates, it fell from just over two thirds of total production in 1700 to half by the century's end.[81] Decline, however, was not uniform. Private brewing remained widespread on farms, at country houses and in institutions.[82] In some regions, too, like the West Riding of Yorkshire, its practice continued;[83] but in southern England, in poor agricultural parishes, it was clearly declining. The labourers' budgets collected by the Reverend David Davies in Barkham, Berkshire, in the late 1780s show the brewing of beer only for special occasions – or in one instance to nourish a nursing mother – and that, due to the high price of malt, small beer was ceasing to be one of 'the necessaries of life'. Similarly, Frederick Eden's reports on *The State of the Poor*, published in 1797, found the poorest labourers in the south unable to afford 'the indulgence of malt liquor'.[84] It must be said, however, that it has been suggested that their researches, prompted as they were by concern for the poor's reduced state, overstated the decline of beer consumption, as those surveyed might have been reluctant to reveal their drinking in the public house.[85] More generally, whether the living standards of the labouring classes in the period of early industrialization did or did not actually deteriorate, these were not, on the whole, years of rising real wages, as had been the case in the early eighteenth century, to fuel alcohol consumption.[86] And now, with tea, there was a real alternative drink. Its consumption had spread over the course of the eighteenth century, both geographically and socially to all classes, to become a new staple beverage.[87]

Beer consumption nevertheless remained high in this period, but over the course of the first half of the nineteenth century levels fluctuated, principally again in relation to working-class spending power. The fall in the years from 1815 is consistent with high prices and, similarly, the decline in the 1840s corresponds to years of economic difficulty. The rise in the early 1830s must in part be attributed to the creation of thousands of new beer outlets under the provisions of the Beer Act of 1830, as will be examined in the next chapter. Substantial advances in real wages from the late 1850s then underpinned rising consumption to the mid 1870s of over six pints a week per head. Per capita spirit consumption also peaked in those years, at one fifth of a pint per week.[88]

## 'A distinct advance in sobriety'

These words form the key conclusion on the nation's drinking of a royal commission on licensing, which reported in 1931.[89] This section charts how this situation was arrived at from the peak nineteenth-century years of the mid 1870s. It must be said first of all, however, that *total* consumption of beer and spirits in fact remained high until the First World War. That of beer did fall during the recession of the 1880s, but recovery at the close of the century was marked. It then fell away into the new century before rising again just before the outbreak of war. Spirit consumption showed a similar pattern, but was relatively depressed by increases in duty in 1907 and 1910. But, crucially, those years saw a long-term fall in per capita consumption. For beer this averaged four and a half pints per week in the years immediately before the war, a fall of around one quarter; over the same period per capita spirit consumption halved.[90] In the case of beer this was also accompanied by the beginning of a modest shift in taste to a somewhat weaker beverage. One change was towards mild, sweet ales, particularly in London; another was for light, sparkling, bitter Burton, and Burton-style beers; and a third was for bottled beers.[91]

Of course, this is looking at the whole population. A contemporary treatise on the question of drink by Joseph Rowntree and Arthur Sherwell made an attempt to capture the beer consumption of men, the main drinkers, by making some allowance for groups of non- or more moderate drinkers. The number of abstainers may have risen, which would be consistent with what we know of the temperance movement, to at least three million adults by the end of the century. Children were increasingly non-drinkers, representing at that time about a third of the population. Legally, they were prohibited spirits at first in certain localities and then nationally from 1872, to which beer was added in the 1880s, and they were excluded altogether from licensed premises in 1908 (see Chapter 7 for details). More important, however, was the gradual removal of children from the world of work, the advent of universal elementary education and an increased interest in their welfare, in the context of concern generally about drink and its effects. Women, Rowntree and Sherwell assumed, drank half as much as men. It is in fact extremely difficult to know just how much women did drink, but assuming that their estimate has some validity, average consumption would be nearly six pints a week.[92] Somewhat above the male average of nearly twelve pints a week would be the 'steady artisans', whom Charles Booth in his work on London quoted as drinking four pints a day, which is a substantial amount, but still well below the six to eight daily pints of early-eighteenth-century workers.[93] Nevertheless, at those levels it represented a substantial proportion of working-class earnings. Booth reported even moderate drinkers as spending a quarter of their earnings on drink, whilst thirsty ironworkers in Middlesbrough were said to devote half their wages to it.[94]

One other point to note is that private and institutional consumption, which formerly was important, had all but disappeared by the close of the century. From one fifth of total consumption in 1830 private brewing 'collapsed almost entirely' over the next forty years.[95] Brewing at country houses, for example, declined, especially in the period 1850 to 1870, and had largely ceased altogether by the turn of the century. Beer was already being replaced with cash allowances when from 1887 it was made illegal to pay servants with drink. And Gladstone's replacement in 1880 of malt duty with a tax on beer, which included that brewed privately, on a scale according to the rateable value of the premises used, dealt country-house brewing a further blow.[96] Of institutions, asylums, for example, had provided beer to staff and inmates, the latter getting an average weekly diet of five pints in the mid 1860s. But around the mid 1880s the practice ceased throughout the country as medical and psychiatric opinion turned against its use.[97]

To return to the general population, what explains this fall in per capita consumption? Central, it has been argued, was the relationship of drinking to working-class living standards. As we have seen throughout this history, improvement in the economic fortunes of the poor had led to their increased consumption of alcohol. The peak nineteenth-century drinking years of the 1870s conformed to that pattern. But from this point on there appeared an expanding range of alternative goods to which working-class spending power was now attracted as their price fell. These included imported foodstuffs (grain, meat, dairy products and fruit), ready-made boots, shoes, clothing and household goods. It also included tobacco, particularly cigarettes after 1900. The price of drink, in contrast, remained stable and thus became relatively more expensive. Significantly, when consumption rose in the late 1890s, as the price differential between drink and alternative consumer goods narrowed, it did not return to its mid 1870s peak, suggesting that newer spending patterns had become sufficiently well-established to be maintained at higher prices.[98] Linked to this was the gradual improvement in working-class housing. Although terrible slums survived into the twentieth century, from the late 1870s the process of removing the worst of them had begun and new housing built from those years had to conform to better standards. Such homes could now become the focus for that improved spending power and be places to enjoy leisure time.[99] And there were now more leisure opportunities than the pub: the music hall, the rapid development of the cinema from 1900, day trips and holidays and organized sporting events all absorbed increased working-class spending. These activities did not necessarily exclude drinking, but collectively they progressively reduced its centrality in working-class lives.

It must be said, however, that real poverty remained the lot of many working people – up to one third at the close of the century, according to the surveys of Booth in London and Rowntree in York.[100] But improving living standards for others helped to sustain a feeling that a better life was now possible. It was expressed materially in a more varied diet, a better furnished home, Sunday-best clothes or a day out. And, crucially, that better life was one to be gained at the expense of, rather than expressed through, drinking. Improved material circumstances were linked to important cultural changes which are best understood in the ideal of respectability. For the middle classes, sobriety had become from the late eighteenth and early nineteenth centuries an essential attribute of respectability, along with hard work, thrift and domesticity. This didn't necessarily mean not drinking, but certainly heavy drinking, which had been a common indulgence of the middling sort historically, was no longer condoned.[101] This belief in the virtue of respectability was not, however, confined to the middle classes. Expressed as the linkage of a sense of personal self worth and status with better standards of behaviour, it became an important working-class attribute. But it is not a straightforward concept; rather it is one with 'variations and ambiguities'. As Brian Harrison pointed out, it was never a 'fixed position', rather it was 'a process, a dialogue with oneself and one's fellows'.[102] This is seen in two contrasting attitudes: for some working-class men, committed to the cause of temperance, total abstinence from alcohol was a *sine qua non* of respectability; for many others, in contrast, the enjoyment of a drink clearly did not compromise it. When James Scurrah, one of the committed temperance working men, visited pubs in the northern industrial city of Bradford in the mid 1870s, he aimed to demonstrate the prevalence of drunkenness in contrast to the lack of police action against publicans allowing it. Whilst he certainly did come across 'rough' men and 'loose' women, as he termed them, he found as often as not that all was quiet, that many women were 'respectable' and that the customers included Sunday-school teachers and scholars.[103] As Ellen Ross noted, in a study of the subject in late-Victorian and Edwardian London, the ability to stand one's friends to a drink in the pub demonstrated a popularly understood facet of respectability: the small cash surplus which made it possible.[104] Another study, of workers in Coventry, concluded: 'Respectability and drink amongst the vast majority of the working community were, then, not mutually exclusive categories'.[105] What was essential to a self-perception of respectability was not drinking to excess, save perhaps on permissible special occasions or in the liminal environment of the seaside holiday.

For women, it seems likely that the ideal of respectability was linked with that other Victorian ideal, of home and the woman's place in it, to reduce their drinking from earlier levels. As noted above in relation to Rowntree and Sherwell's estimate that women drank half as much as men, it is in fact very difficult to know how much they drank. This is particularly the case, as will be seen below in Chapter 6, in the late nineteenth century as it excited increased levels of condemnation. But the contemporary view of increased drinking by women is not supported by the evidence. As will be seen in Chapter 3, whilst one can find women in pubs, their use of them almost certainly had declined over the century, even since Scurrah came across them there in the 1870s. Of course, they could drink at home, and the handiness of the off-licence for this was a constant condemnatory refrain, but here again there is no good reason to accept it at face value. Overall, then, for men and women, the widening belief in the ideal, or perhaps ideals, of respectability combined with changing material circumstances in bringing about a continuing reduction in levels of drinking.[106]

This developing trend was accelerated by the First World War in several ways. First, the price of drink increased substantially as a result of tax rises and the escalating cost of raw materials, although this was mitigated by the higher wages of a war economy and the reduced expenditure on food produced by rationing and fixed prices. More important were the reduced strength of the liquor and shortages of supply. In addition, the hours of sale for pubs were severely restricted.[107] Consumption fell markedly, of beer from 27.8 gallons per capita in 1913 to just 10 gallons in 1918 and of spirits from 0.7 gallons to 0.33 per capita.[108] But the crucial point was that after the war had ended, although it did increase from the low of 1918, there was no return to pre-war levels of consumption. The overall trend was clearly downward and the per capita consumption which averaged 13.1 gallons in 1931–8, or two pints a week, was a long way from pre-war levels.[109] Drink's share of total consumer expenditure also went down: allowing for the fall in the value of money it fell from 18.3 per cent in 1900–4 to 6.5 per cent in 1935–8.[110]

One important reason for the persistence of reduced consumption in the interwar years was the depressed state of the great staple industries of coal, iron and steel, and shipbuilding in particular, whose workers provided an important segment of the market for beer and spirits. More broadly, drink continued to become more and more expensive. In real terms the price of beer may have been 40 per cent higher in 1931–3 than ten years earlier and was still 25 per cent higher in 1934–8.[111] The proportion of working-class expenditure on drink declined, as money (for those who had it) was spent on goods and services whose prices fell or were more stable, as had been the case in late-Victorian England. In particular, there was increased spending on leisure, including on its established forms like the seaside or organized sports and on those that emerged in the twentieth century like the cinema or dance halls. The leisure pound also continued to go on tobacco and increasingly too on gambling, as the huge success of the football pools showed. The home also continued to grow in importance as a place of leisure, now furnished with the wireless, with a set in nine out of ten homes by 1939.[112] Those homes continued to improve in quality in these years, which saw both large-scale slum clearance and the building of over four million new houses. Moreover, these new homes were now in suburban areas, where pubs were nothing like as thick on the ground as in the centres of towns and cities.

The drinking that was done displayed elements of both continuity and change. Beer remained the great staple drink, but although its strength recovered from the lows of the war it did not regain its pre-war levels. Bottled beer continued to grow in popularity: its share of the home market doubled from about 10 per cent in 1920 to 20 per cent in 1939.[113] The three leading brands of bottled beers, Guinness, Bass and Whitbread, were actively promoted from the end of the 1920s, notably the former with its famous 'Guinness is Good For You' slogan. But more generally brewers now put greater efforts into advertising to boost consumption, rather than relying, as formerly, on the attraction of the product itself, distinctive labelling and trademarks, notably the famous red triangle of Bass, and a public profile enhanced through support for the local community.[114] In addition to the efforts of individual brewers, a Collective Advertising Campaign was orchestrated by the Brewers' Society from December 1933 with the slogan 'Beer is Best'. Emphasizing the wholesomeness of the ingredients, the link between beer and sport and the role of the pub as a social centre, it aimed to broaden beer's appeal to the middle classes rather than increase sales to its core working-class drinkers. But although it created memorable slogans and images, aggregate expenditure on advertising in relation to sales was modest and marketing and market research remained relatively unsophisticated.[115]

By the close of the nineteenth century, though, advertising and brand labelling had helped Scotch whisky to overtake gin as the most popular spirit, and together they continued to dominate the inter-war market.[116] The significant change was spirit-drinking's decline as a working-class pleasure. The *New Survey of London Life and Labour* in the late 1920s suggested that from being part of the normal drinking habits of the poorest before the war, it had virtually disappeared, except for special occasions or sometimes as a nightcap to round off the evening's beer-drinking.[117] This was to some extent offset by middle-class consumption. In Bolton, Lancashire, in the late 1930s, according to Mass Observation's researches in the pubs there, the only place where there was a significant amount of spirit-drinking was in the lounge of the town's best hotel; working-class pub-goers largely eschewed them.[118] Middle-class preference may also be indicated by the fact that more than half of expenditure on spirits was in off-licences for home consumption, lending some support to the suggestion of a vogue for drinking cocktails in suburbia.[119] Wine consumption remained the preserve of the better-off and continued at low levels. Two trends were notable. First was the growth of Australian and South African imports, encouraged by Churchill's reintroduction in 1927 of a tariff preference for so called Empire wines. Second was the increased popularity of UK wines, or 'sweets', made from native fruits, berries and herbs, but increasingly from imported 'must' of grape juice, raisins and grape sugar, which were half the cost of imported wines. For most people, however, wine still meant port or sherry.[120] Alongside these alcoholic drinks tea further consolidated, in Burnett's words, the 'central place' it had come to occupy 'in the nation's diet and psyche'. Aided by low world prices and low rates of duty, consumption continued to grow in the 1920s and reached all-time peaks in 1929 and 1932, by which time every person in the UK was drinking something like five cups a day.[121]

## Post-war

The 'distinct advance in sobriety' achieved during the inter-war years enabled the government to underpin morale in another world war with an adequate supply of beer, resulting in an increase in consumption. In contrast, that of both spirits and wines fell.[122] But beer consumption too fell again at war's end and overall the key patterns and trends identified in the previous section persisted into the immediate post-war years of economic difficulty, high taxation, material shortages and restrictions on output.[123] But from the late 1950s the country's drink history underwent major changes, which this final section will outline.

Total consumption rose substantially from the 1950s, but within that total there were significant differences between the three main drinks. Per capita beer consumption, from a low in 1958 of 137 pints a year, rose to a peak in 1979 of 217 pints.[124] That of spirits doubled to the end of the 1970s.[125] But the greatest growth was in wine consumption, which quadrupled in the same period from around two and a third bottles a year per adult in 1951 to nine and a third bottles in 1978.[126] From this date it continued to grow and by the mid 1990s stood at around thirty-two gallons per head per year. In contrast, that of spirits stabilized or fell a little, but that of beer declined.[127] The overall result was a significant change in the pattern of consumption. Looking at the twenty years from 1979 to 1999, the amount of both beer and spirits as a proportion of total alcohol drunk fell, from 59.9 per cent to 50.1 per cent and from 23.9 per cent to 19 per cent respectively. In contrast, that of wine increased from 13.8 per cent to 24.6 per cent. The other increased share was that of cider and perry, from 2.4 to 6.3 per cent.[128] Although the modern cider industry dated back to the late nineteenth century, its growth now was principally the result of an appeal to young consumers.[129]

There were also important changes within the three sectors. Traditional draught mild and bitter beer gave way substantially to keg and lager. Keg beer, – that is, beer conditioned in the brewery, filtered, pasteurized and carbonated for consistency, brightness and longevity – had been pioneered on a small scale by Watney in the 1930s, and the company promoted its Red Barrel brand vigorously from the late 1950s. Whitbread introduced Tankard in 1955 and Ind Coope their Double Diamond from 1962. Keg beers took 17 per cent of total beer sales by 1971, helping to end the popularity of bottled beer, whose sales fell from over a third of all beer brewed in 1960 to just 12 per cent in 1979. This promotion of keg prompted consumer reaction, notably what was to become in 1973 the Campaign for Real Ale. More significant was the growth in popularity of lager. Led by Ind Coope with its Skol brand in 1959, sales had risen to 2 per cent of the UK market by 1964. But it was the introduction of draught lager that helped to boost sales to 29.1 per cent in 1979 and within a further decade to over half of total beer sold. By then traditional cask-conditioned beer accounted for just 15 per cent of the market.[130] In spirits, whisky retained its importance with 38 per cent of the market, but gin was eclipsed by vodka, which took 21 per cent by the end of the 1990s, with gin on 12 per cent and rum 9 per cent. Light wines dominated wine sales, with a share of over 86 per cent. Within that, New World wines, with Australia the market leader, increased their share to exceed European wines for the first time in 2003. Port and sherry, the former staples of UK consumption, were now minority tastes.[131]

These were major changes. How do we account for them? Explanation must begin with rising living standards, which produced from the mid 1950s, in the words of one historian of consumption, 'the biggest improvement in the material standards of living in Britain since the Middle Ages'.[132] Spending on alcohol was an essential part of this affluence. Over the whole period from the mid 1960s, real spending on alcohol doubled;[133] but it formed part of a wider context of increased spending generally on leisure, with the biggest rises by far on holidays and catering (eating out and takeaways).[134] Alcohol was inextricably linked to those trends. Foreign holidays encouraged the consumption both of wine and lager. The habit of eating out accustomed people to drinking wine. Higher living standards were also seen in people's homes, which were more comfortable, warmer and, from the advent of television through a range of technological innovations, increasingly equipped with their own entertainment. The trend towards a more home-centred life, discernible in the late nineteenth century, now proceeded apace. Here, too, alcohol became an essential accompaniment. This was especially true of wine-drinking. In 1997 84 per cent of wine was sold by off-licences, 61 per cent of that by supermarkets, which, by making wine accessible and relatively cheap, had done much to promote its consumption. But more beer too was drunk at home: by the mid 1990s packaged beer, in bottles or cans, accounted for over a third of the market.[135] A Mintel survey showed that by 2003 46 per cent of UK adults were doing most of their drinking at home.[136]

A further important influence on trends was that expenditure on drink grew most amongst higher-spending households, which were the greater consumers of wines and spirits.[137] Women's increased consumption, still less than men's but representing a proportionately greater increase, contributed both to the total rise and to the comparatively greater growth of wines and spirits. And although consumption increased amongst women generally, it was greater amongst those on higher incomes and the better educated, reflecting their real occupational and educational gains.[138] In relation to other trends identified, women drank more commonly in restaurants, or in the homes of friends and family, although their drinking in pubs and clubs also rose.[139] In contrast, the fortunes of beer reflected those of its core male, working-class consumers. Thus the market for beer, but not that for other forms of alcohol, never recovered from the recession of 1979 to 1981 and the consequent rise in unemployment, conditions which were repeated in the early 1990s. Especially significant was the massive loss of jobs in the former staple industries of mining, iron and steel, shipbuilding and manufacturing, whose workers provided an important section of beer's consumers and equally of the pub's customers.[140]

Two other groups who increased their consumption were children and young people. Mark Abrams's 1957 study of the teenage consumer, actually those from school-leaving age to their mid 20s, had found that fewer than 40 per cent of males and 10 per cent of females took any alcoholic drink as often as once a week.[141] In contrast, a national survey of adolescents in the mid 1980s found that amongst fifteen-year-olds 52 per cent of boys and 37 per cent of girls were drinking weekly.[142] Research suggested that these levels had changed little from the previous decade, but the early 1990s saw underage drinking increase both in frequency and in quantity. Weekly adolescent drinking doubled in those years and the gap between the sexes disappeared.[143] The European School Survey Project on Alcohol and Other

Drugs (ESPAD), a collaborative effort of independent research teams in some forty countries, in its periodic reports found that frequent and heavy drinking were more common amongst UK teenagers, plus some other northern European countries like Ireland, Belgium, Denmark and the Netherlands.[144] Amongst the young, too, although drinking increased generally, it did so especially amongst those from more affluent backgrounds – thus students, a group whose numbers expanded in the late twentieth century, with both time and money to spend, were amongst the biggest drinkers. As one study of the turn-of-the-millennium night-time economy of pubs, bars and clubs showed, the average UK university city was host to some 50,000 students, each spending some £1,000 a year on entertainment. A study of one such city, Newcastle, found that its key drinking strip, the Bigg Market, was supported by three cash-rich groups, of which two were students and young 'style-oriented' professionals.[145]

As we have seen, for most of the years covered by this history rising living standards led to increased drinking, and the period of the affluent society was no exception. The period which *was* exceptional was that from the later nineteenth century to the mid twentieth – a period of reduced consumption. One response to this point might be that in the second half of the twentieth century the material gains for most people were so pronounced that increased spending could encompass all the things people desired, with no necessity to divert spending. But that would be to ignore an important cultural shift. For people in the earlier period, the better life to which they aspired was one in which moderation and sobriety were essential elements of a respectable life as they would have characterized it. In the second half of the twentieth century, in contrast, the better life was rather one in which material consumption was the paramount goal. This suggestion is paralleled by S. J. D. Green's argument for the decline of protestantism and its rewards: 'the certainty of salvation and the possibility of improvement', in which protestant moralism on sabbatarianism, sex, gambling and drink 'as much reflected aspirational sensibilities as it confounded popular pleasures'. In his view, between 1920 and 1960 the English changed their minds about this as a secularizing country ceased to be protestant.[146]

For the most part, however, drinking has historically formed part of the desirable life for most people, and improvements in living standards have facilitated increased consumption. But, as we have seen, living standards alone cannot explain the drinking trends this chapter has sought to outline. Changes in the demography of drinkers, for example, have also been important. Drinking by children and young people was the norm until well into the nineteenth century. The reversal of its subsequent decline, in the late twentieth century, has had an important impact on consumption. The same is true for drinking by women, with the late twentieth-century rise again especially significant. Succeeding chapters will explore a range of further influences on levels and patterns of drinking, from changes in its production and retail, through examination of its meanings for drinkers, to the impact of anti-drink sentiment and the complex forms of its regulation.

## Abbreviation

PP: Parliamentary Papers

## Notes

1. G. B. Wilson, *Alcohol and the Nation: A contribution to the study of the liquor problem in the United Kingdom from 1800 to 1935* (London: Nicholson and Watson, 1940), pp. 7 and 55–6.
2. A point made by A. L. Martin, *Alcohol, Violence and Disorder in Traditional Europe* (Kirksville, MO: Truman State University Press, 2009), pp. 43–4 in a similar discussion of the statistical evidence.
3. L. Smith and D. Foxcroft, *Drinking in the UK: An exploration of trends* (York: Joseph Rowntree Foundation, 2009), p. 16.
4. Wilson, *Alcohol and the Nation*, pp. 233–71; the demographic question – the age constitution and geographical distribution of the population – he addressed separately on pp. 10–14.
5. J. A. Spring and D. H. Buss, 'Three centuries of alcohol in the British diet', *Nature*, 270 (1977), pp. 567–72.
6. P. Clark, *The English Alehouse: A social history 1200–1830* (London: Longman, 1983), p. 3.
7. J. Burnett, *Liquid Pleasures: A social history of drinks in modern Britain* (London: Routledge, 1999), pp. 179–84.
8. They were responding to a request from a parliamentary inquiry to provide a historical overview of British drinking habits: House of Commons Health Committee, Alcohol, First Report of Session 2009–10, volume II, oral and written evidence, HC 151-II (2010), Ev. 224–7 (Kneale), 231–5 (Withington and McShane) and 239–43 (Nicholls).
9. J. Chartres, 'Spirits in the North-East? Gin and other vices in the long eighteenth century', in H. Berry and J. Gregory (eds), *Creating and Consuming Culture in North-East England, 1660–1830* (Aldershot: Ashgate, 2004), pp. 37–56, on p. 39.
10. J. M. Bennett, *Ale, Beer and Brewsters in England: Women's work in a changing world, 1300–1600* (Oxford: Oxford University Press, 1996), pp. 16–17.
11. Clark, *The English Alehouse*, p. 24; Martin, *Alcohol, Violence and Disorder*, pp. 67–70.
12. P. Slavin, *Bread and Ale for the Brethren: The provisioning of Norwich Cathedral Priory 1260–1536* (Hatfield: University of Hertfordshire Press, 2012), pp. 159–67; B. E. Harris (ed.), *A History of the County of Cheshire* (Oxford: Oxford University Press for the Institute of Historical Research, 1980), vol. 3, p. 180. A range of examples of such evidence is usefully collected in Martin, *Alcohol, Violence and Disorder*, pp. 67–70.
13. Bennett, *Ale, Beer and Brewsters*, p. 17; Clark, *The English Alehouse*, p. 24; C. Dyer, *Standards of Living in the Later Middle Ages: Social change in England, c. 1200–1520* (Cambridge: Cambridge University Press, 1989), p. 157; and see Bennett, p. 189, n. 7 for her questioning of some of Dyer's assumptions to support her point of consumption by most.
14. Bennett, *Ale, Beer and Brewsters*, pp. 43–4; Clark, *The English Alehouse*, p. 32.
15. C. Dyer, 'Changes in diet in the later Middle Ages: The case of harvest workers', *Agricultural History Review*, 36 (1988), pp. 21–37.
16. E. M. Myatt-Price, 'A tally of ale', *Journal of the Royal Statistical Society*, Series A, 28 (1960), pp. 62–7.
17. Clark, *The English Alehouse*, p. 24.
18. Bennett, *Ale, Beer and Brewsters*, pp. 79–81; Clark *The English Alehouse*, pp. 31–2.

19 R. W. Unger, *Beer in the Middle Ages and the Renaissance* (Philadelphia, PA: University of Pennsylvania Press, 2004), p. 98; R. H. Britnell, *Growth and Decline in Colchester, 1300–1525* (Cambridge: Cambridge University Press, 1986), pp. 195–6.
20 Bennett, *Ale, Beer and Brewsters*, pp. 80–1.
21 Clark, *The English Alehouse*, p. 97; L. B. Luu, *Immigrants and the Industries of London 1500–1700* (Aldershot: Ashgate, 2005), pp. 264–5.
22 M. K. James, *Studies in the Medieval Wine Trade* (Oxford: Clarendon Press, 1971), pp. 1–10 and 93. A ton (or tun) consisted of 252 gallons.
23 Dyer, *Standards of Living*, p. 259.
24 James, *Studies in the Medieval Wine Trade*, pp. 15–49.
25 Dyer, *Standards of Living*, pp. 104–8.
26 K. Wrightson, *Earthly Necessities: Economic lives in early modern Britain 1470–1750* (London: Penguin, 2002), pp. 147–8.
27 Martin, *Alcohol, Violence and Disorder*, p. 68.
28 Wrightson, *Earthly Necessities*, pp. 181–200.
29 Georges Edelen (ed.), *William Harrison, The Description of England* (Ithaca, NY: Cornell University Press, 1968), pp. 130 and 138.
30 A. L. Simon, *The History of the Wine Trade in England, vol.2: The progress of the wine trade in England during the fifteenth and sixteenth centuries* (London: The Holland Press, 1964), pp. 44–5 and 160–1.
31 W. B. Stephens, 'English wine imports c. 1603–40, with special reference to Devon ports', in T. Gray, M. Rowe and A. Erskine (eds), *Tudor and Stuart Devon: The common estate and government. Essays presented to Joyce Youings* (Exeter: Exeter University Press, 1992), pp. 141–72, on pp. 141–2 and 161.
32 P. Withington, 'Intoxicants and society in early modern England', *Historical Journal*, 54:3 (2011), pp. 631–57, on pp. 638–41.
33 Wilson, *Alcohol and the Nation*, p. 55; P. Mathias, *The Brewing Industry in England 1700–1830* (Cambridge: Cambridge University Press, 1959), p. 345.
34 C. Muldrew, *Food, Energy and the Creation of Industriousness: Work and material culture in agrarian England, 1550–1780* (Cambridge: Cambridge University Press, 2011), p. 80.
35 Wilson, *Alcohol and the Nation*, p. 363.
36 G. E. Barnett (ed.), *Gregory King, Two Tracts* (Baltimore, MD: Johns Hopkins Press, 1936), pp. 40–1.
37 H. A. Monckton, *A History of English Ale and Beer* (London: The Bodley Head, 1966), pp. 219–23, appendix D; his figures were used by Spring and Buss and in turn by Burnett.
38 Clark, *The English Alehouse*, p. 209; J. Chartres, 'Food consumption and internal trade', in A. L. Beier and R. Finlay (eds), *The Making of the Metropolis: London 1500–1700* (London: Longman, 1986), pp. 168–96, on p. 175.
39 Muldrew, *Food, Energy and the Creation of Industriousness*, p. 80.
40 P. Sambrook, *Country House Brewing in England 1500–1900* (London: Hambledon Press, 1996), p. 229.
41 J. A. L. Lemay and P. M. Zall (eds), *The Autobiography of Benjamin Franklin* (Knoxville, TN: University of Tennessee Press, 1981), p. 46.
42 M. D. George, 'The London coal-heavers: Attempts to regulate waterside labour in the eighteenth and nineteenth centuries', *Economic History* (a supplement to the *Economic Journal*), 1 (1926–1929), pp. 229–48, on p. 232, citing a source of 1769, but there is no reason to suppose it was any less earlier in the century.
43 Edelen, *Harrison*, p. 139.
44 W. L. Sachse (ed.), *The Diary of Roger Lowe of Ashton-in-Makerfield, Lancashire 1663–74* (London: Longmans, Green, 1938), p. 53; the diary is analysed in A. L. Martin, 'Drinking and alehouses in the diary of an English mercer's apprentice, 1663–1674', in M. P. Holt, (ed.), *Alcohol: A social and cultural history* (Oxford: Berg, 2006), pp. 93–105.

45 J. Sumner, 'Status, scale and secret ingredients: the retrospective invention of London porter', *History and Technology*, 24:3 (2008), pp. 289–306; see also Mathias, *The Brewing Industry*, pp. 12–21 and O. McDonagh, 'The origins of porter', *Economic History Review*, Second series, 16:3 (1964), pp. 530–5.
46 Clark, *The English Alehouse*, p. 210; D. Defoe, *A Brief Case of the Distillers* (London: Warner, 1726), p. 47.
47 J. J. Bagley (ed.), *The Great Diurnal of Nicholas Blundell of Little Crosby, Lancashire* (Record Society of Lancashire and Cheshire, 1968), vol. 1, p. 17.
48 Clark, *The English Alehouse*, pp. 210–11; D. Defoe, *The Complete English Tradesman* (New York: Burt Franklin, 1970), vol. 2, p. 220.
49 M. Hori, 'The price and quality of wine and conspicuous consumption in England 1646–1759', *English Historical Review*, 123 (2008), pp. 1457–69.
50 R.C. Latham and W. Matthews (eds), *The Diary of Samuel Pepys* (London: G. Bell and Sons, vol. 6, 1972), p. 151.
51 Stephens, 'English wine imports', p. 161.
52 C. Ludington, *The Politics of Wine in Britain: A new cultural history* (Basingstoke: Palgrave Macmillan, 2013), pp. 23–4 and 49.
53 Ibid., pp. 92–4.
54 On port ibid., pp. 121–43.
55 N. R. Bennett, 'The golden age of the port wine system, 1781–1807', *International History Review*, 12:2 (1990), pp. 221–48; see also his 'The wine growers of the Upper Douro, 1780–1800', *Portuguese Studies Review*, 2:1 (1992–3), pp. 28–45; and 'Port wine merchants: Sandeman in Porto, 1813–1831', *Journal of European Economic History*, 24:2 (1995), pp. 239–69.
56 Defoe, *A Brief Case of the Distillers*, p. 46.
57 K. Harvey, 'Ritual encounters: Punch parties and masculinity in the eighteenth century', *Past and Present*, 214 (2012), pp. 165–203, on pp. 173–4.
58 J. Chartres, 'No English Calvados? English distillers and the cider industry in the seventeenth and eighteenth centuries', in J. Chartres and D. Hey (eds), *English Rural Society 1500–1800* (Cambridge: Cambridge University Press, 1990), pp. 313–42, on p. 317. On smuggling see Clark, *The English Alehouse*, p. 240–1 and Chartres, 'Spirits in the North-East?', pp. 52–3.
59 Chartres, 'No English Calvados?', pp. 318–19; T. S. Ashton, *An Economic History of England: The 18th century* (London: Methuen, 1955), p. 243.
60 Population estimates from L. Schwarz, 'London 1700–1840', in P. Clark (ed.), *The Cambridge Urban History of Britain vol. 2, 1540–1840* (Cambridge: Cambridge University Press, 2000), pp. 641–71, on p. 650, taking the estimated lower total of 600,000 for 1750; E. A. Wrigley, R. S. Davies, J. E. Oeppen and R. S. Schofield, *English Population History from Family Reconstitution 1580–1837* (London: Edward Arnold, 1997), pp. 614–15 for the age distribution of the population.
61 M. D. George, *London Life in the Eighteenth Century* (London: London School of Economics and Political Science, 3rd ed., 1951), p. 29; 2 William & Mary, Sess. 2, c.9.
62 J. Warner, *Craze: Gin and debauchery in an age of reason* (London: Profile Books, 2003), pp. 35–6; and Mathias, *The Brewing Industry*, p. 369.
63 By 12 & 13 William III, c. 11 and 1 Anne St. 2, c.14.
64 Wrightson, *Earthly Necessities*, pp. 230–1.
65 Warner, *Craze*, p. 37.
66 H. Medick, 'Plebeian culture in the transition to capitalism', in R. Samuel and G. Stedman Jones (eds), *Culture, Ideology and Politics: Essays for Eric Hobsbawm* (London: Routledge & Kegan Paul, 1982), pp. 84–113.
67 Warner, *Craze*, pp. 65–82; J. Warner and F. Ivis, 'Gin and gender in early eighteenth-century London', *Eighteenth-Century Life*, 24:2 (2000), pp. 85–105.
68 Clark, *The English Alehouse*, p. 209; Chartres, 'No English Calvados?', pp. 318–20.

69 Ibid., pp. 320–1; Clark, *The English Alehouse*, pp. 83–4 and 242; Ashton, *An Economic History of England*, pp. 57–8; T. S. Ashton, *Economic Fluctuations in England 1700–1800* (Oxford: Clarendon Press, 1959), p. 36; the relevant statutes were 16 George II, c. 8, 17 George II, c. 17 and 24 George II, c. 40.

70 Chartres, 'No English Calvados?', p. 326; Harvey, 'Ritual encounters', p. 174, n. 22.

71 First Report of the Commissioners of Inland Revenue on the Inland Revenue; PP 1857 (1) IV.65, p. 2; Wilson, *Alcohol and the Nation*, pp. 331–5; B. Harrison, *Drink and the Victorians: The temperance question in England 1815–1872*, (Keele: Keele University Press, 2nd ed.,1994), pp. 66–7. The statistics are complicated by the inclusion of spirit-drinking Ireland and Scotland and the exclusion of foreign spirits, illicit distilling and smuggled goods, but the broad trend is probably about right.

72 Chartres, 'No English Calvados?', pp. 320–1.

73 Ludington, *The Politics of Wine*, pp. 144–62; also his '"Claret is the liquor for boys; port for men": How port became the "Englishman's wine," 1750s to 1800', *Journal of British Studies*, 48:2 (2009), pp. 364–90.

74 Wilson, *Alcohol and the Nation*, pp. 394–7.

75 J. Simpson, 'Selling to reluctant drinkers: the British wine market, 1860–1914', *Economic History Review*, 57: 1 (2004), pp. 80–108, on p. 81.

76 Ludington, *The Politics of Wine*, pp. 221–37; J. Simpson, 'Too little regulation? The British market for sherry, 1840–90', *Business History*, 47:3 (2005), pp. 367–82.

77 Ludington, *The Politics of Wine*, pp. 238–56; Harrison, *Drink and the Victorians*, pp. 228–31.

78 Return of Number of Licences for Sale of Beer, Wine and Spirits; PP 1868–69 (429), XXXIV.307.

79 Ludington, *The Politics of Wine*, pp. 255–6; Simpson, 'Selling to reluctant drinkers', pp. 80–3 and 102; Simpson, 'Too little regulation?', p. 367; Simpson's articles should be consulted for the roles of producers and shippers in the failure to create a mass market for wine; Wilson, *Alcohol and the Nation*, pp. 331–3 and 394–6.

80 Mathias, *The Brewing Industry*, p. 375; T. R. Gourvish and R. G. Wilson, *The British Brewing Industry 1830–1980* (Cambridge: Cambridge University Press, 1994), p. 30; Gourvish and Wilson used the estimates, based upon the malt tax, made by Wilson, *Alcohol and the Nation*, pp. 331–3 and 369–70 to produce a series of figures for England and Wales.

81 Monckton, *A History of English Ale and Beer*, p. 219.

82 Sambrook, *Country House Brewing*, pp. 231–4.

83 W. Cudworth, *Condition of the Industrial Classes of Bradford and District* (Bradford: W. Byles, 1887), p. 54; J. James, *The History of Bradford and Its Parish with Additions and Continuation to the Present Time* (London: Longmans, Green, Reader, and Dyer, 1866), p. 85.

84 D. Davies, *The Case of Labourers in Husbandry Stated and Considered* (London: G. G. and J. Robinson, 1795), pp. 8–13; A. G. L. Rogers (ed.), *The State of the Poor: A history of the labouring classes in England, with parochial reports by Sir Frederic Morton Eden, Bart* (London: George Routledge & Sons, 1928), pp. xxvii and 101.

85 Muldrew, *Food, Energy and the Creation of Industriousness*, pp. 68–9.

86 This is not the place to go into the long and complex debate over working-class living standards in this period; the suggestion here is based on C. H. Feinstein, 'Pessimism perpetuated: Real wages and the standard of living in Britain during and after the Industrial Revolution', *Journal of Economic History*, 58:3 (1998), pp. 625–58.

87 Burnett, *Liquid Pleasures*, pp. 52–7.

88 Gourvish and Wilson, *The British Brewing Industry*, pp. 30–1; Wilson, *Alcohol and the Nation*, pp. 331–3.

89 Royal Commission on Licensing (England and Wales) 1929–31, Report; PP 1931–2 (Cmd 3988) XI, p. 8.

90 Gourvish and Wilson, *The British Brewing Industry*, pp. 30–1; Wilson, *Alcohol and the Nation*, pp. 331–3.
91 Gourvish and Wilson, pp. 42–7; see also R. G. Wilson, 'The changing taste for beer in Victorian Britain', in R. G. Wilson and T. R. Gourvish (eds), *The Dynamics of the International Brewing Industry since 1800* (London: Routledge, 1998), pp. 93–104.
92 J. Rowntree and A. Sherwell, *The Temperance Problem and Social Reform* (London: Hodder and Stoughton, 7th ed., 1900), pp. 5–7.
93 C. Booth, *Life and Labour of the People in London, Final Volume, Notes on Social Influences* (London: Macmillan, 1902), p. 70.
94 Ibid; Lady Bell, *At the Works: A study of a manufacturing town* (London: Thomas Nelson & Sons, 1911), p. 342.
95 Gourvish and Wilson, *The British Brewing Industry*, p. 25.
96 Sambrook, *Country House Brewing*, pp. 247–67.
97 N. McCrae, 'The beer ration in Victorian asylums', *History of Psychiatry*, 15:2 (2004), pp. 155–75.
98 A. E. Dingle, 'Drink and working-class living standards in Britain, 1870–1914', *Economic History Review*, Second series 25:4 (1972), pp. 608–22.
99 P. Thompson, *The Edwardians: The remaking of British society* (London: Weidenfeld and Nicolson, 1975), pp. 291–306.
100 D. Read, *England 1868–1914: The age of urban democracy* (London: Longman, 1979), pp. 245–50.
101 Ludington, *The Politics of Wine*, pp. 222–4; L. Davidoff and C. Hall, *Family Fortunes: Men and women of the English middle class, 1780–1850* (London: Hutchinson, 1987), p. 400.
102 P. Bailey, '"Will the real Bill Banks please stand up?" Towards a role analysis of mid-Victorian working-class respectability', *Journal of Social History*, 12:3(1979), pp. 336–53; B. Harrison, *Peaceable Kingdom: Stability and change in modern Britain* (Oxford: Clarendon Press, 1982), p. 161.
103 Records of the Bradford Sunday Closing Association, West Yorkshire Archive Service, Bradford, DB 16/C40/3 and 5; for a short discussion of Scurrah's survey see P. Jennings, 'Liquor licensing and the local historian: The Victorian public house', *Local Historian*, 41:2 (2011), pp. 121–37, on pp. 133–5.
104 E. Ross, '"Not the sort that would sit on the doorstep": Respectability in pre-World War 1 London neighbourhoods', *International Labor and Working-Class History*, 27 (1985), pp. 39–59, on p. 43.
105 B. Beaven, *Leisure, Citizenship and Working-class Men in Britain, 1850–1945* (Manchester: Manchester University Press, 2005), pp. 65–6.
106 For a general survey see F. M. L. Thompson, *The Rise of Respectable Society* (London: Fontana, 1988).
107 A. Shadwell, *Drink in 1914–1922: A lesson in control* (London: Longman, Green, 1923), pp. 81–7.
108 Wilson, *Alcohol and the Nation*, p. 333.
109 Gourvish and Wilson, *The British Brewing Industry*, pp. 335–41.
110 R. Stone and D. A. Rowe, *The Measurement of Consumers' Expenditure and Behaviour in the United Kingdom 1920–1938*, vol. 2 (Cambridge: Cambridge University Press, 1966), pp. 124–5.
111 Gourvish and Wilson, *The British Brewing Industry*, pp. 335–41.
112 S. G. Jones, *Workers at Play: A social and economic history of leisure 1918–1939* (London: Routledge & Kegan Paul, 1986), pp. 3, 10–20 and 44–7; M. Clapson, *A Bit of a Flutter: Popular gambling and English society c. 1823–1961* (Manchester: Manchester University Press, 1992), p. 162; A. J. P. Taylor, *English History 1914–1945* (Harmondsworth: Penguin, 1970), pp. 384 and 391.
113 Gourvish and Wilson, *The British Brewing Industry*, pp. 340–1.

32  *Drinking*

114 J. Reinarz, 'Promoting the pint: Ale and advertising in late Victorian and Edwardian England', *Social History of Alcohol and Drugs*, 22:1 (2007), pp. 26–44.
115 Gourvish and Wilson, *The British Brewing Industry*, pp. 350–6.
116 Burnett, *Liquid Pleasures*, pp. 170 and 174.
117 Sir H. L. Smith, *The New Survey of London Life and Labour, Volume 9, Life and Leisure* (London: P. S. King, 1935), pp. 247–8.
118 Mass Observation, *The Pub and the People: A Worktown study* (London: Cresset Library, 1987), pp. 47–51.
119 R. Stone, *The Measurement of Consumers' Expenditure and Behaviour in the United Kingdom 1920–1938*, vol. 1 (Cambridge: Cambridge University Press, 1954), p. 176; Burnett, *Liquid Pleasures*, p. 174.
120 Stone, *The Measurement of Consumers' Expenditure*, pp. 178–9; Burnett, *Liquid Pleasures*, pp. 152–3.
121 Ibid., pp. 64–5.
122 Ibid., pp. 137–8, 153–4 and 175.
123 Gourvish and Wilson, *The British Brewing Industry*, pp. 364–9.
124 Ibid., pp. 452 and 631.
125 Central Statistical Office, *Social Trends 1980* (London: HMSO, 1979), p. 26.
126 Ibid.
127 Burnett, *Liquid Pleasures*, pp. 138, 154–6 and 176–7.
128 *The Drink Pocket Book* (Henley-on-Thames: NTC, 2000), p. 18.
129 Burnett, *Liquid Pleasures*, p. 158.
130 Gourvish and Wilson, *The British Brewing Industry*, pp. 457–8 and 585; M. Cornell, *Beer: The Story of the Pint* (London: Headline, 2003), pp. 203–5 and 218–20; Monopolies and Mergers Commission: The Supply of Beer; PP 1988–89 (Cm 651) L, p. 10.
131 *The Drink Pocket Book*, p. 14; L. Casini, A. Cavicchi and A. M. Corsi, 'Trends in the British wine market and consumer confusion', *British Food Journal*, 110:6 (2008), pp. 545–58, on p. 545; Burnett, *Liquid Pleasures*, p. 156.
132 J. Obelkevich, 'Consumption', in J. Obelkevich and P. Catterall (eds), *Understanding Post-War British Society* (London: Routledge, 1994), pp. 141–54, on pp. 141–3.
133 J. Appleby, 'Drinking nation: Have we had enough', *British Medical Journal*, 2012; 344; e2634.
134 L. Blow, A. Leicester and Z. Oldfield, *Consumption Trends in the UK, 1975–99* (London: Institute for Fiscal Studies, 2004), pp. 13–14.
135 Burnett, *Liquid Pleasures*, pp. 139 and 155.
136 M. Jayne, G. Valentine and S. L. Holloway, *Alcohol, Drinking, Drunkenness, (Dis) Orderly Spaces* (Farnham: Ashgate, 2011), p. 44.
137 Blow et al., *Consumption Trends*, p. 44.
138 M. Plant, *Women and Alcohol: Contemporary and historical perspectives* (London: Free Association Books, 1997), p. 15; J. Waterson, *Women and Alcohol in Social Context: Mother's ruin revisited* (Basingstoke: Palgrave, 2000), pp. 28 and 41–2; Smith and Foxcroft, *Drinking in the UK*, pp. 83–5.
139 Jayne et al., *Alcohol, Drinking, Drunkenness*, p. 63.
140 Gourvish and Wilson, *The British Brewing Industry*, pp. 581–4; Burnett, *Liquid Pleasures*, p. 138.
141 M. Abrams, *The Teenage Consumer* (London: London Press Exchange, 1959), p. 11.
142 A. Marsh, J. Dobbs and A. White, *Adolescent Drinking* (London: HMSO, 1986), p. ix.
143 T. Newburn and M. Shiner, *Teenage Kicks? Young People and Alcohol: A review of the literature* (York: Joseph Rowntree Foundation, 2001), pp. 27–8; D. Sharp, 'Underage drinking in the United Kingdom since 1970: Public policy, the law and adolescent drinking behaviour', *Alcohol & Alcoholism*, 29:5 (1994), pp. 555–63; Institute of Alcohol Studies, *Adolescents and Alcohol* (St Ives: IAS, 2009), p. 6.

144 J. Aldridge, F. Measham and L. Williams, *Illegal Leisure Revisited: Changing patterns of alcohol and drug use in adolescents and young adults* (London: Routledge, 2011), pp. 13–14, an update of H. J. Parker, J. Aldridge and F. Measham, *Illegal Leisure: The normalization of adolescent recreational drug use* (London: Routledge, 1998).
145 P. Chatterton and R. Hollands, *Urban Nightscapes: Youth cultures, pleasure spaces and corporate power* (London: Routledge. 2003), pp. 126–47; *Changing our 'Toon': Youth, nightlife and urban change in Newcastle* (Newcastle: University of Newcastle upon Tyne, 2001), p. 133. For an overview of research see J. S. Gill, 'Reported levels of alcohol consumption and binge drinking within the UK undergraduate student population over the last 25 Years', *Alcohol & Alcoholism*, 37:2 (2002), pp. 109–20.
146 S. J. D. Green, *The Passing of Protestant England: Secularisation and social change c. 1920–1960* (Cambridge: Cambridge University Press, 2011), pp. 308–16.

## Bibliography

Abrams, M., *The Teenage Consumer* (London: London Press Exchange, 1959).

Aldridge, J., Measham, F. and Williams, L., *Illegal Leisure Revisited: Changing patterns of alcohol and drug use in adolescents and young adults* (London: Routledge, 2011).

Appleby, J., 'Drinking nation: have we had enough', *British Medical Journal*, 2012; 344; e2634.

Ashton, T. S., *An Economic History of England: The 18th century* (London: Methuen, 1955).

—, *Economic Fluctuations in England 1700–1800* (Oxford: Clarendon Press, 1959).

Bailey, P., '"Will the real Bill Banks please stand up?" Towards a role analysis of mid-Victorian working-class respectability', *Journal of Social History*, 12:3 (1979), pp. 336–53.

Beaven, B., *Leisure, Citizenship and Working-class Men in Britain, 1850–1945* (Manchester: Manchester University Press, 2005).

Bennett, J. M., *Ale, Beer and Brewsters in England: Women's work in a changing world, 1300–1600* (Oxford: Oxford University Press, 1996).

Bennett, N. R., 'The golden age of the port wine system, 1781–1807', *International History Review*, 12:2 (1990), pp. 221–48.

—, 'The wine growers of the Upper Douro, 1780–1800', *Portuguese Studies Review*, 2:1 (1992–3), pp. 28–45.

—, 'Port wine merchants: Sandeman in Porto, 1813–1831', *Journal of European Economic History*, 24:2 (1995), pp. 239–69.

Blow, L., Leicester, A. and Oldfield, Z., *Consumption Trends in the UK, 1975–99* (London: Institute for Fiscal Studies, 2004).

Britnell, R. H., *Growth and Decline in Colchester, 1300–1525* (Cambridge: Cambridge University Press, 1986).

Burnett, J., *Liquid Pleasures: A social history of drinks in modern Britain* (London: Routledge, 1999).

Casini, L., Cavicchi, A. and Corsi, A. M., 'Trends in the British wine market and consumer confusion', *British Food Journal*, 110:6 (2008), pp. 545–58.

Chartres, J., 'Food consumption and internal trade' in A. L. Beier and R. Finlay (eds), *The Making of the Metropolis: London 1500–1700* (London: Longman, 1986), pp. 168–96.

—, 'No English Calvados? English distillers and the cider industry in the seventeenth and eighteenth centuries', in J. Chartres and D. Hey (eds), *English Rural Society 1500–1800* (Cambridge: Cambridge University Press, 1990), pp. 313–42.

—, 'Spirits in the North-East? Gin and other vices in the long eighteenth century', in H. Berry and J. Gregory (eds), *Creating and Consuming Culture in North-East England, 1660–1830* (Aldershot: Ashgate, 2004), pp. 37–56.

Chatterton, P. and Hollands, R., *Changing our 'Toon': Youth, nightlife and urban change in Newcastle* (Newcastle: University of Newcastle upon Tyne, 2001).

—, *Urban Nightscapes: Youth cultures, pleasure spaces and corporate power* (London: Routledge, 2003).

Clapson, M., *A Bit of a Flutter: Popular gambling and English Society c. 1823–1961* (Manchester: Manchester University Press, 1992).

Clark, P., *The English Alehouse: A social history 1200–1830* (London: Longman, 1983).

Cornell, M., *Beer: The story of the pint* (London: Headline, 2003).

Davidoff, L. and Hall, C., *Family Fortunes: Men and women of the English middle class, 1780–1850* (London: Hutchinson, 1987).

Dingle, A. E., 'Drink and working-class living standards in Britain, 1870–1914', *Economic History Review*, Second series 25:4 (1972), pp. 608–22.

Dyer, C., 'Changes in diet in the later Middle Ages: The case of harvest workers', *Agricultural History Review*, 36 (1988), pp. 21–37.

—, *Standards of Living in the Later Middle Ages: Social change in England, c. 1200–1520* (Cambridge: Cambridge University Press, 1989).

Feinstein, C. H., 'Pessimism perpetuated: Real wages and the standard of living in Britain during and after the Industrial Revolution', *Journal of Economic History*, 58:3 (1998), pp. 625–58.

George, M. D., 'The London coal-heavers: Attempts to regulate waterside labour in the eighteenth and nineteenth centuries', *Economic History* (a supplement to the *Economic Journal*), 1 (1926–1929), pp. 229–48.

—, *London Life in the Eighteenth Century*, (London: London School of Economics and Political Science, 3rd ed., 1951).

Gill, J. S., 'Reported levels of alcohol consumption and binge drinking within the UK undergraduate student population over the last 25 Years', *Alcohol & Alcoholism*, 37:2 (2002), pp. 109–20.

Gourvish, T. R., and Wilson, R. G., *The British Brewing Industry 1830–1980* (Cambridge: Cambridge University Press, 1994).

Green, S. J. D., *The Passing of Protestant England: Secularisation and social change c. 1920–1960* (Cambridge: Cambridge University Press, 2011).

Harris, B. E. (ed.), *A History of the County of Cheshire* (Oxford: Oxford University Press for the Institute of Historical Research, 1980).

Harrison, B., *Peaceable Kingdom: Stability and change in modern Britain* (Oxford: Clarendon Press, 1982).

—, *Drink and the Victorians: The temperance question in England 1815–1872* (Keele: Keele University Press, 2nd ed., 1994).

Harvey, K., 'Ritual encounters: Punch parties and masculinity in the eighteenth century', *Past and Present*, 214 (2012), pp. 165–203.

Hori, M., 'The price and quality of wine and conspicuous consumption in England 1646–1759', *English Historical Review*, 123 (2008), pp. 1457–69.

James, J., *The History of Bradford and Its Parish with Additions and Continuation to the Present Time* (London: Longmans, Green, Reader, and Dyer, 1866).

James, M. K., *Studies in the Medieval Wine Trade* (Oxford: Clarendon Press, 1971).

Jayne, M., Valentine, G. and Holloway, S. L., *Alcohol, Drinking, Drunkenness, (Dis) Orderly Spaces* (Farnham: Ashgate, 2011).

Jennings, P., 'Liquor licensing and the local historian: The Victorian public house', *Local Historian*, 41:2 (2011), pp. 121–37.
Jones, S. G., *Workers at Play: A Social and Economic History of Leisure 1918–1939* (London: Routledge & Kegan Paul, 1986).
Ludington, C., '"Claret is the liquor for boys; port for men": How port became the "Englishman's wine," 1750s to 1800', *Journal of British Studies*, 48:2 (2009), pp. 364–90.
—, *The Politics of Wine in Britain: A new cultural history* (Basingstoke: Palgrave Macmillan, 2013).
Luu, L. B., *Immigrants and the Industries of London 1500–1700* (Aldershot: Ashgate, 2005).
McCrae, N., 'The beer ration in Victorian asylums', *History of Psychiatry*, 15:2 (2004), pp. 155–75.
McDonagh, O., 'The origins of porter', *Economic History Review*, Second series, 16:3 (1964), pp. 530–5.
Marsh, A., Dobbs, J. and White, A., *Adolescent Drinking* (London: HMSO, 1986).
Martin, A. L., 'Drinking and alehouses in the diary of an English mercer's apprentice, 1663–1674', in M. P. Holt, (ed.), *Alcohol: A social and cultural history* (Oxford: Berg, 2006), pp. 93–105.
—, *Alcohol, Violence and Disorder in Traditional Europe* (Kirksville, MO: Truman State University Press, 2009).
Mass Observation, *The Pub and the People: A Worktown study* (London: Cresset Library, 1987).
Mathias, P., *The Brewing Industry in England 1700–1830* (Cambridge: Cambridge University Press, 1959).
Medick, H., 'Plebeian culture in the transition to capitalism', in R. Samuel and G. Stedman Jones (eds), *Culture, Ideology and Politics: Essays for Eric Hobsbawm* (London: Routledge & Kegan Paul, 1982), pp. 84–113.
Monckton, H. A., *A History of English Ale and Beer* (London: The Bodley Head, 1966).
Muldrew, C., *Food, Energy and the Creation of Industriousness: Work and material culture in agrarian England, 1550–1780* (Cambridge: Cambridge University Press, 2011).
Myatt-Price, E. M., 'A tally of ale', *Journal of the Royal Statistical Society*, Series A, 28 (1960), pp. 62–7.
Newburn, T. and Shiner, M., *Teenage Kicks? Young People and Alcohol: A review of the literature* (York: Joseph Rowntree Foundation, 2001).
Obelkevich, J., 'Consumption', in J. Obelkevich and P. Catterall (eds), *Understanding Post-War British Society* (London: Routledge, 1994), pp. 141–54.
Parker, H. J., Aldridge, J. and Measham, F., *Illegal Leisure: The normalization of adolescent recreational drug use* (London: Routledge, 1998).
Plant, M., *Women and Alcohol: Contemporary and Historical Perspectives* (London: Free Association Books, 1997).
Read, D., *England 1868–1914: The Age of Urban Democracy* (London: Longman, 1979).
Reinarz, J., 'Promoting the pint: Ale and advertising in late Victorian and Edwardian England', *Social History of Alcohol and Drugs*, 22:1 (2007), pp. 26–44.
Ross, E., '"Not the sort that would sit on the doorstep": Respectability in pre-World War 1 London neighbourhoods', *International Labor and Working-Class History*, 27 (1985), pp. 39–59.
Rowntree, J. and Sherwell, A., *The Temperance Problem and Social Reform* (London: Hodder and Stoughton, 7th ed. 1900).

Sambrook, P., *Country House Brewing In England 1500–1900* (London: The Hambledon Press, 1996).
Schwarz, L., 'London 1700–1840', in P. Clark (ed.), *The Cambridge Urban History of Britain vol. 2, 1540–1840* (Cambridge: Cambridge University Press, 2000), pp. 641–71.
Shadwell, A., *Drink in 1914–1922: A lesson in control* (London: Longman, Green, 1923).
Sharp, D., 'Underage drinking in the United Kingdom since 1970: Public policy, the law and adolescent drinking behaviour', *Alcohol & Alcoholism*, 29:5 (1994), pp. 555–63.
Simon, A. L., *The History of the Wine Trade in England, vol.2: The progress of the wine trade in England during the fifteenth and sixteenth centuries* (London: The Holland Press, 1964).
Simpson, J., 'Selling to reluctant drinkers: the British wine market, 1860–1914', *Economic History Review*, 57: 1 (2004), pp. 80–108.
—, 'Too little regulation? The British market for sherry, 1840–90', *Business History*, 47:3 (2005), pp. 367–82.
Slavin, P., *Bread and Ale for the Brethren: The provisioning of Norwich Cathedral Priory 1260–1536* (Hatfield: University of Hertfordshire Press, 2012).
Smith, L. and Foxcroft, D., *Drinking in the UK: An exploration of trends* (York: Joseph Rowntree Foundation, 2009).
Spring, J. A. and Buss, D. H., 'Three centuries of alcohol in the British diet', *Nature*, 270 (1977), pp. 567–72.
Stephens, W. B., 'English wine imports c. 1603–40, with special reference to Devon ports', in T. Gray, M. Rowe and A. Erskine (eds) *Tudor and Stuart Devon: The common estate and government. Essays presented to Joyce Youings* (Exeter: Exeter University Press, 1992).
Stone, R., *The Measurement of Consumers' Expenditure and Behaviour in the United Kingdom 1920–1938*, vol. 1 (Cambridge: Cambridge University Press, 1954).
Stone, R. and Rowe, D. A., *The Measurement of Consumers' Expenditure and Behaviour in the United Kingdom 1920–1938,* vol. 2 (Cambridge: Cambridge University Press, 1966).
Sumner, J., 'Status, scale and secret ingredients: The retrospective invention of London porter', *History and Technology*, 24:3 (2008), pp. 289–306.
Taylor, A. J. P., *English History 1914–1945* (Harmondsworth: Penguin, 1970).
Thompson, F. M. L., *The Rise of Respectable Society* (London: Fontana, 1988).
Thompson, P., *The Edwardians: The remaking of British society* (London: Weidenfeld and Nicolson, 1975).
Unger, R. W., *Beer in the Middle Ages and the Renaissance* (Philadelphia, PA: University of Pennsylvania Press, 2004).
Warner, J., *Craze: Gin and debauchery in an age of reason* (London: Profile Books, 2003).
Warner, J. and Ivis, F., 'Gin and gender in early eighteenth-century London', *Eighteenth-Century Life*, 24:2 (2000), pp. 85–105.
Waterson, J., *Women and Alcohol in Social Context: Mother's ruin revisited* (Basingstoke: Palgrave, 2000).
Wilson, G. B., *Alcohol and the Nation: A contribution to the study of the liquor problem in the United Kingdom from 1800 to 1935* (London: Nicholson and Watson, 1940).

Wilson, R. G., 'The changing taste for beer in Victorian Britain', in R. G. Wilson and T. R. Gourvish (eds), *The Dynamics of the International Brewing Industry Since 1800* (London: Routledge, 1998), pp. 93–104.

Withington, P., 'Intoxicants and society in early modern England', *Historical Journal*, 54:3 (2011), pp. 631–57.

Wrightson, K., *Earthly Necessities: Economic lives in early modern Britain 1470–1750* (London: Penguin, 2002).

Wrigley, E. A., Davies, R. S., Oeppen, J. E., and Schofield, R. S., *English Population History from Family Reconstitution 1580–1837* (London: Edward Arnold, 1997).

# 2   Producers and sellers

**Introduction**

The focus of this chapter is the production and sale of alcoholic drinks. It must be reiterated straightaway, however, that for much of our period and well into the nineteenth century production privately and not for sale was important, by individual households, on farms and at country houses and by institutions such as monasteries, schools, Oxbridge colleges, hospitals, asylums, workhouses and the military. The decline of this private production was an important change. Similarly, the producer and seller was often one and the same individual: from the medieval women brewing domestically and selling small amounts, to the publican brewer trading well into the nineteenth century. The growth of a commercial brewing sector and its relationship to retailers in the so called tied-house system is a further important change.

In highlighting these developments it is important to emphasize the importance of local and regional difference. Publican brewers were already rare in London by the close of the seventeenth century, but traded in other cities and in rural areas for much longer. The pattern of retailing also differed between urban and rural environments and between different types of town. It was always more diverse in towns and cities than in the countryside, but its contours differed between individual towns – for example, in the density of drinking places in relation to population or in the nature and style of establishments. But alongside the local, there was always a wider geographical dimension, as we have already noted with the medieval wine trade or the development of the tastes for hopped beer or a variety of spirits. The drink trade may thus be thought of as global long before the modern concept of globalization came to be applied to it.

The approach taken here is again broadly chronological, examining the different categories of retailer, and on the production side focusing in particular on the brewing industry and its relationship with publicans. This is examined from the development and operation of the tied-house system to the dramatic changes in the relationship at the close of the twentieth century, which saw the rise of pub companies. The diversity of retailing is explored, but particular emphasis is given to the pub, often seen as a quintessentially English institution, with a cultural resonance beyond its economic and social importance. Its relative decline from the late nineteenth century is thus an important change and in the later twentieth century it was to become one, albeit still major, element within an increasingly heterogeneous trade.

## Selling drink in early modern England 1500–1750

At the beginning of the sixteenth century, it is possible to identify three sectors in the retail of drink, each of which had its origins in the medieval period. These were inns, alehouses and taverns, a categorization employed in the first comprehensive survey of drinking places, undertaken in 1577. These sectors were recognized as distinct in law and in licensing practice: inns had a legal obligation to receive travellers and to secure their goods[1]; taverns were subject to a different licensing regime. They were not, however, fixed: establishments could migrate across the boundaries, as alehouses became inns, for example, or taverns reverted to alehouses. With that in mind, the sectors were recognizable to contemporaries and act as a useful organizing principle to historians.[2]

The prime function of inns was to provide accommodation and refreshment for travellers and their horses. Numbers increased with the growth of the economy and the consequent development of long-distance traffic, such that by the end of the fourteenth century they formed an integral part of a road-transport network. There were, for example, twenty inns in York and twelve in Oxford in 1381, and seventeen in late medieval Salisbury. They gradually replaced the hospitality provided in private residences or by monastic houses. When Elizabeth Berkeley, Countess of Warwick, travelled between London, Warwick and the south-west in the early fifteenth century, she stayed at the latter, with dependents on her estates and at inns. The transition from the monastery in particular can be seen in the 'fairly widespread' purpose-building of inns by religious institutions, as, for example, at the George Inn, Norton St Philip, Somerset, by the priory of Hinton Charterhouse in the mid fourteenth century.[3] This expansion of inn provision continued over the fifteenth and sixteenth centuries. Based upon the 1577 survey, John Chartres suggested 3,000 to 3,600 inns for the whole country.[4] Economic growth and the continued expansion of both private and commercial road transport, particularly after the Restoration, more than doubled that number by 1700 to between 6,000 and 7,000. Chartres further estimated, extrapolating from data for four southern and western counties from a War Office survey of accommodation of 1756, up to 19,000 to 20,000 inns by mid century.[5] Their proprietors, the innkeepers, were also known, although less usually, as 'innholders', the name of the London company which replaced the older 'hostelers' in the late fifteenth century.[6] They were often men of wealth and high status. Those of late medieval Hampshire and Wiltshire, for example, were part of the urban elite, often from long-established families. Similarly, in early modern Northampton the principal amongst them became aldermen or mayors and ranked amongst the richest men in the town, like James Bordrigge of the Red Lion, who died in 1743 with personal property valued at over £1,000.[7]

By the mid eighteenth century, a proportion of those inns were actually upgrades from the historically far more numerous category of alehouse. It too had emerged by the late fourteenth century as a more permanent retail outlet, as distinct from occasional selling from the private home, acting as a social centre as well as place of refreshment. Its growth thereafter was linked to the commercialization of brewing and to an increased need for a place for communal recreation with the decline, as a result of post-Reformation hostility, of communal feasts and festivals connected with the church.[8] Based once again on the 1577 survey, estimates have been made of between 20,000 and 24,000 alehouses over the whole country. This also included tipling (or tippling) houses, which seems to have referred to those which did not brew their own ale or beer, such as those of York, which were reminded by the city's corporation in 1594 that they were not allowed to. Numbers from this point expanded significantly, both absolutely and in relation to population. Peter Clark, whilst stressing the fragility of his estimates, suggested 32,000 to 35,000 by the 1630s, with possibly a further 15,000 to 20,000 trading without a licence, which seems to have been common in these early years of regulation. This might represent a great density of drinking places: the port of Southampton had a peak in 1603 of one alehouse for every sixty-one of its inhabitants, whilst an upward trend in numbers in Shrewsbury from the later sixteenth century produced one for every twenty-nine of its people by the 1620s.[9] Growth slowed in the later seventeenth century, but numbers peaked in 1700 at a variously estimated 58,000 alehouses or 60,000 total drink outlets.[10]

The expansion in the number of Shrewsbury alehouse keepers was linked by Clark to poverty. Evidence from other places confirms the picture of a trade made up in large part by the poor, whose deteriorating living standards drove them to take up ale-selling to supplement their incomes. Contemporaries deemed it appropriate that they should be run by poorer members of the community, providing a source of income to those who otherwise might require poor relief and hence burden ratepayers. In Kent nearly a half and in Hertfordshire well over a third of rural alehouse keepers were drawn from the social world of labourers, husbandmen and smallholders. Urban evidence, such as from Norwich, Southampton or York, presents a similar picture. But both here and in rural areas there was also a core of better-off alehouse keepers, from trades such as butcher, baker or yeoman. They were mostly men, although in some places women were a significant minority, typically widowed into the trade. As wives and daughters, however, they made a vital contribution to the running of the business.[11]

The third sector was the tavern, which specialized in the sale of wine. Taverns also dated back to the medieval period of high levels of wine consumption. They were never numerous and mostly urban. In thirty counties in the 1577 survey there were about 339 taverns, which was actually more than the number permitted under legislation of 1553.[12] As wine consumption increased in the early seventeenth century, so did the number of taverns. In an important provincial city like York there were then at least twenty vintners, whilst in the capital one contemporary source gives for the mid 1630s 363 taverns, plus four selling Rhenish wine inhabited solely by Dutchmen. A century later William Maitland in his survey enumerated 447 taverns – compared, however, to nearly 6,000 alehouses.[13]

By that date they would seem already to have begun to lose their earlier distinctiveness. Both innkeepers and alehouse keepers were able to take out a wine licence. Daniel Defoe, in his tour of the country in the 1720s, noted at Bramber in Sussex that the vintner there was more fittingly described as an alehouse keeper, whilst in London in 1740 the Black Boy in Saint Catherine's was described by its proprietor as 'both a Tavern and an Alehouse'.[14]

Alongside these establishments, and indicative of the growing sophistication and diversity of the retail sector generally, the later seventeenth century saw the rise of the coffee house. There were eighty-two by 1663 in the City of London and between four and five hundred by the beginning of the eighteenth century. In smaller numbers they could also be found in provincial towns and cities. Travellers to the Middle East had likened such places to taverns and in consequence they adopted tavern names, typically the Turk's Head. They also sometimes sold alcohol, although they have been characterized by their historians as representing a more sober and respectable alternative to the world of the tavern or alehouse. Maitland gave a figure of 551 by the 1730s, located predominantly in the capital's wealthier districts.[15]

In the retail of alcohol, however, the most significant development was distilled spirits. Their sale grew slowly through the seventeenth century, but increased vastly from the turn of the century onwards. The existing drink retailers naturally took to selling them. Samuel Pepys in September 1667 had called at the Old Swan 'for a glass of strong water'. Surveys of London in 1726 and 1736 showed that about half of those selling spirits were established publicans, and in 1744, when sale was restricted to them, 22,821 throughout the country now took out a spirit licence, roughly two fifths of the total public houses.[16] More common at this time, however, were distinct establishments. Maitland recorded no fewer than 8,659 brandy shops ('brandy' was used as a generic term covering all spirits), comprising over half the total drink retailers in the capital.[17] There were a small number of specialist punch houses, the leading one being James Ashley's London Coffee-House, Punch-house, Dorchester Beer and Welsh Ale Warehouse, as it advertised itself in 1731, although punch too was more widely enjoyed in inns and alehouses.[18]

Londoners seem to have been the principal consumers of gin, but it was drunk in towns around the country. In the 1690s Robert Maddox, a London distiller, had warehouses in York and Exeter, and his inventory listed debtors from over 200 places around the country.[19] But in the capital above all for almost thirty years it was sold quite indiscriminately. Chandlers – general shops selling basic foodstuffs and small beer and household necessities like coal, soap and candles, sometimes run by women – frequently sold gin, as did a range of other traders. Women were to be found more in the lower reaches of the trade, selling from cellars, stalls or wheelbarrows, or simply hawking it about the streets, like an elderly woman called Chapman, sent to prison in January 1737 'for selling spirituous Liquors on the Footway to Chelsea'. It was sold in this way wherever large crowds gathered, notably at public executions and the grisly sequel of the gibbeted corpse.[20] At no other period in England's history has alcohol been so freely available.

In this period the distillers too were permitted to retail. The trade had two branches: the malt distillers, who produced the raw spirit on a relatively large scale and were few in number, and the far more numerous compound distillers, or rectifiers, who redistilled then lowered the spirit with water and added flavourings, such as aniseed or juniper berries. By 1750 there were thirty primary distillers in London and around ten elsewhere in England.[21] The low cost of the raw materials, and hence also of the proof spirit sold on to the rectifiers, enabled the move to a mass market. In Chartres's words, 'It at once committed less capital and offered the probability of a more rapid return'.[22] The result was cheap gin: at three half pence a quartern (quarter of a pint) or half cup it represented slightly more than a thousandth of a typical maid's annual wages.[23] But the measures taken to regulate the trade included the prohibition of retail sale by the distillers, which was finally made effective by legislation of 1751, and which reiterated earlier prohibitions on sale other than in premises licensed by local justices of the peace.[24] With the partial exception of wine, which was not brought under their control until 1792, in law at least the sale of alcohol was now confined to licensed premises.

## The growth of a brewing industry in early modern England

Although gin had become by the mid eighteenth century an important element of the drink trade, beer remained its staple. Over the whole period the organization of brewing underwent a marked transformation from a domestic, particularly female, trade into a large-scale commercial enterprise. At the same time, the foundations were laid for a relationship between the brewers and the retailers – the tied-house system – which was to remain an essential feature of the industry until the end of the twentieth century.

In the medieval period brewing was widespread in both town and country; most households could do it and it was carried on to a large extent by married women. In addition to domestic consumption, ale might be brewed occasionally for sale, or as a more regular supplement to the family income. Judith Bennett attributes the importance of brewing as a female occupation, expressed in the ubiquity of the term brewster, to the fact it was low-status, low-skilled, poorly remunerated and suited to a domestic role. The story, then, in her analysis, is one of women's exclusion from the trade as a result of its transformation in scale, organization, technology and resultant capital requirements.[25] This was brought about by a number of developments from the fourteenth century. The expanding market for ale, and the related growth of retailing in alehouses, demanded more regular brewing on a greater scale. The arrival of hopped beer intensified the process; its qualities meant that greater quantities could be produced more cheaply and it could be stored and transported. All this, however, demanded expenditure on the necessary hops and on more fuel, equipment and storage facilities, costs which women could not meet. The importance of foreign, male brewers in the trade's early development and the growth of brewers' organizations (both for ale and beer) also helped to exclude women, although some few did gain admittance.[26] But their exclusion from brewing may not have been total in this period: in Southampton, for example, a number of widows carried on the brewing business bequeathed to them.[27] Furthermore, in rural areas their withdrawal from brewing, it has been suggested, may have had as much to do with the emergence of different, sometimes better, options for making a living in a situation of greater land availability and labour shortages.[28]

Nevertheless, that brewing became an increasingly commercialized, male-dominated trade is not in doubt. Over the course of the sixteenth and early seventeenth centuries, many towns, but above all London, witnessed the growth of brewing as an important industry. Population growth, the expansion of retailing, the shift in taste towards beer, the export trade from London and the south coast and the general profitability of brewing all combined to this effect. By the late sixteenth century Coventry, for example, had thirteen common brewers with an average production of about 1,000 gallons a week, whilst in London at least twenty-six major brewers were producing over 6,000 gallons a week.[29] Alehouse keepers increasingly obtained their supplies from these brewers, especially in urban areas with higher population densities and the small delivery areas necessary for a bulky product like beer. The relative complexity and expense of brewing beer rather than ale favoured this trend. In addition, the brewer could extend credit, offer allowances for leakage and spoilage, provide free delivery and maintain continuity of supply.[30] By the end of the seventeenth century the common brewers of London, almost two hundred of them, dominated production, with a mere 0.6 per cent of strong beer still brewed by publicans; and in a number of other southern towns like Oxford or Salisbury they were close to complete control. In contrast, over the country as a whole the brewing victualler was still an important figure: nearly 44,000 on average were still brewing each year at the beginning of the eighteenth century, almost three quarters of all the inns and alehouses trading.[31]

## Selling drink 1750–1870: the evolution of the pub

The retail drink trade in the mid eighteenth century was diverse and complex, a product of the range of drinks available, society's growing sophistication and the vital social roles played by drinking places. Diversity and complexity continued to characterize retailing, but by the third quarter of the nineteenth century an institution known as the 'pub' may be said to have arrived. This section charts that emergence, looking at the fortunes of inns, taverns and gin shops, the prevalence and decline of illegal retailing and the creation of a new drinking place: the beerhouse. It also examines the men and women who ran these establishments.

The term 'public house', most likely simply a contraction of 'public alehouse', as this form was also current, was increasingly used from the late seventeenth century. In the 1720s Defoe distinguished 'inns and publick houses', but also paired inns and alehouses under a more general description of 'publick houses of any sort'.[32] This terminological overlap continued throughout the century, as 'public house' became more commonly used – for example, in sale particulars for an 'inn or public house', reflecting the fluidity of trading noted earlier. It is clear, too, in the literature of the period, as, for example, in Fielding's *Joseph Andrews*: 'This Inn, which indeed we might call an Ale-house, had not the words, *The New Inn*, been writ on the Sign'.[33] 'Alehouse' was by then being used more or less pejoratively to denote a particularly basic establishment, along with 'pot house'. Edward Jackson, the vicar of Colton, north of Ulverston, had to make do with a 'paltry pot house' whilst in Langdale in June 1775.[34]

By this time inns, either existing or new, were using for added distinction the designation 'hotel', from the French word, which meant a mansion as well as an inn. The first landlord of the Hotel in Exeter, one of the earliest, which opened in about 1770, was himself of French origin.[35] Its use to denote larger establishments devoted to the provision of accommodation became more common, a process that accelerated when the arrival of the railway from the 1830s spelled the demise of the coaching inn. These hotels were quite clearly a separate entity from the public house.[36] In contrast, a sector which had formerly been separate – the tavern – continued to lose that distinctiveness. Several thousand ordinary publicans were taking out wine licences in 1800.[37] An 1815 guide to eating out in London thus included the Wheatsheaf Tavern in Holborn, famous for its home-brewed ale, and in Red Lion Passage, at the entrance to the square, the Queen's Arms Tavern and Chop-house, 'a public-house regularly licensed' and with 'some good Burton ale'.[38] In this way 'tavern' was coming to be used for public houses more generally.

Looking at public houses as a whole, the century or more down to the 1820s was one of contraction in numbers. If we take the estimate for 1700 of possibly as many as 60,000, this decline was marked, even allowing for its fragility. Statistics for a century later are more accurate. From 1808 publicans had also to take out an excise licence to sell beer, which it seems likely most would do, and in 1810 a little over 49,000 did so.[39] The number of public houses may thus have fallen by as many as 10,000 over the course of the eighteenth century. But it was not uniform across the whole country. The decline in London and in older provincial cities like Bristol or York, in smaller towns and in rural areas generally contrasted with industrializing towns, like Birmingham, Manchester or Sheffield, where numbers rose, although even here their much greater population growth still produced a decline in the ratio of premises to population.[40]

Within the public-house sector a further development in retailing at this time was a new generation of gin, or dram, shops, as they were known, with the revival of gin consumption. These were adaptations or conversions of existing public houses and were opened in towns and cities throughout the country. In 1787 they were said to be 'numerous' in Sheffield; two years later nearly 200 were reported in Manchester; and that number alone was claimed to have been closed down in Plymouth in 1802.[41] The number of public houses taking out a spirit licence increased sharply in the 1820s, from 38,472 in 1825 to 45,675 in 1830.[42] By that year at least, the expression 'gin palace' was being used to describe them by magistrates troubled by their development, and four years later *The Times* was reporting 'another splendid gin-palace' on the Surrey side of Blackfriars Bridge.[43]

In addition to these licensed public houses, the illegal manufacture and sale of spirits was widespread in the early nineteenth century. A study of Manchester at the beginning of the 1830s claimed that three quarters of the 430 licensed houses had gin shops attached to them, but that there were a further 322, by implication illegal, shops which abounded 'in the poorest and most destitute districts'.[44] The Inland Revenue, reporting in the mid 1850s, noted that illicit distillation had 'always been, more or less, carried on in the large Towns of England'.[45] Its current prevalence was linked to the growth of Irish immigration: it was common, for example, in the 1830s and 1840s in the Irish Ancoats and Collyhurst areas of Manchester, where strong community support for it was evidenced in resistance to attempts to stop it.[46] And it was carried out by women in particular. In Bradford, another centre of Irish immigration, Norah Rafter, in a case tried in 1851, had an illicit still in a cellar with five tubs each containing thirty gallons of wash and several gallons of spirits. It was commonly hawked about the streets in bladders: the local Bradford paper over the course of that decade reported fifteen cases of such street sale and twenty-eight of illicit stills.[47] In remote northern areas in the early part of the century illegal whisky was also prevalent, either locally distilled or smuggled from Scotland.[48] In this case, the traffic declined through a combination of the narrowing of the gap in the level of duty between the two countries in the mid 1820s and the efforts of the Excise. Further south, similar official action, prompted by the surge of illicit activity in the 1850s, acted as a check and the cutting off of the industrial outlet for illicit distillers by the removal of duty from methylated spirits further undermined the illegal trade. Detections concerned with illicit distillation now fell sharply and by 1870 the Inland Revenue was claiming that the practice was nearly extinct.[49]

Nor was illicit trading confined to spirits. Those same early and middle years of the nineteenth century also saw a resurgence of illegal beer shops. Unlicensed ale-selling had formerly been common, but its prevalence had declined with the development of a fully functioning licensing system by the eighteenth century. Its renewed incidence was probably due to the failure of the supply of legitimate public houses to match population growth and to the economic hardships experienced by many working people in the early part of the century, which pushed them to seek a cheaper, more basic alternative to the licensed houses.[50] Whilst it is impossible to be precise as to numbers, they were reported from around the country under a variety of names: 'whisht shops' (from the dialect word for 'be silent') in the West Riding of Yorkshire; 'hush shops' there and across in Lancashire; 'wabble shops' in the Midlands –all industrializing, populous regions.[51] But they were also found in more remote areas to cater to a temporary demand, like that of the navvies working on the railway near Harrogate in the late 1840s, whose hush shops were, according to the local paper, 'sod huts' converted into gin palaces and public houses.[52] But whilst such trading was illegal, it should be noted that temporary sale at fairs was quite legitimate.[53] In the mid nineteenth century the 'bush-houses' at the annual fairs at Fazeley and Rugeley in Staffordshire were exciting the disapprobation of the chief constable.[54]

By this time the introduction of free trade in beer had ensured the proliferation of a new, legitimate retail outlet aimed at, and enjoyed by, the working classes: the beerhouse. The 1830 Beer Act, which created it, was designed to open up what was widely perceived as the restrictive licensing system, in the context of moves more generally towards free trade. This movement of opinion had already in fact produced some rather meagre changes to retailing, permitting in 1823 a new 'intermediate' grade of beer between 'strong' and 'table' for off-sale only and in the following year allowing brewers to sell for domestic consumption without a justices' licence. Neither made much impact: in the year to July 1826 there were just fourteen intermediate and 773 retail brewers licensed and, although the number of the latter did rise, their share of total beer brewed was negligible.[55] The 1830 Act was quite another matter. Its more short-term genesis lay in the apparent rise in spirit consumption in the 1820s, the associated growth of gin shops and the desire to promote the healthier and more temperate alternative. It was also an attempt by an unpopular administration, that of the Duke of Wellington, to improve its standing by coming to the aid of depressed agriculture and appealing to the public with the promise of cheap beer.[56]

The Act freed the beer trade by removing the requirement for a justices' licence, a fee to the Excise of two guineas (one if it was solely for the sale of cider or perry) being all that was required to trade. The effect was dramatic. Within a little under three months of the Act coming into effect in October a total of 26,291 licences had been issued. In the first full year of its operation 31,937 licences were taken out, trading alongside 50,547 publicans, the decline in their numbers having been arrested in the 1820s. More than one in three retailers of drink were now beer sellers, and the long decline in the ratio of drinking places to population was halted.[57] In a real sense free trade worked, as the incidence of new beerhouses around the country was broadly relative to the existing provision of public houses, but with the greatest number in those industrial towns like Birmingham, Bradford, Leeds, Manchester and Salford where population growth had outstripped supply and where within just a few years they made up the majority of drinking places.[58] Thereafter, total numbers peaked in 1837 at over 40,000, before falling away to a low in 1843 of 31,227. Growth was then slow until the 1850s. These trends mirrored that for beer consumption, so economic considerations would seem to have been the significant factor. Consumption's great growth from the mid 1860s then saw beerhouse numbers surge to reach over 49,000 by the peak of 1869, trading by then alongside over 69,000 licensed victuallers.[59]

At the same time, the trade in table beer was completely deregulated. This had originally been introduced as an intermediate level of strength between strong and small beer. In 1802 small and table were merged into the single category of table, the weaker brew drunk by children, women and servants. In 1830, shortly after the Beer Act came into effect, a Treasury Order interpreted the 1802 statute to the effect that table beer could be sold without a licence from either justices or the Excise, provided it was for not more than $1\frac{1}{2}$d a quart.[60] It is therefore difficult to get a precise picture of the extent of this particular trade, but it is probably significant that the majority of references to it come from the economically difficult

1840s.[61] In 1861 Gladstone reintroduced the requirement for an excise licence and confined it to off-sale. The number issued then peaked in 1866 at just 2,170.[62]

Like the alehouse of the sixteenth and seventeenth centuries, the new beerhouses provided an economic opportunity to labourers, artisans and small tradesmen. A parliamentary inquiry of 1833 into the new trade, although it did provide some evidence for those hostile to the measure, seeing it as an opportunity for the poor, idle and criminal, supported that more positive conclusion. In Sheffield, for example, the great majority of beerhouses were kept by working men, including, naturally, grinders and cutlers. In Lewes, Sussex, and its neighbourhood they were kept by little tradesmen, blacksmiths, carpenters and the like, or rather their wives who it was said actually ran the business. In the capital keepers of chandlers' shops were the largest group entering the trade, according to one witness.[63] As to the fully licensed houses, looking back to the later seventeenth century, Clark argued for the growing prosperity and respectability of alehouse keepers, evidenced in the trade's greater stability and the personal wealth revealed in probate inventories. There was no longer a flocking to it in difficult times, although the poor did continue to find in drink-selling a living when other options were not possible. As late as the early 1770s those licensed in the Claro division of the West Riding of Yorkshire, covering the Knaresborough and Wetherby districts, still included a small number of the old and infirm.[64] Many moved into victualling from employment in the trade itself or domestic service, men like John Day of the Three Tuns in Northampton, formerly a servant or groom in two aristocratic households. Many also carried on the trade alongside another occupation. In rural areas farming was common, but a range of trades was also pursued: for example, at the turn of the nineteenth century Peter Stubs of the White Bear Inn in Warrington was also a file manufacturer, maltster and brewer.[65] It remained common well into the nineteenth century. In Banbury, Oxfordshire, the beer sellers in particular 'left the bar to their wives while they pursued another trade', but publicans did so too, as builder, blacksmith or coal dealer, for example, amongst several occupations.[66]

Although there remained some degree of difference in status between its two branches, from 1830 the beer trade became the most important route into retailing and consequently the background of publicans tended increasingly to converge on the skilled working and lower middle classes. In Southampton in 1852, for example, the twenty-four new applicants for a full licence were mostly beer sellers or engaged in some other way in the trade, with the remainder comprising an auctioneer, carpenter, carver and gilder, house decorator and two in the coal business.[67] The trade was attractive, too, to men in occupations with a limited life span – the military, sport and the police. Amongst professional footballers, for example, it was one of the four most frequently mentioned post-career employments.[68] That there was never any shortage of entrants to the trade supports a conclusion that for the mid-Victorian publican, as drink consumption reached its century peak, a comfortable living was to be had. The trade itself liked to assert its respectability: as the *Licensed Victuallers' Gazette* opined in May 1880, 'To be a "Licensed Victualler" is, as a rule, a guarantee now-a-days of respectability and position', the more so as respectability could also be gained by 'generosity, gregariousness and affability', all essential qualities for the publican.[69] But others also attested to the trade's respectability. Magistrates at brewster sessions did so, as at Leeds in 1849, asserting, as in previous years, the licensed victuallers' entitlement to their 'confidence and respect'.[70] Their status was demonstrated through their engagement in public affairs, too, as Geoffrey Crossick showed, for example, in his study of Kentish London, and through their own trade bodies. In this the new beer sellers were quick to ape their established brethren. A London-based Friendly Society of Licensed Victuallers had been established in 1794 with its own newspaper, the *Morning Advertiser*.[71] A Metropolitan New Publicans Protection Society, later the Beer Trade Protection Society, was now quickly formed in London with an annual subscription of ten shillings.[72] Local societies followed: when the Leeds Licensed Beersellers' Association sat down for its anniversary dinner at the Crown in Roundhay Road in 1839 it was served, in the words of a local newspaper, 'in a manner which would have reflected credit on a first class hotel'.[73]

The convergence of the background of publicans mirrored the increasing homogeneity of the trade. The inn and the tavern as distinct entities had largely disappeared; the new generation of gin shops were run by licensed publicans; illegal trading had declined markedly; and the new beerhouses provided a legitimate drinking place accessible to the working classes both as retailers and customers. As will be seen in the next chapter, the retreat of the middle and upper classes from public drinking places over the first half of the nineteenth century increased their relative homogeneity as working-class institutions. This is, of course, to generalize and in no way means that the public-house sector was not diverse in the size or nature of individual premises, from large urban gin palaces to little back-street or rural beerhouses, or that publicans were undifferentiated; but it does help to explain why by the late nineteenth century a single term 'pub' came to be used to refer to them. As to the term itself, it is in fact difficult to be precise as to its origin. On the face of it, it is a fairly obvious contraction of public house and must surely have been used as that term itself became common – for example, a diarist writing of a journey in 1812 had noted 'so many handy pubs all the Way'.[74] Not until 1859, however, is it listed in a dictionary of slang as in 'every-day use' in London and the universities of Oxford and Cambridge.[75] A keyword search of the Old Bailey Proceedings shows a growing incidence from its first use in 1876 ('I went to the *pub* and I thought I had missed you'). By the end of the century it had become common usage.[76]

## Selling drink 1870–1960

Just at the point, however, when the institution was becoming known by the name with which it was to assume the character of an English institution, so its long decline began. The number of on-licences in England and Wales peaked in 1869 at 118,499, comprising 69,369 full and 49,130 beer licences, about one for every 192 people, numerically more than ever before but at half the density in relation to population of 1700. Legislation in 1869 returned the beerhouses to magistrates' control. At the first licensing sessions after the Act came into force they seized the opportunity to effect an immediate reduction so that the total fell to 42,590 in 1871. This contraction continued, until by 1901 there were just over 29,000 beerhouses, compared to 73,784 full licences, representing in total one licence for every 316 people.[77] A new century saw numbers continue to fall. During the inter-war years they fell by one tenth to a total of 73,210, and the number of beerhouses fell by a quarter. By the beginning of the 1970s there were around 61,000 pubs, and beerhouse numbers were now negligible, at just 447.[78] There were many reasons for this decline. Over the whole period urban redevelopment and slum clearance steadily reduced the stock of pubs. A study of closures in Halifax, West Yorkshire, documents this process. In the 1960s, for example, an estimated 70 per cent of pub closures were the result of slum clearance and road development.[79] But they were the result, too, of the pub's reduced economic and social role, together with the operation of a more restrictive licensing regime. These important changes will be examined in Chapters 3 and 7.

From the late nineteenth century, however, a growing proportion of those full licences were not in fact pubs. They were granted to an expanding range of other establishments, comprising hotels, concert halls, railway refreshment rooms and restaurants. In London the privilege of members of the Vintners' Company to sell wine was also used (or abused, according to critics) to run a number of wine establishments, known as 'shades', or saloons, as well as clubs like Boodle's and White's.[80] There were also private clubs like the University, Athenaeum or Travellers for the aristocracy, members of parliament and the professions.[81] But much more numerous were clubs for working men. These actually originated at mid century in attempts to provide them with alcohol-free environments; but a combination of the actual preference of working men and the economics of running a club led to most of them selling drink. Charles Booth commented of London clubs towards the end of the century: 'The bar is the centre and support of a working man's club – the pole of the tent'.[82] Or, as the organizing body the Club and Institute Union's historian put it, 'if beer was prohibited there would soon be neither clubs nor Union'.[83] By 1887 there were just under 2,000 clubs, including political, trade, sport and social clubs, which had risen to 8,738 by 1914, 16,463 by 1940 and to almost 24,000 by the early 1970s, peaking at over 27,000 a decade later.[84]

Until a system of registration was introduced in 1902 by the Licensing Act of that year clubs operated outside the licensing system. Since a club was not owned by an individual, but by the body of its members, when a drink was bought, though the member paid in cash, a sale had not taken place since it was his own property.[85] This status presented an opportunity which was taken up by the proprietors of so called bogus clubs. By definition it is difficult to get a clear picture of their prevalence. In Liverpool in 1890, in what was described as the first major Excise prosecution, 198 individuals belonging to twenty-six betting clubs faced charges. The following year in Oldham, this time in an unsuccessful prosecution, in which 519 of 523 summonses were dismissed due to the bench's concern about entrapment by the Excise, the chief constable maintained that a third of the town's clubs were mere drinking dens. In Cardiff, where they flourished due to Sunday closing, introduced in Wales in 1881, 128 were prosecuted in just six years.[86] By this time, the term 'night club' was coming into use – for example, to describe all-night establishments in Soho –[87] and so named they remained an important part of the drinking scene throughout the twentieth century. But infringement of the law governing them, and outright evasion, continued to excite condemnation. In the mid 1920s Home Secretary Sir William Joynson-Hicks declared war on them as part of a clean up London campaign, and in 1949 legislation sought to outlaw all-night so called 'bottle-parties', ostensibly private but actually for profit, for which patrons ordered drinks in advance.[88]

A final but important development was the growth of the off-licence sector, providing a significant contrast over the period with the decline of the pub itself. Of course, there had always been sale for consumption at home, either from publicans, wine and spirit merchants or brewers. Brewers' sale for home drinking was an important part of their business, including for middle-class customers who would not go to the public house. Gales of Hambledon, Hampshire, for example, in the 1870s and 1880s was supplying beer and wines and spirits to farmers, professional families, tradesmen, ladies and officers.[89] In Leeds at this time Tetley's light bitter ale was offered to the middle classes and was said to be 'in great demand among the gentry and leading families of the district'.[90] But in the nineteenth century provision for off-sale was greatly extended. In 1834 an amendment to the Beer Act permitted off-sale for a lower excise fee. To this group were added beer dealers in 1863, when Gladstone permitted them to obtain an off-licence. Their numbers grew together, particularly from the mid 1870s, peaking at the beginning of the 1880s at around 18,000, when an amendment to the law made it easier for magistrates to refuse them, but in 1900 there were still getting on for 17,000, a figure virtually unchanged through the inter-war years.[91] But it was Gladstone who in particular promoted the off-trade in measures at the beginning of the 1860s, which enabled shopkeepers to sell wines and also spirits if they had a spirit dealer's licence.[92] By the beginning of the twentieth century there were over 10,000 outlets for the off-sale of spirits and over 8,500 for wine, figures which grew in the inter-war years to some 9,000 and 12,500 respectively in 1936.[93] One other development in the retail of wine and spirits was the chain. Messrs Gilbey, founded in 1857, created a network of local agencies selling wine, and in 1865 William Winch Hughes founded the Victoria Wine Company, which on his death in 1886 had 98 branches across the southern half of the country. In 1935 it held 147 licences, almost all within a fifty-mile radius of London.[94]

## Brewers and publicans: the tied-house system

At the close of the seventeenth century, over the country as a whole, the publican typically brewed his or her own beer. In contrast, in London above all, with its huge concentrated market and ever-expanding population, but also in a number of other southern towns, the common brewer had come to dominate production. Now, from the 1720s, the growth of porter brewing, a beer 'technically suited to mass production', enabled the capital's larger brewers to expand dramatically at the expense of their smaller competitors. Already by 1748 the top twelve brewers were producing over 40 per cent of the total of strong beer. These great breweries, like Whitbread, Barclay and Truman, were brewing annually over half a million barrels by 1780 and over one million in the new century, by which time the twelve accounted for 80 per cent of strong-beer production.[95] To the industry's historian this represented 'an industrial revolution in brewing', more pronounced than in any other industry, one which consisted in a huge increase in the scale of manufacture rather than any technological advance.[96] The size of the great breweries was one of the wonders of the capital. To a Prussian visitor to Barclay's brewery in 1827, by then having adopted steam power and brewing twelve to fifteen thousand barrels daily, it formed one of the most curious sights in London, which 'the vastness of its dimensions renders almost romantic'.[97]

Alongside this concentration in the industry in London went the development of the so called tie, wherein an individual publican was 'tied' to a particular brewer for exclusive supply of his beer. This arose out of commitments made as an ordinary condition of trade. A publican might become indebted to the brewer, or an aspirant to the trade with insufficient capital might seek financial help to get started. This became more necessary as both the value of public houses and the cost of equipping them increased. It was natural for brewers to offer credit since the incentive was to secure the supply of beer. Further incentives to this loan tie lay in the more effective ability of the brewer to estimate sales, the reduction in delivery costs by concentrating more beer on fewer houses and the maintenance of quality. Further, the number of public houses was contracting over the eighteenth century, which both increased their value and prompted competition amongst brewers to secure outlets for their beer. In this way in the decade after 1800 around eight of ten houses were tied to brewers, although the proportion thereafter did fall. One result was that brewers now began to exploit their own brand name by displaying it on the façade of the premises.[98]

This brewer supply and control of trade developed particularly in the counties surrounding the capital, as local firms sought to counter the threat posed by its big brewers, and in a number of cities around the country like Hull, Liverpool, Nottingham and Norwich. Nationally, by the turn of the century fewer than half of all publicans now brewed their own beer, and by 1822 this had fallen to 42.8 per cent. But there was considerable local and regional variation. In Yorkshire as a whole, for example, in the mid 1820s two thirds of all beer was still brewed by publicans;[99] and in towns like Birmingham, Manchester, Leeds and Sheffield the publican brewer remained the dominant figure. Why this dominance persisted in large urban centres otherwise favourable to the growth of wholesale brewing is not always clear, although it has been suggested that in Birmingham, for example, its tradition of small artisans was influential.[100]

The creation of a new generation of artisan brewers was one of the aims of the promoters of free trade in beer, directed in part at the brewers' perceived monopoly. This did happen: in the year to January 1832 42.1 per cent of beer sellers were brewing, although this represented only a small fraction of total production.

By the close of the free-trade years just one in five beer sellers still brewed.[101] But the key development was that the new beerhouses were increasingly also tied to brewers. Within twenty years a parliamentary inquiry was finding that a very large proportion was, like public houses, the actual property of brewers or tied by advances to them.[102] In the West Riding of Yorkshire, for example, where the brewing publican had been an important figure, local brewers now saw an opportunity in the new trade. As was reported of Michael Stocks of the Shibden Head Brewery, located midway between Bradford and Halifax, his 'interest had been, like that of other brewers, to get hold of beerhouses where he could, both in villages and in populous towns'.[103]

This expansion of the tie after 1830, which comprised full as well as beer licences, whose value had been depressed by the new competitors, was driven, it has been suggested, by several further influences. Tieing houses helped to insulate brewers from the effect of unstable demand for beer, which actually declined from the later 1830s and again in the mid 1850s. Local rivalry between brewers and competitive disadvantages were another spur. This is illustrated by the case of Halifax, where acquisitions by two of the oldest breweries, including Stocks, prompted newer entrants to the trade to secure their own outlets. For these new breweries tied houses brought more predictable sales, ensured quality control and advertised their products to other retailers. Whilst there had been no brewery-owned outlets in 1837, by 1876 37 per cent of public and beerhouses were owned by brewers, by then enjoying the possibility of speculative gains as a more restrictive licensing regime inflated the value of public houses.[104] Over the country as a whole, with the growth of population and the rise in beer consumption from the 1860s, the number of common brewers producing more than a thousand barrels a year increased from 1,436 in 1834 to 2,192 by 1871, a rise of more than half.[105]

The trend towards the tie was, then, already well advanced when the free-trade era came to an end in 1869. Several developments now drove the process forward. One, already in evidence, was the growth of a national market for beer, facilitated by the railway. In this way brewers from Burton on Trent, the premier brewing centre, accounted for almost 8 per cent of England's total beer sales in the late 1860s, rising to almost 12 per cent twenty years later (Figure 2.1).

The movement of Burton brewers into new areas prompted local brewers to secure outlets just as brewers had earlier done in counties around the capital.[106] The ending of free trade also halted the unlimited expansion of public houses. Brewery flotation from the mid 1880s, in which 260 firms sold about £185 million of share capital before 1900, provided finance for further acquisitions and led to a 'scramble for property', inflating prices, particularly in London. There, too, falling beer consumption in the 1880s, bankruptcies amongst publicans due to rising overheads and the incursions of Burton firms led to brewers switching from the loan tie to outright ownership.[107] The final result was that most pubs throughout the country came to be leased or owned by brewery companies. The precise extent is, however, not wholly clear. Hawkins and Pass suggested 90 per cent by 1900, a figure which Gourvish and Wilson felt was too high, whilst acknowledging that such levels were reported for the 1890s by the Royal Commission on Liquor Licensing Laws for a number of cities like Manchester, Liverpool, Bristol,

*Figure 2.1* England's premier brewing centre.
Source: Courtesy of Lynn Pearson.

Plymouth and Hull.[108] John Vaizey cited a Brewers' Society estimate that the percentage tied rose from over 70 in 1886 to as much as 95 per cent in 1913.[109] Whatever the precise extent, it is clear that the great majority of pubs were indeed tied to brewers.

In these tied pubs the publican was typically a tenant, paying rent but keeping the profits. The brewer owned the fixtures and fittings and carried out any alterations and repairs, to the cost of which the tenant might have to contribute.[110] Alternatively, a manager might be employed, sometimes also earning a commission on sales. The system was used in particular in larger cities like Birmingham and Newcastle, but above all in Liverpool, where half the city's publicans were paid managers by the mid 1890s.[111] The trade continued to be attractive in late Victorian and Edwardian England. Robert Roberts put publicans in the premier position in his Salford slum district, along with shopkeepers and skilled tradesmen (Figure 2.2).[112]

Nevertheless, there is increasing evidence at this time that some publicans were struggling. In Newcastle in the mid 1890s about one in ten of the city's pubs was reported as not doing any real trade.[113] The records generated by the redundancy scheme under the Licensing Act of 1904 illustrate clearly how many smaller pubs, particularly beerhouses, were making a poor living. In both rural and urban north Lancashire, for example, some pubs had weekly takings averaging just £9 when those of over £50 were said to be 'fairly respectable'.[114] The continuing fall in per capita beer consumption, the declining social role of the pub and rising overheads, as both central and local taxation increased, worsened their position.

*Figure 2.2* Arthur and Sarah Gray and staff, with neighbouring shopkeeper to the right, at the Black Swan Tavern, Thornton Road, Bradford, c. 1915.

Source: Author's collection.

Worse still was to come during the war. Publicans claimed constantly that they were bearing the brunt of price increases and shortages. Both were real, and although rising wages did offset the former, the latter reduced supplies and forced many pubs to close on some days in the week later in the war.[115] Strained relations between publicans and brewers were exacerbated by the contrast between the former's difficulties and the latter's profits. Little affected in the early part of the war, from 1917 companies enjoyed a 'welcome bonanza' as the enforced move to weaker beer lowered unit costs and consumer demand for what beer there was held up as a result of full employment and the absence of other peacetime leisure pursuits.[116]

After the war, the permanence of reduced consumption levels, made worse by the effects of the depression and high taxation, created for brewers a more difficult trading environment. One result was the continuation of the pre-war trend to concentration in the industry, with the number of UK brewers falling from 2,464 in 1921 to 840 in 1939, and the number of companies more than halving, as they sought first to expand their retailing base, but later to rationalize productive capacity. Nevertheless, profits remained remarkably stable, evidence of the strength of their financial reserves.[117] Publicans, in contrast, continued to face difficulties, especially in the depressed regions, although firmer conclusions must await more detailed research, and there was undoubtedly regional and local variation. In 1924 half of Newcastle's pubs were reported as being unable to pay their way, a situation which persisted through the succeeding decade.[118] Newcastle was, like Birmingham, a city which saw a further shift towards management in the inter-war years, although the majority of publicans nationally, more than 80 per cent, continued to be tenants. The tie was generally extended from draught beers to include bottled and foreign beers, wines, spirits and soft drinks.[119] But it would be misleading to judge the trade solely from its financial rewards. As one York landlady expressed it, voicing the sentiments of most in the city's trade:

> Many times we didn't even have a night off, we just stopped in the pub and played darts with the lads. It was more a friendly, homely atmosphere. All your customers were friends. All my life I've had pleasant memories. I've had fun, I've really enjoyed it. If I went tomorrow, I've no regrets. My husband was the same, he loved the licensed trade. He didn't have hobbies – his work was his hobby.[120]

## Post-war

In brewing and retailing in the 1950s there were key continuities with the world of 1914. Despite contraction and consolidation in the industry, brewing remained dominated by local firms. The pub declined, both in numbers and in social importance, but was still the main working-class place of leisure and, the growth of off-licences and clubs notwithstanding, most beer was still bought there. But the next half century was to see major changes. Five developments in particular must be highlighted. First was the continued decline of the pub. Second, in contrast, were the diversification and multiplication of the broader retail sector. Third was the increased importance of off-sales and of home consumption. Fourth and fifth were the massive changes to the brewing industry and to its relationship with the retail trade and the growth of an entirely new group of pub-owners.

The number of pubs in England and Wales continued to fall, from around 61,000 at the beginning of the 1970s to 51,479 in 2006, according to the trade body the British Beer and Pub Association – a fall in just thirty-five years of some 10,000.[121] Decline was evident in both urban and rural areas. The Halifax study noted above documented closures both in the town itself and in the more rural surrounding districts, with falling numbers in the two decades from 1991 reaching post-war highs.[122] Over the country as a whole, some 300 rural pubs closed in 1999 alone. At the beginning of that decade 29 per cent of rural parishes in Leicestershire, for example, had no pub. In Norfolk, towards its end, there was no pub in 38 per cent of villages, rising to 70 per cent of those with fewer than 500 inhabitants.[123]

In marked contrast to the decline in the numbers of pubs was the rise from the 1960s in the total number of places retailing drink. The provision of alcohol in residential accommodation and restaurants expanded following the introduction in 1961 of licences specific to such premises, combined with a limitation on magistrates' discretion to refuse them. By 1980 there were 20,622 of these new licences, rising to a peak of over 31,000 in 1997.[124] There was also growth from the 1970s of a range of new on-licences, comprising a variety of bars, including wine and café bars, whose precise numbers are, however, difficult to ascertain from the available statistical data.[125] More detailed work does, however, permit some comment. David Gutzke, in a study focusing on the question of drinking by women, looked at wine bars. He cited an estimate of between 500 and 600 of them throughout the country by the end of the 1970s and over 500 in London alone, the main centre for them, by the 1990s.[126] Another growing sector was that of so called branded outlets. One example was the development of restaurant-oriented pubs like Berni, Beefeater, Harvester or Vintage Inns, indicative of the growing importance of food to the sector. By the end of the 1990s, in fact, pubs headed the list of number of meals taken in commercial establishments (not including snacks) at 345.5 million, comprising 248 million in pub restaurants and a further 97 million bar meals.[127] Perhaps the best known example of both the branded pub chain and food orientation was J. D. Wetherspoon, which specialized in converting premises previously put to other uses, such as banks, post offices, cinemas, shops, department stores and hotels.[128] The overall result of these trends was growth in the total of on-licensed premises (other than residential and restaurant) from just over 67,000 in 1980 to almost 82,000 by 2003. If we add to that restaurants and residential licences plus licensed clubs, whose numbers also grew, the total number of places where one could drink had by the turn of the millennium almost reached its nineteenth-century peak at over 110,000 premises. The only declining sector, other than pubs, was that of registered clubs, from over 27,000 in 1983 to fewer than 20,000 twenty years later.[129]

The other important change was the growth of off-sale. This, too, was facilitated by the Licensing Act of 1961, which permitted existing off-licences to open all day, hitherto having been restricted to pub-opening hours with their enforced early-morning and afternoon closing. The equalization of hours for the sale of drink alongside food and other goods now made their sale more attractive to retailers. This was followed by the abolition in 1964 of resale price maintenance, which now permitted price cutting.[130] The total number of off-licences rose from over 28,000 in 1971 to almost 48,000 twenty years later.[131] But of particular significance was the growth of supermarket sales: from just 175 stores in the late

1950s, numbers increased to over 7,000 twenty years later, plus a further 237 superstores.[132] They were especially important to the growth of wine and spirit consumption, both in the ease with which they could be purchased and the fact that women, who increasingly drank them, tended to do the shopping. By 1997 61 per cent of all wine was bought in supermarkets and 84 per cent in all off-licences. Similarly, 60 per cent of average weekly spending on spirits was in off-licences.[133] Together with the growth of packaged beer sales, this underpinned the shift to drinking at home.

Our fourth and fifth changes are in production and ownership. From the late 1950s the pace of concentration in the brewing industry accelerated markedly. Examples included the 1960 creation of Scottish and Newcastle from the merger of Newcastle, Robert Younger and Scottish Breweries; that of the following year between Tetley Walker, Ind Coope and Ansells; and the 1967 creation of Bass Charrington from Bass, Mitchells and Butlers and Charrington.[134] By 1967, according to the Monopolies Commission, the six largest brewers – Bass Charrington, Allied, Whitbread, Watney Mann, Courage and Scottish and Newcastle – between them accounted for nearly 70 per cent of total beer production and owned over half of all the on-licences in the UK.[135] One consequence of concentration was rationalization and greater scale economies of production. Thus the Big Six, as they were known, closed 54 of their 122 breweries between 1958 and 1970. Alongside this were conglomerate mergers linking brewing with wine and spirit wholesalers and shippers, food, tobacco, hotels and restaurants.[136] By the end of the 1980s over 70 per cent of UK pubs were owned by the major brewers, plus they indirectly controlled the free trade through loans and grants.[137] It was this level of concentration in the industry which led to another inquiry by the Monopolies and Mergers Commission into the supply of beer. It concluded that a monopoly existed which operated against the public interest and that the degree of vertical integration – that is, having control over the entire process from purchase of raw materials to sale to the customer – should be reduced in order to encourage lower prices and improve consumer choice. The Department of Trade and Industry endorsed the report, but ultimately watered down its conclusions. Nevertheless, the so called Beer Orders of 1989 did make important changes. Brewers owning more than 2,000 full on-licences were required either to dispose of the brewing business or dispose of, or free the tie on, half of the number of such licences in excess of 2,000 by the end of October 1992. Publicans in tied premises were to be allowed to sell a 'guest' cask-conditioned draught beer and to buy drinks other than beer and alcohol-free and low-alcohol beers from outside the tie.[138]

The succeeding decade witnessed a huge transformation in the industry which continued into the new millennium and whose complex and fast-moving details are beyond the scope of this study. The following are the key changes. First was the separation to a large extent of production from retailing, with only regional brewers such as Greene King maintaining the link, owning in total some 8,500 public houses in 2004. This trend was already evident before the Beer Orders, clearest in the case of Whitbread, which at the beginning of the 1980s had created separate divisions for this sector.[139] Similarly with the second major change, the growth of pub companies, their origin also predated the Beer Orders, but the disposal by brewery companies of large stocks of pubs greatly accelerated their development. The two largest, Enterprise Inns and Punch Taverns, founded in 1991 and 1997, between them owned over 17,000 pubs by 2004.[140] Finally, brewing moved from being national to global in scale, with the old national leaders having been acquired by breweries with worldwide interests – for example, the Danish Carlsberg or Belgian Interbrew – which together came to dominate production.[141] Against this trend, more important symbolically than in the volume of beer produced, was the growth from the early 1970s of small, or 'micro', breweries. Over the next thirty years some 850 new ones opened in the UK, of which more than half were still open at the new millennium.[142]

These outcomes led some commentators to conclude that whilst the intention of the Beer Orders had been 'to remove a complex monopoly rooted in vertical integration – the result has been the growth and development of oligopolistic/ monopolistic presence in both the supply and retailing of beer'.[143] Others have stressed the transforming effects of developments unconnected with the Beer Orders. Gutzke, for example, highlighted overcapacity in the industry as beer consumption contracted and economic, social and demographic changes resulted in the pub's long-term decline. For Gutzke, taking issue with those critical of the Beer Orders, the advent of the pub companies injected new money and, crucially, new ideas into the industry, and, in particular, gave new employment opportunities to women and emphasized their needs as customers, influencing the industry as a whole.[144]

At the close of this history the production and distribution of drink was largely in the hands of global corporations. This was true of wines and spirits as well as beer. But the sellers of drink encompassed a very diverse group, from giant supermarkets to small off-licences, from chains of eateries and hotels to owner-run restaurants and guest houses. The on-licensed sector had also become more heterogeneous, although within it, despite decline, the pub itself remained the main element. Ownership had, however, been transformed, and around half of publicans were now the tenant, lessee or, in around a quarter of cases, the employed manager of a pub company. Nearly a third was independent and just 16 per cent were the tenant/lessee of, or manager for, a brewer.[145] This diversity and the sheer pace of change inevitably make generalization about these individuals hazardous. One survey of managers conducted in 1999 revealed continuities in, for example, their origins in skilled manual or non-manual occupations, or their tendency to have previously worked in the trade; but it also showed change in the greater acceptance of women, either running the business themselves or as the main partner, and in the numbers of younger and often single recruits.[146] Whilst women had always been key figures in the business of selling drink, they finally had begun to be accepted as licensees in their own right.

## Notes

1 W. Blackstone, *Commentaries on the Laws of England, Book the Third* (London: 12th ed., 1794), p. 164.
2 P. Clark, *The English Alehouse: A social history 1200–1830* (London: Longman, 1983), p. 5; J. Brown, 'The Landscape of Drink: Inns, Taverns and Alehouses in Early Modern Southampton' (PhD dissertation, University of Warwick, 2007), pp. 28–9.
3 J. A. Chartres, 'The English inn and road transport before 1700', in H. C. Peyer (ed.), *Gastfreundschaft, Taverne und Gasthaus im Mittelalter* (Munich: R. Oldenbourg, 1983), pp. 153–76; J. Hare, 'Inns, innkeepers and the society of later medieval England, 1350–1600', *Journal of Medieval History*, 39:4 (2013), pp. 477–97; F. Heal, *Hospitality in Early Modern England* (Oxford: Clarendon Press, 1990), p. 55.
4 The lower figure is from Chartres, 'The English inn and road transport', p. 167, the higher from his 'The eighteenth-century English inn: A transient "Golden Age"?', in B. Kümin and B. A. Tlusty (eds), *The World of the Tavern: Public houses in early modern Europe* (Aldershot: Ashgate, 2002), pp. 205–26 on p. 207. The 1577 survey and its difficulties are analysed by Chartres in 'The English inn and road transport', pp. 165–9, Clark, *The English Alehouse*, pp. 41–4 and A. Everitt, 'The English urban inn 1560–1760', in Everitt, *Landscape and Community in England* (London: Hambledon, 1985), pp. 155–208, on pp. 157–8.
5 Chartres, 'The eighteenth-century English inn', pp. 207–8.
6 Royal Commission into Municipal Corporations, Second Report; PP 1837 (239) XXXV.1, p. 163.
7 Hare, 'Inns, innkeepers', pp. 490–5; Everitt, 'The English urban inn', p. 167; see also Clark, *The English Alehouse*, p. 7.
8 Ibid., pp. 29–30; M. Hailwood, *Alehouses and Good Fellowship in Early Modern England* (Woodbridge: The Boydell Press, 2014), pp. 4–6.
9 Clark, *The English Alehouse*, pp. 43–8; Brown, *The Landscape of Drink*, p. 25; H. Murray, *A Directory of York Pubs* (York: Voyager, 2003), p. vii; Chartres, 'The Eighteenth-Century English Inn', p. 207.
10 Clark, *The English Alehouse*, pp. 21 and 44–5; Chartres, 'The eighteenth-century English inn', p. 207.
11 Clark, *The English Alehouse*, pp. 73–87; Hailwood, *Alehouses and Good Fellowship*, pp. 46–7; Brown, 'The landscape of drink', pp. 79–81 and 88–9; S. Wright, '"Churmaids, huswyfes and hucksters": The employment of women in Tudor and Stuart Salisbury', in L. Charles and L. Duffin (eds), *Women and Work in Pre-Industrial England* (London: Croom Helm, 1985), pp. 100–21, on p. 110.
12 Clark, *The English Alehouse*, pp. 11–12; 7 Edward VI, c. 5.
13 P. Withington, 'Intoxicants and the early modern city', in S. Hindle, A. Shepard and J. Walter (eds), *Remaking English Society: Social relations and social change in early modern England* (Woodbridge: The Boydell Press, 2013), pp. 135–63 on p. 149; J. Taylor, *Taylor's Travels and Circular Perambulation, through and by More than Thirty Times Twelve Signes of the Zodiak, of the Famous Cities of London and Westminster* (London, 1636), no pagination; W. Maitland, *The History of London from Its Foundation by the Romans to the Present Time* (Richardson: London, 1739), pp. 519–20.
14 D. Defoe, *A Tour through England and Wales* (London: J. M. Dent & Sons, 1928), vol. 1, p. 130; Old Bailey Proceedings Online, t17400903-6, at www.oldbaileyonline.org, version 7.0 [accessed 30 April 2006].
15 B. Cowan, *The Social Life of Coffee: The emergence of the British coffee house* (London: Yale University Press, 2005), pp. 25, 82 and 154; M. Ellis, *The Coffee-House: A cultural history* (London: Orion, 2005), p. 172 in particular for discussion of sometimes inflated numbers; B. Lillywhite, *London Coffee Houses* (London:

60  *Producers and sellers*

George Allen and Unwin, 1963) lists all known examples from the seventeenth to nineteenth centuries.

16 R. C. Latham and W. Matthews, (eds), *The Diary of Samuel Pepys* (London: G. Bell and Sons, vol. 8, 1974), p. 412; P. Clark, 'The "Mother Gin" controversy in the early eighteenth century', *Transactions of the Royal Historical Society*, 5th Series, 38 (1988), pp. 63–84, on pp. 66–8; First Report of Commissioners of Inland Revenue; PP 1857 (1) IV.65, Appendix 32a.

17 Maitland, *The History of London*, pp. 519–20.

18 K. Harvey, 'Ritual encounters: Punch parties and masculinity in the eighteenth century', *Past and Present*, 214 (2012), pp. 165–203, on pp. 177–8.

19 P. Earle, *The Making of the English Middle Class: Business, society and family life in London, 1660–1730* (London: Methuen, 1989), p. 33; see also Clark, *The English Alehouse*, pp. 240–1 and J. Warner, *Craze: Gin and debauchery in an age of reason* (London: Profile Books, 2003), pp. 39–41 and 202.

20 M. D. George, *London Life in the Eighteenth Century* (London: London School of Economics and Political Science, 3rd ed., 1951), pp. 27–42; L. Davison, 'Experiments in the social regulation of industry: Gin legislation', in L. Davison, T. Hitchcock, T. Keirn and R. B. Shoemaker (eds), *Stilling the Grumbling Hive: The response to social and economic problems in England, 1689–1750* (Stroud: Alan Sutton, 1992), pp. 25–48, on p. 27; Clark, 'The "Mother Gin" controversy', pp. 68 and 84; J. Warner and F. Ivis, 'Gin and gender in early eighteenth-century London', *Eighteenth-Century Life*, 24:2 (2000), pp. 85–105, on pp. 89–90; Warner, *Craze*, pp. 46–54.

21 George, *London Life in the Eighteenth Century*, p. 43; J. J. McCusker, 'The business of distilling in the Old World and the New World during the seventeenth and the eighteenth centuries: The rise of a new enterprise and its connection with colonial America', in J. J. McCusker and K. Morgan (eds), *The Early Modern Atlantic Economy* (Cambridge: Cambridge University Press, 2000), pp. 186–224, on p. 197.

22 J. Chartres, 'No English Calvados? English distillers and the cider industry in the seventeenth and eighteenth centuries', in J. Chartres and D. Hey (eds), *English Rural Society, 1500–1800* (Cambridge: Cambridge University Press, 1990), pp. 313–42, on p. 328.

23 Warner, *Craze*, pp. 35–6.

24 24 George II, c. 40.

25 J. M. Bennett, *Ale, Beer and Brewsters in England: Women's work in a changing world, 1300–1600* (Oxford: Oxford University Press, 1996) is the key work, but women brewers are documented in a number of other studies, for example, K. E. Lacey, 'Women and work in fourteenth and fifteenth century London' and D. Hutton, 'Women in fourteenth century Shrewsbury', in L. Charles and L. Duffin, *Women and Work in Pre-Industrial England* (London: Croom Helm, 1985), pp. 24–82, on p. 51 and pp. 83–99, on pp. 91 and 95; R.H. Britnell, *Growth and Decline in Colchester, 1300–1525* (Cambridge: Cambridge University Press, 1986), pp. 89–90; P. J. P. Goldberg, *Women, Work, and Life Cycle in a Medieval Economy: Women in York and Yorkshire c. 1300–1520* (Oxford: Clarendon Press, 1992), pp. 111–14 and 141–4; M. K. McIntosh, *Working Women in English Society, 1300–1620* (Cambridge: Cambridge University Press, 2005), pp. 140–81.

26 Bennett, *Ale, Beer and Brewsters*, pp. 43–97; M. Ball, *The Worshipful Company of Brewers: A short history* (London: Hutchinson Benham, 1977), p. 62.

27 J. R. Brown, 'Brewers' tales: Making, retailing and regulating beer in Southampton, 1550–1700', *Brewery History*, 135 (2010), pp. 10–39, on p. 20.

28 Suggested in his review of Bennett, *Ale, Beer and Brewsters* by K. Wrightson in *American Historical Review*, 103 (1998), p. 868.

29 Clark, *The English Alehouse*, pp. 106–8; on the industry in London and the role of foreign brewers see L. B. Luu, *Immigrants and the Industries of London 1500–1700* (Aldershot: Ashgate, 2005), pp. 259–99.

30 Clark, *The English Alehouse*, pp. 101–5.
31 P. Mathias, *The Brewing Industry in England 1700–1830* (Cambridge: Cambridge University Press, 1959), pp. 6 and 542–3; Clark, *The English Alehouse*, pp. 183–4.
32 Defoe, *A Tour through England and Wales*, vol. 2, p. 205 and vol. 1, p. 205.
33 H. Fielding, *Joseph Andrews*, ed. M. C. Batteston (Oxford: Clarendon Press, 1967), p. 252.
34 T. E. Casson (ed.), 'The diary of Edward Jackson, Vicar of Colton, for the year 1775', *Transactions of the Cumberland & Westmorland Antiquarian and Archaeological Society*, New Series 40, (1940), pp. 1–45, on p. 13.
35 R. Dymond, 'The old inns and taverns of Exeter', *Devonshire Association Transactions*, 7 (1880), pp. 3–32, on p. 28.
36 P. Jennings, *The Local: A history of the English pub* (Stroud: The History Press, rev. ed., 2011), p. 79.
37 G. B. Wilson, *Alcohol and the Nation: A contribution to the study of the liquor problem in the United Kingdom from 1800 to 1935* (London: Nicholson and Watson, 1940), p. 394; as wine merchants are included in the total figure of 11,014 retail excise licences issued in 1800, it is not possible to be more precise.
38 J. I. Freeman (ed.), *The Epicure's Almanack: Eating and drinking in Regency London* (London: the British Library, 2012), pp. 120–1.
39 By 48 George III, c. 143; Account of Number of Ale, Wine and Spirit Licences issued in England and Wales; PP 1828 (164) XVIII.511.
40 Clark, *The English Alehouse*, pp. 55–9.
41 *Leeds Intelligencer*, 26 June 1787, p. 3 and 18 September 1787, p. 3; Clark, *The English Alehouse*, p. 262; T. Trotter, *An Essay, Medical, Philosophical, and Chemical, on Drunkenness and Its Effects on the Human Body*, ed. R. Porter (London: Routledge, 1988), p. 48.
42 First Report of Commissioners of Inland Revenue; PP 1857, p. 2 and Appendix 32a.
43 Select Committee of the House of Commons on Laws and Regulations which restrict Sale of Beer by Retail; PP 1830 (253) X.I, pp. 38–9; and *Times*, 15 August 1834, p. 3.
44 J. P. Kay, *The Moral and Physical Condition of the Working Classes Employed in the Cotton Manufacture in Manchester* (Didsbury: E. J. Morten, 1969), p. 57.
45 First Report of Commissioners of Inland Revenue; PP 1857, p. 8.
46 M. Turner, 'Drink and illicit distillation in nineteenth-century Manchester', *Manchester Region History Review*, 4:1 (1990), pp. 12–16.
47 *Bradford Observer*, 15 May 1851, p. 5; and *passim*.
48 J. Philipson, 'Whisky smuggling on the border in the early nineteenth century', *Archaeologia Aeliana*, Fourth Series 39 (1961), pp. 151–63; J. Philipson and F. Austin, 'Remains of illicit distilleries in Upper Coquetdale', *Archaeologia Aeliana*, Fourth Series, 38 (1960), pp. 99–112.
49 Philipson, 'Whisky smuggling on the border', p. 154; First Report of Commissioners of Inland Revenue; PP 1857, p. 8; B. Harrison, *Drink and the Victorians: The temperance question in England 1815–1872* (Keele: Keele University Press, 2nd ed. 1994), p. 305; Turner, 'Drink and illicit distillation', p. 16.
50 Clark, *The English Alehouse*, pp. 44, 48–55 and 262.
51 P. Jennings, *The Public House in Bradford, 1770–1970* (Keele: Keele University Press, 1995), pp. 37–8; Report from the Select Committee of the House of Lords appointed to consider the Operation of the Acts for the Sale of Beer; PP 1849 & 1850 (398) XVIII.483, p. 71; Report from the Select Committee on Public Houses; PP 1854 (367) XIV.231, pp. 284–6; and Report from the Select Committee on Public Houses; PP 1852–53 (855) XXXVII.1, pp. 397–8.
52 *Harrogate Advertiser*, 6 November 1847, p. 3.
53 Under the original licensing statute of 5 & 6 Edward VI, c. 25 and also 12 Charles II, c. 24.

## Producers and sellers

54 Report from the Select Committee of the House of Lords appointed to consider the Operation of the Acts for the Sale of Beer; PP 1849 & 1850, p. 34.
55 4 George IV, c. 51 and 5 George IV, c. 54; Account of Number of Brewers and Licensed Victuallers in England, Wales and Scotland; PP 1826–27 (74) XVII.353 and 1830 (190) XXII.161; Report from the Select Committee on the Sale of Beer; PP 1830 (253) X.1, pp. 11–14.
56 For the origins of the Act and its passage see Harrison, *Drink and the Victorians*, pp. 63–84; T. R. Gourvish and R. G. Wilson, *The British Brewing Industry 1830–1980* (Cambridge: Cambridge University Press, 1994), pp. 3–22; Jennings, *The Local*, pp. 57–9; P. Jupp, *British Politics on the Eve of Reform: The Duke of Wellington's administration 1828–1830* (Basingstoke: Macmillan, 1998), pp. 143–4, 274 and 286; N. Mason, "'The sovereign people are in a beastly state": The Beer Act of 1830 and Victorian discourse on working-class drunkenness', *Victorian Literature and Culture*, 29:1 (2001), pp. 109–27; E. Tenbus, 'A draught of discontentment: National identity and nostalgia in the Beerhouse Act of 1830', *Brewery History*, 161 (2015, pp. 2–9).
57 Number of Brewers, Victuallers and Retailers of Beer; PP 1831 (60) XVII.67; Account of Number of Persons in UK licensed as Brewers, and Victuallers; PP 1831–32 (223) XXXIV.27. Note that the number of licences did not correspond to premises as it was not transferable and thus in a given year two or more licences might be granted to proprietors of a single house, for which point see the Return of Beer-houses in Manchester and Salford; PP 1839 (182) XXX.251.
58 Jennings, *The Local*, pp. 62–3.
59 The trend in numbers is derived from the annual Account of the Number of Persons Licensed as Brewers and Victuallers, up to PP 1870 (187) LXI.281.
60 J. Scarisbrick, *Beer Manual (Historical and Technical)* (Wolverhampton: Revenue Series 1, 1892), p. 17; 42 George III, c. 38; Select Committee of the House of Lords on Bill for regulating Sale of Beer and other Liquors on Lord's Day; PP 1847–48 (501) XVI.615, p. 6.
61 Jennings, *The Local*, pp. 68–9.
62 By 24 & 25 Victoria, c. 21; Wilson, *Alcohol and the Nation*, pp. 395–6.
63 Select Committee of the House of Commons on Sale of Beer; PP 1833 (416) XV.1, pp. 253, 183, 229 and *passim*. The evidence was also later used in a hostile way by S. and B. Webb, *The History of Liquor Licensing in England Principally from 1700 to 1830* (London: Frank Cass, 1963), pp. 124–5.
64 Clark, *The English Alehouse*, pp. 200–5; Brewster calendar, Claro 1771, West Yorkshire Archive Service, Wakefield, QE32/22.
65 J. A. Chartres, 'The place of inns in the commercial life of London and Western England 1660–1760' (DPhil dissertation, Oxford University, 1973), pp. 156–66; Everitt, *The English Urban Inn*, p. 185; T. S. Ashton, *An Eighteenth-Century Industrialist: Peter Stubs of Warrington 1756–1806* (Manchester: Manchester University Press, 1939), pp. 1–4.
66 B. Harrison and B. Trinder, *Drink and Sobriety in an Early Victorian Country Town: Banbury 1830–1860* (London: Longmans, *English Historical Review* Supplement 4, 1969), p. 2.
67 List of Persons Applying for Licences, 1852, Southampton Archive Services, D/PM5/3/22/3.
68 T. Mason, *Associated Football and English Society 1863–1915* (Sussex: Harvester, 1980), pp. 18–19; Jennings, *The Local*, pp. 92–3.
69 Quoted in J. Benson, 'Drink, death and bankruptcy: Retailing and respectability in late Victorian and Edwardian England', *Midland History*, 32 (2007), pp. 128–40, on pp. 128 and 138.
70 *Leeds Mercury*, 1 September 1849, p. 12.
71 G. Crossick, *An Artisan Elite in Victorian Society: Kentish London 1840–1880* (London: Croom Helm, 1978), pp. 93–7; Clark, *The English Alehouse*, p. 286.

72 Minute Book of the Beer Trade Protection Society, 1854–1866, Senate House Library, University of London, MS1183.
73 *Northern Star*, 19 October 1839, p. 8.
74 W. B. Crump, *The Leeds Woollen Industry 1780–1820* (Leeds: Thoresby Society, 1931), p. 144.
75 J. C. Hotten, *A Dictionary of Modern Slang, Cant, and Vulgar Words* (London: Hotten, 1859), p. vi.
76 Old Bailey Proceedings Online, t 18760626-265, www.oldbaileyonline.org, version 7.0 [accessed 26 November 2014]; P. Jennings, 'The local: Ideal and reality in the English pub', in R. Snape and H. Pussard (eds), *Recording Leisure Lives: Sports, games and pastimes in 20th century Britain* (Eastbourne: Leisure Studies Association, 2010), pp. 21–39, on pp. 21–4.
77 By the Wine and Beerhouse Act 1869; Account of Number of Persons in UK licensed as Brewers and Victuallers; PP 1870; Wilson, *Alcohol and the Nation*, p. 236.
78 Report of the Departmental Committee on Liquor Licensing; PP 1972–73 (Cmnd 5154) XIV.939, pp. 24–6.
79 P. W. Robinson, 'Ale, beer and public house closures in the Halifax area 1635–2010', *Transactions of the Halifax Antiquarian Society*, 20 (new series) 2012, pp. 68–99, on p. 84.
80 Report from the Select Committee on the Police of the Metropolis; PP 1828 (533) VI.1, pp. 41–4; Report from the Select Committee on Public Houses; PP 1852–53, pp. 14 and 533; Select Committee of the House of Lords on Bill for regulating Sale of Beer and other Liquors on Lord's Day; PP 1847–48, p. 10.
81 R. Thorne, 'Places of refreshment in the nineteenth century city', in A. D. King (ed.), *Buildings and Society: Essays on the social development of the built environment* (London: Routledge & Kegan Paul, 1980), pp. 228–53 on p. 232.
82 J. Taylor, *From Self-help to Glamour: The working men's club* (Oxford: History Workshop Pamphlet 7, 1972); C. Booth, *Life and Labour of the People of London, First Series, vol.1* (London: Macmillan, 1902), pp. 94–106.
83 B. T. Hall, *Our Sixty Years: The story of the working men's club and institute movement* (London: Working Men's Club and Institute Union, 1922), p. 199.
84 Wilson, *Alcohol and the Nation*, p. 384; DCMS Statistical Bulletin, Liquor Licensing England and Wales, July 2003–June 2004 (London: Department for Culture, Media and Sport, 2004), pp. 8 and 25.
85 Report of the Select Committee on the Clubs Registration Bill; PP 1893–94 (314) X.463, p. 5.
86 Ibid., pp. 1–2, 6–11, 20–30, 92–3 and 192.
87 Royal Commission, on Licensing Laws, Second Report; PP 1897 (c. 8523-I) XXXV.7, p. 102.
88 J. Gardiner, *The Thirties: An intimate history* (London: Harper Press, 2010), pp. 628–1; Licensing Act 1949.
89 B. Stapleton and J. H. Thomas, *Gales: A study in brewing, business and family history* (Aldershot: Ashgate, 2000), p. 49.
90 A. Barnard, *The Noted Breweries of Great Britain and Ireland* (London: Sir J. Causton & Sons, 1889–91), vol. 3, p. 240.
91 4 & 5 William. IV, c. 85; Wilson, *Alcohol and the Nation*, pp. 394–7. Refusal was made easier by 43 Victoria, c. 6 and 45 & 46 Victoria, c. 34.
92 By 23 Victoria, c, 27 and 24 & 25 Victoria, c. 21. This facility was extended to beer dealers by 26 & 27 Victoria, c. 33.
93 Wilson, *Alcohol and the Nation*, pp. 394–7.
94 Harrison, *Drink and the Victorians*, p. 230; and A. Briggs, *Wine for Sale: Victoria wine and the liquor trade* (London: B. T. Batsford, 1985), p. 9.
95 Mathias, *The Brewing Industry*, pp. 12–21 and 26.

## Producers and sellers

96 P. Mathias, 'An industrial revolution in brewing, 1700–1830', in P. Mathias, *The Transformation of England: Essays in the economic and social history of England in the eighteenth century* (London: Methuen, 1979), pp. 209–30.
97 E. M. Butler (ed.), *A Regency Visitor: The English tour of Prince Pückler-Muskau described in his letters 1826–1828* (London: Collins, 1957), pp. 236–7.
98 Mathias, *The Brewing Industry*, pp. 117–38.
99 D. W. Gutzke, *Protecting the Pub: Brewers and Publicans Against Temperance* (Woodbridge: Boydell, 1989), p. 129; Gourvish and Wilson, *The British Brewing Industry*, pp. 70–5; E. M. Sigsworth, *The Brewing Trade during the Industrial Revolution: The case of Yorkshire* (York: Borthwick Papers, 1967), p. 3.
100 Gourvish and Wilson, *The British Brewing Industry*, pp. 70–5; A. Crawford, M. Dunn and R. Thorne, *Birmingham Pubs 1880–1939* (Gloucester: Alan Sutton, 1986), p. 4.
101 Gourvish and Wilson, *The British Brewing Industry*, p. 68.
102 Select Committee of the House of Lords to consider Operation of Acts for Sale of Beer; PP 1849 & 1850, p. iv.
103 *Bradford Observer*, 23 February 1869, p. 4.
104 Gutzke, *Protecting the Pub*, pp. 18–19; P. W. Robinson, *The Emergence of the Common Brewer in the Halifax District* (Halifax: Halifax Antiquarian Society, 1982), pp. 77–8.
105 Gourvish and Wilson, *The British Brewing Industry*, p. 111.
106 Gutzke, *Protecting the Pub*, pp. 20–1. For Burton see C. C. Owen, *"The Greatest Brewery in the World": A history of Bass, Ratcliff & Gretton* (Chesterfield: Derbyshire Record Society, 1992).
107 Ibid., pp. 15–16 and 22–4.
108 K. H. Hawkins, and C. L. Pass, *The Brewing Industry: A study in industrial organization and public policy* (London: Hargreaves, 1979), p. 27; Gourvish and Wilson, *The British Brewing Industry*, pp. 267–8.
109 J. Vaizey, *The Brewing Industry 1886–1951* (London: Pitman and Sons, 1960), p. 17.
110 E. A. Pratt, *The Licensed Trade: An independent survey* (London: Murray, 1907), pp. 97–105 and 305–8.
111 Ibid., pp. 106–28 and 308–13; Royal Commission on Liquor Licensing Laws, First Report; PP 1897 [C. 8356] XXXIV.253, pp. 239, 309 and 447–9; Royal Commission on Liquor Licensing Laws, Third Report; PP 1898 [C. 8694] XXXVI.9, p. 4; A. Mutch, 'Shaping the public house, 1850–1950: Business strategies, state regulation and social history', *Cultural & Social History*, 1:2 (2004), pp. 179–200; 'Magistrates and public house managers, 1840–1914: Another case of Liverpool exceptionalism?', *Northern History*, 40:2 (2003), pp. 325–42; 'Public houses as multiple retailing', *Business History*, 48:1 (2006), pp. 1–19.
112 R. Roberts, *The Classic Slum: Salford life in the first quarter of the century* (Harmondsworth: Penguin, 1973), pp. 17–18 and 120–1.
113 Royal Commission on Liquor Licensing Laws, First Report; PP 1897 [C. 8356], pp. 305 and 311.
114 Compensation Reports 1907–1909, Lancashire Record Office, Preston, QAD 6/1.
115 Gourvish and Wilson, *The British Brewing Industry*, pp. 318–23; Wilson, *Alcohol and the Nation*, p. 275; H. Carter, *The Control of the Drink Trade in Great Britain: A contribution to national efficiency during the Great War 1915–1918* (London: Longmans, Green, 2nd ed., 1919), pp. 240–1.
116 Gourvish and Wilson, *The British Brewing Industry*, pp. 332–5.
117 Ibid., pp. 335–50. The figure for companies included Eire.
118 B. Bennison, 'Not so common: The public house in North East England between the wars', *Local Historian*, 25:1 (1995), pp. 31–42, on p. 33.
119 Gourvish and Wilson, *The British Brewing Industry*, pp. 346, 409 and 441–5.
120 M. Race, *Public Houses, Private Lives: An oral history of life in York pubs in the mid-twentieth century* (York: Voyager, 1999), p. 121.

121 British Beer and Pub Association, Pub Numbers, November 2006, at http://www.beerandpub.com/content.asp?id_Content=345 [accessed 7 February 2007].
122 Robinson, 'Ale, beer and public house closures', pp. 87–8 and 96.
123 J. C. Everitt and I. R. Bowler, 'Bitter-sweet conversions: Changing times for the British pub', *Journal of Popular Culture*, 30:2 (1996), pp. 101–22, on p. 103; J. D. Pratten and C. J. Lovatt, 'Can the rural pub survive? – A challenge for management or a lost cause', *Management Research News*, 25:1 (2002), pp. 60–72, on pp. 63–4.
124 By the Licensing Act 1961; DCMS Statistical Bulletin Liquor Licensing, p. 9.
125 Much space could be taken up discussing how in more recent times the various retail outlets for alcohol have been classified, including the for some vital, and for others pointless, question of what exactly constitutes a pub. My concern is to try and provide some basis for historical analysis. I used the market analyst CGA Strategy for this at http://www.cgastrategy.co.uk/products/drinksplaces.shtml [accessed 16 February 2009].
126 D. W. Gutzke, *Women Drinking Out in Britain since the Early Twentieth Century* (Manchester: Manchester University Press, 2014), pp. 134–5.
127 R. Mansukhani, *The Pub Report: British pubs in the 1980s* (Euromonitor, 1985), pp. 113–23; J. Burnett, *England Eats Out: A social history of eating out in England from 1830 to the present* (Harlow: Pearson Education, 2004), p. 291.
128 Gutzke, *Women Drinking Out*, pp. 150–9; P. Jones, 'Enter the superpub', *Town & Country Planning*, 65 (1996), pp. 110–12.
129 DCMS Statistical Bulletin Liquor Licensing, p. 8.
130 J. P. Lewis, *Freedom to Drink: A critical review of the development of the licensing laws and proposals for reform* (London: Institute for Economic Affairs, 1985), p. 36.
131 DCMS Statistical Bulletin Liquor Licensing, p. 8.
132 Gourvish and Wilson, *The British Brewing Industry*, p. 456.
133 J. Burnett, *Liquid Pleasures: A social history of drinks in modern Britain* (London: Longman, 1999), pp. 155 and 177.
134 G. Hall, 'Mergers and the product mix: A case-study of the brewing industry', in K. Cowling, P. Stoneman, J. Cubbin, J. Cable, G. Hall, S. Domberger and P. Dutton, *Mergers and Economic Performance* (Cambridge: Cambridge University Press, 1980), pp. 214–37, on p. 215.
135 The Monopolies Commission: A Report on the Supply of Beer; PP 1968–69 (216) XL, pp. 50–1; Hawkins, and Pass, *The Brewing Industry*, p. 59.
136 For details see Gourvish and Wilson, *The British Brewing Industry*, pp. 447–97.
137 D. Preece, 'Change and continuity in UK public house retailing', *Services Industries Journal*, 28:7–8 (2008), pp. 1107–24, on p. 1109.
138 Gourvish and Wilson, *The British Brewing Industry*, pp. 596–8; Monopolies and Mergers Commission: The Supply of Beer; PP 1988–89 (cm. 651) L.
139 A. Mutch, *Strategic and Organizational Change: From production to retailing in UK brewing 1950–1990* (Abingdon: Routledge, 2006), p. 142.
140 Preece, 'Change and continuity', pp. 1113–14; J. D. Pratten, 'The development of the modern UK public house Part 3: The emergence of the modern public house 1989–2005', *International Journal of Contemporary Hospitality Management*, 19:7 (2007), pp. 612–18, on p. 614.
141 For this whole process see J. Christensen, 'Consolidating the global brewing industry, 1992–2012', *Brewery History*, 157 (2014), pp. 20–44, on pp. 27–9.
142 M. Cornell, *Beer: The Story of the Pint* (London: Headline, 2003), pp. 220–2.
143 G. Steven, V. Steven and D. Preece, 'Turbulence in the UK brewing and public house retailing sector: The role and response of capital and the implications for staff, (Proceedings of the 16th AIRAANZ conference, Queenstown, New Zealand, February 2002), at www.airaanz.org/2002-conference-main-html [accessed 20 June 2012).
144 Gutzke, *Women Drinking Out*, pp. 164–9.

145 Mutch, *Strategic and Organizational Change*, p. 151; British Beer and Pub Association, Pub Numbers.
146 A. Mutch, 'Where do public house managers come from? Some survey evidence', *International Journal of Contemporary Hospitality Management*, 13:2 (2001), pp. 86–92; Gutzke, *Women Drinking Out*, pp. 167–9.

## Bibliography

Ashton, T. S., *An Eighteenth-Century Industrialist: Peter Stubs of Warrington 1756–1806* (Manchester: Manchester University Press, 1939).
Ball, M., *The Worshipful Company of Brewers: A short history* (London: Hutchinson Benham, 1977).
Bennett, J. M., *Ale, Beer and Brewsters in England: Women's work in a changing world, 1300–1600* (Oxford: Oxford University Press, 1996).
Bennison, B., 'Not so common: The public house in North East England between the wars', *Local Historian*, 25:1 (1995), pp. 31–42.
Benson, J., 'Drink, death and bankruptcy: Retailing and respectability in late Victorian and Edwardian England', *Midland History*, 32 (2007), pp. 128–40.
Briggs, A., *Wine for Sale: Victoria wine and the liquor trade* (London: B. T. Batsford, 1985).
Britnell, R. H., *Growth and Decline in Colchester, 1300–1525* (Cambridge: Cambridge University Press, 1986).
Brown, J., 'The landscape of drink: Inns, taverns and alehouses in early modern Southampton' (PhD dissertation, University of Warwick, 2007).
—, 'Brewers' tales: Making, retailing and regulating beer in Southampton, 1550–1700', *Brewery History*, 135 (2010), pp. 10–39.
Burnett, J., *Liquid Pleasures: A social history of drinks in modern Britain* (London: Longman, 1999).
—, *England Eats Out: A social history of eating out in England from 1830 to the present* (Harlow: Pearson Education, 2004).
Carter, H., *The Control of the Drink Trade in Great Britain: A contribution to national efficiency during the Great War 1915–1918* (London: Longmans Green, 2nd ed., 1919).
Chartres, J. A., 'The place of inns in the commercial life of London and Western England 1660–1760' (DPhil dissertation, Oxford University, 1973).
—, 'The English inn and road transport before 1700', in H. C. Peyer (ed.), *Gastfreundschaft, Taverne und Gasthaus im Mittelalter* (Munich: R.Oldenbourg, 1983), pp. 153–76.
—, 'No English Calvados? English distillers and the cider industry in the seventeenth and eighteenth centuries', in J. Chartres and D. Hey (eds), *English Rural Society, 1500–1800* (Cambridge: Cambridge University Press, 1990), pp. 313–42.
—, 'The eighteenth-century English inn: A transient "Golden Age"?', in B. Kümin and B. A. Tlusty (eds), *The World of the Tavern: Public houses in early modern Europe* (Aldershot: Ashgate, 2002), pp. 205–26.
Christensen, J., 'Consolidating the global brewing industry, 1992–2012', *Brewery History*, 157 (2014), pp. 20–44.
Clark, P., *The English Alehouse: A social history 1200–1830* (London: Longman, 1983).
—, 'The "Mother Gin" controversy in the early eighteenth century', *Transactions of the Royal Historical Society*, 5th Series, 38 (1988), pp. 63–84.
Cowan, B., *The Social Life of Coffee: The emergence of the British coffee house* (London: Yale University Press, 2005).

Crawford, A., Dunn, M. and Thorne, R., *Birmingham Pubs 1880–1939* (Gloucester: Alan Sutton, 1986).
Crossick, G., *An Artisan Elite in Victorian Society: Kentish London 1840–1880* (London: Croom Helm, 1978).
Crump, W. B., *The Leeds Woollen Industry 1780–1820* (Leeds: Thoresby Society, 1931).
Davison, L., 'Experiments in the social regulation of industry: Gin legislation', in Davison, L., Hitchcock, T., Keirn, T. and Shoemaker, R. B (eds)., *Stilling the Grumbling Hive: The response to social and economic problems in England, 1689–1750* (Stroud: Alan Sutton, 1992), pp. 25–48.
Dymond, R., 'The old inns and taverns of Exeter', *Devonshire Association Transactions*, 7 (1880), pp. 3–32.
Earle, P., *The Making of the English Middle Class: Business, society and family life in London, 1660–1730* (London: Methuen, 1989).
Ellis, M., *The Coffee-House: A cultural history* (London: Orion, 2005).
Everitt, A., 'The English urban inn 1560–1760', in Everitt, *Landscape and Community in England* (London: Hambledon, 1985), pp. 155–208.
Everitt J. C. and Bowler, I. R., 'Bitter-sweet conversions: Changing times for the British pub', *Journal of Popular Culture*, 30:2 (1996), pp. 101–22.
Gardiner, J., *The Thirties: An intimate history* (London: Harper Press, 2010).
George, M. D., *London Life in the Eighteenth Century* (London: London School of Economics and Political Science, 3rd ed., 1951).
Goldberg, P. J. P., *Women, Work, and Life Cycle in a Medieval Economy: Women in York and Yorkshire c. 1300–1520* (Oxford: Clarendon Press, 1992).
Gourvish, T. R. and Wilson, R. G., *The British Brewing Industry 1830–1980* (Cambridge: Cambridge University Press, 1994).
Gutzke, D. W., *Protecting the Pub: Brewers and publicans against temperance* (Woodbridge: Boydell, 1989).
—, *Women Drinking Out in Britain since the Early Twentieth Century* (Manchester: Manchester University Press, 2014).
Hailwood, M., *Alehouses and Good Fellowship in Early Modern England* (Woodbridge: The Boydell Press, 2014).
Hall, B. T., *Our Sixty Years: The Story of the working men's club and institute movement* (London: Working Men's Club and Institute Union, 1922).
Hall, G., 'Mergers and the product mix: A case-study of the brewing industry', in K. Cowling, P. Stoneman, J. Cubbin, J. Cable, G. Hall, S. Domberger and P. Dutton (eds), *Mergers and Economic Performance* (Cambridge: Cambridge University Press, 1980), pp. 214–37.
Hare, J., 'Inns, innkeepers and the society of later medieval England, 1350–1600', *Journal of Medieval History*, 39:4 (2013), pp. 477–97.
Harrison, B., *Drink and the Victorians: The temperance question in England 1815–1872* (Keele: Keele University Press, 2nd ed. 1994).
Harrison, B. and Trinder, B., *Drink and Sobriety in an Early Victorian Country Town: Banbury 1830–1860* (London: Longmans, *English Historical Review* Supplement 4, 1969).
Harvey, K., 'Ritual encounters: Punch parties and masculinity in the eighteenth century', *Past and Present*, 214 (2012), pp. 165–203.
Hawkins, K. H. and Pass, C. L., *The Brewing Industry: A study in industrial organization and public policy* (London: Hargreaves, 1979).
Heal, F., *Hospitality in Early Modern England* (Oxford: Clarendon Press, 1990).

Hutton, D., 'Women in fourteenth century Shrewsbury', in L. Charles and L. Duffin (eds), *Women and Work in Pre-Industrial England* (London: Croom Helm, 1985), pp. 83–99.

Jennings, P., *The Public House in Bradford, 1770–1970* (Keele: Keele University Press, 1995).

—— 'The local: Ideal and reality in the English pub', in R. Snape and H. Pussard (eds), *Recording Leisure Lives: Sports, games and pastimes in 20th century Britain* (Eastbourne: Leisure Studies Association, 2010), pp. 21–39.

——, *The Local: A history of the English pub* (Stroud: The History Press, rev. ed., 2011).

Jones, P., 'Enter the superpub', *Town & Country Planning*, 65 (1996), pp. 110–12.

Jupp, P., *British Politics on the Eve of Reform: The Duke of Wellington's administration 1828–1830* (Basingstoke: Macmillan, 1998).

Lacey, K. E., 'Women and work in fourteenth and fifteenth century London', in Charles and Duffin (eds), *Women and Work*, pp. 24–82.

Lewis, J. P., *Freedom to Drink: A critical review of the development of the licensing laws and proposals for reform* (London: Institute for Economic Affairs, 1985).

Lillywhite, B., *London Coffee Houses* (London: George Allen and Unwin, 1963).

Luu, L. B., *Immigrants and the Industries of London 1500–1700* (Aldershot: Ashgate, 2005).

McIntosh, M. K., *Working Women in English Society, 1300–1620* (Cambridge: Cambridge University Press, 2005).

McCusker, J. J., 'The business of distilling in the Old World and the New World during the seventeenth and the eighteenth centuries: The rise of a new enterprise and its connection with colonial America', in J. J. McCusker and K. Morgan (eds), *The Early Modern Atlantic Economy* (Cambridge: Cambridge University Press, 2000), pp. 186–224.

Mansukhani, R., *The Pub Report: British pubs in the 1980s* (Euromonitor, 1985).

Mason, N., '"The sovereign people are in a beastly state": The Beer Act of 1830 and Victorian discourse on working-class drunkenness', *Victorian Literature and Culture*, 29:1 (2001), pp. 109–27.

Mason, T., *Associated Football and English Society 1863–1915* (Sussex: Harvester, 1980).

Mathias, P., *The Brewing Industry in England 1700–1830* (Cambridge: Cambridge University Press, 1959).

——, 'An industrial revolution in brewing, 1700–1830', in P. Mathias, *The Transformation of England: Essays in the economic and social history of England in the eighteenth century* (London: Methuen, 1979), pp. 209–30.

Murray, H., *A Directory of York Pubs* (York: Voyager, 2003).

Mutch, A., 'Where do public house managers come from? Some survey evidence', *International Journal of Contemporary Hospitality Management*, 13:2 (2001), pp. 86–92.

——, 'Magistrates and public house managers, 1840–1914: Another case of Liverpool exceptionalism?', *Northern History*, 40:2 (2003), pp. 325–42.

——, 'Shaping the public house, 1850–1950: Business strategies, state regulation and social history', *Cultural & Social History*, 1:2 (2004), pp. 179–200

——, 'Public houses as multiple retailing', *Business History*, 48:1 (2006), pp. 1–19.

——, *Strategic and Organizational Change: From production to retailing in UK brewing 1950–1990* (Abingdon: Routledge, 2006).

Owen, C. C., *"The Greatest Brewery in the World": A history of Bass, Ratcliff & Gretton* (Chesterfield: Derbyshire Record Society, 1992).

Philipson, J., 'Whisky smuggling on the border in the early nineteenth century', *Archaeologia Aeliana*, Fourth Series 39 (1961), pp. 151–63.

Philipson, J. and Austin, F., 'Remains of illicit distilleries in Upper Coquetdale', *Archaeologia Aeliana*, Fourth Series, 38 (1960), pp. 99–112.

Pratten, J. D., 'The development of the modern UK public house Part 3: The emergence of the modern public house 1989–2005', *International Journal of Contemporary Hospitality Management*, 19:7 (2007), pp. 612–18.

Pratten, J. D. and Lovatt, C. J., 'Can the rural pub survive? – A challenge for management or a lost cause', *Management Research News*, 25:1 (2002), pp. 60–72.

Preece, D., 'Change and continuity in UK public house retailing', *Services Industries Journal*, 28:7–8 (2008), pp. 1107–24.

Race, M., *Public Houses, Private Lives: An oral history of life in York pubs in the mid-twentieth century* (York: Voyager, 1999).

Roberts, R., *The Classic Slum: Salford life in the first quarter of the century* (Harmondsworth: Penguin, 1973).

Robinson, P. W., *The Emergence of the Common Brewer in the Halifax District* (Halifax: Halifax Antiquarian Society, 1982).

—, 'Ale, beer and public house closures in the Halifax area 1635–2010', *Transactions of the Halifax Antiquarian Society*, 20 (new series) 2012, pp. 68–99.

Sigsworth, E. M., *The Brewing Trade during the Industrial Revolution: The case of Yorkshire* (York: Borthwick Papers, 1967).

Stapleton, B. and Thomas, J. H., *Gales: A Study in Brewing, Business and Family History* (Aldershot: Ashgate, 2000).

Steven, G., Steven, V. and Preece, D., 'Turbulence in the UK brewing and public house retailing sector: The role and response of capital and the implications for staff (Proceedings of the 16th AIRAANZ conference, Queenstown, New Zealand, February 2002), at www.airaanz.org/2002-conference-main-html [accessed 20 June 2012).

Taylor, J., *From Self-help to Glamour: The working men's club* (Oxford: History Workshop Pamphlet 7, 1972).

Tenbus, E., 'A draught of discontentment: National identity and nostalgia in the Beerhouse Act of 1830', *Brewery History*, 161 (2015), pp. 2–9.

Thorne, R., 'Places of refreshment in the nineteenth century city', in A. D. King (ed.), *Buildings and Society: Essays on the social development of the built environment* (London: Routledge & Kegan Paul, 1980), pp. 228–53.

Turner, M., 'Drink and illicit distillation in nineteenth-century Manchester', *Manchester Region History Review*, 4:1 (1990), pp. 12–16.

Vaizey, J., *The Brewing Industry 1886–1951* (London: Pitman and Sons, 1960).

Warner, J., *Craze: Gin and debauchery in an age of reason* (London: Profile Books, 2003).

Warner, J. and Ivis, F., 'Gin and gender in early eighteenth-century London', *Eighteenth-Century Life*, 24:2 (2000), pp. 85–105.

Webb, S. and B., *The History of Liquor Licensing in England Principally from 1700 to 1830* (London: Frank Cass, 1963).

Wilson, G. B., *Alcohol and the Nation: A contribution to the study of the liquor problem in the United Kingdom from 1800 to 1935* (London: Nicholson and Watson, 1940).

Withington, P., 'Intoxicants and the early modern city', in S. Hindle, A. Shepard and J. Walter (eds), *Remaking English Society: Social relations and social change in early modern England* (Woodbridge: The Boydell Press, 2013), pp. 135–63.

Wright, S., '"Churmaids, huswyfes and hucksters": The employment of women in Tudor and Stuart Salisbury' in Charles and Duffin (eds), *Women and Work*, pp. 100–21.

# 3 Places and spaces

**Introduction**

The previous chapter outlined the development of the sale of drink. Here the focus is on the variety of establishments and settings as places and spaces. By place I mean the architecture and internal layout and design of premises, and I follow Amanda Flather's definition of space as 'an arena of social action'. Accordingly, 'A place is transformed into a space by the social actors who constitute it through everyday use'.[1] This chapter is concerned, then, with the ways in which individuals and groups used drinking places, and it pays attention in particular to their social class, sex and age. The use of these places was of course shaped by economic, social, cultural, political and legal influences, some of which are discussed here, whilst others receive attention elsewhere in this book. The structure is broadly chronological, whilst acknowledging that matters of continuity and change as usual make difficult the assigning of neat boundaries in time, and is organized into three parts. The first looks at the categories of drinking place identified in the previous chapter – the inns, taverns, alehouses and gin shops of early modern England – down to the early years of Victoria's reign, by which time the beerhouse had become an important addition to the drinking scene. The second concentrates on the pub, which emerged as a distinct entity in the mid nineteenth century, tracing its history from this heyday through its slow decline from the later nineteenth century through the inter-war years. The third looks at the post-war decades, during which the pub's central importance as a social institution continued to diminish, the diversity of places in which to enjoy a drink grew and women became increasingly important customers.

Two points need to be kept in mind in what follows. The first, to reiterate, is the fluidity of the boundaries between, and indeed within, categories throughout the period covered in this book – between, for example, early modern inns, taverns and alehouses, city-centre gin palaces and back-street beerhouses, or modern pubs and bars. Migration could occur across categories, as when an alehouse upgraded to an inn, for example, or where a tavern also sold beer as an alehouse. As will be seen, even basic beerhouses adopted features from the gin palace. Equally, customers did not confine their drinking to one particular type of drinking place, but chose them according to circumstances and wants. The second is that in categorizing and generalizing, as one must in a work such as this, one should not forget the individuality of these drinking places and spaces, formed as they were of a complex and subtle mix of influences, including architecture and design, the character of the individuals running them, the customers and their various actions and interactions.

## Early modern to early Victorian England

For Alan Everitt, the years from the reign of Elizabeth to that of Victoria constituted the 'golden age' of the inn, during which it played a vital role in the economic, social and political life of the country.[2] It was a role which was enhanced with the growth of the economy and the related development of towns and transport, particularly after the Restoration. The inn's importance, then, in the estimation both of Everitt and fellow historian of the institution John Chartres, was at its peak in the late eighteenth century, from when decline was relatively swift, and the 'golden age' was passing by the 1830s.[3]

Throughout these years, inns were a key feature of towns great and small. Two types of design have been identified, both with medieval origins. There was the courtyard plan, in which a central yard was enclosed by two or more storeys of public and private rooms, sometimes galleried to provide independent access to them. This type was dominant in London, economizing as it did on space on the major thoroughfares. Examples included the Bull and Mouth in St Martin's Le Grand, the Belle Sauvage on Ludgate Hill and the George Inn in Southwark, which, unusually, survived to become a property of the National Trust. More numerous was the block, or gatehouse, plan in which the public rooms faced the front and the yard was to the rear, accessed from the street through an arched entrance or from a parallel back lane. Surviving examples of this type include the George at Stamford or those in the inn-keeping town of Stony Stratford, Buckinghamshire, on the London to Chester road.[4] Inns in towns on key routes such as these could be grand establishments and as such impressed contemporaries. William Harrison noted in the late sixteenth century the 'great and sumptuous inns', before going on to laud how they competed with each other 'for goodness of entertainment of their guests, as about fineness and change of linen, furniture of bedding, beauty of rooms, service at the table, costliness of plate, strength of drink, variety of wines, or well using of horses'.[5] Defoe commented similarly on the scale and quality of the inns in towns on the 'great northern road' like Stamford, Grantham or Doncaster; and in the county town of Northampton, the George, with forty-one expensively furnished rooms, was 'more like a palace than an inn'.[6]

Not all inns, however, were of the scale and luxury of those palatial establishments. More modest, and more typical, was an inn like the Spread Eagle at Midhurst, west Sussex, on a through route from London close to the coast, able at the close of the seventeenth century to sleep at least twenty-five people in nine bedrooms, each given an individual name, as was the custom at this time.[7] Travellers' tales, as they will, paint a rather more basic picture of their inn. A Dutch visitor staying at the White Swan at Gravesend was 'tolerably well accommodated and regaled', but had to sleep on a 'hard bench' as 'the English fleas were very aggressive'. And Celia Fiennes found near Sheffield that the 'poor sorry Inn' had 'just one good bed for us Gentlewomen'.[8] More than a century later, in 1818, when Halifax gentlewoman Anne Lister stayed at a Malton inn the chambermaid found the first room to be occupied and on entering instead a small back room, 'the bed was literally smoking from some gentleman who had just left it'.[9]

Catering for travellers such as these and their horses was the inn's primary function, offering refreshment en route and overnight accommodation. They were the points of arrival and departure for scheduled coach services, for which at their peak in the 1830s some 700 mail and 3,300 stage coaches were in operation in Great Britain as a whole. In London the great coaching inns functioned in the way of the railway termini which succeeded them, like the Bull and Mouth, the 'Euston of the era of road travel', with over fifty mail- and stagecoaches departing northwards every twenty-four hours.[10] Innkeepers also kept coaches for hire, whilst wealthier travellers used their own, changing horses at inns as they journeyed.[11] Poorer people might use a carrier's cart, but many simply walked, although the inferior treatment which they received at inns as pedestrians seems to have been a common enough source of complaint. William and Dorothy Wordsworth experienced this in the summer of 1802 when continuing their journey on foot from the Three Tuns at Thirsk, Yorkshire, and leaving their luggage behind. Having treated them well as post-chaise travellers, the landlady on their departure, as Dorothy noted, now 'threw out some saucy words in our hearing'.[12] The Radical Samuel Bamford fared worse at the Bedford Arms, Woburn, in 1820, where a drink and breakfast were actually refused him, an incident he recollected with the hope that 'like scores of their arrogant brotherhood' they had been humbled into civility by 'those great levellers, the railways'.[13]

Inns were equally important in the carriage of goods, offering the same facilities for the carrier and his horse, providing storage space and acting as a deposit and collection point. Commercial directories provided information on the inns used by carriers for particular destinations. In addition to their vital role in the country's transport infrastructure, they were important to the economy in providing a base for a wide variety of trading activities. They functioned as markets for the sale of produce, raw materials and finished goods. Blacksmiths, wheelwrights and butchers based themselves at inns, as did the itinerant providers of a wide range of services, including dentists, opticians, quacks, vets, portraitists, tailors and tutors. Other business routinely transacted in them included banking, the settlement of accounts, sealing of deals, payment of rents, leasing of property, creditors' and shareholders' meetings, job interviews and auctions of all manner of property.[14]

Inns also provided accommodation for much of the judicial and administrative business of the country. Quarter, petty and licensing sessions, manorial and coroners' courts and courts martial were all convened there. Local government bodies and the agents of central government such as the Excise and Post Office used them. They were important for the billeting of soldiers, the provision of which was a much resented legal obligation on innkeepers, and for recruitment. In contrast to billeting, which cost them money despite the government allowance, their vital role in the political life of the country was welcomed by innkeepers. A study of seventeenth-century Norwich has shown how as 'cornerstones of the expanding public sphere' inns like the Maid's Head in Tombland or the King's Head abutting the market place 'facilitated participation in political events, channelled rumours, news and information, and provided a space for the disseminational expression of public opinion'.[15] Elections came to be especially profitable: in the tiny Cornish borough of Grampound in 1727 one party spent almost £1,300 'for the freemen to drink', and to the innkeepers of Exeter at the 1790 election the three candidates were reputed to have distributed some £34,000.[16]

Finally, inns were hugely important in social life. They provided the venues for theatrical and musical performances, dancing assemblies, and dinners for celebrations, such as coronations and royal births, military and naval victories. An annual dinner was also enjoyed there by members of the proliferating range of clubs and societies. They included lodges of masons, friendly societies, trade clubs, county societies and clubs for what would later be termed hobbies, such as floral or animal and bird societies.[17] In the growth of those centres of the polite, leisured life the spas, inns played a vital role, particularly in the northern spas of Scarborough, Harrogate, Buxton and Matlock. Landlords promoted the resorts and their inns were centres of communal life.[18] Innkeepers were also great promoters of sporting events and as such played an important role in the development of prize-fighting, horse-racing and cricket. The 'most significant cricketing entrepreneur of the period', John Nyren of the Hambledon Club, kept the public house that was to become the Bat and Ball and came to innkeeping through his cricketing connections. In racing innkeepers organized plates and arranged subsidiary entertainments like dinners and balls. These also included cockfights, and other blood sports like bull- and badger-baiting took place at inns.[19]

The provision of all these services meant that the inn and the more substantial public house in the early modern period were regularly frequented by, in addition to a range of tradesmen and skilled workers, the middling sort and the gentry. The latter groups included women as travellers and diners and at some of the social events, such as balls or concerts. But from the late eighteenth century the middling sort and the gentry in particular began to withdraw from these spaces as the roles of the inn outlined here began to diminish and disappear. For many of the activities alternative accommodations were developed: theatres and assembly rooms for the social functions; warehouses, commercial halls, auction houses, exchanges, estate agencies and lawyers' offices for trading and commercial services; court houses and other public buildings for judicial and administrative processes.[20] This varied both geographically and in its timing. The same was true of the carriage of goods beyond the reach of the railway.[21] But it was the spread of the railway from the 1830s which, as Bamford had foreseen, spelled the end of the coaching inn.

The gentry and the middling sort also patronized the tavern, the specialist establishment for the sale of wine and food. Samuel Pepys noted in May 1662 how 'many ladies and persons of Quality' had come to the Triumphe Tavern at Charing

Cross to see 'some portugall Ladys' there before the arrival in England of Charles II's bride-to-be, Catherine of Braganza. Pepys in fact was a great frequenter of taverns. In February 1668, for example, he reported enjoying at the Bear Tavern in Drury Lane 'an excellent ordinary after the French manner' – that is, with the courses served separately.[22] They could be substantial premises, with ten rooms or more common in the capital, and a number were in fact converted from the private residences of the wealthy.[23] Others were more basic: Pepys again at the Three Cranes Tavern, Old Bailey, was with a wedding party in the 'best' room, crammed 'in such a narrow dogghole ... that it made me loathe my company and victuals; and a sorry poor dinner it was too'.[24] Like inns they were places to transact business or to consult professional men. They were patronized by politicians and writers, too. The Mermaid in Bread Street was renowned for its club of poets and dramatists, established by Raleigh, and including Shakespeare, Jonson, Beaumont, Webster and Donne.[25] And in the mid eighteenth century Samuel Johnson and James Boswell enjoyed their own and other writers' company at the Mitre Tavern in Fleet Street.[26]

As a distinct institution, however, the tavern declined over the course of the eighteenth century. This was partly a result of competition from the coffee house. Boswell and Johnson often went to them and indeed the latter encouraged their use of a room at the Turk's Head coffee house in the Strand because the mistress of the house was 'a good civil woman and wants business'.[27] But probably more significant, it has been suggested, was falling wine consumption and the fact that inns and more substantial public houses, with comparable if not superior accommodation, sold wine.[28]

Whilst, as we saw, the corollary of this decline was that the name of tavern came to be applied generally to public houses, a class of tavern that offered facilities for sexual encounters continued to trade. Pepys had used them in this way, although on one occasion he and Doll Lane didn't have sex at the Dog Tavern as there were only chairs in the room.[29] A century later Boswell took a room at the Shakespeare's Head, a tavern in Covent Garden, and had sex with two women he paid with a bottle of sherry.[30] Covent Garden was notorious for commercial sex. Magistrate Sir John Fielding inveighed against the 'brothels and irregular taverns' there, where prostitutes appeared 'at the windows ... in an indecent manner for lewd purposes'. Dockyard towns like Chatham, Plymouth and Portsmouth were supplied with similar establishments.[31] The parliamentary inquiry of 1772, to which Fielding gave this evidence, called for restriction in the grant of wine licences, but, although that power was placed in the hands of magistrates in 1792, the preservation of the rights of the Vintners' Company to trade afforded legitimate cover for their survival. The chief magistrate of Bow Street, Sir Nathaniel Conant, noted again, in 1816, its use for 'a higher kind of hotels, kept for the reception of men and women, for purposes which one cannot be blind to'.[32] Named wine saloons, six were reported in St James in the 1840s, including one frequented by shopmen and young gentlemen, where at two o'clock one morning Superintendent Beresford found around thirty to forty prostitutes, 'some of them with their Dresses so low that they might be said to be almost half naked'.[33]

But there were comparatively few such establishments. The alehouse was by far the most numerous type of drinking place. From its origins in the late medieval period it came in the sixteenth and seventeenth centuries 'to occupy a central place in early modern English society'.[34] Although there were some larger, mainly urban alehouses, they were generally smaller and much more basic establishments than inns and taverns. In the late medieval period their status was proclaimed by an ale-stake, a pole with a bush hanging at the end which signified that brewing had taken place and ale was now available. From the late sixteenth century, however, alehouse keepers increasingly replaced the temporary pole with the permanent sign of an inn.[35] Other than the sign, however, there was little externally that distinguished them from private houses. This was replicated internally, as, typically, the private quarters of the alehouse keeper and his family overlapped with the public drinking space. Often the main drinking room was the kitchen with its fire. Fixtures and fittings were also basic, 'little different from the ordinary furniture of a poor household', comprising trestle tables, benches, stools and a few chairs. Drinking vessels were of earthenware, stone and wood, or pewter in more respectable houses. The basic layout of a couple of rooms was common into the eighteenth century. This fact, and the domestic nature of the space and its overlapping of the public and the private, is nicely conveyed at the Bull and Butcher in Smithfield in 1767, where the landlady had hung washing to dry in the tap room.[36] By this time, however, alehouses generally were becoming more substantial and many were making the transition to inn status.[37] Towards the close of the eighteenth century, at a superior public house like the King's Arms in Arundel Street off the Strand, customers in the parlour enjoyed the comfort of stuffed leather benches fixed to the wall and drank off mahogany tables.[38]

The customers of the alehouse have attracted particular interest from historians of early modern England. Its cumulative effect has been, in Mark Hailwood's words, a 'broadening out of the profile of the alehouse crowd'.[39] This has shifted from a picture dominated by the male poor to one in which the middling and upper ranks of society and women made greater use of its spaces.[40] One should not, however, overemphasize difference in interpretation of the evidence. Whilst Peter Clark found that the 'great majority' of customers were indeed 'recruited from the bottom half of the social order' and were mostly young married or middle aged men, gentlemen, members of the clergy, substantial farmers and merchants were to be found there too, as were women, either with their husbands or in groups of other married women on special occasions.[41] More recent studies have suggested a greater presence for these groups. Flather's work on Essex in the late sixteenth and early seventeenth centuries showed that a quarter of alehouse customers were from the middling and upper ranks and over a third were women. Bernard Capp, looking at the late Stuart period, similarly found that women were present in alehouses in a variety of circumstances, with their husbands and at celebrations, yes, but also seeking refreshment after a visit to the market, or young single women in a mixed group of friends or 'with a respectable young man at a respectable time of day'. Patricia Fumerton, studying alehouse ballads, also noted the presence of women. But as all three historians averred, this was still in the context of a mostly male environment. For Flather this was a male-dominated drink culture, 'in which men lingered for longer, more freely and frequently over their drinking than women'. Capp too stressed that although there was space for women in alehouses, they had to use it, if they valued their good name, by adhering to the conventions. And for Fumerton, the ballads expressed men's freedom 'from the self-binding constraints of societal and, especially, familial obligations, most notably, to the wife'.[42] That freedom might include seeking other sexual partners, but, as Hailwood has suggested, this might also have appealed to single unmarried, and perhaps even married, women. In the end, he stresses the variety of the gendered forms of alehouse sociability: as husband and wife or with a new sexual partner, but also in mixed company without a sexual dimension, with siblings and kin or in single-sex groups.[43]

The alehouse performed, if in a more humble way, some of the functions of the inn, providing food and lodging and supporting the economy by offering a venue for trading goods, sealing business deals or recruiting labour.[44] But for the great mass of drinking places, even as their designation as alehouse was paralleled by, and ultimately gave way, to that of public house, their key role was recreational and social. Essential elements were talk, games and music. The mid-seventeenth-century diary of Roger Lowe, an apprentice shopkeeper of Ashton-in-Makerfield in Lancashire, which mentions some forty-seven different alehouses, makes this clear. Thus we find him there arguing about religion, or talking 'about tradeinge and how to get wives' or making 'a sett of Bowleinge' for a wager.[45] Bowling was common but alehouse keepers also kept footballs and cudgels for the sport of customers. A great variety of games were played inside, of which backgammon, cards or shove-halfpenny are still known today, and in which, as Lowe exemplified, gambling was common.[46] As for music, Pepys at the Cock alehouse in the Strand was entertained with harp and violin.[47] Ballad-singing was popular and the ballad sheets themselves, mass produced from the later sixteenth century, were often used to decorate the walls of the alehouse.[48] Itinerant musicians and singers visited alehouses, like Mary Saxby, making a living in mid-eighteenth-century London with another girl singing ballads at feasts and fairs 'for a few pence and a little drink'.[49]

Joining the more basic alehouse at the poorer end of the retail trade from the late seventeenth century was the gin shop. As we saw, gin was in fact sold in a variety of places, but until the trade was confined to licensed public houses by the middle of the eighteenth century gin shops flourished, known by a variety of alternative names: strong water, brandy, geneva or distiller's shops, as they appear, for example, in the proceedings of the Old Bailey. It is difficult to get a clear picture of what they were like, but their particular prevalence in London's poorer, and in some cases most notorious, districts, in the lanes, courtyards and alleys of the East End and south of the river, suggests they were pretty basic establishments. Their space as 'shops', where you bought the drink but did not necessarily linger, is further evidenced by references to a counter. Some were located in cellars, like the one in Church Lane, St Giles, run by one Richard Blunt with his wife and sister in the mid 1730s until, that is, he was sentenced to transportation for theft.[50]

But they often provided rooms, including for commercial sex, like the low taverns of Covent Garden, as upstairs at a brandy shop in Wapping in 1716 when Robert Pritchard's offer of 6d to Judith Brooks 'to let him lie with her' was refused.[51] But the gin shops, and the chandler's shops, were used by women more generally than for prostitution, particularly young, single, working women.[52]

The basic nature of the place and its popularity with women were features of the new generation of gin, or dram, shops, or spirit vaults as they were now also known, which developed in London and provincial towns from the 1780s. A diarist in Hull observed one Storm's dram shop there in 1784, where 'Several of the poor people came ... called for a Dram which they paid for and drank of immediately'.[53] But the physical space of the gin shop now began to change as its proprietors incorporated features then transforming retailing more generally, like plate glass and gas lighting. By the late 1820s, by which time numbers had risen substantially, the clerk of the peace for Middlesex was bemoaning 'the conversion of what used to be quiet respectable public-houses, where the labouring population could find the accommodation of a tap-room or parlour, in which to take the meals or refreshment they might require, into flaring dram-shops having no accommodation for persons to sit down'.[54] In 1834 the members of the parliamentary select committee inquiring into drunkenness amongst the labouring classes were treated to a description of the process by George Wilson, a grocer of Tothill Street, not far from Westminster Abbey:

> it was converted into the very opposite of what it had been, a low dirty public-house, with only one doorway, into a splendid edifice, the front ornamented with pilasters, supporting a handsome cornice and entablature, and balustrades (*sic*), and the whole elevation remarkably striking and handsome; the doorways were increased in number from one, and that a small one only three or four feet wide, to three, and each one of them eight to 10 feet wide; the floor was sunk so as to be level with the street; and the doors and windows glazed with very large single squares of plate glass, and the gas fittings of the most costly description; the whole excited the surprise of the neighbourhood.[55]

Wilson had been especially struck by its apparent appeal to women, and his observation was further supported by evidence to the inquiry of fourteen 'leading gin-shops' around the capital, where in one week over 40 per cent of customers seen to enter were women.[56]

Similar conversions, of varying degrees of transformation, were carried out in towns across the country, as in Leeds, for example, where the bench similarly complained of 'highly respectable innkeepers' who had converted part of their premises to dram shops.[57] As Dickens had noted them in London, so Mrs Gaskell in *Mary Barton* described one in Manchester where 'the light which streamed from its enlarged front windows, made clear the interior of the splendidly fitted up room, with its painted walls, its pillared recesses, its gilded and gorgeous fittings up'.[58] She called it a gin palace, the term that came to be generally applied to these establishments, the product of developments in retailing, the concentrated market offered in urban environments and the rise in spirit consumption.[59]

By the early nineteenth century, then, drinking places and spaces were changing. Inns were still important, but that importance was beginning to contract even before the advent of the railway brought about a much more rapid diminution. Some were rebranded, or rebuilt as hotels, as the Bull and Mouth, for example, became the Queen Hotel in 1830.[60] Others became in effect public houses, the name now taken by the great mass of drinking places, including taverns which had also been subsumed into their ranks. The term alehouse was still used but generally for the most basic town or village establishment. A new generation of gin shops was developing in ways which, as will be seen, would have an important influence on what came to be known as the pub. It was to this picture that an entirely new category of drinking place was added in 1830: the beerhouse.

Beerhouses traded alongside the many small public houses as more basic establishments. They were often created simply by converting a cottage or small shop; as we saw, many beer sellers traded alongside another business. Newer housing developments, however, now often made provision for a beerhouse. Internally, they followed the arrangement of rooms of existing small public houses, with often just a parlour and tap room (Figure 3.1).

But the purpose-building of premises, the effect of introducing minimal rateable values in legislation of 1834 and 1840 and the aspiration of many beerhouse keepers to a full licence all tended to make them more substantial properties.[61] In this way, although overall they continued to be more basic than fully licensed houses and there was still a measure of distinctiveness about them, physically the public house was becoming a more inclusive category.

The other major contribution to that development was the growing homogeneity of the customers. Beerhouses were always working-class institutions. As one witness to an early parliamentary inquiry into them put it, 'I do not think a respectable character ever enters them'.[62] Since the middling and upper classes were withdrawing from the worlds of the inn and the superior public house, the custom of public drinking places generally was by the early years of Victoria's reign becoming more, if not wholly, working-class. As a witness to another parliamentary inquiry of 1852 put it, explaining the need for alternative facilities for respectability to be able to purchase wine, 'no person above the rank of a labouring man or artisan, would venture to go into a public house'.[63]

## The pub and the people

This section takes its title from the famous Mass Observation study of the pub in 'Worktown', in fact Bolton, Lancashire, in the late 1930s, still one of the most interesting and useful studies of the institution.[64] The pub, as a recognizable single type, albeit one which exhibited considerable variation, had by the mid nineteenth century evolved from several more or less distinct drinking places. But at this moment of its creation, and when its numbers in fact reached a peak, so its importance in English society began a long decline, one which steepened in the latter

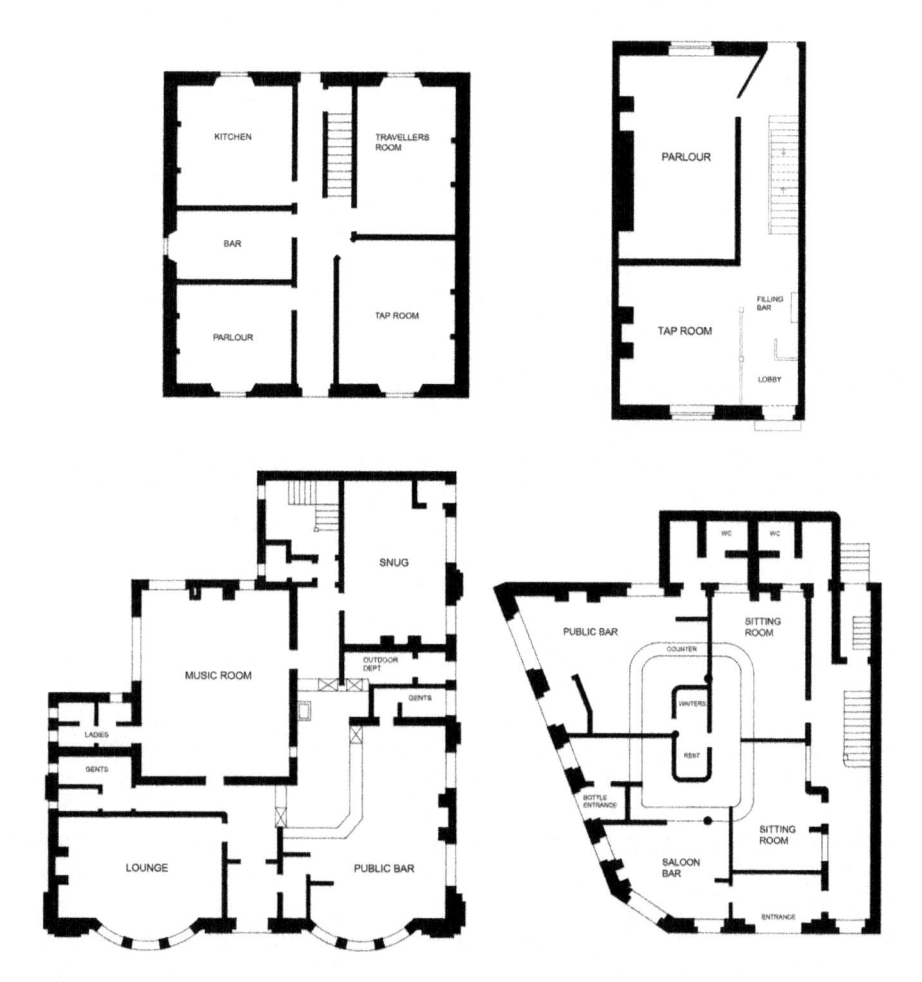

*Figure 3.1* Schema of pub interiors, clockwise from top left: fully licensed mid-Victorian pub; early beerhouse; late-century urban pub; inter-war improved house.

Source: Plans drawn by William Sutherland RIBA RIAS for the author.

part of the twentieth century. I look at the architecture and design of pubs and at the people who frequented them and what they did there.

Externally, mid-Victorian pubs continued to be distinguished from private houses chiefly by their signs. Indeed, both fully licensed premises and beerhouses were often converted from one or more houses or cottages. The innovations of the gin shops, however, now gave many a more distinctive appearance, which might be further emphasized by advertisements for the products of brewers.[65] Internally, they inherited the divisions of the inn, tavern and alehouse. Little beerhouses, as was noted, might offer just a couple of public rooms. An 1864 plan for converting a joiner's shop in Preston into a two-room beerhouse shows a bar with counter serving a vault, and a bar parlour. A more substantial house, aspiring perhaps to a full licence, would have more and a greater variety of rooms.[66] By this time the innovations of the gin palace, the gin-palace style, as it might usefully be termed, were also becoming widespread. Bar-counter service became common, whereas the term 'bar' had formerly referred to the private office of the publican. This was made clear in an 1833 architectural guide in its differentiation between the office, or store, type of bar of an inn and the counter of a public house, where many customers drank standing up or came in for off-sales.[67] Similarly, although the original gin palaces tended to have a single large space, like the Jolly Gardeners in Lambeth Walk, described by the barman in 1855 as having no tap room or parlour, just the bar,[68] the more common public-house layout of several rooms incorporated its typical fixtures and fittings. Thus the newly built Clarendon Hotel of 1846, also in London, had in the tap room traditional furniture of deal tables, wooden forms and settles around the walls, and in the parlour mahogany settles and seats stuffed with horse hair. But the bar itself was fitted up with a 'painted and panelled' counter with a metal top and twelve brass spirit taps plus a seven-motion beer engine with ivory handles, and the 'fine plate chimney-glass' in its mahogany frame was matched by the plate-glass lining of the Spanish-mahogany door leading to the bar parlour (Figure 3.1).[69]

These lavish interiors reached their apotheosis in a number of pubs in larger cities at the close of the century: pubs like the Salisbury in St Martin's Lane, London, with its electric lamps supported by bronze nymphs, reflected in its decorated glass and mirrors, or the Woodman in Easy Row, Birmingham, which featured stained glass, sumptuous woodwork and tiles painted with old scenes of the city. A distinctive appearance for some of the city's pubs, as also at Newcastle, was created with the use of tile and terracotta, or its glazed variant known as faience. In Portsmouth a similar distinction was achieved by the use of a half-timbered style in several of the city's pubs.[70] But pubs of such palatial splendour were in a minority. At the other end of the scale, many were considerably more basic, with few rooms and rudimentary sanitary arrangements. In the Yorkshire port and resort of Whitby, for example, in 1904, when the police made objection to several pubs, the Neptune in Haggersgate had just a bar and tap room, and although the Plough in Baxtergate had four rooms, they were said to be low, dark and poorly ventilated. At the Cleveland Arms the toilet was overlooked by another private dwelling; it had no flush and the waste ran in an open channel to the main drain.[71] Such an arrangement was not uncommon: in Blackburn in 1893 fewer than 10 per cent of pubs had modern toilet facilities.[72] Nevertheless, one may still think of them all as pubs by this time. All, to a greater or lesser extent, had internal arrangements of separate rooms, and all adopted some form of decoration, however basic; and in the use of mirrors and glass and the fixtures and fittings we can see elements of the gin-palace style. At the Ancient Druids Inn, a little beerhouse in Westgate, Bradford, on the edge of one of the city's poorest districts, there was a glazed partition to the entrance passage, a plate-glass mirror behind the bar in the tap room, and in the parlour, lit by three fancy gas brackets, were a racing print in gilt and a spring timepiece.[73]

The customers of these Victorian and Edwardian pubs were predominantly working-class and male, meriting the description of 'masculine republic'.[74] As Robert Roberts put it in his memoir of his Salford slum district, 'To the great mass of manual workers the local public house spelled paradise'. But this picture needs to be qualified in two ways. It was by no means wholly working-class. Roberts also noted that the premier pub there was frequented by shopkeepers and foremen, who took up the 'Best Room', whilst artisans occupied the vault, in Lancashire a basic room like the tap room. And in addition to social distinction within the pub, each of the sixteen in the district had its own particular status, for the working class itself was not undifferentiated.[75] Similarly, in rural east Kent, whilst some pubs relied entirely on labourers' trade, in others a private or saloon bar was patronized by village farmers, farm bailiffs and tradesmen and also skilled workers like craftsmen and gardeners.[76]

Nor were they wholly male. Women formed a significant minority of customers. Susan Kling's study of pub culture in the capital concluded that women's presence in pubs was 'an ordinary occurrence'.[77] A contemporary survey, like the one we saw of gin palaces in the mid 1830s, of some 200 pubs in all parts of the capital in the mid 1880s, found that over a third of those entering were women, although, like the 8 per cent who were children, they may have come for off-sale.[78] And at the close of the century Charles Booth's survey found women in pubs. In the East End Monday was recognized as ladies' day, when they still had a little money left over.[79] Some pubs there had women's bars, and in the West End, too, some opened special ladies' bars to accommodate better-off women.[80] But the unequal and circumscribed nature of women's use of the pub is indicated by the very fact that such bars were separate. Furthermore, it invited misogynistic comment. The East End pubs which women patronized were called 'cowsheds' from the local epithet for women. Similarly, Cow Shed or Duck Pen were nicknames in Birmingham for the rooms in pubs where older women sat, away from their husbands.[81] Booth's informants mostly felt that women's drinking and use of the pub was increasing, but this view was contradicted by journalist Arthur Shadwell, who felt that 'so far from women having recently taken to frequenting the public-house they have never frequented it less'.[82] Overall this conclusion makes more sense when set in the context of what we know about the growth over the century of the ideals of respectability and women's proper place in the home. It may also depend to some extent upon where we look. Roberts in Salford observed that 'few respectable wives visited public houses'. Rowntree in York similarly found 'a comparatively small amount of public-house drinking done by women in the more respectable working-class districts'. And in rural east Kent few women went to the pub unless with their husband on Saturday night; it was not thought to be respectable, a view tellingly reinforced by the fact that London women down for the hop-picking did.[83]

For many women, in the end the pub could be as much a source of pain as of pleasure. Men's use of it often gave rise to tension as they spent time and money there which could have gone on their families. In Edwardian London, as Ellen Ross expressed it, wives were in a 'continuous tug-of-war with pubs' for the housekeeping money. A variety of stratagems might be used to obtain it, from accompanying their spouse, like Ann Jasper of Hoxton, whose local landlord would push the change in her direction, or making arrangements with obliging publicans to limit husbands' spending, to physically dragging the offending husband out of the pub. But the aggression was more commonly in the other direction. As one London magistrate put it, 'If I were to sit here from Monday morning till Saturday to protect women that had got brutal and drunken husbands, I should not get through half of them'.[84]

Looking at the recreational and social role of the pub, there were continuities with the world of the alehouse in the key activities of talking, playing games and enjoying music, but there was also change. Talk no doubt exhibited many recurring elements. In the alehouses of Pudsey in the West Riding of Yorkshire in the 1820s it was characterized, in the memory of former Chartist Joseph Lawson, as village gossip, 'spinning long yarns of various sorts and cracking jokes'.[85] In rural East Anglian pubs work was the chief topic of conversation as men went over the day's tasks in minute detail.[86] Most pubs were very much neighbourhood meeting places and in poor districts in particular their density was such that a pub was literally only yards away. A study of Birmingham mapped this, using newspaper reports of court proceedings which gave addresses, to conclude that 'to a considerable extent people did visit pubs in their immediate neighbourhood'.[87] In this context local gossip and work naturally loomed large in the conversation. Sport was also a popular topic and its centrality to pub conversation may have increased with the growth of organized sport over the course of the century. Gambling, linked to sport, was also popular, probably more so once the electric telegraph was able to provide starting-price odds and speedy results for betting on horses.[88] Sport's popularity was reflected in the space given over to it in newspapers, whose circulation expanded enormously, particularly from the middle of the century, and they were commonly available in pubs. In this way current affairs may also have assumed more salience, but newspapers' reporting of crime and, within the boundaries of convention, sexual scandal probably loomed as large. Although, when Mass Observation listened to pub conversation in late-1930s Bolton, news of any sort was low down the list: sport and betting, jobs and money were far and away the most common topics.[89]

Some older pub games, like skittles or quoits, retained their popularity, particularly in rural areas, whilst in towns cards and newer games – dominoes, darts and, in some pubs, billiards – were more important.[90] Sport continued to be linked to the pub. In Edwardian Norwich publicans organized bowling clubs and a firm of brewers ran the Anchor League.[91] But the case of football shows how the close link between the pub and sport was weakening by the late nineteenth century. Although some teams were based at pubs, the real locus of the game was the ground: as one Blackburn publican complained in 1883, football was bad for business for all but a few pubs.[92] The cinema also affected trade: one Bradford landlord explained that whereas before people had stayed all evening, now they just called in on their way to and from the picture house.[93] These activities did not necessarily exclude drinking, but collectively they progressively reduced its centrality in working-class lives.

The musical life of pubs too exhibited elements of continuity and change. Informal singing remained common and itinerant musicians provided accompaniment, or performance in their own right.[94] Growing towns offered a ready market for more organized entertainments, like the 'free and easy' or 'harmonic meeting', which featured both amateur and professional talent. And from the 1830s pubs increasingly provided purely professional entertainment. Charles Rice, a part-time professional comic singer in London, recorded in his diary at this time performances at thirty-three pubs with dedicated concert rooms.[95] Some styled these rooms 'music halls', like the one at the Bermondsey Hotel in Bradford at the close of the 1840s, which could accommodate around 500 people. From this developed the music hall proper, as did the proprietor of the Bermondsey when its licence was refused, opening the purpose-built Royal Colosseum within a year.[96] Pub music thrived into the twentieth century. Pubs in York, for example, usually had a piano, but customers would play on accordion, ukulele, violin or even penny whistle.[97] Mechanized forms appeared: the Polyphon, for example, in the late nineteenth century, which played over a thousand tunes; between the wars the wireless and the gramophone; and after the war the jukebox and television.[98]

Of course, the music halls, just like the cinema, were competitors to the pub and also contributed to the diminution of its centrality in working-class leisure. Similarly, the pub's importance as a meeting place was lessening. Its use for official purposes declined steadily, surviving only in rural areas, as in East Anglia, for example, where coroners' courts and meetings of parish councils were still held there into the twentieth century.[99] In this, as in political life, as we will see in Chapter 7, legislation also played a part in removing these activities from the world of the public house. For other purposes, however, although the likes of trades unions and friendly societies sometimes moved to alternative premises, the pub remained essential up to the First World War. Around 1900 over two thirds of the branches of the Manchester Unity of Oddfellows and the Ancient Order of Foresters and over 80 per cent of those of the Amalgamated Society of Engineers still met on licensed premises.[100] In Edwardian Norwich at least a hundred fishing clubs were connected to pubs and the club meetings of canary breeders were invariably held at them.[101] But for some a further competitor was now the home: as one contemporary study of the working class in south London noted, 'quieter spirits' would send out to the pub for a pint, often then 'spreading their enjoyment over a couple of hours'.[102]

This last development was linked, as we saw, to the growth of working-class respectability. But the pub itself had become by the First World War a more orderly space. This had, however, been a long process. Into the Victorian period pubs were associated with crime, prostitution and blood sports. Henry Mayhew documented all of these for the capital at mid century. He cited, for example, police statistics showing that over 350 public and beerhouses were the resorts of thieves and prostitutes, and was told of dogfights at beerhouses and rat pits at around forty pubs.[103] The relatively unregulated beerhouses were often cited in this respect, and their return to magistrates' control in 1869 led to the refusal of licences to many. In Halifax, for example, 26 were closed in this way, of which no fewer than seventeen were frequented by prostitutes and two more were described as disorderly or badly conducted.[104] The more restrictive licensing regime, together with commercial pressures, as we will see in Chapter 7, aided the move to orderliness. When, in 1897, the licensee of the Imperial Wreath in Manchester was prosecuted for harbouring, as it was termed, prostitutes the *Manchester Guardian* could opine that 'the time has long passed for a house of this kind to exist in the centre of the city'.[105] Although individual pubs could still be used by criminals and prostitutes, and some no doubt were sometimes drunken and disorderly, the overall tone of 'the ordinary public house at the corner of any ordinary East End street' was as Booth, certainly no friend to drink, found it at the close of the century:

> There, standing at the counter, or seated on the benches against wall or partition, will be perhaps half-a-dozen people, men and women, chatting together over their beer – more often beer than spirits – or you may see a few men come in with no time to lose, briskly drink their glass and go. Behind the bar will be a decent middle-aged woman, something above her customers in class, very neatly dressed, respecting herself and respected by them. The whole scene comfortable, quiet and orderly.[106]

Orderliness and respectability were generally also the tone in the working men's club, which flourished now as another alternative to the pub. As one member put it, 'The great thing about club life is the absence of a "floating population" – strangers who can come in and kick up a row or misbehave themselves'.[107] As places, they showed the same variety as the pub, ranging from the 'humble village club', with just one or two rooms and perhaps thirty members, to urban clubs like one at Leeds with 1,400 members, or Bolton, which had no fewer than twenty-seven rooms, a gymnasium and a garden. Their members enjoyed a range of activities very much like those at the pub: chatting and smoking, playing games like draughts or dominoes, reading the newspapers or preparing for Saturday night's free and easy. At the latter wives and daughters might be admitted, but in general the club was, and long remained, a more exclusively male space than the pub.[108]

In contrast, women's use of pubs increased, beginning with the First World War. They were now part of the workforce in large numbers and the resulting income, plus greater independence and the desire for company, drew them into the pub. To some extent this represented greater use by existing customers. This was the finding of an investigative committee set up in Birmingham to examine the issue in response to the hostility which it aroused in some quarters. Allegations of increased intemperance were unfounded it reported, but munitions workers with money to spend 'caused a visible concentration of numbers at particular times'.[109] But there was evidence, too, of new custom and of greater use by women further up the social scale.[110]

These trends persisted into the inter-war years (Figure 3.2).[111] They were supported by moves to improve the physical environment of the pub. Chiefly this

*Figure 3.2* Pub interior, Bolton, 1938, photographed by Humphrey Spender, showing the gin-palace style and the presence of women.

Source: Courtesy of Bolton Council.

came about as a result of improved living standards generally, with customers coming to expect greater comfort and modern facilities, including toilets, and licensing magistrates insisting on them (Figure 3.1). But it was also part of a self-conscious movement of pub 'improvement' on the part of some brewers. This had its origins in late-nineteenth-century efforts to create a more civilized drinking place and their implementation in those areas where pubs were placed under state control during the war, which I will examine in Chapters 6 and 7. But as a general policy it was taken up more significantly in the inter-war years. For these brewers, men like Sydney Nevile of Whitbread and Edwyn Barclay of Barclay Perkins in London and William Waters Butler of Mitchells and Butlers of Birmingham, it would both demonstrate the social responsibility of the industry and be good for business. As Nevile, the de facto spokesman for the movement, argued, sobriety was 'commercially, as well as socially, desirable'; accordingly, 'a policy of improvement and good service' was the way forward.[112] The wider intellectual context of the movement has been the subject of some debate, particularly its location in pre-war transatlantic Progressive thinking and its aim to address the deleterious consequences of industrialization with scientific enquiry and an interventionist approach to the problems identified, a thesis advanced by David Gutzke.[113] But whatever the precise nature of its intellectual roots, or the exact motivations of its proponents, its practical outcomes were the provision of food, new pub designs, the encouragement of a wider clientele and the creation in the pub of a 'venue for respectable family leisure'. Exemplifying the approach was Mitchells and Butlers, which spent £1.7m on 142 pubs, like the British Oak at Stirchley, with car parking, gardens, bowling greens and a playground, and inside an assembly room for food, concerts, meetings and functions.[114] In the end, however, self-conscious improvement of the reformers' type had limited practical effect. In total some 5,900 pubs were built or rebuilt between the wars, concentrated in the second half of the 1930s, representing about 7 per cent of the existing stock in 1921. This was a huge investment but it was only a fraction of that in general improvement. Moreover, it was geographically localized, with Birmingham and London together accounting for one sixth of the total, two thirds of which in turn were in suburban or rural locations.[115]

By the outbreak of war, then, there were new pubs, mostly built in a neo-Tudor or neo-Georgian style, which attempted to recreate a version of the traditional inn, with little in the way of modernist design.[116] But overall the stock of pubs remained in the inter-war years, and into the 1950s, recognizably Victorian, both externally and internally. One innovation, however, approved by the improvers, and which became common, was the 'lounge', sometimes called a smoke room, a 'gender-neutral' space which appealed to some working-class and, in some places, middle-class couples and women drinkers (Figure 3.1).[117] The Second World War then saw a rise in the use of pubs, particularly by young women. This was based on increased spending power and freedom from familial and neighbourhood constraints when they were relocated to a new area. It reflected also, it has been argued, women's belief in their right to leisure as equal contributors to the war effort.[118]

The war years represented the final acceptance of the pub as a legitimate, even respectable place of leisure – the goal, if not wholly the achievement, of the improvers. That acceptance is reflected in the adoption of a term to characterize it, which had come into use in the 1930s: the 'local'.[119] As the *Brewers' Journal* noted in April 1942 of the term's increasing use, it was 'a neighbourly, part-of-us phrase'.[120] In contrast to the First World War, when, as we will see, drink and the pub were perceived as threats to the war effort, now, in the context of a more sober nation, maintaining the supply of beer was seen as good for morale. As Tom Harrisson of Mass Observation put it, arguing for immediate publication of *The Pub and the People*, it would remind people of 'one small section of the thing we are fighting for'.[121]

## Post-war

Mass Observation had reached two key conclusions about the pub at the close of the 1930s. The first was its central importance in social life, more than any other institution. But the second was its decline, playing 'a smaller part in the life of the town than it had ever done'.[122] This became increasingly the case in the post-war years. In Chapter 2 I outlined how the number of pubs fell. Crucial to the pub's declining importance was the erosion of its male working-class base as heavy and manufacturing industry collapsed from the late 1970s. This also contributed to the decline of the club from this time, a sharp contrast to its post-war heyday when 'thousands of working men's clubs were at the centre of many local communities with people queuing before opening time to lay claim to their favourite seats'.[123]

At the same time, working-class people continued the trend of the inter-war years to move to suburban private or council housing. Although some new pubs were built to serve these estates, they were not ubiquitous as in the old central districts. But although the pub's importance lessened, one should not in the end overstate the case. In the 1990s going to the pub remained the most common free-time activity outside the home, with 65 per cent of adults having done so within the previous three months.[124]

Physically, there had been significant changes to the pub. They continued to be refurbished as living standards rose and health-and-safety regulations became stricter. Interiors were opened out, often into a single large space, ending the traditional multi-roomed layout. This permitted greater supervision of the drinking spaces by staff and dispensed with the need for waiters. Diminishing numbers of manual workers also meant less demand for basic rooms like a vault or tap room.[125] But the open layout did not prevent customers from forming social spaces, as one study showed. There was the 'public space' of the middle-aged regulars at the bar; the 'negotiable space' of the non-seating areas by various groups of customers; and the 'closed social space where couples sat alone.[126] Typically, they were fitted out in 'traditional' style with stained oak furniture and decorated with horse brasses. Some were designed according to a particular theme, notably 'Irishness' as in the Scruffy Murphy or O'Neill's concepts, where 'every stereotype of Irish nationality imaginable' was introduced in what one study described as 'the hyperreal pub in a postmodern market'.[127] But in addition to the changes made to existing pubs, an important trend was the opening of entirely new premises, like those of J. D. Wetherspoon, whose design strategy often mixed references to traditional pub culture with contemporary interiors.[128]

Accompanying these developments were important changes in the profile of customers, two of which will be highlighted here. One was their increasing use by the young. The inter-war years had seen an ageing of the pub's customers, a trend which continued into the immediate post-war years. A survey of more than 400 London pubs found that both men and women were middle-aged or elderly. Young people were more interested in the cinema, dancing and sport.[129] This now changed. By 1970 a study of three Lancashire towns found that the pub had become the only public meeting place regularly mentioned by young people; cinema, dance hall and church hall had all declined.[130] This was linked to the increasingly young age at which alcohol was being consumed, based in turn on increased disposable income and changing aspirations. It may also have been facilitated by the relaxation of police supervision of pubs.[131] Young people also used drinking places in different ways, as observers were noting from the mid 1980s. Rather than stay in one place for most of the night, a round or 'circuit' was made of a number of pubs and bars by groups of from three to twenty people, spending just twenty minutes in each. In place of the old community local, where customers stayed most of the night, drinking places were now, it was argued, 'fashion items', places for the staging of self, emancipation from the older generation and distancing from its values.[132] The expansion of the night-time economy of bars and clubs in town and city centres was based to a large extent in catering for this age group.

It was based, too, in the second important development in the customer base: the greater amount of public drinking by women. In contrast to the years after the First World War, women's use of pubs seems to have fallen after the Second, a conclusion stressed by Gutzke, arguing that the post-war ideology extolling home, family and her rightful place and the betrayal of wartime rhetoric of equality of sacrifice had together driven them away.[133] This persisted for some time. A 1970 survey found that only just over a quarter of women visited a pub at least once a month.[134] And, as in the past, women's use of pub space was circumscribed. In an East Anglian village in the early 1980s, although the pub studied was an important social centre for working-class women, who had a darts team, their use was only acceptable at certain times and only if accompanied by a man.[135] A feminist study of the pub drew upon its author's experience of hostility to portray its culture of misogyny, within which a woman's place was marginal.[136] From this time, however, the economic and social bases of the male-dominated pub were eroded and women began to achieve greater economic independence and equality. By the mid 1990s more than half of all women reported visiting a pub within the previous three months.[137] And on the supply side pubs were being made more attractive to women, both physically and, for example, in their greater orientation towards food sales and accessibility for children. Of particular importance was the development of new types of drinking place, like the wine bar or so called female friendly chains like Pitcher & Piano or All Bar One. J. D. Wetherspoon, the best known of these, sought to appeal to women with its pubs' layout, décor and, not least, clean and attractive toilets.[138]

At the close of this history, then, two developments stood out. One was the increased diversity of places to drink. The pub was still the most numerous, with the category of community pubs or locals approaching 40,000 premises in a market survey of 2003, exceeding the 25,500 of all other categories, such as circuit bars, themed pubs, pub-restaurants, café bars or wine bars. But both were exceeded by the almost 80,000 other places in which to drink: from restaurants, hotels, guest houses, nightclubs, working men's and sports clubs to university and college bars.[139] The other development was the presence of women in these places and spaces, almost certainly more than at any point in the previous five-hundred years.

## Notes

1 A. Flather, *Gender and Space in Early Modern England* (Woodbridge: The Boydell Press, 2007), pp. 1–2.
2 A. E. Everitt, 'The English urban inn, 1560–1760', in Everitt, *Landscape and Community in England* (London: Hambledon, 1985), pp. 155–208, on p. 156; for a European perspective see B. Kümin, *Drinking Matters: Public houses and social exchange in early modern Central Europe* (Basingstoke: Palgrave Macmillan, 2007).
3 J. Chartres, 'The eighteenth-century English inn: A transient "Golden Age"?', in B. Kümin and B. A. Tlusty (eds), *The World of the Tavern: Public houses in early modern Europe* (Aldershot: Ashgate, 2002), pp. 205–26, on p. 226; see also his 'The place of inns in the commercial life of London and Western England 1660–1760' (Dphil dissertation, Oxford University, 1973). Although they pioneered detailed historical

study, Everitt and Chartres were by no means the first to write of the inn. From the mid-Victorian period there developed a voluminous antiquarian literature on the subject and a smaller, more scholarly, contribution, for which see Everitt, 'The English urban inn', pp. 206–7 and W. E. Tate, 'Public house bibliography', *Local Historian*, 8:4 (1968), pp. 126–30. For works on inns, and also pubs and beerhouses, see D. W. Gutzke, *Alcohol in the British Isles from Roman Times to 1996* (London: Greenwood Press, 1996), pp. 113–39.

4 W. A. Pantin, 'Medieval inns', in E. M. Jope (ed.), *Studies in Building History* (London: Odhams, 1961), pp. 166–91; J. A. Chartres, 'The capital's provincial eyes: London's inns in the early eighteenth century', *London Journal*, 3:1 (1977), pp. 24–39; Everitt, 'The English urban inn', p. 162.

5 G. Edelen (ed.), *William Harrison, The Description of England* (Ithaca, NY: Cornell University Press, 1968), pp. 397–406.

6 D. Defoe, *A Tour through England and Wales* (London: J. M. Dent & Sons, 1928), vol. 2, pp. 86, 103 and 181; Everitt, 'The English urban inn', p. 188.

7 J. Pennington, 'Inns and taverns of Western Sussex, 1500–1700: A documentary and architectural investigation', in Kümin and Tlusty, *The World of the Tavern*, pp. 116–35, on p. 126.

8 M. Exwood and H. L. Lehman (eds), *The Journal of William Schellink's Travels in England 1661–1663* (London: Royal Historical Society, Camden Fifth Series 1, 1993), p. 33; C. Morris (ed.), *The Journeys of Celia Fiennes* (London: Cresset Press, 1947), p. 95.

9 H. Whitbread (ed.), *'I Know My Own Heart': The diaries of Anne Lister 1791–1840* (London: Virago, 1988), p. 65.

10 H. W. Hart, 'Sherman and the Bull and Mouth', *Journal of Transport History*, 5:1 (1961), pp. 12–21; Chartres, 'The capital's provincial eyes'.

11 Chartres, 'The Eighteenth-Century English Inn', p. 218.

12 H. Darbishire (ed.), *Journals of Dorothy Wordsworth* (London: Oxford University Press, 1958), p. 191.

13 W. H. Chaloner (ed.), *The Autobiography of Samuel Bamford* (London: Frank Cass, 1967), vol. 2, pp. 130–1.

14 Chartres, 'The eighteenth-century English inn', pp. 219–21; Everitt, 'The English urban inn', pp. 171–3; P. Jennings, *The Local: A history of the English pub* (Stroud: The History Press, rev. ed., 2011), pp. 39–47 for the whole of this section on the role of inns.

15 F. Williamson and E. Southard, 'Drinking houses, popular politics and the middling sorts in early seventeenth-century Norwich', *Cultural & Social History*, 12:1 (2015), pp. 6–26, on p. 21.

16 H. L. Douch, *Old Cornish Inns and Their Place in the Social History of the County* (Truro: D. Bradford Barton, 1966), p. 33; R. Newton, *Eighteenth Century Exeter* (Exeter: University of Exeter, 1984), pp. 81–2.

17 P. Clark, *British Clubs and Societies 1580–1800: The Origins of an Associational World* (Oxford: Clarendon Press, 2000), pp. 2 and 164.

18 P. Hembry, *The English Spa 1560–1815: A social history* (London: Athlone Press, 1990), p. 202 and *passim*.

19 Chartres, 'The eighteenth-century English inn', pp. 224–5.

20 P. Clark, *The English Alehouse: A social history 1200–1830* (London: Longman, 1983), p. 10.

21 A. Everitt, 'Country carriers in the nineteenth century', in *Landscape and Community in England*, pp. 279–307.

22 R. C. Latham and W. Matthews (eds), *The Diary of Samuel Pepys* (London: G. Bell and Sons, vol. 3, 1970), p. 92 and (vol. 9, 1976), p. 78.

23 Clark, *The English Alehouse*, p. 12.

24 Latham and Matthews, *The Diary of Samuel Pepys,* (vol. 3, 1970), p. 16.

25 Clark, *The English Alehouse*, p. 13.
26 F. A. Pottle (ed.), *Boswell's London Journal* (London: Heinemann, 1950), pp. 278 and 282.
27 Ibid., p. 307.
28 Clark, *The English Alehouse*, p. 14.
29 Latham and Matthews, *The Diary of Samuel Pepys*, (vol. 9, 1976) p. 78; also, for example, (vol. 7, 1972), pp. 359 and 385–6 and (vol. 8, 1974), p. 3.
30 *Boswell's London Journal*, pp. 263–4.
31 Report from a Committee of the House of Commons, appointed to enquire into the several Burglaries and Robberies committed in London and Westminster, reprinted as Appendix 8 to the Report on the Nightly Watch and Police of the Metropolis; PP 1812 (127) II.95.
32 Select Committee of the House of Commons on the State of the Police of the Metropolis; PP 1816 (510) V.1, p. 24; for the law on the sale of wine see chapter 7.
33 Select Committee of the House of Lords on Bill for regulating the Sale of Beer and other Liquors on Lord's Day; PP 1847–48 (501) XVI.615, pp. 58–9.
34 M. Hailwood, *Alehouses and Good Fellowship in Early Modern England* (Woodbridge: The Boydell Press, 2014), p. 3.
35 Clark, *The English Alehouse*, pp. 65–8.
36 Ibid., pp. 197–8; Old Bailey Proceedings Online, t17670218-20 at www.oldbaileyonline.org, version 7.0, [accessed 10 July 2006].
37 Clark, *The English Alehouse*, pp. 195–7.
38 M. Thale (ed.), *The Autobiography of Francis Place (1771–1854)* (Cambridge: Cambridge University Press), p. 37.
39 Hailwood, *Alehouses and Good Fellowship*, p. 179.
40 Ibid., pp. 179–81 summarizes that historiography.
41 Clark, *The English Alehouse*, pp. 123–32.
42 Flather, *Gender and Space*, pp. 110–21; B. Capp, 'Gender and the culture of the English alehouse in late Stuart England', in A. Kornohen and K. Lowe (eds), *The Trouble with Ribs: Women, men and gender in early modern Europe* (Helsinki: Helsinki Collegium for Advanced Studies, 2007), pp. 103–27; P. Fumerton, 'Not home: Alehouses, ballads, and the vagrant husband in early modern England', *Journal of Medieval and Early Modern Studies*, 32:3 (2002), pp. 493–518; see also T. Reinke-Williams, 'Women, ale and company in early modern London', *Brewery History*, 135 (2010), pp. 88–106.
43 Hailwood, *Alehouses and Good Fellowship*, pp. 209–14.
44 Ibid., pp. 20–1.
45 W. L. Sachse (ed.), *The Diary of Roger Lowe of Ashton-in-Makerfield, Lancashire 1663–74* (London: Longmans, Green, 1938), pp. 28, 37 and 52; the diary is analysed in A. L. Martin, 'Drinking and alehouses in the diary of an English mercer's apprentice, 1663–1674', in M. P. Holt (ed.), *Alcohol: A social and cultural history* (Oxford: Berg, 2006), pp. 93–105.
46 Clark, *The English Alehouse*, pp. 154–5.
47 Latham and Matthews, *The Diary of Samuel Pepys*, (vol. 2, 1970), p. 89.
48 Clark, *The English Alehouse*, pp. 155–6.
49 T. Hitchcock, *Down and Out in Eighteenth-Century London* (London: Hambledon, 2004), p. 69.
50 Old Bailey Proceedings Online, t17301014-7, t17330510-3 and t17370420-31; W. Maitland, *The History of London from Its Foundation by the Romans to the Present Time* (London: Richardson, 1739), pp. 519–20; J. Warner, *Craze: Gin and debauchery in an age of reason* (London: Profile Books, 2003), pp. 45–6.
51 Old Bailey Proceedings Online, t17160517-34, among several examples.
52 J. Warner and F. Ivis, 'Gin and gender in early eighteenth-century London', *Eighteenth-Century Life*, 24:2 (2000), pp. 85–105.

53 G. Jackson, *Hull in the Eighteenth Century: A study in economic and social history* (London: Oxford University Press, 1972), p. 286.
54 *Times*, 1 December, 1829, p. 3.
55 Select Committee of the House of Commons on Inquiry into Drunkenness among the Labouring Classes of UK; PP 1834 (559) VIII.315, p. 274.
56 Ibid., pp. 3 and 274–5.
57 *Leeds Mercury*, 9 and 23 September 1837, p. 7.
58 C. Dickens, 'Gin-shops', in *Sketches by Boz* (Harmondsworth: Penguin, 1995), pp. 214–20; E. Gaskell, *Mary Barton* (Harmondsworth: Penguin, 1970), pp. 87–8.
59 Jennings, *The Local*, pp. 82–3.
60 Hart, 'Sherman and the Bull and Mouth'.
61 Jennings, *The Local*, pp. 66–7.
62 Select Committee of the House of Commons on Sale of Beer; PP 1833 (416) XV.1, p. 11.
63 Select Committee of the House of Commons on Wine Duties; PP 1852 (495) XVII.1, pp. 523–4.
64 Mass Observation, *The Pub and the People: A Worktown study* (London: Cresset Library, 1987). For an assessment of the usefulness of this study to the history of the pub and drinking see P. Jennings, 'Mass Observation's *The Pub and the People*' in R. Snape and H. Pussard (eds), *Recording Leisure Lives: Histories, archives and memories of leisure in 20th century Britain* (Eastbourne: Leisure Studies Association, 2009), pp. 131–42.
65 P. Mathias, *The Brewing Industry in England 1700–1830* (Cambridge: Cambridge University Press, 1959), pp. 137–8.
66 G. Brandwood, A. Davison and M. Slaughter, *Licensed to Sell: The history and heritage of the public house* (London: English Heritage, 2004), pp. 28–9.
67 J. C. Loudon, *An Encyclopaedia of Cottage, Farm, and Villa Architecture and Furniture* (London: Longman, Orme, Brown, Green & Longman, 1839), pp. 675–90.
68 Old Bailey Proceedings Online, t18550409-507.
69 M. Girouard, *Victorian Pubs* (London: Yale University Press, 1984), pp. 44–5.
70 Ibid., pp. 94–100 and 110–97; A. Crawford, M. Dunn and R. Thorne, *Birmingham Pubs 1880–1939* (Gloucester: Alan Sutton, 1986), pp. 7–39; L. F. Pearson, *The Northumbrian Pub: An architectural history* (Morpeth: Sandhill Press, 1989); R. C. Riley and P. Eley, *Public Houses and Beerhouses in Nineteenth Century Portsmouth* (Portsmouth: Portsmouth City Council, 1983), p. 15; Brandwood, Davison and Slaughter, *Licensed to Sell*, pp. 57–75.
71 C. Waters, *A History of Whitby's Pubs, Inns and Taverns* (Whitby: author, 1992) where these details are noted in an alphabetical list.
72 D. W. Gutzke, *Pubs and Progressives: Reinventing the public house in England 1896–1960* (De Kalb, Il: Northern Illinois University Press, 2006), p. 9.
73 P. Jennings, *The Public House in Bradford, 1770–1970* (Keele: Keele University Press, 1995), p. 176.
74 B. Harrison, *Drink and the Victorians: The temperance question in England 1815–1872* (Keele: Keele University Press, 2nd ed., 1994), p. 47.
75 R. Roberts, *The Classic Slum: Salford life in the first quarter of the century* (Harmondsworth: Penguin, 1973), pp. 120–1.
76 M. Winstanley, 'The rural publican and his business in East Kent before 1914', *Oral History*, 4:2 (1976), pp. 63–78, on pp. 73–5.
77 S. M. Kling, 'Spare time … Pub culture in nineteenth century London: A social and cultural history of working class pub patronage' (PhD dissertation, UCLA, 2001), pp. 159–206 and particularly p. 191.
78 *Times*, 16 April 1885, p. 9.

79 C. Booth, *Life and Labour of the People in London Third Series Religious Influences* (London: Macmillan 1902), vol.1, p. 54 and vol. 5, p. 19 and *Final Volume: Notes on social influences and conclusion*, pp. 61–4.
80 Charles Booth Online Archive, British Library of Political and Economic Science, Police Notebooks B 352, p. 33, at www.booth.lse.ac.uk [accessed 1 September 2005]; Royal Commission on Liquor Licensing Laws, Third Report; PP 1898 [C. 8694] XXXVI.9, p. 171; F. Fisher, 'Privacy and supervision in the modernised public house, 1872–1902', in B. Martin (ed.), *Designing the Modern Interior: From the Victorians to today* (Oxford: Berg, 2009), pp. 41–52, on this and on the spaces of London pubs generally.
81 Booth, Police Notebooks, B346, p. 41 and B 347, p. 121; C. Chinn, *They Worked All Their Lives: Women of the urban poor in England, 1880–1939* (Manchester: Manchester University Press, 1988), pp. 66 and 120–1.
82 A. Shadwell, *Drink, Temperance and Legislation* (London: Longmans, Green, 1902), p. 89. On women in pubs in this period see also B. Gleiss, 'Women in public houses: A historic analysis of the social and economic role of women patronising English public houses, 1880s–1970s' (DPhil dissertation, University of Vienna, 2009), pp. 41–69; D. W. Gutzke, *Women Drinking Out in Britain since the Early Twentieth Century* (Manchester: Manchester University Press, 2014), pp. 14–51; Jennings, *The Local*, pp. 112–18.
83 Roberts, *The Classic Slum*, p. 175; B. S. Rowntree, *Poverty: A Study of Town Life* (London: Macmillan, 1903), p. 325; Winstanley. 'The rural publican', p. 73.
84 E. Ross, 'Survival networks: Women's neighbourhood sharing in London before World War 1', *History Workshop*, 15 (1983), pp. 4–27, on p. 16; *Love and Toil: Motherhood in outcast London, 1870–1918* (Oxford: Oxford University Press, 1993), p. 44; '"Fierce questions and taunts": Married life in working-class London 1870–1914', *Feminist Studies*, 8:3 (1992), pp. 575–602, on p. 591.
85 J. Lawson, *Progress in Pudsey* (Firle: Caliban Books, 1978), pp. 83–4.
86 G. E. Evans, *The Days That We Have Seen* (London: Faber and Faber, 1975), pp. 154–5.
87 W. M. Bramwell, *Pubs and Localised Communities in Mid-Victorian Birmingham* (London: Occasional Paper 22, Department of Geography and Earth Science, Queen Mary College, University of London, 1984), pp. 7–22.
88 M. J. Huggins, 'The first generation of street bookmakers in Victorian England: Demonic fiends or "decent fellers"?', *Northern History*, 36 (2000), pp. 129–45.
89 Mass Observation, *The Pub and the People*, pp. 186–91.
90 Lawson, *Progress in Pudsey*, pp. 83–4; Winstanley. 'The rural publican', p. 71; Evans, *The Days That We Have Seen*, p. 142; Jennings, *The Public House in Bradford*, pp. 57–8. For details and excellent illustrations see A. Taylor, *Played at the Pub: The pub games of Britain* (Swindon: English Heritage, 2009).
91 C. B. Hawkins, *Norwich: A social study* (London: Philip Lee Warner, 1910), p. 314.
92 T. Collins and W. Vamplew, *Mud, Sweat and Beers: A cultural history of sport and alcohol* (Oxford: Berg, 2002), pp. 12–15.
93 *Yorkshire Observer*, 21 April 1914, p. 7.
94 P. Jennings, 'The pub as a music centre in mid-Victorian Bradford', *Bradford Antiquary*, Third series, 6 (1992), pp. 22–32, on pp. 22–3.
95 L. Senelick (ed.), *Tavern Singing in Early Victorian London: The diaries of Charles Rice for 1840 and 1850* (London: Society for Theatre Research, 1997), pp. 14–15 and passim.
96 Jennings, 'The pub as a music centre', pp. 24–9.
97 M. Race, *Public Houses, Private Lives: An oral history of York Pubs in the Mid-Twentieth Century* (York: Voyager, 1999), pp. 93–101; see also S. Moss, '"A harmonizing whole"? Music, Mass Observation and the interwar public house', in The Subcultures Network (ed.), *Subcultures, Popular Music and Social Change* (Newcastle upon Tyne: Cambridge Scholars, 2014), pp. 105–20.

*Places and spaces* 93

98 Girouard, *Victorian Pubs*, pp. 196–7; Race, *Public Houses, Private Lives*.
99 Evans, *The Days That We Have Seen*, p. 146.
100 E. A. Pratt, *The Policy of Licensing Justices* (London: King & Son, 1909), p. 22.
101 Hawkins, *Norwich*, pp. 313–15.
102 A. Paterson, *Across the Bridges OR Life by the South London River-Side* (London: Garland, 1980), p. 214.
103 H. Mayhew, *London Labour and the London Poor* (London: Frank Cass, 1967), vol. 1, pp. 15 and 451–2, vol. 3, pp. 5–11 and vol. 4, p. 375; Jennings, *The Local*, pp. 114–15 and 126–7.
104 P. W. Robinson, 'Ale, beer and public house closures in the Halifax area 1635–2010', *Transactions of the Halifax Antiquarian Society*, 20 (new series) 2012, pp. 68–99, on p. 80.
105 Cited in J. Parke, 'The social functions of public-houses in Manchester and Preston, c. 1840–1914', (MA Dissertation, Lancaster University, 1977), p. 64.
106 Booth, *Life and Labour, First Series, vol. 1*, pp. 113–14.
107 L. Marlow, 'A menace to sobriety? The drink question and the working man's club, c. 1862–1906', in H. van Voss and F. L. van Holthoon (eds), *Working Class and Popular Culture* (Amsterdam: Stichting Beheer, 1988), pp. 109–20, on p. 112; E. Selley, *The English Public House as It Is* (London: Longmans, Green, 1927), p. 161–4.
108 H. Solly, *Working Men's Social Clubs and Educational Institutes* (London: Simpkin, Marshall, Hamilton, Kent, 2nd ed., 1904), p. 67; R. L. Cherrington, 'The development of working men's clubs: A case study of implicit cultural policy', *International Journal of Cultural Policy*, 15:2 (2009), pp. 187–99, on pp. 193–4.
109 H. Carter, *The Control of the Drink Trade in Britain: A contribution to national efficiency during the Great War* (London: Longmans Green, 2nd ed., 1919), pp. 113–14.
110 D. W. Gutzke, 'Gender, class and public drinking in Britain during the First World War', *Histoire sociale/ Social History*, 27:54 (1994), pp. 367–91.
111 Gutzke, *Women Drinking Out*, pp. 14–51.
112 S. O. Nevile, *Seventy Rolling Years* (London: Faber and Faber, 1958), pp. 53–67.
113 There is not space here to examine that debate in detail but see Gutzke, *Pubs and Progressives* and 'W. Waters Butler and the making of a progressive brewer in Britain', *Histoire sociale/Social History*, 48:96 (2015), pp. 137–60 and the debate between Gutzke and A. Mutch in the latter's 'Shaping the public house, 1850–1950: Business strategies, state regulation and social history', *Cultural & Social History*, 1:2 (2004), pp. 179–200; response of Gutzke, 'Progressivism and the history of the public house 1850–1950', *Cultural & Social History*, 4:2 (2007), pp. 235–60; Mutch, 'Improving the public house in Britain, 1920–1940: Sir Sydney Nevile and "social work"', *Business History*, 52:4 (2010), pp. 517–35 and comment by Gutzke, 'Sydney Nevile: Squire in the slums or progressive brewer', *Business History*, 53:6 (2011), pp. 960–9 and Mutch's response, 'Sydney Nevile: Squire in the slums or progressive brewer? A response to David Gutzke', on pp. 970–5. See also the review of *Pubs and Progressives* by Matthew Hilton in *English Historical Review*, 122 (2007), pp. 852–3.
114 Gutzke, *Pubs and Progressives*, pp. 85–95; Crawford, Dunn and Thorne, *Birmingham Pubs*, pp. 48–57 and 92–3; B. Oliver, *The Renaissance of the English Public House* (London: Faber and Faber, 1947), pp. 80–92.
115 Gutzke, *Pubs and Progressives*, pp. 210–11 and 246–8.
116 These improved pubs are particularly well documented. In addition to the above, see E. E. Williams, *The New Public-House* (London: Chapman and Hall, 1924); C. Aslet, 'Beer and skittles in the improved public house', *Thirties Journal*, 4 (1984), pp. 2–9; R. Thorne, 'Good service and sobriety: The improved public house', *Architectural Review*, 159 (1976), pp. 107–11; Brandwood, Davison and Slaughter, *Licensed to Sell*, pp. 50–2 and 78–88.

## Places and spaces

117 Gutzke, *Women Drinking Out*, pp. 27–8; A. Davies, *Leisure, Gender and Poverty: Working-class culture in Salford and Manchester, 1900–1939* (Buckingham: Open University Press, 1992), pp. 62–3.
118 C. Langhamer, '"A public house is for all classes, men and women alike": Women, leisure and drink in Second World War England', *Women's History Review*, 12:3 (2003), pp. 423–43; Gutzke, *Women Drinking Out*, pp. 55–65.
119 See M. Gorham, *The Local* (London: Cassell, 1939).
120 B. Glover, *Brewing for Victory: Brewers, beer and pubs in World War II* (Cambridge: Lutterworth Press, 1995), pp. 14–28. For the idea of the local see P. Jennings, 'The local: Ideal and reality in the English pub', in R. Snape and H. Pussard (eds), *Recording Leisure Lives: Sports, games and pastimes in 20th century Britain* (Eastbourne: Leisure Studies Association, 2010), pp. 21–39.
121 Mass Observation, *The Pub and the People*, p. xv.
122 Ibid., pp. 17, 74 and 218.
123 Cherrington, 'The development of working men's clubs', p. 187; she also explores other reasons for their decline.
124 Social Trends 27 (London: HMSO, 1997), p. 220.
125 Jennings, *The Local*, pp. 215–16.
126 M. A. Smith, *The Pub and the Publican* (Salford: Centre for Leisure Studies, University of Salford, 1981).
127 J. C. Everitt and I. R. Bowler, 'Bitter-sweet conversions: Changing times for the British pub', *Journal of Popular Culture*, 30:2 (1996), pp. 101–22; A. Williams, 'The postmodern consumer and the hyperreal pub', *Hospitality Management* 17 (1998), pp. 221–32, on pp. 228–9.
128 C. Rountree and R. Ackroyd, 'More than just a shop that sells beer? J D Wetherspoon and the pub authenticity-value aesthetic', in M. Hailwood and D. Toner (eds), *Biographies of Drink: A case study Approach to our historical relationship with alcohol* (Newcastle upon Tyne: Cambridge Scholars, 2015), pp. 100–35.
129 F. Zweig, *Labour, Life and Poverty* (London: Gollancz, 1948), pp. 25–30.
130 E. Roberts, *Women and Families: An oral history, 1940–1970* (Oxford: Blackwell, 1995), pp. 62–3.
131 Jennings, *The Local*, p. 223.
132 L. Gofton, 'On the town; drink and the "new lawlessness"', *Youth and Policy*, 29 (1990), pp. 33–9; L. Gofton and S. Douglas, 'Drink and the city', *New Society*, 20 (1985), pp. 502–4.
133 Gutzke, *Women Drinking Out*, pp. 62–5.
134 M. Bradley and D. Fenwick, *Public Attitudes to Liquor Licensing Laws in Great Britain* (London: HMSO, 1974), pp. 13 and 55.
135 G. Hunt and S. Satterlee, 'Darts, drink and the pub: The culture of female drinking', *Sociological Review*, 35:3 (1987), pp. 575–601.
136 V. Hey, *Patriarchy and Pub Culture* (London: Tavistock, 1986), pp. 33–4; see also A. Whitehead, 'Sexual antagonism in Herefordshire', in D. L. Barker and S. Allen (eds), *Dependence and Exploitation in Work and Marriage* (London: Longman, 1976), pp. 169–203. For its persistence in rural pubs in particular see M. Leyshon, '"No place for a girl": Rural youth, pubs and the performance of masculinity', in J. Little and C. Morris (eds), *Critical Studies in Rural Gender Issues* (Aldershot: Ashgate, 2005), pp. 104–22.
137 Social Trends 27, p. 220.
138 This is discussed in detail in Gutzke, *Women Drinking Out*, pp. 146–93.
139 *Pub Visiting, Leisure Intelligence, August 2004* (London: Mintel International, 2004), p. 19.

# Bibliography

Aslet, C., 'Beer and skittles in the improved public house', *Thirties Journal*, 4 (1984), pp. 2–9.

Bramwell, W. M., *Pubs and Localised Communities in Mid-Victorian Birmingham* (London: Occasional Paper 22, Department of Geography and Earth Science, Queen Mary College, University of London, 1984).

Brandwood, G., Davison, A. and Slaughter, M., *Licensed to Sell: The history and heritage of the public house* (London: English Heritage, 2004).

Capp, B., 'Gender and the culture of the English alehouse in late Stuart England', in A. Kornohen and K. Lowe (eds), *The Trouble with Ribs: Women, men and gender in early modern Europe* (Helsinki: Helsinki Collegium for Advanced Studies, 2007), pp. 103–27.

Carter, H., *The Control of the Drink Trade in Britain: A contribution to national efficiency during the Great War* (London: Longmans Green, 2nd ed., 1919).

Chartres, J., 'The place of inns in the commercial life of London and Western England 1660–1760' (DPhil dissertation, Oxford University, 1973).

—, 'The capital's provincial eyes: London's inns in the early eighteenth century', *London Journal*, 3:1 (1977), pp. 24–39.

—, 'The eighteenth-century English inn: A transient "Golden Age"?', in B. Kümin and B. A. Tlusty (eds), *The World of the Tavern: Public houses in early modern Europe* (Aldershot: Ashgate, 2002), pp. 205–26.

Cherrington, R. L., 'The development of working men's clubs: A case study of implicit cultural policy', *International Journal of Cultural Policy*, 15:2 (2009), pp. 187–99.

Chinn, C., *They Worked All Their Lives: Women of the urban poor in England, 1880–1939* (Manchester: Manchester University Press, 1988).

Clark, P., *The English Alehouse: A social history 1200–1830* (London: Longman, 1983).

—, *British Clubs and Societies 1580–1800: The origins of an associational world* (Oxford: Clarendon Press, 2000).

Collins, T. and Vamplew, W., *Mud, Sweat and Beers: A cultural history of sport and alcohol* (Oxford: Berg, 2002).

Crawford, A., Dunn, M. and Thorne, R., *Birmingham Pubs 1880–1939* (Gloucester: Alan Sutton, 1986).

Davies, A., *Leisure, Gender and Poverty: Working-class culture in Salford and Manchester, 1900–1939* (Buckingham: Open University Press, 1992).

Douch, H. L., *Old Cornish Inns and Their Place in the Social History of the County* (Truro: D. Bradford Barton, 1966).

Evans, G. E., *The Days That We Have Seen* (London: Faber and Faber, 1975).

Everitt, A. E., 'The English urban inn, 1560–1760', in Everitt, *Landscape and Community in England* (London: Hambledon, 1985), pp. 155–208.

—, 'Country carriers in the nineteenth century', in Ibid., pp. 279–307.

Everitt, J. C. and Bowler, I. R., 'Bitter-sweet conversions: Changing times for the British pub', *Journal of Popular Culture*, 30:2 (1996), pp. 101–22.

Fisher, F., 'Privacy and supervision in the modernised public house, 1872–1902', in B. Martin (ed.), *Designing the Modern Interior: From the Victorians to today* (Oxford: Berg, 2009), pp. 41–52.

Flather, A., *Gender and Space in Early Modern England* (Woodbridge: The Boydell Press, 2007).

Fumerton, P., 'Not home: Alehouses, ballads, and the vagrant husband in early modern England', *Journal of Medieval and Early Modern Studies*, 32:3 (2002), pp. 493–518.

Girouard, M., *Victorian Pubs* (London: Yale University Press, 1984).

Gleiss, B., 'Women in public houses: A historic analysis of the social and economic role of women patronising English public houses, 1880s – 1970s' (DPhil dissertation, University of Vienna, 2009).

Glover, B., *Brewing for Victory: Brewers, beer and pubs in World War II* (Cambridge: Lutterworth Press, 1995).

Gofton, L., 'On the town; drink and the "new lawlessness"', *Youth and Policy*, 29 (1990), pp. 33–9.

Gofton, L. and Douglas, S., 'Drink and the city', *New Society*, 20 (1985), pp. 502–4.

Gorham, M., *The Local* (London: Cassell, 1939).

Gourvish, T. R. and Wilson, R. G., *The British Brewing Industry 1830–1980* (Cambridge: Cambridge University Press, 1994).

Gutzke, D. W., 'Gender, class and public drinking in Britain during the First World War', *Histoire sociale/ Social History*, 27:54 (1994), pp. 367–91.

—, *Alcohol in the British Isles from Roman Times to 1996* (London: Greenwood Press, 1996).

—, *Pubs and Progressives: Reinventing the public house in England 1896–1960* (De Kalb, Il: Northern Illinois University Press, 2006).

—, 'Progressivism and the history of the public house 1850–1950', *Cultural & Social History*, 4:2 (2007), pp. 235–60.

—, 'Sydney Nevile: Squire in the slums or progressive brewer?', *Business History*, 53:6 (2011), pp. 960–9.

—, *Women Drinking Out in Britain since the Early Twentieth Century* (Manchester: Manchester University Press, 2014).

—, 'W. Waters Butler and the making of a progressive brewer in Britain', *Histoire sociale/ Social History*, 48:96 (2015), pp. 137–60.

Hailwood, M., *Alehouses and Good Fellowship in Early Modern England* (Woodbridge: The Boydell Press, 2014).

Harrison, B., *Drink and the Victorians: The temperance question in England 1815–1872* (Keele: Keele University Press, 2nd ed., 1994).

Hart, H. W., 'Sherman and the Bull and Mouth', *Journal of Transport History*, 5:1 (1961), pp. 12–21.

Hembry, P., *The English Spa 1560–1815: A social history* (London: Athlone Press, 1990).

Hey, V., *Patriarchy and Pub Culture* (London: Tavistock, 1986).

Hitchcock, T., *Down and Out in Eighteenth-Century London* (London: Hambledon, 2004).

Huggins, M. J., 'The first generation of street bookmakers in Victorian England: Demonic fiends or "decent fellers"?', *Northern History*, 36 (2000), pp. 129–45.

Hunt, G. and Satterlee, S., 'Darts, drink and the pub: The culture of female drinking', *Sociological Review*, 35:3 (1987), pp. 575–601.

Jackson, G., *Hull in the Eighteenth Century: A study in economic and social history* (London: Oxford University Press, 1972).

Jennings, P., 'The pub as a music centre in mid-Victorian Bradford', *Bradford Antiquary*, Third series, 6 (1992), pp. 22–32.

—, *The Public House in Bradford, 1770–1970* (Keele: Keele University Press, 1995).

—, 'Mass Observation's *The Pub and the People*' in R. Snape and H. Pussard (eds), *Recording Leisure Lives: Histories, archives and memories of leisure in 20th century Britain* (Eastbourne: Leisure Studies Association, 2009), pp. 131–42.

—, 'The local: Ideal and reality in the English pub', in R. Snape and H. Pussard (eds), *Recording Leisure Lives: Sports, games and pastimes in 20th century Britain* (Eastbourne: Leisure Studies Association, 2010), pp. 21–39.

—, *The Local: A history of the English pub* (Stroud: The History Press, rev. ed., 2011).

Kling, S. M., 'Spare time ... Pub culture in nineteenth century London: A social and cultural history of working class pub patronage' (PhD dissertation, UCLA, 2001).

Kümin, B., *Drinking Matters: Public houses and social exchange in early modern Central Europe* (Basingstoke: Palgrave Macmillan, 2007).

Langhamer, C., '"A public house is for all classes, men and women alike": Women, leisure and drink in Second World War England', *Women's History Review*, 12:3 (2003), pp. 423–4.

Leyshon, M., '"No place for a girl": Rural youth, pubs and the performance of masculinity', in J. Little and C. Morris (eds), *Critical Studies in Rural Gender Issues* (Aldershot: Ashgate, 2005), pp. 104–22.

Marlow, L., 'A menace to sobriety? The drink question and the working man's club, c. 1862–1906', in H. van Voss and F. L. van Holthoon (eds), *Working Class and Popular Culture* (Amsterdam: Stichting Beheer, 1988), pp. 109–20.

Martin, A. L., 'Drinking and alehouses in the diary of an English mercer's apprentice, 1663–1674', in M. P. Holt (ed.), *Alcohol: A social and cultural history* (Oxford: Berg, 2006), pp. 93–105.

Mass Observation, *The Pub and the People: A Worktown study* (London: Cresset Library, 1987).

Mathias, P., *The Brewing Industry in England 1700–1830* (Cambridge: Cambridge University Press, 1959).

Moss, S., '"A harmonizing whole"? Music, Mass Observation and the interwar public house', in The Subcultures Network (ed.), *Subcultures, Popular Music and Social Change* (Newcastle upon Tyne: Cambridge Scholars, 2014), pp. 105–20.

Mutch, A., 'Shaping the public house, 1850–1950: Business strategies, state regulation and social history', *Cultural & Social History*, 1:2 (2004), pp. 179–200.

—, 'Improving the public house in Britain, 1920–1940: Sir Sydney Nevile and 'social work', *Business History*, 52:4 (2010), pp. 517–35.

—, 'Sydney Nevile: Squire in the slums or progressive brewer? A response to David Gutzke', *Business History*, 53:6 (2011), pp. 970–5.

Newton, R., *Eighteenth Century Exeter* (Exeter: University of Exeter, 1984).

Oliver, B., *The Renaissance of the English Public House* (London: Faber and Faber, 1947).

Pantin, W. A., 'Medieval inns', in E. M. Jope (ed.), *Studies in Building History* (London: Odhams, 1961), pp. 166–91.

Parke, J., 'The social functions of public-houses in Manchester and Preston, c. 1840–1914', (MA Dissertation, Lancaster University, 1977).

Pearson, L. F., *The Northumbrian Pub: An architectural history* (Morpeth: Sandhill Press, 1989).

Pennington, J., 'Inns and taverns of Western Sussex, 1500–1700: A documentary and architectural investigation', in Kümin and Tlusty (eds), *The World of the Tavern*, pp. 116–35.

Race, M., *Public Houses, Private Lives: An oral history of York pubs in the mid-twentieth century* (York: Voyager, 1999).

Reinke-Williams, T., 'Women, ale and company in early modern London', *Brewery History*, 135 (2010), pp. 88–106.

Riley, R. C. and Eley, P., *Public Houses and Beerhouses in Nineteenth Century Portsmouth* (Portsmouth: Portsmouth City Council, 1983).

Roberts, E., *Women and Families: An oral history, 1940–1970* (Oxford: Blackwell, 1995).

Roberts, R., *The Classic Slum: Salford life in the first quarter of the century* (Harmondsworth: Penguin, 1973).

Robinson, P. W., 'Ale, beer and public house closures in the Halifax area 1635–2010', *Transactions of the Halifax Antiquarian Society*, 20 (new series 20) 2012, pp. 68–99.

Ross, E., 'Survival networks: Women's neighbourhood sharing in London before World War 1', *History Workshop*, 15 (1983), pp. 4–27.

—, '"Fierce questions and taunts": Married life in working-class London 1870–1914', *Feminist Studies*, 8:3 (1992), pp. 575–602.

—, *Love and Toil: Motherhood in outcast London, 1870–1918* (Oxford: Oxford University Press, 1993).

Rountree, C. and Ackroyd, R., 'More than just a shop that sells beer? J D Wetherspoon and the pub authenticity-value aesthetic', in M. Hailwood and D. Toner (eds), *Biographies of Drink: A case study approach to our historical relationship with alcohol* (Newcastle upon Tyne: Cambridge Scholars, 2015), pp. 100–35.

Selley, E., *The English Public House as It Is* (London: Longmans, Green, 1927).

Shadwell, A., *Drink, Temperance and Legislation* (London: Longmans, Green, 1902).

Smith, M. A., *The Pub and the Publican* (Salford: Centre for Leisure Studies, University of Salford, 1981).

Tate, W. E., 'Public house bibliography', *Local Historian*, 8:4 (1968), pp. 126–30.

Taylor, A., *Played at the Pub: The pub games of Britain* (Swindon: English Heritage, 2009).

Thorne, R., 'Good service and sobriety: The improved public house', *Architectural Review*, 159 (1976), pp. 107–11.

Warner, J., *Craze: Gin and debauchery in an age of reason* (London: Profile Books, 2003).

Warner, J. and Ivis, F., 'Gin and gender in early eighteenth-century London', *Eighteenth-Century Life*, 24:2 (2000), pp. 85–105.

Waters, C., *A History of Whitby's Pubs, Inns and Taverns* (Whitby: author, 1992).

Whitehead, A., 'Sexual antagonism in Herefordshire', in D. L. Barker and S. Allen (eds), *Dependence and Exploitation in Work and Marriage* (London: Longman, 1976), pp. 169–203.

Williams, A., 'The postmodern consumer and the hyperreal pub', *Hospitality Management* 17 (1998), pp. 221–32.

Williams, E. E., *The New Public-House* (London: Chapman and Hall, 1924).

Williamson, F. and Southard, E., 'Drinking houses, popular politics and the middling sorts in early seventeenth-century Norwich', *Cultural & Social History*, 12:1 (2015), pp. 6–26.

Winstanley, M., 'The rural publican and his business in East Kent before 1914', *Oral History*, 4:2 (1976), pp. 63–78.

Zweig, F., *Labour, Life and Poverty* (London: Gollancz, 1948).

# 4  Meanings

**Introduction**

This chapter is concerned with what drinking means to the drinker. This is not to suggest that this is a novel preoccupation in this history. In the discussion of the relationship between drinking and living standards importance was attached to economic considerations, such as levels of disposable income and the relative cost of drinks, but crucial too was cultural change in notions of what constituted a better life: sobriety and moderation or conspicuous consumption. Nonetheless, greater emphasis has been placed hitherto on economic variables, including developments in the supply of drink, and social influences – for example, shifts in the age structure of the population; and succeeding chapters will pay attention to the impact of anti-drink sentiment and regulation. But the meanings of drinking are sufficiently important to merit a discrete chapter.

That importance has been recognized in what is now a considerable literature. There is not space here to review it in detail, but one common theme might usefully be highlighted to begin with: an appreciation of the positive role which alcohol has played in people's lives in contrast to emphasis on its negative consequences for the individual and society. Thus E. M. Jellinek, exemplifying the latter, with his development of the concept of alcoholism as a disease, concerned himself with the symbolic function of drinking, at that time – the immediate post-war years – in his view 'the most neglected' topic in alcohol and alcoholism research.[1] But it was the work of a number of anthropologists, such as Dwight Heath, Mary Douglas and Mac Marshall, which was important in that it placed emphasis on the positive, or constructive, aspects of drinking and took forward the exploration of its cultural significance. In their view, specialists on alcohol had focused on pathology, so that inevitably the problematic aspects were highlighted. But they found that in most cultures alcohol consumption was part of normal behaviour – in celebrations, for example – and most people drank without discernible suffering.[2] Historians too have recognized the importance of this insight. Notable here was Brian Harrison's 1971 study of Victorian temperance, by definition concerned with drink as a problem, which, drawing upon the findings of social anthropologists, devoted space to discussion of what drinking meant to people.[3]

In organizing the discussion which follows I have made use of the categories of Harrison and Heath in particular to create four sections, dealing in turn with the physical, psychological, symbolic and ritual and social meanings of drinking. Within each category the aim is to locate those meanings historically, highlighting elements of continuity and change.

## Physical

For much of our period, and for most people, drink was the chief quencher of thirst, meeting the body's basic need for liquid. For the poorest, water, despite its dangers, may also have served that purpose, as we saw in Chapter 1. Rod Phillips has gone further, arguing that for many the amounts of ale, beer or wine consumed were below what was needed for rehydration and that in consequence water must have been drunk.[4] Beyond the quenching of thirst, it formed an essential item of daily diet and was valued as a source of energy and strength. It was seen as particularly vital to the effective performance of hard, physical labour.[5] We saw this with harvest workers, and the same was true of industrial labour. The forge men at Low Moor ironworks in the West Riding of Yorkshire in the mid nineteenth century drank each shift between one and three gallons of home-brewed beer, with water in addition.[6] It also kept out the cold, as the late-seventeenth-century 'Praise of Yorkshire Ale' put it:

> The tattered beggar being warmed with ale,
> Nor rain, hail, frost, nor snow can him assail.[7]

Serving at Ypres in the summer of 1917, Harry Patch recalled the morning rum ration after the 'endless' night, either on watch or trying to keep warm in the cold night air:

> Rum was brought up in a big pottery jar. I don't know what the measure was meant to be exactly because they poured a bit into the lid of your mess tin and you drank out of that. It burnt all the way down, especially if you weren't a drinker, but it warmed you up beautifully.[8]

Whilst the pleasure of the warming effect has persisted across time, the dietary centrality, its role as thirst-quencher and as imparter of strength have all declined with a richer diet, a much greater variety of liquid refreshment from which to choose, including safe water, and modern notions of bodily fitness.

In addition to these basic effects, throughout much of our period the general health-giving properties of drink throughout the lifecycle were valued at all levels of society. It was seen as beneficial to nursing mothers. As one mother of four of a gentry family put it in 1768, 'As I am a nurse, I take great care of myself and drink porter like any fishwoman'.[9] It also offered a more general tonic: the Norfolk clergyman James Woodforde, for example, took a glass of port as 'a strengthening Cordial twice a day'.[10] These beliefs persisted well into the twentieth century and continued to encompass all drinks. For Mass Observation's Bolton respondents, reasons of health and/or beneficial physical effects, were the most commonly cited reasons for drinking beer.[11] Gordon's gin, according to an advertisement of 1938, had 'medicinal properties'. Martini and Rossi's dry and sweet vermouths, first introduced into the UK in the 1930s, promoted their health-giving properties alongside their links to physical and sexual attractiveness. Guinness, which introduced its 'good for you' slogan in 1929, was still keeping the doctor away forty years later.[12] This preventive role also had specific applications. In the deadly cholera outbreaks of the mid nineteenth century, spirits were taken to ward off the disease and to assuage the fear it engendered.[13] Similarly, stonemason John Dickinson in the Washburn Valley in Yorkshire in the cold and snow of May 1891 drank 'a lot of whisky' to ward off the influenza then causing deaths and distress in the district.[14] It was used as an antiseptic. The Reverend George Woodward of Berkshire in the mid eighteenth century used rum on a scraped shin, which 'assuaged the swelling', and also recommended holding hot red wine on a piece of cloth against the wound as 'extremely painful' but 'infallible'.[15] And it offered hope of a cure for every ailment or disease, either by itself or as one ingredient in a remedy. From the seventeenth century medical books began to be written in English, rather than Latin, making information on remedies much more widely available.[16] English men and women made extensive use of them. Parson Woodforde took rum for 'wind cholic' and for her vomiting gave his niece Nancy half a pint of rum and later more rum with rhubarb and ginger.[17]

Lay opinions such as these persisted well into modern times, but alcohol also continued to be an important tool of the medical profession through the nineteenth century. In the 1820s Yorkshire physician John Simpson could take two bottles each of port and claret to a gentleman who was 'rather indisposed'.[18] Indeed, it has been argued that alcohol reached 'a zenith of therapeutic fashion' in the middle years of the century for a variety of conditions, including pneumonia, rheumatic fever and typhus, with prescriptions of up to three pints of brandy a day for several days to a month.[19] In 1876 Disraeli was still prescribed port wine for his bronchitis, asthma and gout.[20] But by this time scientific research and temperance advocacy, and the two combined as medical temperance, were challenging with some success its efficacy in prevention, restoration and prescription.[21] Its use in hospitals, for example, declined. In the General Hospital, Birmingham, this was significant from the 1860s, although it was linked there to cost rather than therapeutics.[22] In seven leading London hospitals the line of rising expenditure on milk crossed that of falling expenditure on alcohol in 1878.[23] In 1907 eminent physicians Sir Victor Horsley and Mary Sturge published *Alcohol and the Human Body* 'to put forward the present state of knowledge of alcohol solely on the basis of experimental, anatomical, and statistical evidence', although it was at the time criticized for its one-sidedness (Horsley was a teetotaller) and its methodology.[24] During the First World War, however, a Scientific Advisory Committee was set up to review existing research. Its 1918 report, *Alcohol: Its Action on the Human Organism*, and others which followed, expressed a unified medical-scientific view of the alcohol problem, one which favoured a 'moderationist paradigm', where small or moderate quantities were held to have little effect on the capacity to function normally, rather than teetotalism or prohibition.[25] Over the succeeding century more effective remedies and further developments in experimental science brought about the replacement of alcohol in medicine.[26] Belief in its preventive qualities, however, has persisted, both in the lay mind and in the scientific, with, for example, the suggested benefits to the heart of red wine.[27]

## Psychological

One cannot always, of course, easily separate the psychological from the physical. Harry Patch's rum ration must surely have done more than warm his body, helping to relieve the tension and boredom of life at the front. Alcohol was seen as a remedy for mental as well as physical ailments. Seventeenth-century manuals offered many for lethargy or melancholia which included wine amongst the ingredients.[28] Cider too was said to be an aid to 'banishing melancholy', in addition to being good for stomach ailments and generally for promoting longevity.[29] David Livingstone's wife Mary took brandy to steady her nerves on her mother's recommendation, and her otherwise 'prim' sister-in-law, Emily Moffat, confided to her father that for what the wives of missionaries had to endure wine was 'a real godsend, no matter what temperance friends say'.[30] The benefits to the mind were also promoted into the twentieth century. An advertisement for Dubonnet Tonic Wine of 1903 included 'depression' amongst the ills for which it was 'invaluable', and Guinness, similarly, was also good for 'nerves'.[31]

More generally drink has been seen as providing escape or oblivion, a motive to which I shall return when looking at drunkenness in the next chapter. But we can note here, too, that those seeking solace or consolation have always found it in drink. As John Taylor, the so called water poet, put it in the seventeenth century, ale 'doth comfort the heavy and troubled mind; it will make a weeping widow laugh and forget sorrow for her deceased husband'.[32] Samuel Johnson expressed it in well-known lines, drinking 'to throw myself away, to get rid of myself', observing that 'he who makes a beast of himself gets rid of the pain of being a man'.[33] Branwell Brontë noted ruefully of a last night at the Royal Hotel in Kendal, Westmorland, before taking up a post as tutor: 'I took a half-year's farewell of old friend whisky'.[34] And in this mid-seventeenth-century drinking song, drink is linked to the ultimate consolation or oblivion:

> Drink today and drowne all sorrow,
> You shall perhaps not doe it tomorrow.
> Best while you have it use your breath,
> There is no drinking after death.[35]

Drink and sex were also linked. It could itself be the object of desire, in the words of another song, 'the mistress I love'.[36] In early modern England it was praised, especially wine, for its aphrodisiac properties, opening 'every woman's door' according to one seventeenth-century ballad. The same sentiments were expressed by Bolton pub goers: three pints improved one man's virility, whilst another 'ladykiller' said that 'If tha comes in 'ere and pays for who tha fancies a couple o' stouts tha's no need to get wed'.[37] It was believed to be an aid to conception and a cure for impotence, although as the well-known lines from *Macbeth* testified, whilst 'it provokes the desire … it takes away the performance'.[38] The connection between drinking and sex, in the sense of reducing inhibitions or provoking desire, has been a constant throughout history, although not necessarily in a positive way. For one Edwardian working-class woman the fear of pregnancy was paramount: 'It's all go … and tonight, when you think you've finished, he'll come home drunk and start again; I do hope he doesn't make another beer baby'.[39] An element of courage might be involved in finding a sexual partner and alcohol was often used to bolster it more widely. As the detective Jack Whicher confided to Dickens when in a tight spot, 'I couldn't do better than have a drop of brandy-and-water to keep my courage up'.[40]

## Symbolic and ritual

The symbolism of drinking has been evident throughout human history, linked to life itself. For the Egyptians, Osiris, god of the underworld was also the source of all life on earth and credited with bestowing both wine and beer on humans. Dionysus, the Greek god of wine was also a god of vegetation, fertility and friendship, acknowledged as having given to humanity all the goodness of wine, which was drunk in his honour. Jews and Christians traced wine to a mortal, Noah, the first man to plant a vineyard. Wine was integrated into Jewish festivities and elevated in Christianity to a central position in its ritual of the communion.[41] Its importance for fertility was seen, for example, in the cider districts of southern and western England, where in a ceremony described as a 'veritable sacrament' by its historian, health was drunk to the apple trees and cider sprinkled over them, rituals which continued into the nineteenth and even twentieth centuries.[42]

Drinking was an essential element in the key ceremonies in life of marriage, christening and burial. The rite of marriage, in A. Lynn Martin's words, brought together all those elements we have noted: 'the Christian symbolism of wine, the symbolic connection between alcohol and sexuality, fertility, regeneration, and life, the role of alcohol in conception and pregnancy' as well as praise (and condemnation) for its erotic effects.[43] The bride-ale in early modern England included the wedding itself and the ceremonial drinking in the church that sometimes followed it, but most commonly referred to the feasting after the ceremony. Guests would contribute food and drink and also money for the couple's future.[44] The bonds of kinship, community and friendship were in these ways expressed symbolically. The connection to the church was ended with the Reformation, but drinking and feasting continued to be essential to a wedding. Henri Misson, visiting England in the late seventeenth century, commented of weddings of the middling sort in London how afterwards all repaired to a tavern or a friend's house for dinner. And before bed the couple were given a good posset of milk, wine, egg yolks, sugar and spices.[45] But the poor also had their celebrations, with varying degrees of alcoholic indulgence. A study of late medieval and early modern London showed that their marriages were sometimes actually contracted in an inn, tavern or alehouse, with drink of course on hand afterwards, as William Dichand and Joan Qualley's was at the Swan in 1491, the marriage later being solemnized in church. Such contracts were usually made by couples less strictly under parental control and, in a late example of this practice, at Otley in the West Riding of Yorkshire in 1652, it was, significantly, without the consent of the bride's father.[46] In the nineteenth century changes to drinking habits naturally found expression in the festivities. As John O'Neil, a 'respectable' power-loom weaver of Clitheroe, Lancashire, noted of his daughter's wedding in January 1862, 'It passed off very quietly and nobody got drunk'.[47] But, in contrast, in Bradford in 1889 an Irish wedding party of forty to fifty young men and women packed into the bar parlour of the Sun Hotel in George Street, one of the town's poorest districts, were still going strong on Saturday night a week after the wedding.[48] Pre-wedding rites of passage – the stag and hen party – developed in more recent times, but drinking was equally central to them. They became increasingly adventurous, evolving from single nights to several days and migrating overseas as premarital tours, including to Eastern Europe, where the drink was cheap.[49]

Christenings, in contrast, were, according to Misson, more restrained affairs, with just a glass of wine and a piece of special cake.[50] 'Wetting the child's head' was one of the hundreds of 'drinking usages' discovered by temperance campaigner John Dunlop in the early nineteenth century.[51] Its northern version, 'weshin t'bairn's head', was still being described as 'not so much a feast as a free drinking' in the Edwardian period, when the bed-ale for friends and neighbours was still celebrated in some rural districts.[52] Not only babies were christened. When the *Bradford Courier and West Riding Advertiser* was launched in July 1825 the proprietors christened the paper. The 'priest', the Dr Simpson whose prescription we saw earlier, named it and 'threw the punch upon it, wishing it all success'.[53] And ships, of course, have similarly been named and launched with drink.

Funerals, lastly, were also accompanied by drinking. In the early modern period friends, kin and guests went to the deceased's house for a drinking prior to the funeral and afterwards in the church, although with the Reformation this gave way to the home or alehouse. It was at once 'hospitality given by the dead to the living', as from Elizabeth Stow, the mother of the chronicler, who in her will left ten shillings for 'my children and fryndes to drincke withal after my buryall', and 'a ritual means to perpetuate a view of community beyond the grave'.[54] This pattern of drinking before and after the funeral was still present in the nineteenth century to invite disapproval. As one Manchester informant to Edwin Chadwick's 1843 inquiry into interment put it, 'The occasion of a funeral is commonly looked to, amongst the lowest grade, as the occasion of "a stir"'. And from London it was reported that drink was freely offered to the undertaker's men to the detriment of the proper performance of their duties, even reeling in with the coffin.[55] In late-nineteenth-century Liverpool, drinking at Irish wakes in particular prompted condemnation of 'drunken revels by the side of the corpse' and efforts by the Catholic clergy to deter them.[56]

In addition to these key life events, drinking was an essential accompaniment to holidays and special occasions. These were more common in the early modern period than subsequently. Shrove Tuesday, for example, before the fast began, was 'a day of great gluttony, surfeiting and drunkenness', according to one protestant preacher.[57] Widespread, if regionally diverse, were all manner of ales, like the bride-ale already noted. The most common was the church-ale of the patron saint, for which parishioners cooperated in planning, brewing and in the preparation of food, 'a central focus of piety and popular culture, charity and play, cooperation and community' as Judith Bennett describes them.[58] They also raised money for the parish church. Charitable ales like this were common, like the clerk-ale for the parish clerk and bid-ales and Whitsun-ales for the poor, or the herd-ale for the cowherd. Help-ales gave thanks for rural tasks completed with the help of neighbours. Rural labour was also celebrated, for example, in the lamb-ale at the annual shearing.[59] Although isolated examples persisted into the eighteenth and nineteenth centuries, these festivals declined as a result of the Reformation. They were held to profane the Lord's Day, to be Catholic and heathen and to promote disorder.[60]

Despite the disappearance of these ales, there remained plenty of opportunities for celebration. Although religious holidays may have declined, so called Saint Monday, the extra day after the weekend taken by workers to recover from, or continue, drinking, was still popular in the mid nineteenth century in some trades in some districts. One Midlands potter recalled that neither they nor the colliers worked much on Monday, drinking 'plenteously' instead. The practice declined as the Saturday half-holiday movement developed and working-class economic prospects improved, although it persisted in some specific work situations, such as small unmechanized workshops, even into the twentieth century.[61] But Christmas was, and has remained, the key holiday. It was not forgotten when far from home. On Cook's first voyage in 1768 Joseph Banks noted of the day that 'all good Christians that is to say all hands got abominably drunk so that at night there was scarce a sober man on the ship'.[62] In London at Christmas in the 1820s, according to one observer, 'In every broad thoroughfare, and in every close alley, there was drunkenness abroad'.[63] All classes enjoyed Christmas. In mid-Victorian York on Christmas Eve 'between eleven and twelve o'clock roistering parties of "fast" young men disturbed the ordinary quiet of the citizens'. And in the working-class home of William Bell, the party brought the police round. Neil Armstrong, in his study of Christmas from which these examples are taken, argued that the early Victorian emphasis on toasts and drinking gradually disappeared from the festival's iconography as it was reconfigured as one for children.[64] Whilst children in modern times remain at the heart of the promotion and celebration of Christmas, drinking is hardly neglected.

Special events also called for celebration. Royalty always provided an excuse for drinking. At the Restoration of Charles II, which was also his birthday, 29 May 1660, John Evelyn noted the 'fountaines running with wine' in the capital.[65] Despite George IV's unpopularity, his coronation was not ignored – as one inhabitant observed in Manchester, 'men, women and children [lie] dead drunk in the streets'.[66] On the occasion of military and naval victories, or on the conclusion of peace, patriotism was fuelled with plenty of alcohol. The Leeds antiquarian and diarist Ralph Thoresby enjoyed the cavalcade on the celebration of peace in 1713, but retired before the feast, 'dreading the usual attendants, drunkenness and quarrelling'.[67] Contrast this with VE Day in London, in a greatly changed drinking context, when 'There were drunks about, but none seemed violent or even unduly rowdy'.[68] More generally, feasts and fairs for much of this history were occasions for drinking. In rural areas the annual hiring fairs for the employment of agricultural workers and servants were important days for pleasure and drinking and inevitably excited opposition, as from the police at Driffield in the East Riding of Yorkshire in 1858 to the 'surging sea of drunkenness'.[69] But attempts to suppress them failed, as it was recognized that they provided a useful release from an otherwise dull life tied to farms and, in addition, benefited the local economy, and they flourished into the 1920s.[70]

Drink at the fairs had another important significance: exchange between the bargainers 'symbolized good commercial intentions'.[71] In this way drink was connected to the world of work as much as to that of pleasure. In the later seventeenth century French traveller Jorevin de Rochefort had observed how 'no kind of business is transacted in England without the intervention of pots of beer'.[72] Landlords and employers were expected to treat tenants and workers. The Shackletons of Lancashire in the mid eighteenth century offered drink to their tenants on rent day and, after their work was done, sheep-shearers, hay-makers, mowers and stonemasons were treated to drink and music in the servants' hall. Mr Shackleton, unfortunately, failed sometimes to maintain the necessary social distance by getting drunk with them. Family birthdays similarly involved hospitality to the local community.[73] Work itself afforded many occasions for drinking rituals. Harvest workers drank at the sharpening of the sickle and scythe;[74] building workers drank at the rearing when the roof was put in place, like the masons and joiners on Joseph Rogerson's new home at Pudsey, near Leeds, 'in great spirits in expectation of plenty of Ale & a good Supper';[75] and shipwrights drank at the caulking and laying of the keel and the launch itself.[76] The last example is from John Dunlop's researches, which also documented such rituals as the footings and loosings at the beginning and end of employment or apprenticeship, when the worker or apprentice was obliged to buy food and drink for the other men. Dunlop felt that many were in fact of recent origin, but that they were widespread. But he also suggested that their incidence was declining, in part as many masters and foreman were now using their influence to end them, rather than tolerating or even encouraging them as once they had.[77]

The intimate connection of drink and the workplace would seem then to have declined over the course of the century. In Bradford, for example, by the 1880s, according to a contemporary study, 'The practice, once freely indulged in, of fetching in beer to workshops and warehouses is almost totally abolished'.[78] Both rituals and general drinking, however, persisted in some trades to the end of the century. Charles Booth found the silk-hat and tailoring trades in London still full of 'queer customs' connected with drinking, like footings or fines for breaches of shop law, or, if seen out with a female friend, 'putting her in the pitcher', although all were said to be dying out by this time.[79] On the eve of the First World War workers at a Coventry bicycle-component factory were still enjoying beer fetched in from the local pub, and some stampers in hot weather could drink as much as sixteen pints in a single shift.[80] As we will see in Chapter 7, the war raised the issue of drink and work to one of national importance.

Drink was also essential to the construction and expression of identity. This applied to the nation itself, a fact which several scholars have explored across a range of countries. It has been fundamental, for example, to French identity, 'in much the same way as being born in France, fighting for liberty or speaking French'.[81] The chosen drink might change, as conceptions of the nation changed, as in Mexico, where the traditional pre-conquest drink of pulque was replaced in the twentieth century with tequila and its more modern connotations as the authentic expression of Mexican identity.[82] For the English, cider had in the late seventeenth and early eighteenth century acquired patriotic symbolism as the country's wine.[83] And during the late-eighteenth- and early-nineteenth-century wars with France it was through drinking port that national identity was expressed, including by the Scots in an interval between their identification with French claret and native whisky.[84] But it was beer that became the national drink of the English, as expressed evocatively by Sydney Smith in 1823: 'what two ideas are more inseparable than Beer and Britannia!' John Bull and St George, agricultural prosperity and the yeomen of England, hatred and contempt for the French, intensified during more than a century of conflicts, and anti-Catholicism: all were evoked by beer.[85] As the chorus of one patriotic drinking song expressed it:

> Let us sing our own treasures, old England's good cheer,
> The profits and pleasures of stout British beer,
> Your wine-tippling dram-sipping fellows retreat,
> But your beer-drinking Britons can never be beat.[86]

Early in the Second World War an advertisement for Worthington beer, illustrated with a glass of beer with a man's smiling face contained within it, ended its evocation of English spirit, 'When the hour is grave', thus: 'And if the waiting be hard, seek fortitude and clear, calm thought over a Worthington – the golden brew that has nurtured generations of the yeoman of England'.[87]

The pub in particular shared in these associations. Hundreds of them after all have been named after members of the royal family, military and naval heroes and their celebrated victories, notably Nelson and Wellington, but others now more obscure like Lords Rodney and Clyde. Writers on the inn and the pub in the twentieth century have often extolled the importance of the institution to national identity. As Thomas Burke began his 1930 volume: 'To write of the English inn is almost to write of England itself … as familiar in the national consciousness as the oak and ash and the village green and the church spire'.[88] Although this expresses the familiar linkage of Englishness to the rural, the urban pub for some also expressed elements of the national character. One writer on those of London saw its Englishness in the domesticity of its welcome, the solidity of its architecture, the happiness and contentment of its customers and the poetic spirit 'so essentially a part of the English character'.[89] And a modern popular history of the pub proclaimed: 'The pub is an institution unique to England, and there is nothing more English'.[90] This is not strictly true, of course; by the nineteenth century the pub in Ireland too stood at the centre of Irish identity for a wide spectrum of its society.[91] One might argue that beer's declining share of total national drink consumption and the fall in pub numbers have together undermined the connection between beer and Britannia. To some extent they have, but just as declining wine consumption in France has not diminished how wine characterizes Frenchness, so beer and the pub are still part of what the English perceive as their national identity. Nevertheless, the connection is perhaps weakening: John Major's evocation of late-twentieth-century England as a country of 'long shadows on county cricket grounds' and 'warm beer' struck a somewhat risible note.[92] And drink's late-twentieth-century associations with football violence at home and abroad, notably in the Heysel Stadium riot of 1985, tended to foreground the darker side of Beer and Britannia.

Within England, drinking has been linked more particularly with specific local and regional identities. In football, for example, until the 1960s locally based or regional brewers advertised at clubs, 'anchoring their position in local working-class culture'.[93] Newcastle Brown was one such brew and in north-east England, it has been argued, 'Alcohol and sociability are well known hallmarks of consumption and popular culture'.[94] More broadly, the historical association of the 'North' with a particular set of features of what constitutes being working class, based in an urban and industrial world, naturally included a fondness for beer. The Keighley brewer Timothy Taylor played on this with its slogan 'Originally Brewed for Men of the North'. As this suggests, the connection of drinking with masculinity has also been an important one. Regional, masculine and also class identity were united in Reg Smythe's cartoon creation, in 1957, of Andy Capp in (initially) the northern edition of the *Daily Mirror*. 'Indolent, cloth-capped ... pint glass never far away', he became, in Dave Russell's words, 'one of the great universal figures of dissolute working-class masculinity'.[95]

The links between gender and drinking may be seen throughout the period covered by this history. Drinking was a central element in what has been termed homosocial bonding, the seeking of enjoyment with, and a preference for, company of the same sex. In early modern England, for one historian, 'The deliberately extravagant consumption of large amounts of drink in the context of the group appears to have functioned as a test of manhood not unlike a trail of strength, or a feat of bravery'. Whilst for another, drinking was a means to test the limits of the self-control deemed essential to the acquisition of 'honourable manhood'.[96] In the eighteenth century the masculinity of port was contrasted with French effeminacy.[97] These traits continued into modern male working-class culture where the ability to drink a lot but to be able to 'take' or 'hold' it was what was prized.[98] Similarly, group bonding in the early modern alehouse or tavern is echoed in modern settings. For participants in the premarital stag tours noted earlier, bonding was established 'somewhat predictably through drinking alcohol and gazing on, talking about, or actually pursuing, women'.[99] And for the members of a university football team, observed in another ethnographic study, 'being able to drink, and engaging in the collective bonding that this facilitated, was the key marker to being accepted into the group and becoming identified as one of the lads'. The shared activity of its consumption made possible the construction of 'the imagined borders of the men's community, keeping them distinct from "otherness" and supporting and nurturing their individualities'.[100] It performed those functions for women, too. A study of so called New Wave Girls from a comprehensive school in the south of England in the 1980s found that their regular group underage drinking in a variety of settings and the telling of drinking stories 'were crucial aspects of their promenade as a youth cultural group', setting them apart from the other girls in their school who only went into a pub with a boyfriend.[101]

Drink has always been expressive of class, status and political identities. Throughout much of this history drinking wine was confined largely to the better-off. For Pepys, as we saw, his wine cellar was a symbol of his status and success. A Yorkshire gentlewoman noted in her diary in 1819 how people of higher social status drank wine not beer.[102] Beer was the drink of working people. Gladstone's efforts to wean them to wine came to nothing and, as we saw in Chapter 1, the growth of wine consumption in the late twentieth century was still disproportionately amongst those in higher income groups. Thus it was in a self-consciously proletarian way that under the Labour governments of the 1960s and 1970s beer and sandwiches were offered to union leaders at 10 and 11 Downing Street. And when Roy Jenkins left Labour to form the SDP with his fellow members of the Gang of Four his fondness for fine wines was used in efforts to set Labour voters against him.[103] In earlier years particular drinks similarly denoted specific political affiliations. During the Civil War wine was identified with the Cavaliers and beer with the common people and the Roundheads, with allegations that Cromwell was linked to the brewing trade. After the Restoration claret, reportedly Charles I's last drink before his execution, became the choice of the Tories, whilst the Whigs opted for port.[104]

## Sociability

One of the key meanings of drinking is to be found in sociability – drinking in the company of others. It was of paramount importance throughout this history. Phil Withington argued for this importance for the early modern period, expressed as it was by contemporaries in the idea of 'company', which comprised 'quite formal associational bodies' from urban corporations to theatrical or musical troupes, recurring habitual and voluntary groupings of men and women and accidental, occasional or transitory encounters.[105] In the same way, Mark Hailwood stressed the centrality of 'good fellowship' in the culture of the alehouse, a potent form of social bonding, formed of communal merriment and with free-spending excess its guiding principle.[106] Shorn of such alcoholic excess, it was 'good fellowship' or 'pleasant, sociable companionship' which in the mid nineteenth century the

Reverend Henry Solly was seeking to offer in the club movement for working men.[107] But, as we saw, for most club members drinking was a necessary accompaniment to that companionship. In the same way, Mass Observation noted the 'two aspects of pub-going – social and alcoholic – that cannot really be separated from each other'.[108] But the study also observed those who preferred to drink alone, a figure, it has to be said, not generally met with in the historical record. It called him the 'silent regular' and was rather hesitant in its assessment, speculating that they 'may be simply chaps who drop in for a drink on their way from somewhere, and who have no interest in getting into contact with other drinkers in the pub'. Here, in a large pub at a street corner on a main road,

> 2 men with pints, talking together in undertones. Man in cap, scarf, shiny baggy blue suit, comes in, says nothing to the others, and orders "Pint o' mild (stranger) ...
>
> ... An old man, wearing clean corduroy trousers, blue jacket, cap and scarf, comes in. He does not say anything but is a regular, and has a pint drawn for him right away; he stays at the bar. The stranger takes a last swig and goes, no one having spoken to him; he does not say goodnight.[109]

That 'somewhere' may, of course, have been work, as when Marc Riboud photographed this moment in the George, a pub close to the law courts and the Infirmary in Leeds, in 1954 (Figure 4.1).

To return to sociability, in the previous chapter we encountered various elements of it in the perennial pastimes in drinking places of talk, music and games, together with their importance for more formal associational life. Here I would like to focus on two key rituals associated with public drinking: toasts, or the drinking of healths, and the practice of treating, or buying rounds. In the seventeenth century the drinking of healths provoked the denunciations of those who perceived its encouragement to heavy drinking and drunkenness. Early in the century William Prynne published his *Healthes; Sicknesse* to prove 'the Drinking and Pledging of Healths to be Sinfull and utterly Unlawful unto Christians' and these sentiments were voiced through the century. In his *A Discourse of Drinking Healths* the Bishop of Cork and Rosse inveighed against the 'Evil of this Prevailing CUSTOM' so productive of drunkenness. He cited examples of proclaiming loyalty or fidelity to the monarch, reminding his readers that Charles II had actually issued a proclamation forbidding them to toast the success or prosperity of an affair, or absent friends.[110] Henri Misson noted its prevalence and that it would be considered very rude, especially amongst middling people, to sit down at table without drinking someone's health.[111] In the seventeenth century the expression 'toast' also came into use for the practice.[112] It continued. Both loyalists and Radicals in the late eighteenth and early years of the nineteenth century shared a love of toasting. In December 1818 126 of the 'principal inhabitants' of Manchester dined in honour of the magistrates for their repression of the march of the Blanketeers and heading off of the so called Ardwick conspiracy, getting

*Figure 4.1* A drink after work, the George, Great George Street, Leeds, 1954, photographed by Marc Riboud for *Picture Post*.

Source: Courtesy of Marc Riboud.

through no fewer than thirty-eight loyal toasts. In contrast, a dinner to celebrate Henry Hunt's first visit to the town the following month opened with toasts to 'The source of all power, the People' and the Rights of Man, and included further toasts to 'the immortal memory' of revolutionary martyrs Hampden, Sydney and Russell. Radicals in this way asserted ritually their own brand of popular patriotism against the officially sanctioned shibboleths of King and Church and Glorious Constitution, showing how potent the ritual could be.[113]

By the time Mass Observation was watching Bolton drinkers in the late 1930s the drinking of healths was not altogether dead, but it was much diminished, surviving only in the simple expression of 'good health'. They thought it 'very probable', however, that they continued to find expression in the ritual of treating – or buying, or standing – rounds, when each man in turn buys a round of drinks for the whole group. It was a ritual 'of fundamental importance in the life of a pub'. As a barman explained it:

> Treating. Firmly established custom. Sign of friendship ... Convenience to waiters and turns to pay are carefully watched. Missing your turn would cause social stigma, anyone so behaving would be called mean, a sponger etc. People remember who pay, and expect to pay next even if weeks elapse before their next meeting.[114]

Its importance is illustrated when the practice was prohibited during the First World War. Of the various restrictions introduced, the ban on treating was the only one to be rescinded once the war was over. Whilst it lasted it provoked resentment, and at best grudging acceptance, in the face of appeals to patriotism.[115] No doubt aggrieved were farm labourer William Parrington and his two female companions, to whom he asked, in the usual style, on entering the Burlington Arms in Keighley one Saturday night in December 1916, 'Now, lasses, what are you going to have?' They were seen by plain-clothes policemen and fined, along with the landlord and the barman, £25 in total.[116] Treating's persistence in the pub at the turn of the millennium was observed by social anthropologist Kate Fox as 'the sharing and reciprocal exchange of drinks', a means of preventing aggression between groups and an expression of the English devotion to taking one's turn. It was still an activity governed by rules. In 1916 Parrington had bought the drinks for the women and in Fox's observations couples were treated as one individual and only the man was expected to buy. The stigma attached to attempts to avoid one's 'shout' continued too.[117]

In the meanings of drinking, then, there were elements of both continuity and change. Sociability and the importance of celebration and ritual were important examples of the former. What changed were the amount of drinking done and the prevalence of drunkenness, both of which declined from the later nineteenth century, as we saw and will explore further in the next chapter. Of the latter, the health-giving and medicinal properties attributed to alcoholic drinks had largely ceased to be supported by the late twentieth century. Much diminished too were the once close links between drink and work, either as thirst-quencher and strength-builder, or in rituals. Drinking, however, was still a feature of certain occupations, as the statistics of liver-cirrhosis mortality demonstrated, with publicans and bar staff, entertainers and musicians, merchant seamen and members of the armed forces amongst the later-twentieth-century's high-risk groups.[118] In general, though, work and alcohol had become separated, as drinking was transformed into a more purely recreational activity over the nineteenth and into the twentieth century, although, as we saw, it was still important to some, as one might suggest of the drinker in the George, in marking the boundary between the two spheres. But the key continuity was that drinking was, and is, an intensely meaningful activity.

## Notes

1 E. M. Jellinek, 'The symbolism of drinking: A culture-historical approach, ed. for publication by R. E. Popham and C. D. Yawney', *Journal of Studies on Alcohol*, 38:5 (1977), pp. 849–66, on p. 852.
2 D. B. Heath, 'Anthropological perspectives on alcohol: An historical review', in M. W. Everett, J. O. Waddell and D. B. Heath (eds), *Cross-Cultural Approaches to the Study of Alcohol: An interdisciplinary perspective* (The Hague: Mouton, 1976), pp. 41–101 and *Drinking Occasions: Comparative perspectives on alcohol and culture* (Philadelphia, PA: Brunner/Mazel, 2000); M. Douglas, *Constructive Drinking: Perspectives on drink from anthropology* (Cambridge: Cambridge University Press, 1987); M. Marshall, *Beliefs, Behaviors, and Alcoholic Beverages: A cross-cultural survey* (Ann Arbor, MI: University of Michigan Press, 1979). Also of note are M. Adler, 'From symbolic exchange to commodity consumption: Anthropological notes on drinking as a symbolic practice', in S. Barrows and R. Room (eds), *Drinking: Behavior and belief in modern history* (Berkeley, CA: University of California Press, 1991), pp. 376–98; I. and G. de Garine (eds), *Drinking: Anthropological approaches* (Oxford: Bergahn Books, 2001); T. M. Wilson (ed.), *Drinking Cultures: Alcohol and identity* (Oxford: Beg, 2005).
3 B. Harrison, *Drink and the Victorians: The temperance question in England 1815–1872* (Keele: Keele University Press, 2nd ed., 1994), pp. 42–3.
4 R. Phillips, *Alcohol: A history* (Chapel Hill, NC: University of North Carolina Press, 2014), pp. 79–80.
5 J. Warner, 'Good help is hard to find: A few comments about alcohol and work in preindustrial England', *Addiction Research*, 2:3 (1995), pp. 259–69.
6 W. Cudworth, *Round About Bradford* (Bradford: Thomas Brear, 1876), pp. 51–2.
7 By Giles Worthington, quoted in A. L. Martin, *Alcohol, Sex, and Gender in Late Medieval and Early Modern Europe* (Basingstoke: Palgrave, 2001), pp. 3–4. Of course, I am here concerned with experience and belief rather than what science tells us about drink's effects.
8 H. Patch with R. van Emden, *The Last Fighting Tommy: The life of Harry Patch, last veteran of the trenches 1898–2009* (London: Bloomsbury, 2008), p. 76.
9 A. Vickery, *The Gentleman's Daughter: Women's lives in Georgian England* (London: Yale University Press, 1998), p. 109.
10 J. Beresford (ed.), *The Diary of a Country Parson: The Reverend James Woodforde* (Oxford: Clarendon Press, vol. 3, 1927), p. 174.
11 Mass Observation, *The Pub and the People: A Worktown study* (London: Cresset Library, 1987), p. 42.
12 P. Dade, *Drink Talking: 100 years of alcohol advertising* (London: Middlesex University Press, 2008), pp. 26, 42–3, 45 and 90.

13 In Merthyr Tydfil for example, see W. R. Lambert, 'Drink and work-discipline in industrial South Wales, c. 1800–1870', *Welsh History Review*, 7:2 (1974), pp. 289–306, on p. 291.
14 R. Harker (ed.), *Timble Man: Diaries of a Dalesman* (Nelson: Hendon, 1988), p. 68.
15 D. Gibson (ed.), *A Parson in the Vale of White Horse: George Woodward's letters from East Hendred, 1753–1761* (Gloucester: Alan Sutton, 1982), p. 113.
16 L. H. Curth, 'The medicinal value of wine in early modern England', *Social History of Alcohol and Drugs*, 18 (2003), pp. 35–50; and also with T. M. Cassidy, '"Health, strength and happiness": Medical constructions of wine and beer in early modern England', in A. Smyth (ed.), *A Pleasing Sinne: Drink and Conviviality in Seventeenth-Century England* (Cambridge: D. S. Brewer, 2004), pp. 143–59.
17 Beresford, *The Diary of a Country Parson*, (vol. 3, 1927), p. 274 and (vol. 2, 1926), p. 217.
18 *The Journal of Dr John Simpson of Bradford 1825* (Bradford: City of Bradford Metropolitan Council Libraries Division, 1981), p. 15.
19 J. H. Warner, 'Physiological theory and therapeutic explanation in the 1860s: The British debate on the medical use of alcohol', *Bulletin of the History of Medicine*, 54:2 (1980), pp. 235–57, on p. 236.
20 Harrison, *Drink and the Victorians*, p. 299.
21 Ibid., pp. 298–300; J. Woiak, '"A medical Cromwell to depose King Alcohol": Medical scientists, temperance reformers, and the alcohol problem in Britain', *Histoire sociale/Social History*, 27:54 (1994), pp. 337–65.
22 J. Reinarz and R. Wynter, 'The spirit of medicine: The use of alcohol in nineteenth-century medical practice', in S. Schmid and B. Schmidt-Haberkamp (eds), *Drink in the Eighteenth and Nineteenth Centuries* (London: Pickering & Chatto, 2014), pp. 127–39, on pp. 136–7.
23 N. Longmate, *The Waterdrinkers: A history of temperance* (London: Hamish Hamilton, 1968), p. 176.
24 Sir V. Horsley and M. D. Sturge, *Alcohol and the Human Body: An introduction to the study of the subject and a contribution to national health* (London: Macmillan, 2nd ed., 1909), p. xxv; Longmate, *The Waterdrinkers*, p. 178.
25 Woiak, '"A medical Cromwell"', pp. 360–5.
26 Reinarz and Wynter, 'The spirit of medicine', p. 139.
27 Phillips, *Alcohol*, pp. 315–16.
28 Curth, 'The medicinal value of wine', p. 44.
29 V. de Palma, 'Drinking cider in paradise: Science, improvement, and the politics of fruit trees', in Smyth, *A Pleasing Sinne*, pp. 161–77, on pp. 175–6.
30 M. Forster, *Good Wives? Mary, Fanny, Jennie and Me, 1845–2001* (London: Chatto & Windus, 2001), pp. 53 and 71.
31 Dade, *Drink Talking*, pp. 17 and 26.
32 K. Thomas, *Religion and the Decline of Magic: Studies in popular beliefs in sixteenth and seventeenth century England*, (London: Weidenfeld and Nicolson, 1971), p. 19.
33 Quoted in A. Taylor, *Bacchus in Romantic England* (Basingstoke: Macmillan, 1999), p. 5.
34 W. Gérin, *Branwell Brontë* (London: Thomas Nelson & Sons, 1961), p. 164.
35 V. Gammon, *Desire, Drink and Death in English Folk and Vernacular Song, 1600–1900* (Aldershot: Ashgate, 2008), pp. 163–8.
36 Ibid., p. 110.
37 Martin, *Alcohol, Sex, and Gender*, p. 50; Mass Observation, *The Pub and the People*, p. 46.
38 Martin, *Alcohol, Sex, and Gender*, pp. 42–3; *Macbeth*, II.III.24–5.
39 E. Hall, *Canary Girls and Stockpots* (Luton: WEA Luton Branch, 1977), p. 15.
40 K. Summerscale, *The Suspicions of Mr Whicher* (London: Bloomsbury, 2008), p. 44.
41 Jellinek, 'The symbolism of drinking'; Phillips, *Alcohol*, in chs 1–3.

42 J. R. Harris, 'Origin and meaning of apple cults', *Bulletin of the John Rylands Library*, 5:1–2 (1919), pp. 29–74; W. Minchinton, 'Cider and folklore', *Folk Life*, 13:1 (1975), pp. 66–79.
43 Martin, *Alcohol, Sex, and Gender*, p. 51.
44 J. M. Bennett, 'Conviviality and charity in medieval and early modern England', *Past and Present*, 134 (1992), pp. 19–41, on pp. 31–3.
45 H. Misson, *M. Misson's Memoirs and Observations in his Travels over England. With Some Account of Scotland and Ireland* (London: D. Browne, 1719), pp. 351–3.
46 S. McSheffrey, *Marriage, Sex, and Civic Culture in Late Medieval London* (Philadelphia, PA: University of Pennsylvania Press, 2006), pp. 128–34; F. Morrell and D. Peel, *All Saint's Parish Church Otley: Historical Notes* (Otley: All Saints Parish Church, n. d.), p. 13.
47 M. Brigg (ed.), *The Journals of a Lancashire Weaver, 1850–60, 1860–64, 1872–75 (John O'Neil)*, (Record Society of Lancashire and Cheshire, vol. 122, 1982), p. 132.
48 *Bradford Observer*, 8 October 1889, p. 7.
49 See A. Eldridge and M. Roberts, 'Hen parties: Bonding or brawling', *Drugs, Education, Prevention and Policy*, 15:3 (2008), pp. 323–8; T. Thurnell-Read, 'What happens on tour: The premarital stag tour, homosocial bonding and male friendship', *Men and Masculinities*, 15:3 (2012), pp. 249–70.
50 Misson, *Misson's Memoirs*, p. 35.
51 J. Dunlop, *The Philosophy of Artificial and Compulsory Drinking Usage in Great Britain and Ireland* (London: Houlston and Stoneman, 6th ed., 1839), p. 190.
52 E. M. Wright, *Rustic Speech and Folk-Lore* (London: H. Milford, Oxford University Press, 1913), pp. 267–8.
53 *The Journal of Dr John Simpson*, p. 71.
54 F. Heal, *Hospitality in Early Modern England* (Oxford: Clarendon Press, 1990), pp. 371–5.
55 Supplementary Report on the results of a special Inquiry into the practice of Interment in Towns; PP 1843 (509) XII.395, pp. 60 and 64.
56 J-M. Strange, *Death, Grief and Poverty in Britain, 1870–1914* (Cambridge: Cambridge University Press, 2005), pp. 87–9.
57 R. Hutton, *The Rise and Fall of Merry England: The ritual year 1400–1700* (Oxford: Oxford University Press, 1994), p. 19.
58 Bennett, 'Conviviality and charity', pp. 24–33.
59 Ibid., G. Edelen (ed.), *William Harrison, The Description of England* (Ithaca, NY: Cornell University Press, 1968), p. 36; F. A. Carrington, 'Ancient ales in the county of Wiltshire, and the diocese of Sarum', *Wiltshire Archaeological and Natural History Magazine*, 2:2 (1855), pp. 191–204; T. G. Barnes, 'County politics and a Puritan cause célèbre: Somerset church ales, 1633', *Royal Historical Society Transactions*, 5th Series 9 (1959), pp. 103–22, on pp. 106–7.
60 Bennett, 'Conviviality and charity', pp. 35–6; Hutton, *The Rise and Fall of Merry England*, pp. 143–6.
61 C. Shaw, *When I Was A Child by 'An Old Potter'* (Wakefield: SR Publishers, 1969), p. 31; D. A. Reid, 'The decline of Saint Monday 1766–1876', *Past and Present*, 71 (1976), pp. 76–101.
62 R. Hough, *Captain James Cook* (London: Hodder and Stoughton, 1994), p. 70.
63 Charles Knight, quoted in R. V. French, *Nineteen Centuries of Drink in England: A history* (London: National Temperance Publication Depot, 2nd ed., n. d.), p. 345.
64 N. Armstrong, *Christmas in Nineteenth-century England* (Manchester: Manchester University Press, 2010), pp. 30 and 62–3.
65 E. S. de Beer (ed.), *The Diary of John Evelyn* (London: Oxford University Press, 1959), p. 406.
66 E. Griffin, *England's Revelry: A history of popular sports and pastimes 1660–1830* (Oxford: Oxford University Press, 2005), pp. 93–5 and see also pp. 77–8.

67 Rev. J. Hunter, *The Diary of Ralph Thoresby, F. R. S.: Author of the topography of Leeds (1677–1724)* (London: H. Colburn and R. Bentley, 1830), vol. 2, p. 189.
68 A. Calder, *The People's War: Britain 1939–1945* (London: Pimlico, 1969), pp. 567–9.
69 G. Moses, *Rural Moral Reform in Nineteenth-Century England: The crusade against adolescent farm servants and hiring fairs* (Lampeter: Edwin Mellen Press, 2007), p. 121.
70 S. Caunce, 'The hiring fairs of Northern England, 1890–1930: A regional analysis of commercial and social networking in agriculture', *Past and Present*, 217 (2012), pp. 213–46, on pp. 221–7.
71 Moses, *Rural Moral Reform*, p. 120–1.
72 Quoted in French, *Nineteen Centuries of Drink*, p. 224.
73 Vickery, *The Gentleman's Daughter*, pp. 203 and 214–15.
74 D. H. Morgan, 'The place of harvesters in nineteenth-century village life', in R. Samuel (ed.), *Village Life and Labour* (London: Routledge & Kegan Paul, 1975), pp. 27–72, on p. 32.
75 W. B. Crump (ed.), *The Leeds Woollen Industry 1780–1820* (Leeds: Thoresby Society, 1931), p. 126.
76 Dunlop, *The Philosophy of Artificial and Compulsory Drinking Usage*, p. 176.
77 Ibid., pp. 306–8.
78 W. Cudworth, *Condition of the Industrial Classes of Bradford and District* (Bradford: W. Byles, 1887), p. 86.
79 C. Booth, *Life and Labour of the People in London, First series, Poverty, vol. 4 and Second Series, Industry, vol. 3* (London: Macmillan, 1902), pp. 143–4 and 27–8.
80 B. Beaven, *Leisure, Citizenship and Working-class Men in Britain, 1850–1945* (Manchester: Manchester University Press, 2005), p. 64.
81 M. Demossier, *Wine Drinking Culture in France: A national myth or a modern passion* (Cardiff: University of Wales Press, 2010), p. 1.
82 D. Toner, *Alcohol and Nationhood in Nineteenth-Century Mexico* (London: University of Nebraska Press, 2015).
83 A. L. Martin, *Alcohol, Violence, and Disorder in Traditional Europe* (Kirksville, MO: Truman State University Press, 2009), p. 64.
84 C. Ludington, *The Politics of Wine in Britain: A new cultural history* (Basingstoke: Palgrave Macmillan, 2013), pp. 172–5.
85 Harrison, *Drink and the Victorians*, p. 61.
86 Gammon, *Desire, Drink and Death*, p. 145.
87 S. O. Rose, *Which People's War? National Identity and Citizenship in Wartime Britain 1939–1945* (Oxford: Oxford University Press, 2003), p. 154.
88 T. Burke, *The English Inn* (London: Longmans, Green, 1930), p. 7.
89 M. McLaren, 'The London public-house', *London Mercury*, May 1928, pp. 30–8.
90 M. Jackson, *The English Pub* (London: Collins, 1976), p. 5.
91 B. Kadel, 'The pub and the Irish nation', *Social History of Alcohol and Drugs*, 18 (2003), pp. 69–84, on pp. 82–3.
92 John Major, Speech to Conservative Group in Europe, 22 April 1993, at www.johnmajor.co.uk/page1086.html [accessed 25 April 2015].
93 N. McRae, 'Football and beer in the 1960s: Transformation in the British brewing industry and its impact on local identity', *Sport in History*, 28:2 (2008), pp. 236–58.
94 B. Lancaster, 'The North East, England's most distinctive region?', in B. Lancaster, D. Newton and N. Vall (eds), *An Agenda for Regional History* (Newcastle: Northumbria University Press, 2007), pp. 23–41, on p. 32.
95 D. Russell, *Looking North: Northern England and the national imagination* (Manchester: Manchester University Press, 2004), p. 270.

96 A. Shepard, '"Swil-bols and tos-pots": Drink culture and male bonding in England, c. 1560–1640', in L. Gowing, M. Hunter and M. Rubin (eds), *Love, Friendship and Faith in Europe, 1300–1800* (Basingstoke: Palgrave Macmillan, 2005), pp. 110–30, on p. 122; E. A. Foyster, *Manhood in Early Modern England: Honour, sex and marriage* (London: Longman, 1999), p. 40.
97 Ludington, *The Politics of Wine*, p. 155.
98 L. Gofton, 'On the town; drink and the "new lawlessness"', *Youth and Policy*, 29 (1990), pp. 33–9, on p. 35.
99 Thurnell-Read, 'What happens on tour', p. 265.
100 B. Clayton and J. Harris, 'Our friend Jack: Alcohol, friendship and masculinity in university football', *Annals of Leisure Research*, 11:3–4 (2008), pp. 311–30, on p. 328. Similar findings were reported for another group of male students in B. Gough and G. Edwards, 'The beer talking: Four lads, a carry out and the reproduction of masculinities', *Sociological Review*, 46:3 (1998), pp. 409–35. For young men in rural pubs see M. Leyshon, '"No place for a girl": Rural youth, pubs and the performance of masculinity', in J. Little and C. Morris (eds), *Critical Studies in Rural Gender Issues* (Aldershot: Ashgate, 2005), pp. 104–22.
101 S. J. Blackman, 'The school: "Poxy Cupid!": An ethnographic and feminist account of a resistant female youth culture: The New Wave Girls', in T. Skelton and G. Valentine (eds), *Cool Places: Geographies of youth cultures* (London: Routledge, 1998), pp. 207–28, on p. 216.
102 H. Whitbread (ed.), *I Know My Own Heart: The diaries of Anne Lister (1791–1840)*, (London: Virago Press, 1988), p. 95.
103 A. Beckett, *When the Lights Went Out: What really happened to Britain in the Seventies* (London: Faber and Faber, 2010), p. 290; D. Johnson, 'Mixing politics and drink', *Times*, 3 December 1996, p. 16.
104 A. McShane Jones, 'Roaring royalists and ranting brewers: The politicisation of drink and drunkenness in political broadside ballads from 1640 to 1689', in Smyth, *A Pleasing Sinne*, pp. 69–87, on pp. 85–7; C. C. Ludington, '"Be sometimes to your country true": The politics of wine in England, 1660–1714', in Smyth, *A Pleasing Sinne*, pp. 89–106; and see also his *The Politics of Wine*.
105 P. Withington, 'Company and sociability in early modern England', *Social History*, 32: 3 (2007), pp. 291–307.
106 M. Hailwood, *Alehouses and Good Fellowship in Early Modern England* (Woodbridge: The Boydell Press, 2014).
107 H. Solly, *Working Men's Social Clubs and Educational Institutes* (London: Simpkin, Marshall, Hamilton, Kent, 2nd ed., 1904), pp. 153–4.
108 Mass Observation, *The Pub and the People*, p. 254.
109 Ibid., pp. 149–50.
110 French, *Nineteen Centuries of Drink*, pp. 190–1; P. Browne, *A Discourse of Drinking Healths* (London: H. Clements, 1716).
111 Misson, *Misson's Memoirs*, pp. 69–70.
112 French offered origins for the term 'toast' in *Nineteen Centuries of Drink*, pp. 282–3.
113 J. Epstein, 'Radical dining, toasting and symbolic expression in early nineteenth-century Lancashire: Rituals of solidarity', *Albion*, 20:2 (1988), pp. 271–91, on pp. 276–81.
114 Mass Observation, *The Pub and the People*, pp. 176–83.
115 See chapter 7 for resentment and unpopularity, but general acceptance. R. Duncan, *Pubs and Patriots: The drink crisis in Britain during World War One* (Liverpool: Liverpool University Press, 2013), pp. 105–7 and 224.
116 *Keighley News*, 16 December 1916, p. 5.
117 K. Fox, *Watching the English: The hidden rules of English behaviour* (London: Hodder & Stoughton, 2004), pp. 255–9.
118 M. A. Plant, *Drinking Careers: Occupations, drinking habits, and drinking problems* (London: Tavistock, 1979), pp. 31–4, showing standardized mortality ratios.

# Bibliography

Adler, M., 'From symbolic exchange to commodity consumption: Anthropological notes on drinking as a symbolic practice', in S. Barrows and R. Room (eds), *Drinking: Behavior and belief in modern history* (Berkeley, CA: University of California Press, 1991), pp. 376–98.

Armstrong, N., *Christmas in Nineteenth-century England* (Manchester: Manchester University Press, 2010).

Barnes, T. G., 'County politics and a Puritan cause célèbre: Somerset church ales, 1633', *Royal Historical Society Transactions*, 5th Series 9 (1959), pp. 103–22.

Beaven, B., *Leisure, Citizenship and Working-class Men in Britain, 1850–1945* (Manchester: Manchester University Press, 2005).

Beckett, A., *When the Lights Went Out: What really happened to Britain in the Seventies* (London: Faber and Faber, 2010).

Bennett, J. M., 'Conviviality and charity in medieval and early modern England', *Past and Present*, 134 (1992), pp. 19–41.

Blackman, S. J., 'The school: "Poxy Cupid!": An ethnographic and feminist account of a resistant female youth culture: The New Wave Girls', in T. Skelton and G. Valentine (eds), *Cool Places: Geographies of youth cultures* (London: Routledge, 1998), pp. 207–28.

Burke, T., *The English Inn* (London: Longmans, Green, 1930).

Calder, A., *The People's War: Britain 1939–1945* (London: Pimlico, 1969).

Carrington, F. A., 'Ancient ales in the county of Wiltshire, and the diocese of Sarum', *Wiltshire Archaeological and Natural History Magazine*, 2:2 (1855).

Caunce, S., 'The hiring fairs of Northern England, 1890–1930: A regional analysis of commercial and social networking in Agriculture', *Past and Present*, 217 (2012), pp. 213–46.

Clayton, B. and Harris, J., 'Our friend Jack: Alcohol, friendship and masculinity in university football', *Annals of Leisure Research*, 11:3–4 (2008), pp. 311–30.

Crump, W. B., (ed.), *The Leeds Woollen Industry 1780–1820* (Leeds: Thoresby Society, 1931).

Curth, L. H., 'The medicinal value of wine in early modern England', *Social History of Alcohol and Drugs*, 18 (2003), pp. 35–50.

—, and Cassidy, T. M., '"Health, strength and happiness": Medical constructions of wine and beer in early modern England', in A. Smyth (ed.), *A Pleasing Sinne: Drink and conviviality in seventeenth-century England* (Cambridge: D. S. Brewer, 2004), pp. 143–59.

Dade, P., *Drink Talking: 100 years of alcohol advertising* (London: Middlesex University Press, 2008).

De Garine, I. and G. (eds), *Drinking: Anthropological approaches* (Oxford: Bergahn Books, 2001).

Demossier, M., *Wine Drinking Culture in France: A national myth or a modern passion* (Cardiff: University of Wales Press, 2010).

De Palma, V., 'Drinking cider in paradise: Science, improvement, and the politics of fruit trees', in Smyth (ed.), *A Pleasing Sinne* pp. 161–77.

Douglas, M., *Constructive Drinking: Perspectives on drink from anthropology* (Cambridge: Cambridge University Press, 1987).

Duncan, R., *Pubs and Patriots: The drink crisis in Britain during World War One* (Liverpool: Liverpool University Press, 2013).

Eldridge, A. and Roberts, M., 'Hen parties: Bonding or brawling', *Drugs, Education, Prevention and Policy*, 15:3 (2008), pp. 323–8.

Epstein, J., 'Radical dining, toasting and symbolic expression in early nineteenth-century Lancashire: Rituals of solidarity', *Albion*, 20:2 (1988), pp. 271–91.

Forster, M., *Good Wives? Mary, Fanny, Jennie and Me, 1845–2001* (London: Chatto & Windus, 2001).

Fox, K., *Watching the English: The hidden rules of English behaviour* (London: Hodder & Stoughton, 2004).

Foyster, E. A., *Manhood in Early Modern England: Honour, sex and marriage* (London: Longman, 1999).

Gammon, V., *Desire, Drink and Death in English Folk and Vernacular Song, 1600–1900* (Aldershot: Ashgate, 2008).

Gérin, W., *Branwell Brontë* (London: Thomas Nelson & Sons, 1961).

Gofton, L., 'On the town; drink and the "new lawlessness"', *Youth and Policy*, 29 (1990), pp. 33–9.

Gough, B. and Edwards, G., 'The beer talking: Four lads, a carry out and the reproduction of masculinities', *Sociological Review*, 46:3 (1998), pp. 409–35.

Griffin, E., *England's Revelry: A history of popular sports and pastimes 1660–1830* (Oxford: Oxford University Press, 2005).

Hailwood, M., *Alehouses and Good Fellowship in Early Modern England* (Woodbridge: The Boydell Press, 2014).

Harris, J. R., 'Origin and meaning of apple cults', *Bulletin of the John Rylands Library*, 5:1–2 (1919), pp. 29–74.

Harrison, B., *Drink and the Victorians: The temperance question in England 1815–1872* (Keele: Keele University Press, 2nd ed., 1994).

Heal, F., *Hospitality in Early Modern England* (Oxford: Clarendon Press, 1990).

Heath, D. B., 'Anthropological perspectives on alcohol: An historical review' in M. W. Everett, J. O. Waddell and D. B. Heath (eds), *Cross-Cultural Approaches to the Study of Alcohol: An interdisciplinary perspective* (The Hague: Mouton, 1976), pp. 41–101.

—, *Drinking Occasions: Comparative perspectives on alcohol and culture* (Philadelphia, PA: Brunner/Mazel, 2000).

Horsley, Sir V. and Sturge, M. D., *Alcohol and the Human Body: An introduction to the study of the subject and a contribution to national health* (London: Macmillan, 2nd ed., 1909).

Hough, R., *Captain James Cook* (London: Hodder and Stoughton, 1994).

Hutton, R., *The Rise and Fall of Merry England: The ritual year 1400–1700* (Oxford: Oxford University Press, 1994).

Jackson, M., *The English Pub* (London: Collins, 1976)

Jellinek, E. M., 'The symbolism of drinking: A culture-historical approach, ed. for publication by R. E. Popham and C. D. Yawney', *Journal of Studies on Alcohol*, 38:5 (1977), pp. 849–66.

Kadel, B., 'The pub and the Irish nation', *Social History of Alcohol and Drugs*, 18 (2003), pp. 69–84.

Lancaster, B., 'The North East, England's most distinctive region?', in B. Lancaster, D. Newton and N. Vall (eds), *An Agenda for Regional History* (Newcastle: Northumbria University Press, 2007), pp. 23–41.

Lambert, W. R., 'Drink and work-discipline in industrial South Wales, c. 1800–1870', *Welsh History Review*, 7:2 (1974), pp. 289–306.

Leyshon, M., '"No place for a girl": Rural youth, pubs and the performance of masculinity', in J. Little and C. Morris (eds), *Critical Studies in Rural Gender Issues* (Aldershot: Ashgate, 2005), pp. 104–22.

Longmate, N., *The Waterdrinkers: A history of temperance* (London: Hamish Hamilton, 1968).

Ludington, C., '"Be sometimes to your country true": The politics of wine in England, 1660–1714', in Smyth (ed.), *A Pleasing Sinne*, pp. 89–106.

—, *The Politics of Wine in Britain: A new cultural history* (Basingstoke: Palgrave Macmillan, 2013).

McRae, N., 'Football and beer in the 1960s: Transformation in the British brewing industry and its impact on local identity', *Sport in History*, 28:2 (2008), pp. 236–58.

McShane Jones, A., 'Roaring royalists and ranting brewers: The politicisation of drink and drunkenness in political broadside ballads from 1640 to 1689', in Smyth (ed.), *A Pleasing Sinne*, pp. 69–87.

McSheffrey, S., *Marriage, Sex, and Civic Culture in Late Medieval London* (Philadelphia, PA: University of Pennsylvania Press, 2006).

Marshall, M., *Beliefs, Behaviors, and Alcoholic Beverages: A cross-cultural survey* (Ann Arbor, MI: University of Michigan Press, 1979).

Martin, A. L., *Alcohol, Sex, and Gender in Late Medieval and Early Modern Europe* (Basingstoke: Palgrave, 2001).

—, *Alcohol, Violence, and Disorder in Traditional Europe* (Kirksville, MO: Truman State University Press, 2009).

Mass Observation, *The Pub and the People: A Worktown study* (London: Cresset Library, 1987).

Minchinton, W., 'Cider and folklore', *Folk Life*, 13:1 (1975), pp. 66–79.

Morgan, D. H., 'The place of harvesters in nineteenth-century village life', in R. Samuel (ed.), *Village Life and Labour* (London: Routledge & Kegan Paul, 1975), pp. 27–72.

Morrell, F. and Peel, D., *All Saint's Parish Church Otley: Historical notes* (Otley: All Saints Parish Church, n. d.)

Moses, G., *Rural Moral Reform in Nineteenth-Century England: The crusade against adolescent farm servants and hiring fairs* (Lampeter: Edwin Mellen Press, 2007).

Patch, H., with R. van Emden, *The Last Fighting Tommy: The life of Harry Patch, last veteran of the trenches 1898–2009* (London: Bloomsbury, 2008).

Phillips, R., *Alcohol: A history* (Chapel Hill, NC: University of North Carolina Press, 2014).

Plant, M. A., *Drinking Careers: Occupations, drinking habits, and drinking problems* (London: Tavistock, 1979).

Reid, D. A., 'The decline of Saint Monday 1766–1876', *Past and Present*, 71 (1976), pp. 76–101.

Reinarz, J. and Wynter, R., 'The spirit of medicine: The use of alcohol in nineteenth-century medical practice', in S. Schmid and B. Schmidt-Haberkamp (eds), *Drink in the Eighteenth and Nineteenth Centuries* (London: Pickering & Chatto, 2014), pp. 127–39.

Rose, S. O., *Which People's War? National Identity and Citizenship in Wartime Britain 1939–1945* (Oxford: Oxford University Press, 2003).

Russell, D., *Looking North: Northern England and the national imagination* (Manchester: Manchester University Press, 2004).

Shepard, A., '"Swil-bols and tos-pots": Drink culture and male bonding in England, c. 1560–1640', in L. Gowing, M. Hunter and M. Rubin (eds), *Love, Friendship and Faith in Europe, 1300–1800* (Basingstoke: Palgrave Macmillan, 2005), pp. 110–30.

Strange, J-M., *Death, Grief and Poverty in Britain, 1870–1914* (Cambridge: Cambridge University Press, 2005).

Summerscale, K., *The Suspicions of Mr Whicher* (London: Bloomsbury, 2008).

Taylor, A., *Bacchus in Romantic England* (Basingstoke: Macmillan, 1999).

Thomas, K., *Religion and the Decline of Magic: Studies in popular beliefs in sixteenth and seventeenth century England*, (London: Weidenfeld and Nicolson, 1971).

Thurnell-Read T., 'What happens on tour: The premarital stag tour, homosocial bonding and male friendship', *Men and Masculinities*, 15:3 (2012), pp. 249–70.

Toner, D., *Alcohol and Nationhood in Nineteenth-Century Mexico* (London: University of Nebraska Press, 2015).

Vickery, A., *The Gentleman's Daughter: Women's lives in Georgian England* (London: Yale University Press, 1998).

Warner, J., 'Good help is hard to find: A few comments about alcohol and work in preindustrial England', *Addiction Research*, 2:3 (1995), pp. 259–69.

Warner, J. H., 'Physiological theory and therapeutic explanation in the 1860s: The British debate on the medical use of alcohol', *Bulletin of the History of Medicine*, 54:2 (1980), pp. 235–57.

Wilson, T. M., (ed.), *Drinking Cultures: Alcohol and identity* (Oxford: Beg, 2005).

Withington, P., 'Company and sociability in early modern England', *Social History*, 32:3 (2007), pp. 291–307.

Woiak, J., '"A medical Cromwell to depose King Alcohol": Medical scientists, temperance reformers, and the alcohol problem in Britain', *Histoire sociale/Social History*, 27:54 (1994), pp. 337–65.

Wright, E.M., *Rustic Speech and Folk-Lore* (London: H. Milford, Oxford University Press, 1913).

# 5 Drunks

**Introduction**

Of the myriad functions and meanings of drinking, one of the most important is undoubtedly displayed in getting drunk. Accordingly, a chapter is devoted here to drunks. But we are immediately faced with a basic problem of definition: what constitutes being drunk? This of course depends upon who is doing the defining. The point was nicely put by the head constable of Liverpool in his report for 1909, taking 'a concrete case of a man seen in a public-house and said to have departed from sobriety'. His state might be interpreted in ten different ways: from a total abstainer's perception of him as 'beastly drunk', through varying shades of opinion such as 'drunk but able to take care of himself' or 'slightly under the influence', to the man himself – 'painfully sober: almost in a state of collapse for want of a drink'.[1] Such individual perceptions are in turn derived from social and cultural influences. In this regard, for example, the drunkenness of women or the poor has always been more readily perceived, and subject to greater condemnation, than that of men or the wealthy. The former will be considered later in this chapter; the latter was, for example, a common Radical grievance in the early nineteenth century, as voiced here by Fergus O'Connor, provoking laughter in a speech at Huddersfield in 1839, contrasting how the police kicked the poor drunk 'in the gutter to prevent him falling' with the way in which the wealthy one was escorted carefully home 'like a basket of eggs'.[2]

On the other hand, drunks generally have often been treated indulgently. A study of London's East End at the close of the nineteenth century, a period of widespread anti-drink sentiment, noted rather the 'amused sympathy' which drunkenness aroused in the general public, as when 'a friendly onlooker will plead in defence of a poor creature too far gone to tell the tram conductor his destination': 'Bless yer, 'e ain't drunk; 'e's only got a bit of a booze'.[3] The enduring comedic figure of the drunk is also testament to this indulgence. Dickens created several memorable drunks: Squeers alighting 'to stretch his legs' at every halt on the coach journey to Yorkshire; Dick Swiveller, who the previous night had had 'the sun very strong in his eyes'; and Mrs Gamp, about whom a smell of spirits lingered, even though she was 'never able to do more than taste it'.[4] Such figures recur through the music hall,[5] from the characters portrayed by Frank Randle or

Freddy Frinton to the routines of Billy Connolly and Father Jack's heartfelt cry of 'Drink!'. Indulgence has also extended to their treatment in the courts. Although strictly in law drunkenness was no defence for crime, juries in the eighteenth and nineteenth centuries in practice could view it as a mitigating factor. Thus Ruth Woodward, charged with bigamy at the Old Bailey in 1737, pleaded she was too drunk to remember the wedding, and the jury, ignoring a reminder as to the law, acquitted her. Deaths in pub brawls involving drunken men were viewed with comparative tolerance by the courts well into the nineteenth century, even though the wider climate of opinion was shifting towards greater condemnation of the effects of drinking.[6]

Not only is the perception of the drunken state variable, the behaviour of those experiencing it also is not fixed. This was the influential insight of two US anthropologists in their concept of 'drunken comportment': the fact that it is learned behaviour and that what people do when they are drunk varies between societies and in the same societies over time in different situations and circumstances. Drunken behaviour, they argued, whilst it might be different from that of a person's sober self, was characterized by the same 'healthy respect for certain socially sanctioned limits'.[7] This chapter begins, then, with the problem of definition, goes on to the question of why people get drunk and then suggests a history of drunkenness, focusing on the nineteenth and early twentieth centuries as arguably constituting a watershed in its prevalence.

## Defining drunk[8]

The vocabulary of drunkenness richly conveys the ubiquity of the experience over time, its physical consequences and its degrees.[9] A writer in the *Gentleman's Magazine* in 1770 listed eighty-seven terms for the condition, as he put it, 'of an Honest Fellow, and no Flincher, under the Effects of Good Fellowship', which were expressive of many aspects of the drunken state. These ranged from the resulting emotional state, from 'fuddled' to 'hot-headed', or 'pot-valiant', 'maudlin' or 'cheary'; to its physical effects, as in 'got glass eyes', 'sees double' or 'lost his leggs'; or, metaphorically, 'been among the Philistines' or 'came home by the villages' (as opposed to by the fields and consequently not meeting anyone).[10] This, however, is quite a modest list when compared with the 228 terms compiled by Benjamin Franklin in 1737.[11] In addition to the more obviously indigenous 'Been at an Indian Feast', it shared terms like 'skin full' or 'half seas over' with the later list. It also cited 'Piss'd in the Brook', a term still found in a modern dictionary of slang, which as 'pissed', or one of its many variants, such as 'on the piss', 'piss-artist', 'piss-head' or 'piss-up', is perhaps now the most common in use, amongst hundreds listed. The language is constantly evolving, with new terms being coined, like 'arseholed' from the 1960s, 'banjo'd' or 'banjoed' from the 1970s and 'bladdered' from the early 1990s.[12] Local and regional variation has added to the richness: in the nineteenth century 'noggy' or 'corky', for example, were used for slight intoxication in respectively the Craven district and southern parts of the West Riding of Yorkshire, whilst in the East Riding 'knoppy', 'noppy' or 'nappy' were in use to describe this particular state.[13] Degrees of drunkenness like this were identified explicitly in an 1859 dictionary of slang, in use in London and apparently the universities of Oxford and Cambridge, which listed fifty terms divided into three categories. These went from mild intoxication ('beery', 'boozy', 'elevated', 'lushy', 'stewed' or 'tight') to a higher or more intense state ('blued out', 'ploughed' or 'obfuscated') through to the 'climax of fuddlement' ('sewed up' or 'regularly scammered').[14]

Greater precision on drunken states was sought by scientists through the nineteenth century. As one authoritative study, published in 1909, explained, the symptoms referable to the nervous system, commonly known as drunkenness or intoxication, followed a large dose of alcohol taken at one sitting within two to four hours in more or less rapid sequence. Beginning with a person becoming for a short time 'conversational', talking 'freely, and more or less at random', this 'stage of stimulation develops into noisiness and emotional excitement as the cerebral control becomes increasingly paralysed'. Narcosis begins and 'dulness [sic] and heaviness' succeed. Vomiting may now intervene, getting rid of some of the excess alcohol, or the person simply falls asleep; but, if not, serious unconsciousness, coma and death may result.[15] Seventy years later a special report from the Royal College of Psychiatrists charted a similar trajectory of effects on the brain, linked now to blood levels of alcohol, beginning at 50 mg per cent with the majority of individuals feeling 'carefree and released from many of their ordinary anxieties and inhibitions', on through 'clumsiness and emotional lability' at 100 to 'obvious impairment of parts of brain controlling movement and emotional behaviour' at 200 and so to confusion, passing-out and progressive stupor from 300.[16] These characteristics are subject to variation. There are, for example, significant differences between men and women in their handling of alcohol, as the latter are 'more physiologically compromised' by it, due to weight differences, tissue saturation, stomach enzymes and the percentage of fat to water in the body.[17] There is also a link to diet. Foods high in carbohydrates tend to delay absorption of alcohol into the bloodstream. It has thus been argued, for example, that the starchy diet of medieval populations would have mitigated its effects.[18]

The criminal-justice system usually took a view of drunkenness as at the more extreme end of the spectrum. Seventeenth-century magistrates were advised in the standard guide to their powers and duties that it meant that 'the same legs which carry a man into the house cannot carry him out again'.[19] The law itself, as will be seen, later defined it more narrowly than simply 'drunk', as drunk in the highway or other public place, or drunk and disorderly or drunk and incapable, and this stricter definition remained the common perception, as the nineteenth-century rhyme had it:

> Not drunk is he, who from the floor
> Can rise again and ask for more.
> But drunk is he who prostrate lies,
> Without the power to speak or rise.[20]

In contrast, for drunk-driving in the later twentieth century the qualifying blood–alcohol level might actually correspond to what is perceived by the driver, or indeed by onlookers, as relatively mild intoxication. In a similar way, the modern definition of binge drinking, rather than the prolonged 'bender' it formerly meant, is consuming twice the recommended daily guidelines for low-risk drinking, equating to four and three pints of ordinary-strength lager or four and three glasses of wine for men and women respectively. For many drinkers this would not in fact constitute a heavy drinking session, and the phrase 'heavy episodic drinking' has been preferred.[21]

Defining drunk is therefore not an easy task. Science and human perception tell us that the symptoms of intoxication are manifest from the beginning of consumption. At what point this becomes something called drunkenness is culturally determined. Since culture is subject to historical change, what is perceived as drunk will also differ over time. It may be legally defined, as in the blood–alcohol level at which driving under the influence of drink becomes a criminal offence or if it is in a public place or combined with being either disorderly or incapable, being in charge of a variety of dangerous objects or being responsible for a child. But the law itself is similarly subject to historical change. This chapter certainly acknowledges the complexity of the whole question, but takes as its definition a common-sense, if you like, view of a more advanced stage of intoxication, one going beyond the mild state as categorized in the 1859 dictionary or the carefree one described for the Royal College of Psychiatrists to reach the former's 'obfuscated' or the latter's 'obvious impairment' – or as eighteenth-century moral reformers were advised in 'judging when a man is drunk' to use 'prudence and caution':

> Though a man that cannot stand upon his legs, or that reels or staggers as he goes along the streets, and is heard to faulter remarkably in speech, unless in case of some known natural infirmity or defect, may ordinarily be presumed to be drunk.[22]

In so doing, however, it will also consider in particular those more advanced stages, when through disorderly behaviour or incapacity an individual was brought into contact with the police.

## Getting drunk

Before I attempt to chart a history of drunkenness, this section asks why do people get drunk? It does not, however, claim to get to grips with the large psychological literature on this; rather it offers a series of general motivations to enable us to make some sense historically of the experience.[23] First is the all important context of sociability, or good fellowship, which was explored in the previous chapter. Getting drunk could simply follow in the ordinary course of drinking events, whether it be a routine social occasion or a more special celebration. Pepys experienced both, of the latter noting after celebrating Charles II's coronation: 'no sooner a-bed … but my head begun to turne and I to vomitt'. He woke up next day to find himself 'wet with my spewing' and with his 'head in sad taking'.[24]

Second is the experience itself. Altering consciousness, getting 'out of it', as the author of a cultural history of intoxication described it, is 'its own justification'.[25] In this context the power, force or violence of many of the expressions for drunkenness – plastered, or smashed, for example – is suggestive, it has been argued, of how 'part of the pleasure of drunkenness is the pleasure involved in destroying everyday consciousness'.[26] For the US philosopher and psychologist William James, intoxication was a religious experience, wherein its

> power to stimulate the mystical faculties of human nature, usually crushed to earth by the cold facts and dry criticisms of the sober hour ... brings its votary from the chill periphery of things to the radiant core. It makes him for the moment one with truth.[27]

Similarly, for writers and artists in the nineteenth century, intoxication, in James Nicholls's words, 'shared with art (albeit imperfectly) the capacity to transform and redeem the fleeting ephemera of the everyday'. The association of creativity with excess and rebellion against the mundane and conformist has continued to exercise a powerful cultural fascination.[28]

Getting 'out of it' might thus be undertaken with deliberation, if perhaps in a rather more mundane way than allusions to art or religion might suggest. The Yorkshire clergyman Oliver Heywood saw, and lamented, an incident in the late 1670s, when six young men at an alehouse in Halifax made a 'solemn vow and oath' that they would drink till they were drunk and the first to be dead drunk would pay for all the rest.[29] From the 1990s drunkenness amongst young people has similarly been viewed as a 'determined' pursuit of altered states, a 'psychoactive high' like that from taking illicit drugs, where getting 'out of your head' or 'off your face', it has been argued, is 'virtually a prerequisite for the active search for individualized hedonistic excess'.[30] Yet, at the same time, it has also been contended, following the idea of 'drunken comportment', that although the intention is to lose control, it is a 'controlled loss of control', a 'calculated hedonism' from which one will ultimately return to the pressures of day-to-day life, work, education and family.[31] A study of US college students 'getting wasted' found that whilst adventure and unpredictability were certainly being sought in heavy drinking, they pursued strategies to avoid trouble, to protect their fellows from harm and, in the end, to not compromise their studies.[32]

A third reason is to seek oblivion or escape. A number of historians have seen this motive as a key to understanding drunkenness historically. Keith Thomas argued how in the sixteenth and seventeenth centuries 'the poor took to drink to blot out some of the horror of their lives'.[33] Similarly, Jessica Warner saw gin in the first half of the eighteenth century 'numbing countless thousands to the fatigue, hunger and cold that was the lot of London's working poor'.[34] Thus it was that drink as the quickest way out of Manchester, or indeed anywhere else, became a common saying. A key objection to the oblivion thesis is that some of these periods of exceptionally heavy drinking, like the early eighteenth century, or the 1870s, were actually ones of relative prosperity for the labouring classes, when rising incomes provided the necessary financial means to drink to excess. In the former period gin became a luxury for the poor, but it was their only luxury, and since their lives remained fundamentally uncertain, saving for the future was eschewed in favour of a 'more meaningful expenditure' in consumption. In this view, heavy drinking was at once an affirmation, rooted in an existing culture of drinking, and a solace.[35] In times of hardship for the poorest, like the late sixteenth and early seventeenth centuries, or the early nineteenth, it was amongst the better paid that heavy drinking prevailed, as in 1830s Bolton, for example, where the reduced consumption of impoverished weavers was contrasted with that of better-paid skilled workers like file-cutters, carters, railwaymen or the police.[36] But if the escape thesis is open to question, oblivion or solace for the troubled individual, as we saw in the previous chapter, could indeed be an important function of drunkenness.

For a final observation, we turn from the solitary drinker to group intoxication. Here, the related ideas of 'time-out' from the expected norms of behaviour, or of carnival, have been used to try and explain the nature of the experience.[37] The drunkenness of the seaside holiday has been characterized in this way, since in the liminal environment which resorts represented 'the usual constraints on respectability and decorum in public behaviour might be pushed aside in the interests of holiday hedonism and carnivalesque escape from the petty restrictions of everyday life'.[38] In addition to the occasional release from the day-to-day, carnival has also been seen as a form of inversion where 'Momentarily the social order is turned upside down'. Since this occurs, however, in the '"unreal" context of recreational time and space, it has the effect of reinforcing the social order when "real" time and space are re-entered'.[39] Consider this outing to the Yorkshire spa town of Ilkley in the summer of 1900. Over two days waggonette parties of women, organized from pubs, made the trip from the industrial city of Leeds, some dozen miles to the south east. According to the local paper, these 'undesirable trippers' got drunk on the first day, made 'abundant use of disgusting language' and stole toys and china from shopfronts, although it wasn't deemed worthwhile to arrest them. The following day, once again, several women were 'so drunk as to be unable to stand' and there were a couple of instances of 'sudden illness'.[40] Similarly, an ethnographic study of young working-class women towards the end of the twentieth century found that one of the attractions for them of getting drunk was to please themselves as they wished rather than as society ordained. As one put it: 'When you're completely ratted you feel so fucking brilliant, dead in control like ... You just think fuck it ... I'm enjoying myself'.[41]

## A history of drunkenness

At various times contemporaries and subsequent historians have identified what they saw as the emergence of a new kind of drunkenness in England. In the mid sixteenth century it was attributed to the adoption by the English of foreign habits, as for the writer and adventurer George Gascoigne, viewing it as 'a monstrous plant, lately crept into the pleasant orchards of England'.[42] Gin in the early eighteenth century was similarly said to produce a different kind of drunkenness. Lord Chesterfield contrasted its joylessness and silent indulgence with 'the old English sort of drunkenness, which proceeded from hospitality and good fellowship'.[43] For W. E. H. Lecky, the Victorian historian of eighteenth-century England, with gin 'The fatal passion for drink was at once, and irrevocably, planted in the nation'.[44] Modern historians have expressed similar views. Roy Porter, albeit in less apocalyptic terms, saw the introduction of gin, along with porter, as ushering in 'a new drink problem'.[45] And for Wolfgang Schivelbusch gin represented the 'industrialization of drinking', an acceleration as modern life in general speeded up.[46] 'Binge' drinking by the young at the turn of the millennium has also been viewed in this way, as something qualitatively different.

Beliefs in a new kind of drunkenness, by both contemporaries and historians, imply that drunkenness has a history, one in which its incidence and intensity might rise and fall. At least one nineteenth-century temperance reformer and twentieth-century psychiatrist have thought so in delineating such a history.[47] But can one say with any degree of certainty that at this period or another England was a more or less drunken nation? Levels of consumption might offer one piece of evidence, but, as we saw in Chapter 1, charting them poses numerous difficulties. What we were reasonably confident in suggesting in the end, however, was that in the past levels of consumption were much higher than prevailed for much of the twentieth century. But in themselves they do not necessarily indicate the prevalence of drunkenness, including for some of the reasons noted above: the relationship to diet of the medieval period, for example, or the relative strengths of what was being drunk. Historians have been cautious. Looking at the late sixteenth and early seventeenth centuries, Peter Clark felt that despite the absence of quantifiable evidence the torrent of contemporary criticism of drunkenness together with the growth in the number of alehouses probably indicated an actual rise in drunkenness.[48] For Nicholls, in contrast, there is no compelling evidence of any significant increase at that time; the reasons for that criticism lay elsewhere than in its actual increase – in the rise of Puritanism and the fear of political instability.[49] Where it seems we can be reasonably confident is in asserting that drunkenness was common at all levels of society and remained so through the sixteenth, seventeenth and eighteenth centuries, whether or not we see the Elizabethan and early Stuart period or the gin era as witnessing an actual increase in its incidence or intensity.

This confidence is based in a picture necessarily built up from 'scattered and incidental contemporary references'.[50] All occupational and social groups got drunk. Some were especially prone to it. Soldiers and sailors are the obvious examples here, drawn from amongst the young male population most likely in any case to indulge, provided with generous rations and brought together in long periods of enforced inaction. According to one historian, 'Drunkenness was epidemic in the British army during the eighteenth century' and it was well into the succeeding century before any improvement was effected.[51] So too with sailors: drunkenness was the chief cause of accidents and several deaths on Cook's voyages of exploration.[52] But it was widespread in civilian society, too. In the seventeenth century the diarist John Evelyn twice noted the custom of a host providing for the intoxication of one's servants.[53] Oliver Heywood tells us of the drunken vicar of Otley falling off his horse.[54] The Sussex village shopkeeper Thomas Turner in the 1750s noted a party at the rector's house 'drinking like horses' and indeed reported of himself in his very first diary entry, 'went to bed drunk'.[55] In the 1780s John Byng, later Viscount Torrington, himself no stranger to alcohol, observed 'a bevy of Welsh squires intoxicating themselves' at the Three Cranes in Chepstow, whilst a foreign traveller, Carl Moritz, pondered the farmers on the coach from Northampton to London, with faces 'bloated and discoloured by their copious use of ale and brandy', awaking from their slumbers to discuss sheep, 'the first and last topic of their conversation'.[56] Drunkenness amongst the elite was also common throughout these centuries. In late seventeenth-century Oxford St John's was singled out by one diarist as a 'debauched college' with much drunkenness, and one fellow of All Souls died at a London tavern after 'immoderate drinking'.[57] A century later things were the same, but at Cambridge this time, with 'hard drinking ... almost as prevalent there as it was in country society'.[58] Amanda Vickery's study of Georgian women from commercial, professional and gentry families – the 'genteel' of northern England – found that amongst their menfolk 'drunken disorder was latent in almost every evening gathering'.[59] Amongst both the middle and upper classes at this time the three-bottle man, in the contemporary phrase, was not unusual.[60]

Undoubtedly drunkenness remained common in the nineteenth century: the contemporary evidence is overwhelming. Friedrich Engels reported of Manchester in the 1840s how on Saturday evenings 'intemperance may be seen in all its brutality'.[61] Dostoevsky, visiting London in 1862, was similarly struck by how everyone was 'in a hurry to drink himself into insensibility'.[62] One could multiply individual instances *ad nauseam*, as any reading of the newspapers of this time will evidence. Nor was it confined to the lower orders. The 'men in respectable positions' returning home drunk in 1857 on the omnibus to the Leeds suburb of Headingley 'to the disgust of all decent people' were common enough.[63] But from the late eighteenth century this began to change and the nineteenth century was to see a long-term decline in levels of drunkenness. This may seem a rather paradoxical statement given that this was a century which also saw the growth of an organized temperance movement and an associated torrent of criticism of heavy drinking and drunkenness akin to that of the late sixteenth and early seventeenth centuries. But many contemporaries also were aware of change across all classes: the pleased surprise of the well-to-do at the orderly behaviour of the crowds attending the Great Exhibition in London in 1851 is evidence for this.[64] It is on this change that I would like to focus here as it represents what seems to have been in the nineteenth century a real break with the drunken past.

There is rather more evidence from the nineteenth century than before on which to base an assessment. A succession of parliamentary inquiries, although concerned with perceived problems, heard ample testimony of improvement.[65] At the

1816 inquiry into policing in London the chief clerk at the Bow Street office and five of seven magistrates who expressed an opinion took the view that drunkenness amongst the lower orders had declined or at least was no worse. The former had 'no doubt as to greater habits of sobriety among journeymen workmen and mechanics than ten years ago' and that 'those excessive scenes of drunkenness which I have formerly observed are not by any means so frequent'.[66] Francis Place put this same view before the 1834 committee inquiring into drunkenness amongst the labouring classes. Chaired as it was, however, by a teetotaller and seeking to reach a conclusion that it was indeed increasing, it ignored him and others who offered contrary testimony, including one of the new commissioners of the metropolitan police.[67] As a Radical working man, Place was especially irritated by the charges levelled at his class and defended them as being without hope of betterment, a point which we noted earlier, the wonder being not that they should get drunk occasionally, but 'that it should be only occasional'.[68]

Two major inquiries, into intemperance and the licensing system respectively, chart the decline over the course of the rest of the century, whilst again fully acknowledging, it must be said, its prevalence. The former, reporting towards the end of the 1870s, a decade of high levels of consumption, concluded that drunkenness was

> less common than formerly among the more respectable portion of the working classes, and that the increase has taken place chiefly, either in the lowest grades of society, or among those whose advance in education has not kept pace with the increase of their wages.

It thus acknowledged a rise with the growth of the economy, but overall felt that there was 'no evidence to prove that the country is, in this respect, in worse condition than it was 30 years ago'.[69] And the Royal Commission on the Liquor Licensing Laws, which reported at another time of relative prosperity, some twenty years later, whilst asserting that a 'gigantic evil' remained, concluded that: 'Most persons who have studied the question are of opinion that actual drunkenness has materially diminished in all classes of society in the last 25 or 30 years'.[70]

In addition to the reports of inquiries such as these, there is similar testimony from a variety of sources. A journalist who visited the dram shops of Bradford at the close of the 1860s and found there 'nothing but downright drinking and utter debasement' painted a rather different picture by the mid 1880s. He found now, reporting on how 'Bradford Takes Refreshment', 'just as much of sunshine as of shade in the general picture';[71] and a study of social conditions in late-Edwardian Oxford observed how 'drinking has greatly diminished here as elsewhere'.[72] At this time, too, in London south of the river, 'Only a small minority drank frequently to excess'.[73] Even temperance believers might concede that the more disorderly drunkenness had diminished, even if in their view drinking itself had not. As one prominent spokesman, Thomas Whittaker, put it, 'Habitual drinking, continual and frequent, has taken the place of occasional bouts of brutal drunkenness'.[74]

We have also for the nineteenth century statistics of police action against drunkenness. As a sin, drunkenness had been punishable in early modern England by church courts, but it became a criminal offence in legislation of 1606. The offence was simply that a person, or persons, 'shall be drunk' and of drunkenness 'shall be lawfully convicted' and thus liable for a fine of five shillings or in default to be placed in the stocks for six hours.[75] Although only 'drunk' was specified, in practice it meant drunk and disorderly or drunk and incapable. Although there is evidence in places of action in both church and secular courts against drunks in the early part of the seventeenth century in particular, overall they were neither numerous nor sustained.[76] In the later seventeenth and through the eighteenth centuries, the use of church courts declined and it became an offence with which secular courts too seldom dealt. But towards the end of the eighteenth century this began to change. As historian of the police Clive Emsley put it, 'men of property in England appear to have developed a new threshold for order maintenance ... and sought improved policing to achieve this'.[77] Although the development of policing from this time was a piecemeal and protracted process, and not geographically complete until the mid 1850s, wherever improvements were made drinking places and disorderly drunks were their target.[78] The law also was modernized, first in local legislation, for London, for example, in 1829 against 'disorderly persons' and those found at night 'lying in any Highway' and then in 1839 specifically covering anyone found 'drunk in any street or public thoroughfare' and 'while drunk ... guilty of any riotous or indecent behaviour'. These provisions were incorporated into the Town Police Clauses Act of 1847, which it was open to any local authority to adopt. Second, in 1872 an important general Licensing Act brought the law into its modern form, covering anyone drunk in any highway or public place, drunk and committing riotous or disorderly behaviour and drunk in charge, including of horses, carriages, steam engines and loaded firearms.

Using these laws, tens of thousands of drunken men and women were processed by the police, courts and prisons in Victorian and Edwardian England and Wales. In the peak years for proceedings – the mid 1870s and the Edwardian period – there were annually over 200,000 for offences of drunkenness, which represented typically around a fifth to a quarter of all cases with which magistrates dealt. Nor does this include offences, such as assault, where drink was a likely contributory factor but where the drunkenness was not proceeded against. And as many as a third or more of those in prison had been convicted of drunkenness.[79] However, what is noteworthy for my argument here is a decline in the *rate* of proceedings over this period. New forces could record very high rates indeed, as did those of London and Liverpool, of over 250 per 10,000 people in the early 1830s and 1840s. But by the time we have a run of national statistics, from 1857, this was already much lower at over 40 per 10,000. This rose then to a peak in 1875 of nearly 85, but after that year a long-term decline set in.[80]

Of course, one must be cautious about making inferences from these figures. The statistics, as contemporaries were well aware, do not represent the actual amount of drunkenness: as the editor of the first compilation of judicial statistics commented, the figures were 'a distant indication only of the extent of this vice'.[81]

They were indicators of police action, which was subject to a great variety of influences. There was the law itself: the changes introduced in the Licensing Act of 1872 and a further Act of 1902 themselves inflated the number of proceedings. There were operational practicalities, such as changes in official procedures or the actual availability of officers. Drunks could be difficult to deal with and their family and friends were liable to get involved. As one London officer noted of a great crowd in Battersea Park Road one Saturday night in 1888 and the efforts of his colleague to take into custody a drunk and disorderly man in the face of the rescue attempts of his drunken wife, 'no persons assisted the constable, just the reverse'.[82] Public opinions were important influences, of those wanting more stern enforcement of the law and those resisting it. Finally, there was the willingness of magistrates to convict. Accordingly, there were sharp fluctuations in the number of proceedings from year to year and between different localities. Such local particularities are nicely illustrated in a detailed study of the Westmorland towns of Kirby Stephen and Kirby Lonsdale. Police in the former were much more likely to arrest or summons drunks, whereas those in the latter concerned themselves more with vagrants, reflecting local priorities respectively for the temperance cause and the tourist trade.[83] Similarly, police priorities might change over time. A study of Crewe suggested that the fall in drunkenness proceedings after 1900 was produced by the police prosecuting instead public-order offences such as street gambling, criminal damage, obscenity and vagrancy (all of which might be committed whilst under the influence of alcohol). When proceedings fell in turn for all public-order offences from 1910, this was the result of a shift in resources to the policing of driving-related offences, the number of which increased exponentially.[84] Nevertheless, one can, if cautiously, cite the falling rate of proceedings nationally as indicating a decline in the actual overall incidence of drunkenness, for the following reasons. The pattern for proceedings corresponds with trends in consumption. When this rose so too did proceedings, as in the 1870s or again in the late 1890s. This in turn corresponded to periods of prosperity. But, as with the rate of proceedings, whilst total consumption fluctuated, per capita consumption fell. At the same time, anxiety over drinking and drunkenness remained high in late Victorian and Edwardian England, as we will see in the next chapter, and the police certainly continued to process drunks, suggesting again that the falling rate of proceedings reflected a real decline in public disorderly or incapable drunkenness, which was what the law and the police dealt with.[85]

Who were these drunks who attracted the attentions of the police? They were overwhelmingly from the labouring classes; rarely did a middle- or upper-class drunk fall foul of the law. When they did, as in a controversial Liverpool case of 1879, the differential operation of the system might continue to confirm those old Radical accusations. There, four well-connected young men involved in a carriage accident whilst returning from the Grand National were in fact convicted of drunkenness and, significantly, of assaulting a police officer with a whip. But the case was deliberately held early in the morning before any reporters were in court and in any case the newspapers later complied with a request not to publicize it.[86] But these men were unusual in actually coming to court.

Taking educational background as an indicator of social status, in Sheffield, of a sample of 515 individuals arrested during 1863–4 228 had 'none', 276 'imperfect' and only eleven an educational background described as 'good'; only one whose occupation was listed was described as a 'gentleman' and seventy-seven were unemployed.[87] Certain occupations contributed disproportionately to the statistics: the rate overall of proceedings was highest in seaports and mining counties in the late Victorian and Edwardian period.[88] Local evidence tends to confirm that over the century those taken up by the police were drawn more and more from the 'lowest grades of society', to use the phrase of the Lords committee. In Oxford, for example, in 1911, of the 110 people proceeded against (in a total population of around 53,000), one third were 'members of the derelict bands of tramps who pass through Oxford in such large numbers'; and of sixty-one drunks charged in 1910 in the rural North Riding of Yorkshire around Bedale and Masham no fewer than forty were described as 'tramping' or 'tramping labourer'.[89]

The majority of offenders were men, but women always formed a significant minority. Their share of those proceeded against actually fell over the century, from over 30 per cent in towns and cities in the 1830s and 1840s to a little over 20 per cent by the Edwardian period. But looked at another way, drunkenness became more of a female crime, rising from 21.7 per cent of total female convictions in 1857 to a high in 1875 of 43.9 per cent, remaining high thereafter. Their rate of proceedings, however, was declining in line with that of men, which rather belied the increasing concern with female drunkenness at this time.[90] Those women who were prosecuted were more likely to be repeat offenders. In 1910, whilst women accounted for only 20 per cent of those convicted, 14 per cent of those women made up 43 per cent of those with twenty or more convictions.[91] A number of women with huge numbers of convictions became the subject of rather prurient contemporary fascination, like Jane Cakebread, who by the age of sixty-five in 1895 had made a total of 278 court appearances. For one of these, a constable had seen her around midnight, surrounded by a mob and using very bad language. Taken into custody, she became violent and tried to bite him. In court, in 'her usual plausible style', as the news report had it, she claimed to be very weak and not used to liquor. To laughter in court, she alleged that whilst in her cell singing hymns the inspector had let officers in to 'bang her about'. On receiving her sentence she blessed the magistrate. In South Wales Emma Retallick was known as Pontypridd's own Jane Cakebread, with almost 200 court appearances by 1909.[92] As we will see in the next chapter, such women were to be the subject of attempts to 'reform' them.

They were still to be found after the war, still the object of prurience and community mythologizing, like Nancy 'Dickybird', apparently a terror to the police in north Manchester in the 1920s with 173 convictions, who later put the beautiful singing for which she was named to good use in the Salvation Army.[93] But by this time the long-term trends over the previous century, including the effects of the First World War, had finally produced a markedly more sober nation. Consumption levels and proceedings for drunkenness were now substantially below pre-war levels. The latter stood at 54 per 10,000 people in 1911, but had fallen to 23 in 1921 and to just 12 in 1931.[94] The Royal Commission on Licensing, reporting in that year, was emphatic that 'by almost universal consent, excessive drinking in this country has been greatly, even spectacularly, diminished'.[95] This was a view shared by many commentators. The *New Survey of London Life and Labour* concluded that 'drunkenness had become markedly the exception even in those districts where formerly it had been almost the rule'.[96] Or as Richard Hoggart saw it, in his study of working-class life in Leeds, whilst drink was 'still regarded as the main pitfall for a working class husband', overall there was 'little violent drunkenness, and much less drinking of all kinds'.[97]

What had produced this long-term change? The police had clearly acted against drunkenness, but it is unlikely that they contributed much to the decline. In any case, they dealt only with a fraction of those actually drunk and their actions were always, as a study of policing in London argued, 'tempered by weakness, fear, realism, tolerance, familiarity and humanitarianism'.[98] We must look to wider changes for an explanation. The impact of industrialization must loom large in any answer; but its consequences in the short term, in the view of Brain Harrison, were complex. In some ways it enhanced drink's attractions – for example, for men in new occupations like iron smelting subject to new extremes of heat and cold or for migrants from rural areas to the strangeness, squalor but also the attractions of the new industrial towns. In other ways it helped to reduce drunkenness – for example, by creating a new class of employers using novel methods of production who had a direct interest in sobriety.[99] But one long-term material consequence of industrialization was crucial: improved working-class living standards. It was this which brought about, particularly from the 1870s, as was argued in Chapter 1, the fall in per capita consumption which continued into the twentieth century. It provided the essential material support to the belief that a better life, to however limited an extent – a better-furnished home, a Sunday suit, a day out – was possible and that money could buy these, or even be saved, rather than blown on the immediate pleasure of a drunken 'spree'. But improvements in material circumstances do not by themselves provide the answer. As I also argued, the widening belief in the ideal, or ideals, of respectability was a crucial change. For the middle classes, drunkenness, which had been a common indulgence of the middling sort historically, was much diminished and certainly was no longer condoned. And for working men and women, too, not drinking to excess was essential to a self-perception of respectability, except perhaps on permissible special occasions or in the liminal environment of the seaside holiday.

There had, then, been a real change, and general consumption, and drunken excess, remained at historically low levels beyond the Second World War. The subsequent rise in consumption engendered, as will be seen in the next chapter, growing concern from a public-health perspective. This naturally included the consequences for individual health of heavy alcohol consumption, concern which took in habitual drunken offenders, including vagrant drunks.[100] But anxiety about the public drunkenness so prevalent in previous centuries has in the latter half of the twentieth century focused primarily on the young. This was apparent immediately after the war and was linked to what was perceived as a growing general problem of juvenile delinquency, itself dating back to the war years. For example, in a survey of twenty cities the number of convictions for drunkenness of males under twenty-one was shown to have doubled between 1950 and 1957. In the latter year around 15 per cent of all convictions were accounted for by service personnel, and indeed part of the reason for the overall problem was said to be the deleterious effect of high wages amongst the young, combined with the postponement of adult responsibility enforced by national service.[101] Youthful drunkenness remained both apparent, and a reason for society's anxiety, for the remainder of the century and beyond. In the 1980s it focused on drunken football supporters and the so called lager lout, who inhabited, it was claimed, not just the more traditionally drunken urban areas, but small towns and rural communities.[102]

But it is the phenomenon of binge drinking in cities by young men and women which has aroused the greatest amount of concern. This too was apparent from the 1980s. With the growth of the night-time economy, the number of drinking places proliferated and with them the number of youthful revellers. City centres played host to huge numbers of mostly young people. In Leeds, for example, by the new millennium there were often in excess of 100,000 people in the city centre at the weekend. In Nottingham, another key proponent of the night-time economy, the capacity of pubs, bars and clubs was 111,000. In Newcastle over 200 licensed premises could cater for nearly 100,000 drinkers.[103] By this time 'Dean', a police officer in what was referred to as a major north-east city, was describing two o'clock on a Sunday morning in apocalyptic terms reminiscent of Engels or Dostoevsky, with 'literally thousands and thousands of mostly young kids, and they're mostly drunk out of their minds' (Figure 5.1). He noted in particular

*Figure 5.1* Out of it: young man in Newton Abbot, Devon, 2014; still from the documentary film *A Royal Hangover*, directed by Arthur Cauty.

Source: Courtesy of Arthur Cauty.

'young girls, no more than eighteen years old, who can't stand up, can't speak'.[104] Images of such young women in particular became an essential feature of media coverage of the issue, as prurience once again was combined with traditional disapproval of the drunkenness of women.[105]

The disorder produced by these numbers of drinkers and levels of drunkenness was well documented in a number of studies. The Youth Lifestyles Survey at the close of the 1990s classified 39 per cent of 18– 24-year-olds as 'binge drinkers', defined as getting very drunk at least once a month, of whom 60 per cent admitted involvement in criminal and/or disorderly behaviour during or after drinking.[106] A Home Office research study showed that most young adults whilst out drinking had experienced or witnessed assaults or fighting.[107] Indeed, it has been argued that the disorder, or threat of it, is part of the attraction, in a 'powerful atmosphere of dangerous adventure'.[108] And yet, perhaps, one should make some caveats. Nearly two thirds of young people were not classified as binge drinkers. Of those who were, given the thousands who drank to excess in the night-time economy's bars and clubs, the overwhelming majority came through the experience unscathed other than with the usual physical after-effects of intoxication. Moreover, it was likely to be for them, however it might appear to others, a positive experience, be it simply getting 'out of it', affirming an identity or 'time out' from the mundane world.

There are thus continuities in the history of drunkenness, from the reasons for indulging to the physical consequences of doing so. The experience of Samuel Pepys at the end of coronation day is one all too common throughout history. But, as this chapter has sought to demonstrate, there have been important changes in overall levels of drunkenness. As Brian Harrison and Barrie Trinder asserted in their pioneering 1969 study of temperance and drink in Banbury, Oxfordshire, 'Early Victorian England differs from modern England nowhere more markedly than in the scale of its public drunkenness and violence'.[109] Since they wrote those words the experience of the later twentieth and early twenty-first centuries may have modified the conclusion somewhat, but it is in the end only a modification of what remains a fair assessment of the change which took place over the course of the nineteenth and early twentieth centuries.

## Notes

1 G. B. Wilson, *Alcohol and the Nation: A contribution to the study of the liquor problem in the United Kingdom from 1800 to 1935* (London: Nicholson and Watson, 1940), p. 284.
2 *Northern Star*, 30 November 1839, p. 1.
3 Mrs B. Bosanquet, *Rich and Poor* (London: Macmillan, 1899), p. 134.
4 C. Dickens, *Nicholas Nickleby* (London: Penguin, 1999), p. 64; *The Old Curiosity Shop* (London: Collins, 1953), p. 29; *Martin Chuzzlewit* (London: Odhams, n. d.), p. 298;
5 For music hall see G. Stedman Jones, 'The "cockney" and the nation, 1780–1988', in D. Feldman and G. Stedman Jones (eds), *Metropolis London: Histories and representations since 1800* (London: Routledge, 1989), pp. 272–324, on pp. 294–6.

6 Old Bailey Proceedings Online, 7 September 1737, trial of Ruth Woodward (t17370907-15), at www.oldbaileyonline.org [accessed 13 June 2011]; D. Rabin, 'Drunkenness and responsibility for crime in the eighteenth century', *Journal of British Studies*, 44:3 (2005), pp. 457–77; J. A. Bars, 'Defining murder in Victorian London: An analysis of cases 1862–1892' (DPhil dissertation, Oxford University, 1995), pp. 212–25; M. J. Wiener, *Men of Blood: Violence, manliness and criminal justice in Victorian England* (Cambridge: Cambridge University Press, 2004), pp. 258–9 and 270; for the whole complex question of drunkenness and criminal responsibility see P. Handler, 'Intoxication and criminal responsibility in England, 1819–1920', *Oxford Journal of Legal Studies*, 33:2 (2013), pp. 243–62.

7 C. MacAndrew and R. B. Edgerton, *Drunken Comportment: A social explanation* (Chicago: Aldine, 1969), pp. 13–14, 53 and 85.

8 For another attempt see, B. A. Tlusty, 'Defining "drunk" in early modern Germany', *Contemporary Drug Problems*, 21:3 (1994), pp. 427–51.

9 One compilation, drawing upon a variety of historical sources, discovered some 2,000 words for drunkenness, see O. Mendelsohn, *Nicely, Thank You (Drunk 2000) Times: A frolic with some synonyms* (Melbourne: The National Press PTY., 1971).

10 'Observations on drunkenness' in *Gentleman's Magazine*, December 1770, pp. 559–60.

11 For his *Pennsylvania Gazette*, cited in H. G. Levine, 'The vocabulary of drunkenness', *Journal of Studies on Alcohol*, 42:11 (1981), pp. 1038–51.

12 T. Thorne, *Dictionary of Contemporary Slang* (London: A & C Black, 2005).

13 J. Wright, *English Dialect Dictionary* (Oxford: English Dialect Society, 6 vols 1898–1905); J. E. and P. A. Crowther (eds), *The Diary of Robert Sharp of South Cave: Life in a Yorkshire village 1812–1837* (Oxford: Oxford University Press, 1997), pp. 176 and 566.

14 J. C. Hotten, *A Dictionary of Modern Slang* (London: Hotten, 1859).

15 Sir V. Horsley and M. D. Sturge, *Alcohol and the Human Body* (London: Macmillan, 1909), pp. 79–80.

16 Royal College of Psychiatrists, *Alcohol and Alcoholism* (London: Tavistock Publications, 1979), p. 31.

17 M. Plant, *Women and Alcohol: Contemporary and historical perspectives* (London: Free Association Books, 1997), pp. 69–70.

18 J. Warner, 'Before there was "alcoholism": Lessons from the medieval experience with alcohol', *Contemporary Drug Problems* 19:3 (1992), pp. 409–29, on pp. 414–16.

19 This was Michael Dalton's *Countrey Justice*, which went through many editions, cited in J. A. Sharpe, *Crime in Seventeenth-century England: A county study* (London: Longman, 1983), p. 54.

20 G. W. E. Russell (ed.), *Sir Wilfrid Lawson: A memoir* (London: Smith, Elder and Co, 1909), p. 124.

21 M. and M. Plant, *Binge Britain: Alcohol and the national response* (Oxford: Oxford University Press, 2006), pp. viii–xii.

22 L. Radzinowicz, *A History of English Criminal Law and its Administration from 1750, vol. 3, Cross-Currents in the Movement for the Reform of the Police* (London: Stevens and Sons, 1956), p. 496 and also in *vol. 2, The Clash Between Private Initiative and Public Interest in the Enforcement of the Law* (London: Stevens and Sons, 1956), p. 437.

23 For psychology see R.G. Smart, 'Psychological theories of drinking' in J. S. Blocker, D. M. Fahey and I. R. Tyrrell (eds) *Alcohol and Temperance in Modern History. An International Encyclopedia, vol. 2* (Santa Barbara, Denver, Oxford: ABC Clio, 2003), pp. 503–5.

24 R. C. Latham and W. Matthews (eds), *The Diary of Samuel Pepys* (London: G. Bell and Sons, vol. 2, 1970), p. 87.

25 S. Walton, *Out of It: A cultural history of intoxication* (London: Hamish Hamilton, 2001), p. 204.
26 Levine, 'Vocabulary of drunkenness', p. 1039.
27 W. James, *The Varieties of Religious Experience: A study of human nature* (London: Longmans, Green, 1941), p. 387.
28 J. C. Nicholls, 'Gin Lane revisited: Intoxication and society in the gin epidemic', *Journal for Cultural Research*, 7:2 (2003), pp. 125–46, on pp. 138–40. See also with S. J. Owen (eds), *A Babel of Bottles: Drink, drinkers and drinking places in literature* (Sheffield: Sheffield Academic Press, 2000); P. Withington, 'Introduction: Cultures of intoxication', *Past and Present* (2014), Supplement 9, pp. 9–33, on p. 25.
29 J. Horsfall Turner (ed.), *The Rev. Oliver Heywood BA 1630–1702: His autobiography, diaries, anecdote and event books* (Brighouse: A. B. Bayes, 1881), vol. 2, p. 257.
30 F. Measham, 'The decline of ecstacy, the rise of "binge" drinking and the persistence of pleasure', *Probation Journal*, 51:4 (2004), pp. 309–26, on p. 318; 'The "Big Bang" approach to sessional drinking: Changing patterns of alcohol consumption amongst young people in North West England', *Addiction Research*, 4:3 (1996), pp. 283–99, on p. 297; F. Measham and K. Brain, '"Binge" drinking, British alcohol policy and the new culture of intoxication', *Crime, Media, Culture*, 1:3 (2005), pp. 262–83; S. Winlow and S. Hall, *Violent Night: Urban leisure and contemporary culture* (Oxford: Berg, 2006), p. 104.
31 M. Martinic and F. Measham, 'Extreme drinking', in M. Martinic and F. Measham (eds), *Swimming with Crocodiles: The cultures of extreme drinking* (Abingdon: Routledge, 2008), pp. 1–12, on pp. 8–9; K. J. Brain, *Youth, Alcohol, and the Emergence of the Post-Modern Alcohol Order* (London: Institute of Alcohol Studies, 2000), pp. 8–9.
32 T. Vander Ven, *Getting Wasted: Why college students drink too much and party so hard* (London: New York University Press, 2011), pp. 165–73.
33 K. Thomas, *Religion and the Decline of Magic: Studies in popular beliefs in sixteenth and seventeenth century England* (London: Weidenfeld and Nicolson, 1971), p. 19.
34 J. Warner, *Craze: Gin and debauchery in an age of reason* (London: Profile Books, 2003), pp. ix–x.
35 H. Medick, 'Plebeian culture in the transition to capitalism', in R. Samuel and G. Stedman Jones (eds), *Culture, Ideology and Politics: Essays for Eric Hobsbawm* (London: Routledge & Kegan Paul, 1982), pp. 84–113.
36 G. Hirschfelder, 'The myth of "misery alcoholism" in early industrial England: The example of Manchester', in S. Schmid and B. Schmidt-Haberkamp (eds), *Drink in the Eighteenth and Nineteenth Centuries* (London: Pickering & Chatto, 2014), pp. 91–101, on pp. 94–6.
37 MacAndrew and Edgerton, *Drunken Comportment*, pp. 96 and 169; P. Borsay, *A History of Leisure: The British experience since 1500* (Basingstoke: Palgrave Macmillan, 2006), pp. 79 and 226–8.
38 J. Walton, *The British Seaside: Holidays and resorts in the twentieth century* (Manchester: Manchester University Press, 2000), p. 96.
39 Borsay, *A History of Leisure*, p. 79.
40 *Ilkley Gazette*, 1 September 1900, p. 5.
41 T. M. Barnes Powell, 'Young women and alcohol: Issues of pleasure and power' (PhD dissertation, York University, 1997), pp. 188 and 191.
42 J. Nicholls, *The Politics of Alcohol: A history of the drink question in England* (Manchester: Manchester University Press, 2009), pp. 12–13.
43 L. Davison, 'Experiments in the social regulation of industry: Gin legislation, 1729–1751', in L. Davison, T. Hitchcock, T. Keirn and R. B. Shoemaker (eds), *Stilling the Grumbling Hive: The response to social problems in England 1688–1750* (Stroud: Alan Sutton, 1992), pp. 25–48, on pp. 32–3.

44 W. E. H. Lecky, *A History of England in the Eighteenth Century* (London: Longmans, Green, 2nd ed. vol. 6, 1887), p. 479.
45 Thomas Trotter, *An Essay, Medical, Philosophical, and Chemical, On Drunkenness, and Its Effects on the Human Body*, ed. R. Porter (London: Routledge, 1988), Porter's introduction, p. xi.
46 W. Schivelbusch, *Tastes of Paradise: A social history of spices, stimulants, and intoxicants* (New York: Pantheon, 1992), p. 153.
47 R. V. French, *Nineteen Centuries of Drink in England: A history* (London: National Temperance Publication Depot, 2nd ed., n. d.); M. M. Glatt, 'The English drink problem: Its rise and decline through the ages', *British Journal of Addiction*, 55:1 (1958), pp. 51–67.
48 P. Clark, *The English Alehouse: A social history 1200–1830* (London: Longman, 1983), pp. 108–10.
49 Nicholls, *The Politics of Alcohol*, pp. 16–17.
50 An approach suggested by B. Harrison, *Drink and the Victorians: The temperance question in England 1815–1872* (Keele: Keele University Press, 2nd ed. 1994), p. 24.
51 P. E. Kopperman, '"The cheapest pay": Alcohol abuse in the eighteenth-century British army', *Journal of Military History*, 60:3 (1996), pp. 445–70; A. R. Skelley, *The Victorian Army at Home: The recruitment and terms and conditions of the British regular, 1859–1899* (London: Croom Helm, 1977), pp. 128–50.
52 R. Hough, *Captain James Cook* (London: Hodder and Stoughton, 1994), p. 55.
53 E. S. de Beer (ed.), *The Diary of John Evelyn* (London: Oxford University Press, 1959), pp. 342 and 528.
54 Turner, *Oliver Heywood*, p. 273.
55 D. Vaisey (ed.), *The Diary of Thomas Turner 1754–1765* (Oxford: Oxford University Press, 1984), pp. 1 and 141.
56 C. B. Andrews (ed.), *The Torrington Diaries* (London: Eyre and Spottiswoode, 1934), vol. 1, p. 26; R. Nettel (ed.), *Journeys of a German in England: Carl Philip Moritz, a walking tour of England in 1782* (London: Eland Books, 1983), p. 214.
57 E. Cockayne, *Hubbub: Filth, noise and Stench in England 1600–1770* (New Haven: Yale University Press, 2007), p. 46; see also P. Withington, 'Renaissance drinking cultures in popular print', in J. Herring, C. Regan, D. Weinberg and P. Withington (eds), *Intoxication and Society: Problematic pleasures of drugs and alcohol* (Basingstoke: Palgrave Macmillan, 2013), pp. 135–52.
58 George Pryme, first Professor of Political Economy and MP for the borough, cited in French, *Nineteen Centuries of Drink*, p. 318.
59 A. Vickery, *The Gentleman's Daughter: Women's lives in Georgian England* (London: Yale University Press, 1998), p. 213.
60 C. Ludington, *The Politics of Wine in Britain: A new cultural history* (Basingstoke: Palgrave Macmillan, 2013), pp. 183–220.
61 F. Engels, *The Condition of the Working Class in England* (Oxford: Oxford University Press, 1993), p. 138.
62 F. Dostoevsky, *Summer Impressions*, trans. and ed. K. Fitzlyon (London: John Calder, 1955), pp. 60–1.
63 *Leeds Mercury* 28 November 1857, p. 7.
64 F. M. L. Thompson, *The Rise of Respectable Society* (London: Fontana, 1988), p. 261.
65 A. Shadwell, *Drink, Temperance and Legislation* (London: Longmans, Green, 1902), pp. 43–53 noted this evidence in an analysis of 'The decline of drunkenness' by an author, lecturer and social reformer who sought to put the point of view of the moderate drinker.
66 Report from the Committee on the State of the Police of the Metropolis; PP 1816 (510) V.1, pp. 42, 59, 68, 76, 86, 100, 110 and 186.

67 Select Committee on Inquiry into Drunkenness among Labouring Classes of the UK; PP 1834 (559), VIII.315, pp. 25 and 173–4; see also B. Harrison, 'Two roads to social reform: Francis Place and the "Drunken Committee" of 1834', *Historical Journal*, 11:2 (1968), pp. 272–300.

68 M. Thale (ed.) *The Autobiography of Francis Place 1771–1854* (Cambridge: Cambridge University Press, 1972), p. xxiv.

69 Report and Minutes of Evidence of the Select Committee of the House of Lords for inquiring into the Prevalence of Habits of Intemperance, and the Effects of recent Legislation; PP 1878–79 (113), X.469, pp. xxxiii–xxxv and xxxviii.

70 First Report of Her Majesty's Commissioners Appointed to Inquire into the Operation and Administration of the Laws Relating to the Sale of Intoxicating Liquors; PP 1899 [C.-9379], XXXV.1, p. 2.

71 J. Burnley, *Phases of Bradford Life* (Bradford: Thomas Brear, 1870), pp. 145–56; *Bradford Observer*, 18 January 1886, p. 6.

72 C. V. Butler, *Social Conditions in Oxford* (London: Sidgwick & Jackson, 1912), p. 218.

73 A. Paterson. *Across the Bridges OR Life by the South London River-Side* (London: Edward Arnold, 1911), p. 214.

74 Cited in R. Duncan, *Pubs and Patriots: The drink crisis in Britain during World War One* (Liverpool: Liverpool University Press, 2013), pp. 19–20.

75 4 James 1, c. 5.

76 On church courts see J. Addy, *Sin and Society in the Seventeenth Century* (London: Routledge, 1989), pp. 107–12; M. Ingram, *Church Courts, Sex and Marriage in England, 1570–1640* (Cambridge: Cambridge University Press, 1987), pp. 100 and 116–7; D. Carlile, '"A comon and sottish drunkard you have been" – prosecutions for drunkenness in the York courts c. 1660–1725', *York Historian*, 16 (1999), pp. 32–44. On criminal courts, see for example Sharpe, *Crime in Seventeenth-century England*, pp. 54–5 and 183; D. Underdown, *Fire from Heaven: The life of an English town in the seventeenth century* (London: Harper Collins, 1992), pp. 72 and 104.

77 C. Emsley, *The English Police: A political and social history* (London: Longman, 2nd ed. 1996), p. 5.

78 P. Jennings, 'Policing drunkenness in England and Wales from the late eighteenth century to the First World War', *Social History of Alcohol and Drugs*, 26:1 (2012), pp. 69–92, on p. 72.

79 Based upon the Annual Judicial Statistics, England and Wales; PP.

80 Select Committee into Drunkenness; PP 1834 (559), p. 437; Return of the Number of Persons taken into Custody for Drunkenness and Disorderly Conduct by Metropolitan and City of London Police 1831–43; PP 1844 (217), XXXIX.265; Select Committee of the House of Lords on the Bill for regulating the Sale of Beer and Other Liquors on the Lord's Day; PP 1847–48 (501), XVI.615, p. 16; the figures from the Annual Judicial Statistics from 1857 are set out in Jennings, 'Policing drunkenness', pp. 79–82.

81 Judicial Statistics, England and Wales, 1857; PP 1857–58 (2407), LVII.383, p. ix.

82 Old Bailey Proceedings Online, trial of George Russell, t18880702-700, at www.oldbaileyonline.org, version 7.0 [accessed 13 June 2011]; Jennings, 'Policing drunkenness', pp. 73–9.

83 G. N. Woolnough, 'The policing of petty crime in Victorian Cumbria' (PhD dissertation, Keele University, 2013), pp. 219–21 and 360–3.

84 B. S. Godfrey, D. J. Cox and S. Farrell, *Criminal Lives: Family life, employment and offending* (Oxford: Oxford University Press, 2007), pp. 54–5.

85 For policing see also S. Petrow, *Policing Morals: The Metropolitan Police and the Home Office 1870–1914* (Oxford: Clarendon Press, 1994), pp. 213–20; for an assertion of faith in the utility of police statistics for this question see Shadwell, *Drink, Temperance and Legislation*, pp. 57–65 and for a lack of it, or scepticism, see Thompson, *The Rise of Respectable Society*, p. 330; D. Beckingham, 'Geographies

of drink culture in Liverpool: Lessons from the drink capital of nineteenth-century England', *Drugs: Education, prevention and policy,* 15:3 (2008), pp. 305–13; V. A. C. Gatrell, 'The decline of theft and violence in Victorian and Edwardian England', in V. A. C. Gatrell, B. Lenman, and G. Parker (eds) *Crime and the Law: The social history of crime in Western Europe since 1500* (London: Europa, 1980), pp. 238–370, on p. 291.

86 J. Pinfold, 'Dandy rats at play: the Liverpudlian middle-classes and horse-racing in the nineteenth century', in M. Huggins and J. A. Mangan (eds), *Disreputable Pleasures: Less virtuous Victorians at play* (London: Frank Cass, 2004), pp. 57–79, on pp. 64–5.

87 Harrison, *Drink and the Victorians,* p. 376.

88 G. B. Wilson, 'A statistical review of the variations during the last twenty years in the consumption of intoxicating drinks in the United Kingdom, and in the convictions for offences connected with intoxication, with a discussion of the causes to which these variations may be ascribed',' *Journal of the Royal Statistical Society,* 75 (1912), pp. 183–247, on pp. 225–7.

89 Butler, *Social Conditions in Oxford,* p. 216; North Riding Constabulary Charge Book, Hang Division of Hang East Petty Sessional District, commencing 1 January 1910, Ripon Museum Trust.

90 Return; PP 1844 (217); Abstract of return of the number of persons taken into custody for drunkenness and disorderly conduct in each city and town in the United Kingdom in each year 1841 to 1851; PP 1852–53 (531), LXXXI.295; Judicial Statistics, 1857–1913.

91 L. Zedner, *Women, Crime and Custody in Victorian England* (Oxford: Clarendon Press, 1991), pp. 228–9.

92 Sir L. Radzinowicz, *A History of English Criminal Law and its Administration, vol. 5, The Emergence of Penal Policy* (London: Stevens and Sons, 1986), p. 301; T. Holmes, 'Habitual inebriates', *Contemporary Review,* 75 (May, 1899), pp. 740–6; *Times,* 26 August 1890, p. 10; D. James, '"Drunk and riotous in Pontypridd": Women, the police courts and the press in South Wales coalfield society, 1899–1914', *Llafur,* 8:3 (2002), pp. 5–12, on p. 11.

93 A. Davies, *Leisure, Gender and Poverty: Working-class culture in Salford and Manchester, 1900–1939* (Buckingham: Open University Press, 1992), pp. 70–2.

94 T. R. Gourvish and R. G. Wilson, *The British Brewing Industry 1830–1980* (Cambridge: Cambridge University Press, 1994), pp. 335–9, 358 and 363–9; G. P. Williams and G. T. Brake, *Drink in Great Britain 1900–1979* (London: B. Edsall, 1980), p. 263, in a chapter which surveys the whole question of drunkenness from 1900 to 1939.

95 Royal Commission on Licensing (England and Wales) Report; PP 1931–2 (Cmd 3988), XI, pp. 13 and 22.

96 Sir H. Llewellyn Smith, *The New Survey of London Life and Labour, vol. 9, Life and Leisure* (London: P. S King & Son, 1935), pp. 272–4.

97 R, Hoggart, *The Uses of Literacy* (Harmondsworth: Penguin, 1958), pp. 94–6.

98 S. Inwood, 'Policing London's morals: The metropolitan police and popular culture, 1829–1850', *The London Journal,* 15:2 (1990), pp. 129–46; for this point see also Jennings, 'Policing drunkenness'.

99 Harrison, *Drink and the Victorians,* p. 41.

100 B. Thom, *Dealing with Drink: Alcohol policy and social reform from treatment to management* (London: Free Association Books, 1999), pp. 85–104.

101 *Drunkenness among Persons Aged under 21 in England and Wales 1950–1957, Fifth Annual Report* (London: Christian Economic and Social Research Foundation, 1958), pp. 6 and 14; *Drunkenness among Persons Aged under 21 in England and Wales 1950–1955* (London: Economic Research Council, 1956), p. 5.

102 Nicholls, *The Politics of Alcohol,* pp. 216–17; B. Osgerby, *Youth in Britain since 1945* (Oxford: Blackwell, 1998), pp. 162–3.

103 P. Chatterton and R. Hollands, 'The London of the North? Youth cultures, urban change and nightlife', in R. Unsworth and J. Stillwell (eds), *Twenty-first Century Leeds: Geographies of a regional city* (Leeds: Leeds University Press, 2004), pp. 265–90, on p. 277; J. E. McGregor, *Drink and the City: Alcohol and alcohol problems in urban UK since the 1950s* (Nottingham: Nottingham University Press, 2012), pp. 156–7; P. Chatterton and R. Hollands, *Changing Our 'Toon': Youth, nightlife and urban change in Newcastle* (Newcastle: University of Newcastle, 2001), p. 20.
104 Winlow and Hall, *Violent Night*, pp. 176–7.
105 V. Berridge, *Demons: Our changing attitudes to alcohol, tobacco, and drugs* (Oxford: Oxford University Press, 2013), pp. 233–4; K. Day, B. Gough and M. McFadden, '"Warning!: alcohol can seriously damage your feminine health": A discourse analysis of recent British newspaper coverage of women and drinking', *Feminist Media Studies*, 4:2 (2004), pp. 165–83.
106 N. Stratford and W. Roth, *The 1998 Youth Lifestyles Survey: Technical report* (London: National Centre for Social Research, 1999).
107 R. Engineer, A. Phillips, J. Thompson and J. Nicholls, *Drunk and Disorderly: A qualitative study of binge drinking among 18 to 24 year olds* (London: Home Office Research, Development and Statistics Directorate, 2003).
108 D. Hobbs, P. Hadfield, S. Lister and S. Winlow, *Bouncers: Violence and governance in the night–time economy* (Oxford: Oxford University Press, 2003), pp. 37 and 46.
109 B. Harrison and B. Trinder, *Drink and Sobriety in an Early Victorian Country Town: Banbury 1830–1860* (London: Longmans, *English Historical Review* Supplement 4, 1969), p. 1.

## Bibliography

Addy, J., *Sin and Society in the Seventeenth Century* (London: Routledge, 1989).
Barnes Powell, T. M., 'Young women and alcohol: Issues of pleasure and power' (Dphil dissertation, York University, 1997).
Bars, J. A., 'Defining murder in Victorian London: An analysis of cases 1862–1892' (PhD dissertation, Oxford University, 1995).
Beckingham, D., 'Geographies of drink culture in Liverpool: Lessons from the drink capital of nineteenth-century England', *Drugs: Education, prevention and policy*, 15:3 (2008), pp. 305–13.
Berridge, V., *Demons: Our changing attitudes to alcohol, tobacco, and drugs* (Oxford: Oxford University Press, 2013).
Borsay, P., *A History of Leisure: The British experience since 1500* (Basingstoke: Palgrave Macmillan, 2006).
Brain, K. J., *Youth, Alcohol, and the Emergence of the Post-Modern Alcohol Order* (London: Institute of Alcohol Studies, 2000).
Carlile, D., '"A comon and sottish drunkard you have been" – prosecutions for drunkenness in the York courts c. 1660–1725', *York Historian*, 16 (1999), pp. 32–44.
Chatterton, P. and Hollands, R., *Changing Our 'Toon': Youth, nightlife and urban change in Newcastle* (Newcastle: University of Newcastle, 2001).
—, 'The London of the North? Youth cultures, urban change and nightlife', in R. Unsworth and J. Stillwell (eds), *Twenty-first Century Leeds: Geographies of a regional city* (Leeds: Leeds University Press, 2004), pp. 265–90.
Clark, P., *The English Alehouse: A social history 1200–1830* (London: Longman, 1983).
Cockayne, E., *Hubbub: Filth, noise and stench in England 1600–1770* (New Haven, CT: Yale University Press, 2007).

Davies, A., *Leisure, Gender and Poverty: Working-class culture in Salford and Manchester, 1900–1939* (Buckingham: Open University Press, 1992).

Davison, L., 'Experiments in the social regulation of industry: Gin legislation, 1729–1751', in L. Davison, T. Hitchcock, T. Keirn and R. B. Shoemaker (eds), *Stilling the Grumbling Hive: The response to social problems in England 1688–1750* (Stroud: Alan Sutton, 1992), pp. 25–48.

Day, K., Gough, B. and McFadden, M., '"Warning!: alcohol can seriously damage your feminine health": A discourse analysis of recent British newspaper coverage of women and drinking', *Feminist Media Studies*, 4:2 (2004), pp. 165–83.

Duncan, R., *Pubs and Patriots: The drink crisis in Britain during World War One* (Liverpool: Liverpool University Press, 2013).

Emsley, C., *The English Police: A political and social history* (London: Longman, 2nd ed. 1996).

Gatrell, V. A. C., 'The decline of theft and violence in Victorian and Edwardian England', in V. A. C. Gatrell, B. Lenman, and G. Parker (eds), *Crime and the Law: The social history of crime in Western Europe since 1500* (London: Europa, 1980), pp. 238–370.

Glatt, M. M., 'The English drink problem: Its rise and decline through the ages', *British Journal of Addiction*, 55:1 (1958), pp. 51–67.

Godfrey, B. S., Cox, D. J. and Farrell, S., *Criminal Lives: Family life, employment and offending* (Oxford: Oxford University Press, 2007).

Gourvish, T. R. and Wilson, R. G., *The British Brewing Industry 1830–1980* (Cambridge: Cambridge University Press, 1994).

Handler, P., 'Intoxication and criminal responsibility in England, 1819–1920', *Oxford Journal of Legal Studies*, 33:2 (2013), pp. 243–62.

Harrison, B., 'Two roads to social reform: Francis Place and the "Drunken Committee" of 1834', *Historical Journal*, 11:2 (1968), pp. 272–300.

—, *Drink and the Victorians: The temperance question in England 1815–1872* (Keele: Keele University Press, 2nd ed. 1994).

Harrison, B. and Trinder, B., *Drink and Sobriety in an Early Victorian Country Town: Banbury 1830–1860*, (London: Longmans, *English Historical Review* Supplement 4, 1969).

Hirschfelder, G., 'The myth of "misery alcoholism" in early industrial England: The example of Manchester', in S. Schmid and B. Schmidt-Haberkamp (eds), *Drink in the Eighteenth and Nineteenth Centuries* (London: Pickering & Chatto, 2014), pp. 91–101.

Hobbs, D., Hadfield, P., Lister, S. and Winlow, S., *Bouncers: Violence and governance in the night-time economy* (Oxford: Oxford University Press, 2003).

Hoggart, R., *The Uses of Literacy* (Harmondsworth: Penguin, 1958).

Holmes, T., 'Habitual inebriates', *Contemporary Review*, 75 (May, 1899), pp. 740–6.

Horsley, Sir V. and Sturge, M. D., *Alcohol and the Human Body* (London: Macmillan, 1909).

Hough, R., *Captain James Cook* (London: Hodder and Stoughton, 1994).

Ingram, M., *Church Courts, Sex and Marriage in England, 1570–1640* (Cambridge: Cambridge University Press, 1987).

Inwood, S., 'Policing London's morals: The metropolitan police and popular culture, 1829–1850', *The London Journal*, 15:2 (1990), pp. 129–46.

James, D., '"Drunk and riotous in Pontypridd": Women, the police courts and the press in South Wales coalfield society, 1899–1914', *Llafur*, 8:3 (2002), pp. 5–12.

James, W., *The Varieties of Religious Experience: A study of human nature* (London: Longmans, Green, 1941).
Jennings, P., 'Policing drunkenness in England and Wales from the late eighteenth century to the First World War', *Social History of Alcohol and Drugs*, 26:1 (2012), pp. 69–92.
Jones, G. Stedman, 'The "cockney" and the nation, 1780–1988', in D. Feldman and G. Stedman Jones(eds), *Metropolis London: Histories and representations since 1800* (London: Routledge, 1989), pp. 272–324.
Kopperman, P. E., '"The cheapest pay": Alcohol abuse in the eighteenth-century British army', *Journal of Military History*, 60:3 (1996), pp. 445–70.
Lecky, W. E. H., *A History of England in the Eighteenth Century* (London: Longmans, Green, 2nd ed. vol. 6, 1887).
Levine, H. G., 'The vocabulary of drunkenness', *Journal of Studies on Alcohol*, 42:11 (1981), pp. 1038–51.
Ludington, C., *The Politics of Wine in Britain: A new cultural history* (Basingstoke: Palgrave Macmillan, 2013).
MacAndrew, C. and Edgerton, R. B., *Drunken Comportment: A social explanation* (Chicago: Aldine, 1969).
McGregor, J. E., *Drink and the City: Alcohol and alcohol problems in urban UK since the 1950s* (Nottingham: Nottingham University Press, 2012).
Martinic, M. and Measham, F., 'Extreme drinking', in M. Martinic and F. Measham (eds), *Swimming with Crocodiles: The cultures of extreme drinking* (Abingdon: Routledge, 2008), pp. 1–12.
Measham, F., 'The "Big Bang" approach to sessional drinking: Changing patterns of alcohol consumption amongst young people in North West England', *Addiction Research*, 4:3 (1996), pp. 283–99.
—, 'The decline of ecstacy, the rise of 'binge' drinking and the persistence of pleasure', *Probation Journal*, 51:4 (2004), pp. 309–26.
Measham, F. and Brain, K., '"Binge" drinking, British alcohol policy and the new culture of intoxication', *Crime, Media, Culture*, 1:3 (2005), pp. 262–83.
Medick, H., 'Plebeian culture in the transition to capitalism', in R. Samuel and G. Stedman Jones (eds), *Culture, Ideology and Politics: Essays for Eric Hobsbawm* (London: Routledge & Kegan Paul, 1982), pp. 84–113.
Mendelsohn, O., *Nicely, Thank You (Drunk 2000) Times: A frolic with some synonyms* (Melbourne: The National Press PTY., 1971).
Nicholls, J. C., 'Gin Lane revisited: Intoxication and society in the gin epidemic', *Journal for Cultural Research*, 7:2 (2003), pp. 125–46.
—, *The Politics of Alcohol: A history of the drink question in England* (Manchester: Manchester University Press, 2009).
Nicholls, J. and Owen, S. J., (eds), *A Babel of Bottles: Drink, drinkers and drinking places in literature* (Sheffield: Sheffield Academic Press, 2000).
Osgerby, B., *Youth in Britain since 1945* (Oxford: Blackwell, 1998).
Petrow, S., *Policing Morals: The Metropolitan Police and the Home Office 1870–1914* (Oxford: Clarendon Press, 1994).
Pinfold, J., 'Dandy rats at play: The Liverpudlian middle-classes and horse-racing in the nineteenth century', in M. Huggins and J. A. Mangan (eds), *Disreputable Pleasures: Less virtuous Victorians at play* (London: Frank Cass, 2004), pp. 57–79.
Plant, M., *Women and Alcohol: Contemporary and historical perspectives* (London: Free Association Books, 1997).

Plant, M. and M., *Binge Britain: Alcohol and the national response* (Oxford: Oxford University Press, 2006).
Rabin, D., 'Drunkenness and responsibility for crime in the eighteenth century', *Journal of British Studies*, 44:3 (2005), pp. 457–77.
Radzinowicz, L., *A History of English Criminal Law and its Administration from 1750, vol. 2, The Clash Between Private Initiative and Public Interest in the Enforcement of the Law* (London: Stevens and Sons, 1956).
—, *A History of English Criminal Law and its Administration from 1750, vol. 3, Cross-Currents in the Movement for the Reform of the Police* (London: Stevens and Sons, 1956).
—, *A History of English Criminal Law and its Administration, vol. 5, The Emergence of Penal Policy* (London: Stevens and Sons, 1986).
Russell, G. W. E. (ed.), *Sir Wilfrid Lawson: A memoir* (London: Smith, Elder and Co, 1909).
Schivelbusch, W., *Tastes of Paradise: A social history of spices, stimulants, and intoxicants* (New York: Pantheon, 1992).
Shadwell, A., *Drink, Temperance and Legislation* (London: Longmans, Green, 1902).
Sharpe, J. A., *Crime in Seventeenth-century England: A county study* (London: Longman, 1983).
Skelley, A. R., *The Victorian Army at Home: The recruitment and terms and conditions of the British regular, 1859–1899* (London: Croom Helm, 1977).
Smart, R. G., 'Psychological theories of drinking', in J. S. Blocker, D. M. Fahey and I. R. Tyrrell (eds), *Alcohol and Temperance in Modern History. An International Encyclopedia*, (Santa Barbara, Denver, Oxford: ABC Clio, 2 vols, 2003), pp. 503–5.
Thom, B., *Dealing with Drink: Alcohol policy and social reform from treatment to management* (London: Free Association Books, 1999).
Thomas, K., *Religion and the Decline of Magic: Studies in popular beliefs in sixteenth and seventeenth century England* (London: Weidenfeld and Nicolson, 1971).
Thompson, F. M. L., *The Rise of Respectable Society* (London: Fontana, 1988).
Tlusty, B. A., 'Defining "drunk" in early modern Germany', *Contemporary Drug Problems*, 21:3 (1994), pp. 427–51.
Underdown, D., *Fire from Heaven: The life of an English town in the seventeenth century* (London: Harper Collins, 1992).
Ven, T. Vander, *Getting Wasted: Why college students drink too much and party so hard* (London: New York University Press, 2011).
Vickery, A., *The Gentleman's Daughter: Women's lives in Georgian England* (London: Yale University Press, 1998).
Walton, J., *The British Seaside: Holidays and resorts in the twentieth century* (Manchester: Manchester University Press, 2000).
Walton, S., *Out of It: A cultural history of intoxication* (London: Hamish Hamilton, 2001).
Warner, J., 'Before there was "alcoholism": Lessons from the medieval experience with alcohol', *Contemporary Drug Problems* 19:3 (1992), pp. 409–29.
—, *Craze: Gin and debauchery in an age of reason* (London: Profile Books, 2003).
Wiener, M. J., *Men of Blood: Violence, manliness and criminal justice in Victorian England* (Cambridge: Cambridge University Press, 2004).

Williams, J. P. and Brake, G. T., *Drink in Great Britain 1900–1979* (London: B. Edsall, 1980).

Wilson, G. B., 'A statistical review of the variations during the last twenty years in the consumption of intoxicating drinks in the United Kingdom, and in the convictions for offences connected with intoxication, with a discussion of the causes to which these variations may be ascribed', *Journal of the Royal Statistical Society*, 75 (1912), pp. 183–247.

—, *Alcohol and the Nation: A contribution to the study of the liquor problem in the United Kingdom from 1800 to 1935* (London: Nicholson and Watson, 1940).

Winlow, S. and Hall, S., *Violent Night: Urban leisure and contemporary culture* (Oxford: Berg, 2006).

Withington, P., 'Renaissance drinking cultures in popular print', in J. Herring, C. Regan, D. Weinberg and P. Withington (eds), *Intoxication and Society: Problematic pleasures of drugs and alcohol* (Basingstoke: Palgrave Macmillan, 2013), pp. 135–52.

Withington, P., 'Introduction: Cultures of intoxication', *Past and Present* (2014), Supplement 9, pp. 9–33.

Woolnough, G. N., 'The policing of petty crime in Victorian Cumbria' (PhD dissertation, Keele University, 2013).

Zedner, L., *Women, Crime and Custody in Victorian England* (Oxford: Clarendon Press, 1991).

# 6 Anti-drink

## Introduction

Clearly the drunken state, whilst common and often actively sought throughout history, has also invited condemnation and punishment. This chapter begins with a further examination of the nature of that condemnation of drunkenness in early modern England, before charting the historical development of opposition more broadly to drinking and drinking behaviours. It aims to explore how, as suggested by the US sociologist and historian Joseph Gusfield, drinking behaviours came to be seen as social problems historically and that the ways in which they were conceived as problems varied in different historical circumstances.[1] It will be concerned with the origins and the nature of such opposition to drink, with how those who held such views voiced and enacted their opposition and with what success.

## An 'odious and loathsome Sin' and 'intolerable Hurts and Troubles'

In early modern England drunkenness was widely and vehemently condemned in a torrent of religious texts, medical and educational tracts, advice literature, moral poetry and prose, history, political treatises and ballads. First and foremost, it was a sin. The Bible was quite clear. In its earliest references to the drunken state the consequences for Noah are the exposure of his nakedness and the curse upon his son Ham, and for Lot the committing of incest with his daughters. And in the New Testament Paul assures the Corinthians that drunkards shall not inherit the Kingdom of God.[2] Not only was it a sin itself, although medieval moralists had categorized it as a subset of gluttony, but other sins and abuses might be committed under its influence. The Puritan Philip Stubbes wrote in *The Anatomy of Abuses* of the 'brute beast' who 'in his drunkenness killeth his friend, revileth his lover, discloseth secrets and regardeth no man'.[3] As the 'beastly' epithet makes clear, drunkenness robbed man of the three faculties which in the early modern world view distinguished him as human: reason, speech and conscience. Thus the most common imagery of the drunken state depicted man as animal. The frontispiece to Thomas Heywood's *Philocothonista, or, the Drunkard, Opened, Dissected, and Anatomized* of 1635 featured a tableau of different man-beast hybrids (Figure 6.1). Similarly,

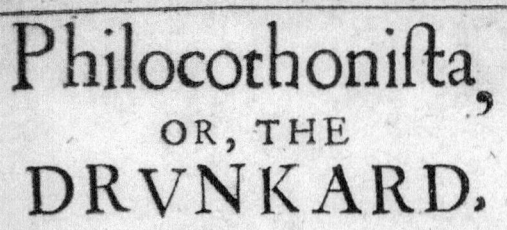

*Figure 6.1* The drunkard as animal: Thomas Heywood's *Philocothonista*.
Source: Courtesy of the Bodleian Libraries, The University of Oxford, Douce HH 227.

Thomas Young's *England's Bane: or, the Description of Drunkenness* of 1617 listed nine stages of excess, each corresponding to an animal, like 'Lyon-drunke' or 'Goate-drunke'.[4]

As sinners, drunks endangered their own souls, but their drinking also posed more corporeal dangers. James Hart, a Northamptonshire physician with 'puritan tendencies', provided in a text of 1633 a doleful catalogue of the consequences of heavy drinking. These comprised those on the drinker's body, including red and watery eyes, a copper nose, carbuncles, rotten teeth, 'filthy and stinking belching' and vomiting; on his health, including fevers, inflammations, gout, epilepsy and apoplexy (stroke) to sudden death; and on his mind, including nightmares and loss of understanding and memory.[5] In the words of another preacher, it was 'a voluntary madness'.[6] But drunks posed a threat also to society, again in Hart's terms, 'swil-bols, tos-pots' and their 'pot companions' swore, were quarrelsome, slanderous, back-biting, murderous, unclean and adulterous, cheated neighbours, wives and children and ignored the dictates of deference by failing to distinguish between superiors and inferiors and to give the former their proper respect. In these ways, in fostering crime and disorder and in undermining family life by failing to work and provide for dependents, drunks posed a threat to the whole social order.[7] And in the drunkenness of women the gender order of society was potentially undermined. As one writer put it in his *A Warning to Drunkards*, 'it is a greater shame to see a drunken woman, than a drunken man'; as 'shamefac'dness and sobriety' were 'an ornament to a woman' so 'impudence and intemperance' disgraced her.[8]

The sinfulness of drunkenness and the social and economic threat it posed were encapsulated in the preamble to the statute of 1606 which created a criminal offence of being drunk:

> Whereas the loathsome and odious Sin of Drunkenness is of late grown into common Use within this Realm, being the Root and Foundation of many other enormous Sins, as Bloodshed, Stabbing, Murder, Swearing, Fornication, Adultery, and such like, to the Great Dishonour of God, and of our Nation, the Overthrow of many good Arts and manual Trades, the Disabling of divers Workmen, and the General Impoverishing of many good Subjects, abusively wasting the good Creatures of God.[9]

This condemnation was paralleled in denunciations of the sites of plebeian heavy drinking: the alehouse, tipling house and tavern. As with the criminalization of drunkenness so statutes of 1552 and 1553 had responded to the 'intolerable Hurts and Troubles to the Commonwealth of this Realm' arising from 'Abuses and Disorders' in the first two and the 'evil Rule' present in the latter.[10] Hostility to the alehouse and tipling house in particular had been growing for decades amongst the higher ranks in society. As perceived sites of drunkenness, disorder, crime, sexual licence and subversion they represented multiple challenges: to religion and morality, law and order, family life and the proper functioning of the economy – apprentices learning their trades, workers working or servants serving. They needed to be contained and controlled.[11]

What underlay these denunciations of drunkenness and drinking places? For although they were not new (such condemnation can be found in the medieval period),[12] they were imbued with greater ferocity and urgency in the sixteenth and early seventeenth centuries. This was the product of the intellectual changes associated with the Reformation and the socially disruptive effects of population growth and economic upheaval which were manifested in widespread poverty and vagrancy, when to some contemporaries, as Keith Wrightson put it, 'it appeared that the very bonds of society were endangered'.[13] With the former came an emphasis on the individual pursuit of a godly life, which included not only proper religious observance but also the cultivation of virtues like thrift and sobriety. With the latter, and linked to that godly life, came 'a new insistence on the duty of every man to work', the product in turn of a novel awareness of the economic importance of labour.[14]

Two strands of opposition to drink are clear. The first was that in the form of drunkenness it was sinful, vicious or immoral. The second was that heavy drinking posed a range of threats to the country's social and economic well-being. The alehouse as a site of such drinking, and its associated adverse consequences, shared in the condemnation. These important features of subsequent anti-drink sentiment and argument were thus already well established by the seventeenth century. There was no sense yet, however, that drinking *per se* was to be opposed, nor was there any denial of the proper function of drinking places as necessary for legitimate refreshment and lodging.

For the moment condemnation followed the existing discourses. Societies for the Reformation of Manners, active chiefly in London from the 1690s to their decline in the 1720s, legitimized their campaign by linking the fate of the nation to the morality of the people, although even in their most active year of 1708 fewer than 5 per cent of the prosecutions initiated were for drunkenness and they were not generally supported by magistrates.[15] In fact, as we saw in the previous chapter, the relative scarcity of prosecutions for drunkenness persisted through the eighteenth century. Alehouses, similarly, continued to be condemned. A piece, for example, in the *Gentleman's Magazine* in September 1736 claimed that no fewer than 120,000 public houses (a huge exaggeration of their number) were corrupting and debauching the nation, ruining 'honest labourers' and fostering crime. Another essay three years later linked disturbances in the Wiltshire textile trade to the proliferation of alehouses there.[16] In the case of alehouses, and in contrast to drunkenness, as will be seen in the next chapter, this did have some practical consequence in contributing to an actual reduction in their number.

## Gin

Such concerns found expression again most significantly in the response to the heavy consumption of gin in the early part of the eighteenth century. Anxiety focused upon the threat it posed to the health of the people and consequently their utility as workers, soldiers and mothers; upon the increase in crime of all kinds and a general disrespect for authority; and on the undermining of home and family life. Taken together the result for the nation would be moral, economic and military decline. These anxieties were vividly expressed in contemporary works such as physician Stephen Hales's *Friendly Admonition to the Drinkers of Brandy* or clergyman Thomas Wilson's *Distilled Spirituous Liquors the Bane of the Nation*. Hales, like his sixteenth- and seventeenth-century predecessors, set out the destructive effects of the poison on both the physical and mental health of the individual, as well as its creation of poverty and crime. The inevitable outcome would be the final ruin of a great nation. Wilson likewise noted its malignant effects on the human body and its deleterious social and economic consequences, fearing within a generation insufficient people to do 'servile offices' or 'cultivate our lands'. Both men noted particularly its consumption by women and both highlighted the consequences for their unborn children, destined, as Wilson saw them, to be weak, sickly and inheriting the mother's love of drink.[17] Hogarth's famous creation of *Gin Lane* expressed all those concerns. In his publicity for the print (and its companion piece *Beer Street*) the artist explained that the aim was 'to reform some reigning Vices peculiar to the lower Class of People, in hopes to render them of more extensive use'.[18] And its central image, of the child falling from the arms of the drunken woman, remains the most powerful expression of how contemporaries viewed gin's effects (Figure 6.2).

Much of this echoed earlier discourses on drunkenness and its consequences, and whilst the special concern over women's drinking may have exhibited a new intensity, it was not itself new. In a similar way gin served to push forward a debate, which also had seventeenth-century origins, on the nature of drunkenness as some sort of addiction or disease. In a work of 1619, for example, it was described as a 'dropsilike disease' and 'almost incurable'. It was still a sin, but one to which you could become addicted, or enslaved, to use the common contemporary way of putting it. One must be wary, however, of falling into anachronism. To become so enslaved was still then a moral failing.[19] Becoming an addict was something one did to oneself, which differs from the modern idea that emphasizes addiction as something that happens to an individual (one becomes addicted). Similarly, earlier conceptions were not necessarily medical, as anything could be termed a disease, like gambling.[20] The moral aspect remained important even as over the course of the eighteenth century a specifically medical understanding developed of heavy drinking as an addictive disorder, even a disease. Thinking upon these lines culminated with the publication in 1804 of naval surgeon Thomas Trotter's *Essay Medical, Philosophical, and Chemical, on Drunkenness and its Effects on the Human Body*, in which he argued that drunkenness was a disease of the mind and consequently fell firmly within the medical domain.[21] Although later temperance reformers continued to emphasize their moral rather than medical influences, the work of Trotter and others, in particular in highlighting the special danger of spirits and the efficacy of abstinence, was an important preparation.[22]

152    *Anti-drink*

*Figure 6.2* Gin Lane by William Hogarth, 1751.
Source: © The Trustees of the British Museum.

## Towards temperance

In the long history of condemnation of the drinking habits and haunts of the labouring population the final quarter of the eighteenth century seems to have been a period, as Peter Clark expressed it, 'with clear signs of renewed anxiety'.[23] For clerical magistrate Henry Zouch, public houses were licensed receptacles for rogues, vagabonds, night-poachers, and dangerous persons of all kinds. It is here that the scanty earnings of the manufacturer and labourer, which ought to be applied to the maintenance of their families at home, are improvidently squandered away.[24]

He went on to link them to the rising level of the poor rate in a further expression of the concerns fuelled by the perceived effects of rising population and economic distress, which fed into the contemporary moves to 'improve', to use their phrase, policing arrangements that we saw in the previous chapter in relation to drunks.

The presence of clergymen amongst the anxious alerts us to the importance of religious movements in the origins of temperance. The Reverend Zouch was an evangelical, a member of a group who were concerned to improve the 'manners' of both the upper and lower classes. Its best-known exponent, William Wilberforce, was instrumental in George III's 1787 Royal Proclamation against 'vice, profaneness and immorality'.[25] Such proclamations were issued by most monarchs, but this one seems to have had a real impact. Although the movement for the reformation of manners did not focus particularly on drinking and drinking places, and its supporters did not practice personal abstinence, the humanitarian impulse which it reflected, and which was also expressed in campaigns against irreligion, gambling, cruel sports and slavery, was in Brian Harrison's view the parent of the later temperance movement. Further, it 'encouraged in the British aristocracy an involvement in moral crusading' essential to its eventual launch and their embrace of a moral code better designed to bolster its legitimacy in turbulent times.[26] Also important were the 'techniques of agitation', which it perfected in its various campaigns.[27] Finally, its stress on the individual and his conscience, on the virtues of self-denial and on the existence of human depravity also helped to lay the ground ideologically for the movement.[28]

These sentiments were shared by Dissenters. Methodism had from the first been anti-spirits and anti-excess. Wesley, in his *Rules of the United Societies*, adopted in 1743, had countenanced their consumption only 'in cases of extreme necessity' and forbade members to buy and sell them.[29] Many Quakers also abstained individually from drinking spirits and condemned drunkenness. In one case, Joseph Ward from near Penistone in the West Riding of Yorkshire travelled through England and Wales to further this cause. To discourage 'that great sin of drunkenness, which is the inlet to many other evils' he visited with a colleague the public houses of, for example, Barnsley and neighbourhood in December 1816 to persuade their hosts not to supply men with more drink than was necessary and to accept that by allowing drinking to excess they were equally culpable in the sight of God, in which endeavour they were apparently received 'civilly'.[30]

In addition to religious echoes of seventeenth-century puritanism there was an intensification of that period's insistence on 'the duty of every man to work'. Where industrialization in the form of foundry or factory developed, so were traditional drinking practices commonly curtailed, including the popular adherence to Saint Monday. But this was a slow process, taking well into the nineteenth century, as the transition from home and workshop, where those practices persisted, to factory-based production was itself slow and uneven.[31] Nevertheless, the heightened attack on wastefulness of time and idleness did prefigure temperance concerns. A sober and disciplined workforce was clearly to be desired by employers. Harrison noted in this context the connection between textile manufacturing and the anti-spirits movement. Yet, as he also affirmed, it is wise to be cautious about any simple causal link between industrialization and temperance reform. Whilst it was indeed strong in Lancashire and Yorkshire, it was to be well supported in, for example, rural Lincolnshire and north Wales, too. Moreover, early teetotallers were sometimes troublesome to employers – for example, in causing disputes with their fellow workers by not cooperating in drinking customs.[32]

The class dimension, then, is more complex than any simple link between temperance and the needs of employers. For the expanding middle classes it was a vehicle both for the expression of their own self-worth, in ideals of hard work and sobriety, and a response to the dangers they saw from the labouring masses of the growing towns and cities. These dangers were all too real to them, witnessing as they did the social and political upheavals of the late eighteenth and the first half of the nineteenth centuries. But an important section of the working classes also, as we have seen, increasingly perceived it to be in their interest. The desire for self-improvement and the related ideal of respectability were to lead many to temperance in the full sense of abstinence and over the century many more to forsake heavy drinking for the pleasures of moderate enjoyment.

Finally, and providing an essential support to any programme of abstinence from alcohol, real alternatives were ever more readily available over the second half of the century: tea and coffee, especially the former, soft drinks and, although its provision was protracted and uneven, clean and safe drinking water.

## Temperance

Although, it must be said at the outset, most people continued to drink, and collectively the nation still drank a lot, the nineteenth century was witness to a well-supported and well-organized temperance movement, which argued and campaigned for total abstinence from alcoholic drinks and later for measures which would prohibit their sale. But more broadly, and in the end more importantly, it saw the widespread acceptance of a generalized temperance sentiment, if I might put it that way, which on the one hand saw drink as an especial problem which society faced and must deal with, hence the Drink Question or Drink or Liquor Problem, as it was variously characterized, and on the other was expressed in personal beliefs and habits of moderation. Overall, as Henry Yeomans fittingly expressed it, the century witnessed 'a new chapter in Britain's relationship with alcohol'.[33] This section examines first the temperance movement and second that generalized temperance sentiment.[34]

The temperance movement was first opposed to spirits. Already in 1795 the evangelical Hannah More had penned 'The Gin-Shop Or, A Peep into a Prison':

> Go where you will throughout the realm,
> You'll find the reigning sin –
> In cities, villages, and towns,
> The monster's name is Gin.[35]

In addition, an anti-spirits movement in the US, responding to the high levels there of consumption, was followed by similar initiatives in the spirit-drinking parts of the UK – Ireland and Scotland – and spread to England in November 1829 when Henry Forbes, a Scottish worsted manufacturer who had settled in Bradford, returned from a business trip to Glasgow.[36] The rationale for the Bradford Society for Promoting Temperance of 1830 specifically cited the success of such societies in the US as its exemplar and justified its creation with a familiar litany of the evils of intemperance: neglect of education, profanation of the Sabbath, declining social habits, corrupted morals, crime and the 'loosening of the bonds that bind man to man'. Members resolved to give up 'ardent spirits', except for medicinal purposes, and by their example and influence 'to affect a change upon the existing habits of the community'.[37]

Other societies were quickly established, in neighbouring Leeds later that year and in the year following in Manchester, Liverpool and London, where it soon was named, again under US influence, the British and Foreign Temperance Society. With about 40 per cent of the membership in Lancashire and Yorkshire, however, its greatest strength, and where it remained, was in the north of England, together with the West Country. This was true also of other patterns of membership, with northern rural counties like Cumberland and Westmorland more strongly represented than their southern counterparts and with the capital itself relatively weak in relation to its enormous population. Its membership was largely middle-class and in 1837 it secured the accolade of royal patronage. It was a movement of all denominations but with Anglicans prominent in its leadership.[38]

It was quickly challenged, however, by a more radical, more working-class movement for total abstinence: teetotalism, as it came to be known after a stuttering Richard Turner declared to a Preston meeting that he would 'be reet down out-and-out t-t-total for ever and ever'. Teetotal societies were formed simultaneously in several places, but that of Preston, like Bradford a textile town, was most vigorous for the new cause. The inherent limitations of focusing on spirits had been highlighted by the 1830 Beer Act's apparent boost to drunkenness and its very real creation of thousands of new beerhouses, which were particularly plentiful in industrial towns and cities. The British and Foreign Temperance Society was criticized by provincial nonconformists for its closeness to the established church and for its lack of vigour, preferring as it did a strategy of leading by example. Teetotallers in contrast wanted to reach out to the drunkard and draw him into the community of abstainers.[39]

These twin aspects of the teetotal movement – reaching out to the drunkard and the creation of a community of abstainers – are seen in their activities. The overall sense of struggle is vividly conveyed by the title of one prominent activist's book: *Life's Battles in Temperance Armour*, the contents of which convey the sometimes violent opposition he and others encountered.[40] There was a constant round of meetings, where Joseph Livesey, the prominent Preston activist, might deliver his famous Malt Lecture, with its 'scientific' demonstrations of the teetotal case, such as igniting the spirits obtained from evaporating a quart of ale.[41] Or reformed drunkards might declare, like woolcomber Thomas Worsnop, with tears rolling down his cheeks, that he would have 'no more *swill*'. As Harrison observed, these meetings combined 'a peculiar form of secularized conversion experience' – as members, whether drunkard or not, took the teetotal pledge to abstain – and the entertainment of a public-house free-and-easy or the music hall.[42] The movement quickly issued its own newspapers to give to their orators the widest possible publicity and to help members keep the faith in the face of general press hostility or indifference.[43] At holiday time tea parties and festivals became popular throughout the manufacturing districts. At Easter 1835, for example, a huge temperance festival was held at Wilsden in the West Riding of Yorkshire, where two-and-a-half-thousand participants from eighteen local societies listened to Livesey and Swindlehurst, 'the king of the reformed drunkards', enjoyed their singing, prayers and refreshments and created, according to one of those present, 'Paradise in miniature'.[44]

The whole range of activity is further illustrated if we look at just one society, that of Halifax, another West Riding textile town. Founded in 1832 as an anti-spirits society, it switched to total abstinence after a visit from Livesey himself, when over 600 members heard the Malt Lecture. There were the regular meetings (outdoors in the summer), anniversary teas, galas, such as the one of 1845 to coincide with the fair (like race meetings, an often drunken event), with tea, music, dancing and games. Tracts and circulars were distributed, petitions sent to government, representations made to the police and to the annual licensing sessions for public houses, links forged with other temperance crusaders, like the visit in 1843 of the Catholic teetotal campaigner Father Mathew, and wider temperance causes supported, like the London Temperance Hostel, founded in 1873. Finally, the movement sought to reach out to the young. A public meeting of a Youths' Temperance Society took place in October 1838, addressed by seven youths, but it does not appear to have survived, although similar efforts were more successful in other places and the British League of Juvenile Abstainers was founded in Edinburgh in 1847. Most important for the longer term was the Band of Hope, founded in Leeds in the same year by the Reverend Jabez Tunnicliffe to teach children the principles of sobriety and teetotalism, as its motto from Proverbs explained: 'Train up a child in the way he should go: and when he is old, he will not depart from it'. A branch was established in Halifax in 1858.[45]

By the 1850s, however, there were signs that the movement was running out of steam. In Bradford both the original middle-class-dominated Temperance Society and the more radical teetotallers, who had in 1843 formed the Bradford Long Pledge Teetotal Association – resolving, that is, neither to serve nor to take (the short pledge) alcohol in any form – were in difficulties and formally dissolved in 1860.[46] More generally, progress towards the goal of a drink-free world still seemed so limited. Most people still drank and consumption was in fact rising. There were more pubs than ever before and their numbers were increasing all the time. Even in the heyday of teetotalism in the late 1830s only a tenth of members were reformed drunkards. The collapse of Father Mathew's campaign seemed to underline the movement's limited achievements. It seemed that the tactic of 'moral suasion', as it was known, was simply not working.[47]

In this context, and drawing once again on the example of the US, where prohibition had been introduced in the state of Maine, the movement turned towards legislative compulsion to achieve the aim of national sobriety. So the organization which, in Harrison's words, 'came to dominate the entire temperance campaign', was founded in Manchester in 1853 as the United Kingdom Alliance for the Suppression of the Liquor Traffic.[48] Most of its supporters were former moral suasionists, with at its core the articulate working men and non-conformists who were so important in the movement, although the new body also accepted non-teetotallers.[49] Moral suasion was not abandoned, any more than the moral suasionists had eschewed campaigning for legislative change, but its foundation did signal a new central strategy.

This strategy for the achievement of prohibition was the so called local veto, giving local ratepayers the opportunity to vote to do away with drink shops. In John Greenaway's analysis this approach to prohibition was a way of meeting 'the obvious charge that prohibition was a dictatorial solution imposed by the state that would be both morally unjustified and impractical' by ensuring that it was both local and democratic. In this way liberalism and prohibition could be reconciled.[50] The measure itself, which was supported by the whole campaigning repertoire of speeches, mass meetings, petitions, canvassing and literature, was the Permissive Prohibition Bill. It was introduced for the first time in 1864, and regularly thereafter, by the Alliance's parliamentary spokesman Sir Wilfrid Lawson, a Radical Liberal MP and considerable landowner in his native Cumberland.[51] He put the Alliance's position clearly in his rejection of the charge of interfering with the liberty of the subject: 'Certainly not. I am going to interfere with the licence of the publican, which is quite a different thing from the liberty of the subject – the licence of a man to do harm to his fellow subjects'.[52]

The campaign was not successful. The Permissive Bill itself was always defeated. Resolutions for a weaker measure of local option, or local control of licensing by an elected local authority or through direct vote, were passed in the 1880s, but they came to nothing. Such was also the local veto's fate when it was adopted by Sir William Harcourt in the Liberal Government of 1892 to 1895.[53] It was modestly successful for Scotland in legislation of 1913, partly, as Greenaway notes, because evidence suggested it would turn out to be dead letter.[54] Prohibition failed for several reasons. Most people did not want it: the Liberal defeat in the general election of 1895 was attributed largely to its negative impact on voters. Most politicians, including many Liberals, were wary of the whole issue. It was easy to portray it as class legislation, directed at the pleasures of the working man, since on the one hand many would not qualify to vote on the issue and on the other the drinking places of the middle and upper classes would not be affected, a point reinforced by the exemptions in the Liberal measure for hotels and railway refreshment rooms. Harcourt's victorious Tory opponent in his Derby constituency in 1895 was actually a supporter of the Church of England Temperance Society, who pitched his appeal to the respectable working man who was entitled to his beer, shouldn't be lumped together with drunks and didn't possess the rich man's cellar.[55] There were doubts as to its practicality, the likelihood that it would be introduced in those areas which least required it (as proved the case in Scotland), the possible consequences for law enforcement and, not least, the political ineptitude displayed by the Alliance, particularly when ministers were at last favourably disposed to legislation.[56]

Although the particular solution to the drink problem of prohibition failed to be enacted, a broad and diverse temperance movement enjoyed widespread support in late Victorian and Edwardian England. Whilst its bedrock was nonconformity, the largest temperance organization was in fact that linked to the established church. It had in the early years of the movement resisted teetotalism, preferring the path of moderation. A Church of England Total Abstinence Society had been founded at the beginning of the 1860s, but had failed to persuade the wider church. The Church of England Temperance Society, founded in 1873, then united advocates of moderation with total abstainers and the society became, in the words of one of its historians, 'the most prestigious anti-drink organization in the Kingdom'. Queen Victoria was its patron and all its bishops acted as vice-presidents, half of whom were teetotal by 1900.[57] By that year the society had 7,000 branches with between 150,000 and 200,000 subscribing members involved in a very wide range of anti-drink activity: sponsoring counter-attractions to pubs, like coffee and cocoa houses, temperance hotels, reading rooms, working men's clubs, sick and benefit societies and penny banks and bands, choirs and music societies. There was a UK Railway Temperance Society aimed at its employees, police court missions to work with drunken cases and a Prison Gate Mission for newly released prisoners.[58]

The Church of England Temperance Society had sections both for women and the young, and these groups need to be highlighted in this survey of the breadth of temperance support and the scale of activities. Lilian Shiman has identified three stages of women's involvement in temperance. In the early years they tended to be in segregated ladies' committees, like those of Blackburn or Leeds, the latter claiming over 400 members in 1839, plus a few independent bodies like the Birmingham Ladies Temperance Association. Then in the mid Victorian period, from around 1860 to 1875, individual women focused on mission work – for example, with the army or navy. But their most extensive involvement came from the 1870s. US influence once again was important with the Gospel Temperance movement and the Independent Order of Good Templars, which had women office holders. The nationwide British Women's Temperance Association, founded in 1876, claimed by 1892 to have 570 branches with 50,000 members. Displaying, however, the capacity for division which characterized the whole temperance movement, it split the following year. Traditionalists set up the Women's Total Abstinence Union, and the rest, under Lady Henry Somerset, renamed themselves the British Women's Temperance Association. Reflecting a desire that the movement take a broader view of reform, they embraced a wide variety of causes other than temperance.[59]

Exceeding all in their numbers, however, were children. The Band of Hope enjoyed its greatest strength in the years from 1870.[60] The movement claimed that over three million children were involved by the turn of the century.

Although this probably is no more than a claim, the largest union, that of Lancashire and Cheshire, already had over 180,000 members in over a thousand societies by the mid 1880s. Effective organization, but above all its sheer energy and innovation underpinned the movement's success. Weekly meetings involved prayers, hymns, songs, lectures, often illustrated with lantern slides, recitations and of course signing the teetotal pledge. There were excursions, parades, picnics and tea parties and regional and national events like the annual UK concerts at the Crystal Palace. Between meetings and events was the continuing enjoyment of regional and national periodicals.[61] Of course, for the working-class children who made up the bulk of the movement's members the events and entertainments must have been for many, if not most, the principal attraction, and for their parents perhaps the possibility of some peace and quiet. But even if those children did not for life adhere to the pledge they had made, they had been exposed to the ideal of a life without drink and to the idea that drink was a problem (Figure 6.3). Exposed in a similar way – and, of course, many were the same individuals – were the 'something like' three quarters of all children attending Sunday school by the late 1880s.[62] And in day schools, too, which all children were compelled to attend from this time, they were taught the virtues of sobriety.

Novelists also helped to disseminate a broad temperance sentiment. There was a specific temperance literature. The best-selling novelist Mrs Henry Wood made her name with *Danesbury House* in 1860, powerfully conveying how drink pervaded society. But novelists more widely, like Anne Brontë in *The Tenant of*

*Figure 6.3* Children against drink outside Sunbridge Road Mission, Bradford, 1906.
Source: Courtesy of Sunbridge Road Mission.

*Wildfell Hall* of 1848 or Thomas Hardy in *The Mayor of Casterbridge* of 1886, vividly portrayed the effects of drink. Literature and the involvement of children were just two of the ways in which a generalized temperance sentiment, beyond the ranks of the organized movement, became widely diffused in society. One example will have to serve here to illustrate this. It is the diary of Ada Jackson, a young woman in a respectable working-class household in Leicester. Her father was a foreman who owned two houses; he drank at home, but in moderation, and does not seem to have gone to the pub. The family used brandy for medicinal purposes. Ada listens on one occasion to a sermon on temperance at her church which she pronounces 'very good'. She likes the fact that her fiancé George, a carpenter and joiner, does not share a drink with her father and similarly notes his returning home early 'before they turn out of the Public Houses'.[63]

## Drink questions and answers

As David Fahey observed, 'Teetotalers and prohibitionists had no monopoly in late Victorian and Edwardian temperance reform. Concern about drink pervaded society'.[64] The common currency of the phrases the Drink Question or the Drink, or Liquor, Problem conveyed this. This concern had grown over the course of the century, but the general critique of drink was sharpened towards the end of the century by several intellectual developments, in turn rooted in economic, social and cultural changes. They had the effect of taking the debate beyond a simple personification of drink as the Demon to an awareness of the complexity of the question, or questions as it might be conceived. This in turn prompted a greater variety of possible answers.

One development was the way in which drink became linked to the contemporary racial discourse of social Darwinism, which saw the world's races and nations locked in a struggle for survival. By the late nineteenth century, although Britain presided over the world's largest empire, the economic advance of the US and the growing economic and military power of Germany were perceived as threats to that position. Anxiety then focused on evidence for the deterioration of the British race, to combat which a drive for so called national efficiency was deemed essential. That evidence was to be found in the poverty, social dependency, disease, crime, violence and drunkenness of the urban working-classes, the 'residuum' as the contemporary phrase termed them.[65]

Within such anxiety present and future mothers were key figures. To one contributor to the recently founded *British Journal of Inebriety*, no subject was of 'more vital importance' than 'the question of national degeneracy'. Having analysed women's conviction statistics for drunkenness in Manchester to demonstrate that most were in their child-bearing years, she opined that they

> were probably giving birth to neurotic, vicious children, tainted with alcoholism and disease, large numbers of whom ... will grow up weak and rickety, to lower still further the standard of national efficiency by adding to the burden of pauperism and crime.[66]

In another piece in the journal the gynaecological surgeon and later president of the Society for the Study of Inebriety, Mary Scharlieb, vividly elaborated a catalogue of the horrors for children taken by their mothers into the public house: the hot and foul atmosphere, the germs in the smokers' spit, the drunken brawls and the quietening dose of gin. She noted too 'The Alcoholic Home' wherein 'the want of thrift, of order, and of cleanliness pervades every nook and corner of the place'.[67]

There was also more interest shown in the broader social and environmental context of heavy drinking, part of a wider perception of the social ills arising from industrialization. This was not in itself novel: they were expressed during the years of the Condition of England Question in the early Victorian period. But by the late nineteenth century urbanization had advanced markedly. By 1891 three quarters of the population lived in towns and over half of them in cities of over 100,000 people.[68] Social investigators like Charles Booth in London or Seebohm Rowntree in York now provided detailed research which showed that poverty was a social condition rather than an individual failing and that the drink problem could not therefore be separated from wider programmes of social amelioration. C. F. G. Masterman's influential 1901 study of 'modern city life in England' devoted a lengthy chapter to 'Temperance Reform'.[69] Another important work, dealing exclusively with drink, was Joseph Rowntree and Arthur Sherwell's massive *The Temperance Problem and Social Reform*, published in 1899 and selling 90,000 copies within five years.[70] Their work, which branded excessive consumption of drink as 'seriously subversive of the economic and moral progress of the nation', singled out as its 'effective causes' the monotony, dullness and misery of working-class lives, the 'absence of adequate provision for social intercourse and healthful recreation', but above all the power of the drink industry and its thirst for profit.[71]

Similarly, there was a long-standing socialist analysis of the issue, going back to Robert Owen and Friedrich Engels, which stressed the environmental causes of heavy drinking. For the Fabian H. Russell Smart drink was 'one of the greatest ramparts of capitalism', and whilst 'the Temperance Party assert that in the main drink is the cause of poverty', for the Socialists 'poverty is the cause of drink'. He noted caustically how the prohibitionist Lawson's wealth derived from grinding 'the Cumberland workers into that monotonous round of penurious toil whose only solace is alcohol'.[72] Teetotal Chartists in the 1830s and 1840s had also emphasized broader social evils in their response to the question.[73] Their belief in the interconnectedness of sobriety and political integrity and in the virtues and benefits to working men of eschewing drink and the pub also found many echoes within the later labour movement, in the views of men like John Burns, Keir Hardie, Philip Snowden and George Lansbury. As the former put it in a lecture at the Free Trade Hall in Manchester in 1904: 'The drinking habits of the poorer classes have everywhere contributed to their political dependence, industrial bondage, personal debasement, civic inferiority, and domestic misery'.[74] Some, however, had always been more sceptical, suspecting that the temperance movement was simply a means to keep the working man in his place by diverting attention away from the root causes of his position towards his own behaviour.[75]

The strength of organized temperance and the more widespread salience of the Drink Question together ensured that drink would be a major political issue. But the passions and divisions of the proponents and the overall complexity of the issue meant that for politicians it was at once complicated and fraught with difficulty. For the emerging labour movement the anti-drink stance of many activists was at odds with the habits of potential supporters who asserted the right of respectable working men to enjoy their legitimate pleasures of beer and pub or club sociability, a position which some Tories were happy to support. Whilst only 3 per cent of Independent Labour Party clubs served alcohol in 1908, the majority of working men's clubs did.[76] For the two major parties at this time drink did to some extent become a party political issue. The Liberals became more closely identified with the cause of temperance, an inevitability given the strength of nonconformity and working-class self-improvement in its support. Similarly, the Tories found themselves aligned with the drink trade given the party's rural bedrock of support and its growing identification with the interests of business and property. But it was never a straightforward alliance: there was much sympathy amongst Conservatives for temperance reform and many feared too close identification with the drink trade. The Liberals for their part continued to enjoy the support of some within those trades and many Liberal politicians, including Gladstone, were equally wary of their temperance supporters.[77]

The fate of drink-related legislation suggests that politicians were right to treat the issue with caution. In the mid 1850s an attempt to reduce drinking hours on Sunday had been modified within a year after rioting in London.[78] The Liberal Government's Licensing Bill of 1871, which included a modest element of licence reduction, had to be withdrawn in the face of widespread and vehement opposition. The successful Act of the following year, although it was a timely updating of a number of aspects of the licensing system (including in the view of some of those in the trade) and passed with the support of members of both parties, illustrated the pitfalls of attempts at reform. On the one hand it failed to persuade its likely supporters in the temperance movement and on the other it amply demonstrated the depth of feeling which the issue could arouse. Gladstone's view of the party's subsequent defeat in the general election of 1874, if exaggerated, was that 'We have been borne down in a torrent of gin and beer'. Its provisions for stricter closing times again provoked widespread rioting, including outside gentlemen's clubs unaffected by them.[79] As we saw, the party's defeat in 1895 was attributed to its drink policy.

As Arthur Balfour put it for the government in responding in 1896 to a question about an inquiry into the subject of licensing, it was indeed 'a thorny and difficult subject'.[80] The ensuing Royal Commission on the Licensing Laws amply illustrated this. Its membership, evenly divided between representatives of the drink trade, temperance and 'neutrals', worked for three years, heard from 259 witnesses to create nine volumes of evidence and produced two reports signed by a majority and minority of its members respectively. Its chairman, Lord Peel, who had originally been a neutral, switched to the temperance camp and sided with the minority.[81] Other than some minor non-contentious changes in the Licensing Act of 1902, little came of it. When Balfour addressed the issue of licence reduction in the Licensing Act of 1904 by creating a mechanism for financial compensation to the trade, it was once again enormously controversial and passed in the face of massive opposition from the temperance movement. And when the succeeding Liberal Government attempted in 1908 to revive the issue and to impose a time limit on compensation another storm of protest ensued, this time from the trade, and the measure was killed by the Tory-dominated House of Lords.[82]

A reduction in the number of licences was one approach to the drink question which met with widespread agreement, albeit the method of achieving it was controversial. But there were two other temperance-minded initiatives which sought to address the pub and its perceived deficiencies. One was to provide alternatives to it; the other was to change its management.

The former had its origins in the movement earlier in the century for what was called rational recreation, to provide more edifying counter-attractions to the pub. Its aspirations were given expression in the report of the 1834 Select Committee on Drunkenness among the Labouring Classes, which recommended the establishment by government, local authorities and residents of public walks, gardens, open spaces, libraries and museums.[83] Over the course of the century much was indeed to be achieved towards this goal, both by private philanthropy and municipal action. But there were moves, too, to create a more specific alternative to the pub. The British Workman movement offered 'public houses without the drink' in a number of cities, but in comparison with hundreds of pubs their numbers were limited: just three, for example, in Bradford or Newcastle. Even the thirty-one in Liverpool in 1878 competed with well over two-thousand pubs.[84] Another similar offering were coffee or cocoa taverns, which were established throughout the country. But again numbers were limited, they sometimes failed and ultimately they were less significant in the cause of reducing drinking than more commercially minded ventures.[85] Working men's clubs had their origins in the same aspiration, in the words of the Objects and Plan of Operations of the Working Men's Club and Institute Union, 'where they can meet for conversation, business, and mental improvement, with the means of recreation and refreshment, free from intoxicating drinks'.[86] As with the British Workmen pubs and the coffee houses, middle-class patronage and an explicit counter-attractionist appeal were key features of the movement, but, as we saw in Chapter 2, the clubs were developed independently by working men, and drink became an integral element both of their appeal and successful operation.

A contrast to the provision of alternatives was reform which looked at the management of pubs. Inspiration was drawn from Scandinavian systems of so called disinterested management, usually known from one exemplar, the town of Gothenburg in Sweden. The central premise was to remove the profit motive from the sale of alcohol, with the pubs themselves run by franchisees or directly by the local authority. The idea was taken up by the Birmingham Liberal politician Joseph Chamberlain, who visited Gothenburg and who had come to the conclusion that the prohibitionists were in fact temperance's worst enemy. He was accordingly not best pleased when Sir Wilfrid Lawson criticized his Gothenburg resolution and helped ensure its defeat in parliament.[87] Municipal control was Chamberlain's favoured option, drawing upon his Birmingham experiences. Although it was never adopted in any systematic way, it continued to find advocates such as Rowntree and Sherwell and within the socialist movement.[88] It was instead taken up in a number of individual experiments and, more significantly, by the People's Refreshment House Association, founded in 1896, and the Central Public House Trust Association of 1901. As the former's chief aims set out: it sought to encourage temperance reform in the management of licensed premises, provide food and non-alcoholic drinks to create 'genuine refreshment houses, not mere drinking dens' and maintain 'cleanliness, comfort and good order'. Managers were paid a fixed salary, deriving no profit from the sale of alcohol.[89] Yet, as with the alternatives to the pub, the overall impact of these efforts was limited. In the whole of England and Wales by 1914 there were approximately 250 trust houses, a negligible number when set against some 90,000 on-licences. The majority were in rural areas rather than the towns and cities, whose pubs were felt to be most in need of reform. In industrial centres like Newcastle, although impressive premises were opened, like the Delaval Arms on the Scotswood Road, with its dining room for 150 workmen, the trust struggled from the outset. Overall, the movement's most important legacy was the principle of pub improvement, which was to have a greater influence during the war and in the post-war years.[90]

Finally, one other strand of anti-drink endeavour which too had at least some tangible, if ultimately modest, outcomes, and which was linked to the social and racial concerns which have been identified, was that which sought to deal with the problem of the habitual drunkard. The nineteenth century saw the continuation, refinement and wide acceptance of the assessment of habitual drunkenness as a disease. The concept had been developed by a number of European theorists over the first half of the century, including the clinical description by the Swede Magnus Huss in 1849 of a condition he called 'chronic alcoholism'.[91] As a disease, it naturally merited medical intervention. The Liberal MP Donald Dalrymple, formerly a surgeon and proprietor of an asylum, having failed with a private bill to provide legal recognition and institutional provision for the treatment of habitual drunkards, secured in 1872 a select committee to consider the question. He had visited North American inebriate asylums and a number of their managers gave evidence to his committee.[92] Its report found that 'occasional drunkenness may, and very frequently does, become habitual, and soon passes into the condition of a disease uncontrollable by the individual, unless indeed some extraneous influence, either punitive or curative is brought into play'. Accordingly it recommended the legal control of an habitual inebriate either in a reformatory or private dwelling.[93] But it was to be another seven years before reservations on libertarian grounds receded and even then the Habitual Drunkards Act which did pass in 1879 was much more limited than the committee had recommended, abandoning any compulsion or provision for public expenditure.[94]

The twin ideas of habitual drunkenness as a disease and the consequent need for treatment continued to gain ground, promoted by medical men actively seeking at this time to increase their professional standing. A Society for Promoting

Legislation for the Cure and Control of Habitual Drunkards had been founded in 1876 by a group of doctors and a lawyer under the presidency of Dr Norman Kerr, medical man and temperance reformer. Under Kerr's presidency too the Society for the Study and Cure of Inebriety was inaugurated in 1884. It promoted the disease view – as Kerr put it, 'a true disease, as unmistakeably a disease as is gout or epilepsy or insanity' – advocated medical approaches to the problem and argued for a joint approach by the state and the medical profession.[95] By this time the social and racial anxieties outlined above had created a climate more amenable to some form of compulsion directed at habitual drunkards who broke the law. The Inebriates Act of 1898 authorized their detention in inebriate reformatories on either of two grounds: if the court was satisfied that the offence was committed under the influence of drink or if drink was a contributory cause and the offender admitted, or the jury found him, to be an habitual drunkard; or if a person had committed a drunkenness offence three times in a twelve-month period. In both cases confinement could be for up to three years. In the event, the climate of opinion which created the legislation did not lead to commensurate practical effect. Two state reformatories were established as annexes to prisons, one each for men and women, and just twelve certified reformatories, divided evenly between those run by local authorities and those by philanthropic or religious bodies. These twelve, in the dozen years for which the system lasted, dealt with a little over 5,000 cases. Clearly the limited amount of provision made available, due chiefly to the unwillingness of local authorities to finance it, was one important reason for the reform's failure. Another reason lay in the reluctance of the courts to use it, arising from problems in interpreting the law and, not least, a justified lack of faith in its effectiveness.[96]

One telling feature of the reformatories was how women made up the great majority of those sent there, reflecting the belief that female drunkenness was increasing and the particular threat it was held to pose to national efficiency. By 1909 78 per cent of committals under the first criteria were women convicted of cruelty towards and/or neglect of their children. But here, too, the system did not achieve its aims, as women were shown to have failed to respond to the reformatory regime on their release. And when the experiment was wound up inebriate women found themselves taken up under the Mental Deficiency Act of 1913, which permitted their transfer to asylums. Indeed the reformatories themselves were simply converted to the new institutions.[97]

By the eve of the First World War, then, one might reasonably conclude that the tangible achievements of a century of temperance campaigning were modest. Prohibition, the goal of one of the pillars of the movement, was still a distant dream. Such legislative changes as were made, as will be seen in the next chapter, were modest and often linked to social and cultural changes unconnected with drink. The only major piece of licensing legislation between the Act of 1872 and the postwar settlement of 1921, the measure of 1904, became law, as Fahey put it, 'despite the opposition of virtually the entire organized temperance movement'. But, as he went on to note, a 'more broadly defined' temperance sentiment was important in shaping the legislation and underlay the government's characterization of it as a temperance measure.[98] This broadly defined temperance sentiment did succeed in establishing for the country that drink was a social problem, even if there was no overall agreement on the solution. For the individual of all classes, sobriety or moderation had come to be seen as acceptable and desirable behaviour, and by the late nineteenth century heavy drinking and drunkenness were in decline. But this had as much to do with changing material circumstances and cultural aspirations, particularly amongst the working class, rather than the urgings of the teetotallers. Furthermore, in 1914 consumption levels were still high and the pub remained the key working-class social institution.

It has been argued, however, that the temperance movement had important social and political consequences beyond the specific question of drink. For Harrison it played an important role in helping to hold English society together in a period of rapid change. It did this both by bringing together the classes in a shared movement and by helping the growth of working-class consciousness, more particularly an outlook that change could be effected within the existing political order. Overall it was a progressive and humanitarian force.[99] But, as he also pointed out, it is possible to interpret its influence in different ways. Its appeal to socialists or feminists was to groups, one might suggest, with little or no voice in the political order as it then existed.[100] Then again, the movement has been viewed as one means to the creation of the stable labour force and mass of consumers required by industrial capitalism – a coercive, negative influence.[101] Yet again, it has been argued by James Roberts in surveying the movement's historiography that there is a measure of validity in both views – that the temperance movement could take on different meanings and appeal to different constituencies at different times and places, attractive to business and labour, for example, in divergent ways. There are, then, in this view, few unqualified generalizations about the movement, its composition, appeal, purposes or methods. Nonetheless, its outcome in England, as we have seen, and in North America and Western Europe was to place the Drink Question at the forefront of society's concerns.[102]

The First World War, in Britain as in other combatant nations, saw that concern come very much to the fore. Drinking by soldiers, their wives and workers aroused concern for allegedly undermining the war effort, although in each case with limited basis in reality.[103] The Chancellor of the Exchequer, Lloyd George, although exaggerating for political effect, underscored the salience of the issue when he declared in a speech early in 1915 that 'Drink is doing us more damage ... than all the German submarines put together'. And to a deputation from the Shipbuilding Employers' Federation: 'We are fighting Germany, Austria and Drink; and as far as I can see, the greatest of these three deadly foes is Drink'.[104] Under the impact of war, then, the concern for national efficiency and generalized temperance sentiment together created a response which combined moral suasion with restrictive measures. The former was embodied in the pledge campaign to abstain from alcohol for the war's duration. It followed the lead of the King, who had, if reluctantly, given up drink 'so that no difference shall be made ... between the treatment of rich and poor in this question'. Whilst a degree of patriotic and moral support did follow, Lloyd George himself later felt that 'unfortunately the

King's example was not adopted widely enough to make any deep impression on the problem itself' and statutory powers thus became necessary.[105] Those statutory powers and their effects are examined in Chapter 7. Some further development of those pre-war initiatives to improve the pub took place under them, within the context of another pre-war solution: state control of the trade, albeit to a limited extent. State purchase of the whole industry, however, whilst discussed, came to nothing in the face of its potential political and financial costs.[106]

## Drink questions in the twentieth century

The First World War may reasonably be presented as a turning point in the history of anti-drink sentiment. For temperance supporters of all views much had been achieved and continued progress might be anticipated with confidence. But in this they were to be disappointed. Once the key wartime changes had been retained in legislation, the Drink Question ceased to be a great overarching issue facing society. It had been presented as such during the conflict, but as Robert Duncan puts it, 'national efficiency had been tested and not found wanting to the challenges of war'.[107] With peace, there was a widespread desire that the controls thought to be vital in wartime should now be dismantled.[108] Moreover, the problem itself had clearly receded: consumption was much reduced and proceedings for drunkenness had fallen dramatically, trends which persisted through the inter-war years.

Drink as an issue, though, did not simply vanish at war's end. The temperance movement continued to play an important part in many lives.[109] This was particularly the case for the young. The Band of Hope kept up the kinds of activity described above. Although it did decline in some areas, in one of its heartlands, the north west, membership actually peaked in the late 1920s. Nevertheless, the long-term picture was one of decline, in parallel with attendance at Sunday schools, in the face of competing leisure attractions for children and the fading of nonconformity.[110] The latter underlay the waning of temperance as a whole. The long-term decline both of nonconformity and temperance then steepened after the Second World War. By the mid 1960s the minutes of the Halifax Society recorded just five members across two annual meetings. As its secretary and treasurer noted finally in 1966, 'we had to face the fact that there is no interest in temperance and none in the work of our society'.[111]

Nor did the issue disappear immediately from politics. Measures for local option continued to be introduced in parliament through the 1920s, although without success. Similarly fruitless were moves to support with legislation disinterested management and pub improvement.[112] The issue as a whole continued to be actively debated, particularly within the Labour Party. A campaign for public ownership of the trade was inaugurated in 1919 to remove the profit motive from its sale, reduce the political influence of the trade and facilitate pub improvement.[113] Measures to support some form of local control or prohibition were also promoted and local option was in fact adopted at the 1920 party conference, which rejected nationalization.[114] Individual Labour politicians remained strongly anti-drink: in 1923 about one-hundred MPs were abstainers, over half the total, and that proportion was virtually unchanged in 1935.[115] But in the end the political sensitivity of the question and the widespread support for moderate enjoyment of alcohol amongst Labour's rank and file, epitomized in the flourishing club movement, ensured that the party, anxious to further position itself as the real alternative to the Conservatives, would seek to take the issue off the political agenda. To this end inquiries were useful: an internal one in 1923 and a royal commission at the end of the decade. The latter's generally positive conclusions on the nation's drinking served to confirm the wisdom of the approach to politicians generally and the issue faded from political view in the 1930s.[116]

That the climate of opinion had changed fundamentally was shown during the Second World War. In contrast to the First, beer and the pub were seen from the outset as essential elements in the war effort. Temperance voices were raised, but were now ignored, and there were no further restrictions. For Lord Woolton, the Minister of Food, the nation was now temperate and, as he expressed it in May 1940, it was 'the business of the Government not only to maintain the life but the morale of the country'.[117] More broadly, the more democratic ethos of the People's War militated against coercive measures.[118]

One area of concern that was expressed during the war, as it had been in the earlier conflict, was drinking by the young, especially women. Drinking by young people of both sexes, and associated problems of public order, became the subject of great concern from the 1950s onwards, as was noted in the previous chapter, and the restrictive measures taken in response will be outlined in Chapter 7. Here the focus will be on two areas of anti-drink feeling and argument which also became prominent in the late twentieth century: the particular issue of drinking and driving and the broader one of drink as a question of public health.

Being drunk in charge of a moving object was not, of course, a novel problem. A Norfolk diarist's entry in the summer of 1792 of one 'Valentine Lound killed by a fall from his horse coming from Cawston sheep show, being very much in liquor' evidences one instance of what seems to have been a common enough event.[119] Similarly, the drunken accidents of carters and coachmen were frequently reported, as when the York Mail overturned one May night in 1831, its driver in a state of 'brutal drunkenness'.[120] Driving a carriage 'furiously so as to endanger the Life and Limb of any Passenger' was included in the general Highways Act of 1835 and driving whilst drunk was specified in relation to hackney carriages in London legislation of 1843, a provision which was taken up elsewhere in by-laws and under the relevant section of the Town Police Clauses Act of 1847. In the 1872 Licensing Act a general offence of drunk in charge of any carriage, horse, cattle or steam engine was created.[121] But the advent of the motor car at the end of the century eventually brought about separate legal treatment in 1925 and 1930, the former referring to 'any mechanically-propelled vehicle' and the latter to driving or attempting to drive whilst 'under the influence of drink or a drug to such an extent as to be incapable of having proper control of the vehicle'.[122]

Despite legislation and an appalling death toll, however, a 'lenient regulatory regime' continued to prevail until the 1960s. Then several developments produced a change. First was the continuing loss of life and press coverage of it; the ever increasing numbers of cars and the perception that existing roads were inadequate. Second were the emergence of cross-party consensus on the issue, outside pressure from doctors and the Pedestrians Association and the impact of scientific work on the effects of alcohol. And third were important departmental shifts, in the Home Office towards support for firmer enforcement and in the Ministry of Transport towards road safety, together with ministerial support for the issue, notably from Conservative Ernest Marples and Labour's Barbara Castle. The result was the Road Safety Act of 1967, which introduced the measure of blood alcohol level and the breathalyzer to test it.[123] Convictions for drinking and driving, which had been increasing before the Act to around 10,000 a year, then rose dramatically over the long term, and although they fell substantially between 1990 and 1994, fluctuated around 80,000 individuals per year thereafter. The number of those killed or seriously injured in drink-drive crashes also fell.[124] To what extent one should attribute improvement to the breathalyzer is of course a complex question, given the number of variables involved, but at the very least it placed the potentially lethal effects of drinking and driving and the consequences of flouting the law firmly in the public mind.

Although the issue of drinking and driving has had a high profile, the key development has been the orientation since the 1970s of anti-drink sentiment around the question of its general impact on public health and the consequent promotion of policies to reduce the harms associated with it. Prior to this, however, the more specific question of the habitual drinker or drunkard had continued to be addressed. The concept of alcoholism as a disease, articulated influentially in the US with the publication of E. M. Jellinek's *Disease Concept of Alcoholism* in 1960 and supported by the World Health Organization, to which he acted as a consultant, underpinned emphasis on the problem as a medical one which affected a minority of the population and was amenable to treatment.[125] In contrast, the public-health approach looked at the whole population, embodying a view of public health as a question of the lifestyle of the individual rather than the environment which he or she inhabited. Instead of the nineteenth century's focus on the impact of polluted water or a lack of effective sanitation, the emphasis now was on the choices of individuals and how they affected their health.[126] In the case of alcohol support was given to this by the findings of the French statistician Sully Ledermann, who had argued in the 1950s that there was a relationship between average per capita consumption and levels of alcohol misuse in a population. The objective, then, should be to reduce overall consumption. This approach was influentially articulated in *Alcohol Control Policies in Public Health Perspective*, published in 1975 and jointly authored by the Finnish Foundation for Alcohol Studies, the Addiction Research Foundation in Toronto and the WHO Regional Office for Europe.[127] In turn it was adopted in the UK, where both consumption levels and the incidence of alcohol-related diseases had been rising since the 1950s, and supported in a number of reports, such as those of the Royal College of Psychiatrists in 1979 on *Alcohol and Alcoholism* and again in 1986 on *Alcohol: Our Favourite Drug*.[128] Although subject to criticism, both of the validity of the statistical correlation and the consequent direction of policy, the basic identification of alcohol consumption as a problem of public health became widely accepted.[129]

A range of control policies were then put forward to effect a reduction in consumption, covering in particular pricing and taxation, availability and promotion.[130] But despite widespread support in the medical, academic and alcohol policy communities, the practical results were limited. Significantly, alcohol education, a policy which all sides could agree upon, was the one to be taken up.[131] One example was the Department of Health and Social Security's 1981 publication *Drinking Sensibly*, which rejected in particular the use of tax rates to regulate consumption and endorsed instead general advice in favour of moderation. This rejection was all the more controversial as it flatly went against the recommendations of a report from the Central Policy Review Staff. Moreover, the report itself had not in fact been made public, but only became available when a leaked copy was published in Sweden.[132] The emphasis on advice was seen, too, in the promotion of safe drinking limits, measured in units of alcohol, which at least had the merit of becoming widely known, even if it did not necessarily lead to drinkers observing them.[133] Similarly, controls on advertising – for example, to prevent drink appealing to the young, or the linkage of its consumption to social or sexual success – were embodied in a voluntary code of practice.[134] This failure to adopt control policies has been attributed to various causes. Crucial was the lack of wider public support for measures which might increase the cost and availability of alcohol and the consequent lack of enthusiasm on the part of politicians. Another was the influence on parliament and government of the drinks industry, together with that of other interested sectors, like tourism. Governments were all too well aware of their economic importance. Within government, too, the issue was complicated by the way it cut across a range of departments, often in conflicting ways.[135]

This public-health movement, which at the turn of the millennium continued its advocacy of a wide range of measures to minimize the risks and reduce the harms associated with alcohol consumption, has been characterized as a 'new temperance movement'.[136] For Yeomans, the new paradigm, in which the consumption of the whole population was problematic, was 'a secular rendering of the religious struggle to lead a virtuous life'. Modern parlance speaks of the risks rather the temptations of drink, but there is continuity with earlier anti-drink movements.[137] There was indeed some organizational continuity, as former temperance or prohibitionist groups repositioned themselves as educational and research bodies. The discourse of public health was also sometimes reminiscent of older rhetoric, as in the title of the 1987 report of the Royal College of Physicians: *A Great and Growing Evil*.[138] As this chapter has shown, one can indeed identify continuities in the ideas and movements against drink: the fear over the consequences of excess for public order is one; the particular concern for the drinking of women is another. But as it has also sought to demonstrate, one should never lose sight of the historical context. Opposition to drink has been articulated in particular ways at different times and, overall, change has been as significant as continuity. The fact that those former temperance and prohibitionist groups repositioned themselves as educational and research bodies shows this clearly. Drink was still held to pose a range of risks to the individual and society, but, the rhetoric of the Royal College notwithstanding, this was not the Demon Drink of the nineteenth century.

**Notes**

1. J. R. Gusfield, *Contested Meanings: The construction of alcohol problems* (Madison, WI: University of Wisconsin Press, 1996), pp. 6 and 12.
2. Genesis 9:21 and 9:32–5. Biblical references are discussed in C. Shrank, 'Beastly metamorphoses: Losing control in early modern literary culture', in J. Herring, C. Regan, D. Weinberg and P. Withington (eds), *Intoxication and Society: Problematic pleasures of drugs and alcohol* (Basingstoke: Palgrave Macmillan, 2013), pp. 193–209, on pp. 203–4.
3. Cited in G. A. Austin, *Alcohol in Western Society from Antiquity to 1800: A chronological history* (Oxford: ABC-Clio Information Services, 1985), p. 180.
4. Shrank, 'Beastly metamorphoses', pp. 195–8; A. Shepard, '"Swil-bols and tos-pots"': Drink culture and male bonding in England, c. 1560–1640', in L. Gowing, M. Hunter and M. Rubin (eds), *Love, Friendship and Faith in Europe, 1300–1800* (Basingstoke: Palgrave Macmillan, 2005), pp. 110–30, on p. 114.
5. Shepard, '"Swill-bols and tos-pots"', p. 111.
6. Austin, *Alcohol in Western Society*, p. 222.
7. Shepard, '"Swill-bols and tos-pots"', p. 110; see also on this A. Smyth, '"It were far better be a *Toad*, or a *Serpent*, than a Drunkard": Writing about drunkenness', in A. Smyth (ed.), *A Pleasing Sinne: Drink and conviviality in seventeenth-century England* (Cambridge: D. S. Brewer, 2004), pp. 193–210, on pp. 200–1; J. Warner, 'Shifting categories of the social harms associated with alcohol: Examples from late medieval and early modern England', *American Journal of Public Health*, 87:11 (1997), pp. 1788–97.
8. J. Warner, 'Before there was "alcoholism": Lessons from the medieval experience with alcohol', *Contemporary Drug Problems*, 19:3 (1992), pp. 409–29 on pp. 421–2 and 'The sanctuary of sobriety: The emergence of temperance as a feminine virtue in Tudor and Stuart England', *Addiction*, 92:1 (1997), pp. 97–111, on p. 101.
9. 4 James I, c. 5.
10. 5 & 6 Edward VI, c. 25 and 7 Edward VI, c. 5.
11. For those points and for what follows see P. Clark, *The English Alehouse: A social history 1200–1830* (London: Longman, 1983), pp. 108–11, 145–51 and 166–9 and 'The alehouse and the alternative society', in D. Pennington and K. Thomas (eds), *Puritans and Revolutionaries: Essays on seventeenth century history presented to Christopher Hill* (Oxford: Clarendon Press, 1978), pp. 47–72; J. A. Sharpe, 'Crime and delinquency in an Essex parish 1600–1640', in J. S. Cockburn (ed.), *Crime in England 1550–1800* (London: Methuen, 1977), pp. 90–109; K. Wrightson, 'Two concepts of order: Justices, constables and jurymen in seventeenth-century England', in J. Brewer and J. Styles (eds), *An Ungovernable People?: The English and their law in the seventeenth and eighteenth centuries* (London: Hutchinson, 1980), pp. 21–46 and 'Alehouses, order and Reformation in rural England, 1590–1660', in E. and S. Yeo (eds), *Popular Culture and Class Conflict 1590–1914: Explorations in the history of labour and leisure* (Brighton: Harvester Press, 1981), pp. 1–27.
12. For this view see A. L. Martin, 'The reform of popular drinking in late medieval and early modern Europe' in D. Kirkby and T. Luckins (eds), *Dining on Turtles: Food, feasts and drinking in history* (Basingstoke: Palgrave Macmillan, 2007), pp. 121–35.
13. K. Wrightson, *English Society 1580–1680* (London: Hutchinson, 1982), p. 149.

172  *Anti-drink*

14 K. Thomas, 'Work and leisure in pre-industrial society', *Past and Present*, 29 (1964), pp. 50–66, on pp. 59–60.
15 R. B. Shoemaker, 'Reforming the city: The Reformation of Manners Campaign in London, 1690–1738', in L. Davison, T. Hitchcock, T. Keirn and R. B. Shoemaker (eds), *Stilling the Grumbling Hive: The response to social and economic problems in England, 1689–1750* (Stroud: Alan Sutton, 1992), pp. 99–120, particularly p. 105; A. Hunt, *Governing Morals: A social history of moral regulation* (Cambridge: Cambridge University Press, 1991), pp. 23–55.
16 *Gentleman's Magazine*, September 1736, vol. 6, p. 537 and January 1739, vol. 9, p. 8.
17 S. Hales, *A Friendly Admonition to the Drinkers of Gin, Brandy and Other Distilled Spirituous Liquors* (London: B. Dod, 4th ed. 1751); T. Wilson (attrib.), *Distilled Spirituous Liquors the Bane of the Nation* (London: J. Roberts, 1736); for more detailed discussion of these anxieties see P. Clark, 'The "Mother Gin" controversy in the early eighteenth century', *Transactions of the Royal Historical Society*, 5th Series 38 (1988), pp. 63–84; L. Davison, 'Experiments in the social regulation of industry: Gin legislation, 1729–1751', in Davison *et al.*, *Stilling the Grumbling Hive*, pp. 25–48; J. Nicholls, *The Politics of Alcohol: A history of the drink question in England* (Manchester: Manchester University Press, 2009), pp. 34–48; J. White, 'The "slow but sure poyson": The representation of gin and its drinkers, 1736–1751', *Journal of British Studies*, 42:1 (2003), pp. 35–64.
18 Quoted in J. C. Nicholls, 'Gin Lane revisited: Intoxication and society in the gin epidemic', *Journal for Cultural Research*, 7:2 (2003), pp. 125–46, on p. 134.
19 Warner, 'Before there was "alcoholism"', p. 419 and '"Resolv'd to drink no more": Addiction as a preindustrial construct', *Journal of Studies on Alcohol*, 55:6 (1994), pp. 685–81.
20 For this whole question see Nicholls, *The Politics of Alcohol*, pp. 59–72 and D. Clemis, 'Medical expertise and the understandings of intoxication in Britain, 1660–1830', in J. Herring, C. Regan, D. Weinberg and P. Withington (eds), *Intoxication and Society*, pp. 33–51; P. Ferentzy, 'From sin to disease: Differences and similarities between past and current conceptions of chronic drunkenness', *Contemporary Drug Problems*, 28 (2001), pp. 363–90, on pp. 365–6 and overall for a critique of Warner's views.
21 T. Trotter, *An Essay, Medical, Philosophical, and Chemical, On Drunkenness, and Its Effects on the Human Body* (London: Routledge, 1988), pp. 8 and 172; see R. Porter's introduction to this edition and also his 'The drinking man's disease: The "pre-history of alcoholism" in Georgian Britain', *British Journal of Addiction*, 80:4 (1985), pp. 385–96.
22 B. Harrison, *Drink and the Victorians: The temperance question in England 1815–1872* (Keele: Keele University Press, 2nd ed., 1994), pp. 89–90.
23 Clark, *The English Alehouse*, p. 254.
24 H. Zouch, *Hints Respecting the Public Police* (London: J. Stockdale, 1786).
25 J. Innes, 'Politics and morals: The Reformation of Manners Movement in later eighteenth-century England', in E. Hellmuth (ed.), *The Transformation of Political Culture in England and Germany in the Late Eighteenth Century* (Oxford: Oxford University Press, 1990), pp. 57–118.
26 Harrison, *Drink and the Victorians*, pp. 90–1.
27 Ibid., pp. 91–2.
28 H. Yeomans, *Alcohol and Moral Regulation: Public attitudes, spirited measures and Victorian hangovers* (Bristol: Policy Press, 2014), pp. 45–6 and 51–2.
29 J. A. Hargreaves, '"Arresting the progress of this degrading and brutalising vice": Temperance, Methodism and Chartism in Halifax and its hinterland', *Transactions of the Halifax Antiquarian Society*, 20 (new series) 2012, pp. 130–60, on p. 130.

30 P. Cooksey (ed.), *The Large and Small Notebooks of Joseph Wood (1750–1821): A Yorkshire Quaker* (Huddersfield: High Flatts Quaker Meeting, 5 vols, 2011), vol. 5, p. 57.4.
31 E. P. Thompson, 'Time, work-discipline, and industrial capitalism', *Past and Present*, 38 ((1967), pp. 56–97; D. A. Reid, 'The decline of Saint Monday 1766–1876', *Past and Present*, 71 (1976), pp. 76–101 and 'Weddings, weekdays, work and leisure in urban England 1791–1911', *Past and Present*, 153 (1996), pp. 135–63.
32 Harrison, *Drink and the Victorians*, pp. 92–4.
33 Yeomans, *Alcohol and Moral Regulation*, p. 59.
34 On temperance key works are Harrison, *Drink and the Victorians*; A. E. Dingle, *The Campaign for Prohibition in Victorian England: The United Kingdom Alliance 1872–1895* (London: Croom Helm, 1980); L. L. Shiman, *Crusade against Drink in Victorian England* (Basingstoke: Macmillan, 1988); W. R. Lambert, *Drink and Sobriety in Victorian Wales c. 1820–c. 1895* (Cardiff: University of Wales Press, 1983). For the Drink Question see J. Greenaway, *Drink and British Politics since 1830: A study in policy making* (Basingstoke: Palgrave Macmillan, 2003); Nicholls, *The Politics of Alcohol*; Yeomans, *Alcohol and Moral Regulation*.
35 Hannah More, *Patient Joe; Wild Robert; Dan and Jane; and the Gin-shop* (London: J. and C. Evans for the Cheap Repository for Moral and Religious Tracts, 1810).
36 Harrison, *Drink and the Victorians*, pp. 97–102.
37 *Leeds Mercury*, 6 February 1830, p. 3.
38 Harrison, *Drink and the Victorians*, pp. 102–6.
39 Ibid., pp. 103–66 for the teetotal movement.
40 T. Whittaker, *Life's Battles in Temperance Armour* (London: Hodder and Stoughton, 1884).
41 See Harrison, *Drink and the Victorians*, pp. 115–19 for a full discussion of the lecture.
42 Ibid., pp. 121–6.
43 B. Harrison, '"A world of which we had no conception." Liberalism and the English temperance press: 1830–1872', *Victorian Studies*, 13:2 (1969), pp. 125–58, on pp. 127–32.
44 *Bradford Observer*, 23 April 1835, p. 5.
45 C. D. McDonald, 'The temperance movement in Halifax: 1832–1966', *Transactions of the Halifax Antiquarian Society*, 20 (new series) 2012, pp. 117–29; A. McAllister, '"The lives and the souls of the children": the Band of Hope in the North West', *Manchester Region History Review*, 22 (2011), pp. 1–18, on p. 4; Proverbs 22:6.
46 L. L. Shiman, 'Temperance and class in Bradford 1830–1860', *Yorkshire Archaeological Journal*, 58 (1986), pp. 173–8.
47 Harrison, *Drink and the Victorians*, p. 195.
48 For the prohibition movement see ibid., pp. 182–241 and Dingle, *The Campaign for Prohibition in Victorian England*.
49 Harrison, *Drink and the Victorians*, p. 209.
50 Greenaway, *Drink and British Politics*, pp. 24–5.
51 For his life and career see G. W. E. Russell (ed.), *Sir Wilfrid Lawson. A Memoir* (London: Smith, Elder, 1909).
52 Ibid., pp. 343–4.
53 Harrison, *Drink and the Victorians*, p. 250; Lord Askwith, *British Taverns: Their history and laws* (London: George Routledge and Sons, 1928), pp. 123–9; J. R. Greenaway, 'The local option question and British politics, 1864–1914' (PhD dissertation, University of Leeds, 1974), p. 11, n. 1 for definitions of local veto and local option and pp. 460–82 for details of proposed measures.
54 Greenaway, *Drink and British Politics*, pp. 85–6.
55 P. Cassidy, 'Temperance and the 1895 general election in the constituency of Derby', *Midland History*, 33:1 (2008), pp. 97–114, on pp. 104 and 110.

## 174  Anti-drink

56 Greenaway, *Drink and British Politics*, pp. 48–52.
57 G. W. Olsen, '"Physician heal thyself": Drink, temperance and the medical question in the Victorian and Edwardian Church of England, 1830–1914', *Addiction*, 89:9 (1994), pp. 1167–76 and 'From parish to palace: Working-class influences on Anglican temperance movements, 1835–1914', *Journal of Ecclesiastical History*, 40:2 (1989), pp. 239–52.
58 L. L. Shiman, 'The Church of England Temperance Society in the nineteenth century', *Historical Magazine of the Protestant Episcopal Church*, 41:2 (1972), pp. 179–95; Olsen, 'From parish to palace', p. 252.
59 L. L. Shiman, '"Changes are dangerous": Women and temperance in Victorian England', in G. Malmgreen (ed.), *Religion in the Lives of English Women, 1760–1930* (Beckenham: Croom Helm, 1986), pp. 193–215; and 'The Blue Ribbon Army: Gospel Temperance in England', *Historical Magazine of the Protestant Episcopal Church*, 50:4 (1981), pp. 391–408.
60 L. L. Shiman, 'The Band of Hope movement: Respectable recreation for working-class children', *Victorian Studies*, 17:1 (1973), pp. 49–74.
61 McAllister, '"The lives and souls of the children"', p. 7; and for the activities see also McAllister, 'Picturing the demon drink: How children were shown temperance principles in the Band of Hope', *Visual Resources*, 28:4 (2012), pp. 309–23.
62 S. J. D. Green, *The Passing of Protestant England: Secularisation and social change c. 1920–1960* (Cambridge: Cambridge University Press, 2011), p. 260.
63 A. Jackson, *The Diary of Ada Jackson 1883* (Leicester: Leicester City Council Living History Unit, 1993).
64 D. M. Fahey, 'Drink and the meaning of reform in late Victorian and Edwardian England', *Cithara*, 13:2 (1974), pp. 46–56, on p. 46.
65 G. R. Searle, *The Quest for National Efficiency: A study in British politics and political thought, 1899–1914* (London: Ashfield Press, 1990), pp. 60–1.
66 F. Zanetti, 'Inebriety in women and its influence on child–life', *British Journal of Inebriety*, 1:2 (1903), pp. 47–57.
67 M. Scharlieb, 'Alcohol and the children of the nation', *British Journal of Inebriety*, 5:2 (1907), pp. 59–71; on this issue see also D. W. Gutzke, '"The cry of the children": The Edwardian medical campaign against maternal drinking', *British Journal of Addiction*, 79:1 (1984), pp. 71–84; D. Wright and C. Chorniawry, 'Women and drink in Edwardian England', *Historical Papers/Communications historiques*, 20:1 (1985), pp. 117–31.
68 P. J. Waller, *Town, City and Nation: England 1850–1914* (Oxford: Oxford University Press, 1983), p. 8.
69 C. F. G. Masterman, *The Heart of the Empire: Discussions of problems of modern city life in England* (London: T. Fisher Unwin, new and popular ed., 1902) and the chapter by N. Buxton and W. Hoare, 'Temperance reform', pp. 165–210.
70 Greenaway, *Drink and British Politics*, pp. 68–70.
71 J. Rowntree and A. Sherwell, *The Temperance Problem and Social Reform* (London: Hodder and Stoughton, 7th ed., 1900), pp. 598–9.
72 H. Russell Smart, *Socialism and Drink* (Manchester: Labour Press Society, n. d.), pp. 3–4 and 14.
73 R. Breton, 'Diverting the drunkard's path: Chartist temperance narratives', *Victorian Literature and Culture*, 41:1 (2013), pp. 139–52; see also B. Harrison, 'Teetotal Chartism', *History*, 58:193 (1973), pp. 193–217.
74 J. Burns, *Labour and Drink* (London: Lees and Raper Memorial Trustees, 1904), p. 5; for labour and drink see J. B. Brown, 'The pig or the stye: Drink and poverty in late Victorian England', *International Review of Social History*, 18:3 (1973), pp. 380–95, on pp. 389–95; P. Catterall, *Labour and the politics of alcohol: The decline of a cause* (London: Institute of Alcohol Studies, 2014), pp. 7–10; Greenaway, *Drink and British Politics*, pp. 56–7.

75 Catterall, *Labour and the Politics of Alcohol*, pp. 5 and 10–11; D. Mutch, 'Intemperate narratives: Tory tipplers, Liberal abstainers and Victorian British Socialist fiction', *Victorian Literature and Culture*, 36:2 (2008), pp. 471–87.
76 Catterall, *Labour and the Politics of Alcohol*, p. 10.
77 For these points and more detailed discussion see Harrison, *Drink and the Victorians*, pp. 274–89.
78 B. Harrison, 'The Sunday Trading Riots of 1855', *Historical Journal*, 8:2 (1965), pp. 219–45.
79 Harrison, *Drink and the Victorians*, pp. 242–73 for the measures; for Gladstone's belief see R. C. K. Ensor, *England 1870–1914* (Oxford: Clarendon Press, 1936), p. 22, n. 1.
80 *Hansard* 4th Series, vol. 37, c. 716 (20 February 1896).
81 D. M. Fahey, 'Temperance and the Liberal Party – Lord Peel's Report, 1899', *Journal of British Studies*, 10:2 (1971), pp. 132–59.
82 Greenaway, *Drink and British Politics*, pp. 81–5.
83 Select Committee on Inquiry into Drunkenness among the Labouring Classes of the UK; PP 1834 (559), VIII.315, p. viii.
84 P. Jennings, *The Public House in Bradford, 1770–1970* (Keele: Keele University Press, 1995), p. 228; B. Bennison, 'Drink in Newcastle', in R. Colls and B. Lancaster (eds), *Newcastle Upon Tyne: A modern history* (Chichester: Phillimore, 2001), pp. 167–92, on pp. 176–7; Select Committee of the House of Lords for inquiring into Prevalence of Habits of Intemperance, Report; PP 1878–79 (113) X.469, p. lx.
85 M. Elliott, 'The Leicester Coffee-House and Cocoa-House Movement', *Transactions of the Leicestershire Archaeological and Historical Society*, 47 (1971–2), pp. 55–61; Harrison, *Drink and the Victorians*, p. 296; R. Thorne, 'Places of refreshment in the nineteenth-century city', in A. D. King (ed.), *Buildings and Society: Essays on the social development of the built environment* (London: Routledge & Kegan Paul, 1980), pp. 228–53, on pp. 244–5; Jennings, *The Public House in Bradford*, p. 228.
86 H. Solly, *Working Men's Social Clubs and Educational Institutes* (London: Simpkin, Marshall, Hamilton, Kent, 2nd ed., 1904), p. 29.
87 J. B. Brown, 'The temperance career of Joseph Chamberlain, 1870–1877: A study in political frustration', *Albion*, 4: 1 (1972), pp. 29–44.
88 Catterall, *Labour and the Politics of Alcohol*, p. 12.
89 *Public House Reform* (Westminster: People's Refreshment House Association, 1912), p. 5.
90 For the movement see D. W. Gutzke, 'Gentrifying the British public house, 1896–1914', *International Labor and Working-Class History*, 45 (1994), pp. 29–43; for a local example B. Bennison, 'Earl Grey's public house reform', *Journal of the Northumberland Local History Society*, 48 (1994), pp. 68–73; J. Rowntree and A. Sherwell, *British 'Gothenburg' Experiments and Public-House Trusts* (London: Hodder and Stoughton, 1901).
91 These developments are beyond the scope of this book, but see W. F. Bynum, 'Chronic alcoholism in the first half of the 19th century', *Bulletin of the History of Medicine*, 42:2 (1968), pp. 160–85 and 'Alcoholism and degeneration in 19th century European medicine and psychiatry', *British Journal of Addiction*, 79:1 (1984), pp. 59–70; A. A. Pruitt, 'Approaches to alcoholism in mid-Victorian England', *Clio Medica*, 9:2 (1974), pp. 93–101; P. McCandless, '"Curses of civilization": Insanity and drunkenness in Victorian Britain', *British Journal of Addiction* 79:1 (1984), pp. 49–58; M. Valverde, *Diseases of the Will: Alcohol and the dilemmas of freedom* (Cambridge: Cambridge University Press, 1998).
92 For US developments see S. W. Tracy, *Alcoholism in America: From Reconstruction to Prohibition* (London: Johns Hopkins University Press, 2005).
93 Select Committee on Plan for Control and Management of Habitual Drunkards; PP 1872 (242) IX.417, pp. iii–iv.

94 R. M. MacLeod, 'The Edge of hope: Social policy and chronic alcoholism 1870–1900', *Journal of the History of Medicine and Allied Sciences*, 22:3 (1967), pp. 215–45, on pp. 218–22; Greenaway, *Drink and British Politics*, p. 36.

95 V. Berridge, 'The Society for the Study of Addiction, 1884–1988', *British Journal of Addiction*, special issue, 85 (1990), pp. 981–1077, on pp. 991–1003; for a concise summary of developments see V. Berridge, *Demons: Our changing attitudes to alcohol, tobacco, and drugs* (Oxford: Oxford University Press, 2013), pp. 60–4.

96 R. W. Branthwaite, 'The Inebriates Act, 1898', *British Journal of Inebriety*, 25 (1927), pp. 5–16, on p. 11; for details of the system see Sir L. Radzinowicz and R. Hood: *A History of English Criminal Law and its Administration from 1750, vol.5, The Emergence of Penal Policy* (London: Stevens and Sons, 1986), pp. 288–315; C. Harding and L. Wilkin, '"The dream of a benevolent mind": The late Victorian response to the problem of inebriety', *Criminal Justice History* 9 (1988), pp. 189–207; J. Mellor, G. Hunt, J. Turner and L. Rees, '"Prayers and piecework": Inebriate reformatories in England at the end of the nineteenth century', *Drogalkohol*, 3 (1986), pp. 92–206; D. Beckingham, 'An historical geography of liberty: Lancashire and the Inebriates Acts', *Journal of Historical Geography*, 36:4 (2010), pp. 388–401.

97 Ibid., p. 400; on the gendered aspect of the system see B. Morrison, 'Controlling the "hopeless": Re-visioning the history of female inebriate institutions c. 1870–1920', in H. Johnston (ed.), *Punishment and Control in Historical Perspective* (Basingstoke: Palgrave Macmillan, 2008), pp. 135–57; G. Hunt, J. Mellor and J. Turner, 'Wretched, hatless and miserably clad: Women and the inebriate reformatories from 1900–1913', *British Journal of Sociology*, 40:2 (1989), pp. 244–70 and 'Women and the inebriate reformatories', in L. Jamieson and H. Corr (eds), *State, Private Life and Political Change* (Basingstoke: Macmillan, 1990), pp. 163–85.

98 Fahey, 'Drink and the meaning of reform', pp. 54–5.

99 Harrison, *Drink and the Victorians*, pp. 350–1.

100 I owe this suggestion to James Kneale.

101 M. Adler, 'From symbolic exchange to commodity consumption: Anthropological notes on drinking as a symbolic practice', in S. Barrows and R. Room (eds), *Drinking: Behavior and belief in modern history* (Berkeley, CA: University of California Press, 1991), pp. 376–98, on pp. 386–8.

102 J. S. Roberts, *Drink, Temperance and the Working Class in Nineteenth-Century Germany* (London: George Allen & Unwin, 1984), pp. 8–10.

103 For assessments of the drink issue during the war see R. Duncan, *Pubs and Patriots: The drink crisis in Britain during World War One* (Liverpool: Liverpool University Press, 2013); S. Mews, 'Urban problems and rural solutions: Drink and disestablishment in the First World War', in D. Baker (ed.), *The Church in Town and Countryside: Studies in church history, vol. 16* (Oxford: Blackwell, 1979), pp. 449–76; Yeomans, *Alcohol and Moral Regulation*, pp. 97–122; Greenaway, *Drink and British Politics*, pp. 91–113. Useful contemporary assessments are H. Carter, *The Control of the Drink Trade in Great Britain: A contribution to national efficiency during the Great War 1915–1918* (London: Longmans, Green, 2nd ed. 1919); A. Shadwell, *Drink in 1914–1922: A lesson in control* (London: Longmans, Green, 1923).

104 Carter, *The Control of the Drink Trade*, pp. 46–50.

105 S. Mews, 'Urban problems and rural solutions', pp. 467–71; Yeomans, *Alcohol and Moral Regulation*, pp. 106–12; Duncan, *Pubs and Patriots*, pp. 78–84; Greenaway, *Drink and British Politics*, pp. 91–7.

106 J. Turner, 'State purchase of the liquor trade in the First World War', *Historical Journal*, 23:3 (1980), pp. 589–615.

107 Duncan, *Pubs and Patriots*, p. 226.

108 Greenaway, *Drink and British Politics*, pp. 116–17.

109 S. G. Jones, *Workers at Play: A social and economic history of leisure 1918–1939* (London: Routledge & Kegan Paul, 1986), p. 170.

110 McAllister, '"The lives and the souls of the children"', pp. 17–18; see also her 'Rational recreation and leisure for children: The Band of Hope in the twentieth century', in R. Snape, H. Pussard and M. Constantine (eds), *Recording Leisure Lives: Everyday leisure in 20th century Britain* (Eastbourne: Leisure Studies Association, 2012), pp. 113–29; Green, *The Passing of Protestant England*, p. 161.
111 McDonald, 'The temperance movement in Halifax', pp. 122–3.
112 Lord Askwith, *British Taverns*, pp. 202–11.
113 A. Greenwood, *Public Ownership of the Liquor Trade* (London: Leonard Parsons, 1920).
114 *Let the People Decide: Some notes on the drink problem* (London: The Liquor (Popular Control) Bill Committee, 1928).
115 S. G. Jones, 'Labour, society and the drink question in Britain, 1918–1939', *Historical Journal*, 30:1 (1987), pp. 105–22, on p. 119; see also Catterall, *Labour and the Politics of Alcohol*.
116 *Labour and the Liquor Trade* (London: Labour Party, 1923); Royal Commission on Licensing (England and Wales) 1929–31, Report, PP 1931–2 (Cmd 3988), XI.
117 B. Glover, *Brewing for Victory: Brewers, beer and pubs in World War II* (Cambridge: Lutterworth Press, 1995), pp. 14–28.
118 See the Introduction to A. Calder, *The People's War: Britain 1939–1945* (London: Pimlico, 1992), pp. 17–19.
119 B. Cozens-Hardy (ed.), *Mary Hardy's Diary* (Norfolk: Norfolk Record Society, vol. 37, 1968), p. 82.
120 *Leeds Mercury*, 14 May 1831, p. 3.
121 6 & 7 Victoria, c.86; 10 & 11 Victoria, c. 89.
122 Criminal Justice Act 1925 and Road Traffic Act 1930.
123 B. Luckin, 'A never-ending passing of the buck? The failure of drink-driving reform in interwar Britain', *Contemporary British History*, 24:3 (2010), pp. 363–84 and 'A kind of consensus on the roads? Drink driving policy in Britain 1945–1970', *Twentieth Century British History*, 21:3 (2010), pp. 350–74.
124 BMA Board of Science, *Alcohol misuse: Tackling the UK epidemic* (London: BMA Board of Science, 2008), pp. 42–4.
125 E. M. Jellinek, *The Disease Concept of Alcoholism* (New Haven, CT: College and University Press, 1960); B. Thom, *Dealing with Drink: Alcohol and social policy from treatment to management* (London: Free Association Books, 1999), p. 209 and generally for this; see also R. Baggott, *Alcohol, Politics and Social Policy* (Aldershot: Avebury, 1990); J. E. McGregor, *Drink and the City: Alcohol and alcohol problems in urban UK since the 1950s* (Nottingham: Nottingham University Press, 2012).
126 Berridge, *Demons*, pp. 165–9.
127 Ibid., p. 191; Finnish Foundation for Alcohol Studies et al., *Alcohol Control Policies in Public Health Perspective* (Helsinki: Finnish Foundation for Alcohol Studies, 1975).
128 Royal College of Psychiatrists, *Alcohol and Alcoholism* (London: Tavistock Publications, 1979*)* and *Alcohol: Our favourite drug* (London: Tavistock Publications, 1986).
129 V. Berridge and B. Thom, 'Research and policy: What determines the relationship?, *Policy Studies*, 17:1 (1996), pp. 23–34, on pp. 27–30.
130 Control policies are set out and evaluated in T. Babor et al., *Alcohol: No ordinary commodity* (Oxford: Oxford University Press, 2003), pp. 102–207.
131 Baggott, *Alcohol, Politics and Social Policy*, pp. 77–9.
132 Nicholls, *The Politics of Alcohol*, pp. 205–11; K. Bruun, (ed.), *Alcohol Policies in the United Kingdom* (Stockholm: Stockholm University, 1982).
133 Nicholls, *The Politics of Alcohol*, pp. 212–13; F. Measham, 'The new policy mix: Alcohol, harm minimisation, and determined drunkenness in contemporary society', *International Journal of Drug Policy*, 17:4 (2006), pp. 258–68, on p. 262.

134 P. Dade, *Drink Talking: 100 years of alcohol advertising* (London: Middlesex University Press, 2008), p. 157
135 Baggott, *Alcohol, Politics and Social Policy*, pp. 152–61; Greenaway, *Drink and British Politics*, pp. 177–9.
136 See for example The Academy of Medical Sciences, *Calling Time: The nation's drinking as a major health issue* (London: Academy of Medical Sciences, 2004); Greenaway, *Drink and British Politics*, p. 176.
137 Yeomans, *Alcohol and Moral Regulation*, p. 221–6.
138 Greenaway, *Drink and British Politics*, p. 176; Nicholls, *The Politics of Alcohol*, p. 213; Royal College of Physicians, *A Great and Growing Evil* (London: Tavistock, 1979).

# Bibliography

Adler, M., 'From symbolic exchange to commodity consumption: Anthropological notes on drinking as a symbolic practice', in S. Barrows and R. Room (eds), *Drinking: Behavior and belief in modern history* (Berkeley, CA: University of California Press, 1991), pp. 376–98.

Askwith, Lord, *British Taverns: Their history and laws* (London: George Routledge and Sons, 1928).

Austin, G. A., *Alcohol in Western Society from Antiquity to 1800: A chronological history* (Oxford: ABC-Clio Information Services, 1985).

Babor, T., Caetano, R., Casswell, S., Edwards, G., Giesbrecht, N., Graham, K., Grube, J. W., Hill, L., Holder, H., Homel, R., Livingston, M., Österberg, E., Rehm, J., Room, R. and Rossow, I. *Alcohol: No ordinary commodity* (Oxford: Oxford University Press, 2003).

Baggott, R., *Alcohol, Politics and Social Policy* (Aldershot: Avebury, 1990).

Beckingham, D., 'An historical geography of liberty: Lancashire and the Inebriates Acts', *Journal of Historical Geography*, 36:4 (2010), pp. 388–401.

Bennison, B., 'Earl Grey's public house reform', *Journal of the Northumberland Local History Society*, 48 (1994), pp. 68–73.

—, 'Drink in Newcastle', in R. Colls and B. Lancaster (eds), *Newcastle Upon Tyne: A modern history* (Chichester: Phillimore, 2001), pp. 167–92.

Berridge, V., 'The Society for the Study of Addiction, 1884–1988', *British Journal of Addiction*, special issue, 85 (1990), pp. 981–1077.

—, *Demons: Our changing attitudes to alcohol, tobacco, and drugs* (Oxford: Oxford University Press, 2013).

—, and Thom, B., 'Research and policy: What determines the relationship?', *Policy Studies*, 17:1 (1996), pp. 23–34.

Branthwaite, R. W., 'The Inebriates Act, 1898', *British Journal of Inebriety*, 25 (1927), pp. 5–16.

Breton, R., 'Diverting the drunkard's path: Chartist temperance narratives', *Victorian Literature and Culture*, 41:1 (2013), pp. 139–52.

Brown, J. B., 'The temperance career of Joseph Chamberlain, 1870–1877: A study in political frustration', *Albion*, 4:1 (1972), pp. 29–44.

—, 'The pig or the stye: Drink and poverty in late Victorian England', *International Review of Social History*, 18:3 (1973), pp. 380–95.

Bruun, K., (ed.), *Alcohol Policies in the United Kingdom* (Stockholm: Stockholm University, 1982).

Buxton, N. and Hoare, W., 'Temperance reform', in C. F. G. Masterman, *The Heart of the Empire: Discussions of problems of modern city life in England* (London: T. Fisher Unwin, new and popular ed., 1902), pp. 165–210.

Bynum, W. F., 'Chronic alcoholism in the first half of the 19th century', *Bulletin of the History of Medicine*, 42:2 (1968), pp. 160–85.

—, 'Alcoholism and degeneration in 19th century European medicine and psychiatry', *British Journal of Addiction*, 79:1 (1984), pp. 59–70.

Calder, A., *The People's War: Britain 1939–1945* (London: Pimlico, 1992)

Carter, H., *The Control of the Drink Trade in Great Britain: A contribution to national efficiency during the Great War 1915–1918* (London: Longmans, Green, 2nd ed. 1919).

Cassidy, P., 'Temperance and the 1895 general election in the constituency of Derby', *Midland History*, 33:1 (2008), pp. 97–114.

Catterall, P., *Labour and the Politics of Alcohol: The decline of a cause* (London: Institute of Alcohol Studies, 2014).

Clark, P. 'The alehouse and the alternative society', in D. Pennington and K. Thomas (eds), *Puritans and Revolutionaries: Essays on seventeenth century history presented to Christopher Hill* (Oxford: Clarendon Press, 1978), pp. 47–72.

—, *The English Alehouse: A social history 1200–1830* (London: Longman, 1983).

—, 'The "Mother Gin" controversy in the early eighteenth century', *Transactions of the Royal Historical Society*, 5th Series 38 (1988), pp. 63–84

Clemis, D., 'Medical expertise and the understandings of intoxication in Britain, 1660–1830', in J. Herring, C. Regan, D. Weinberg and P. Withington (eds), *Intoxication and Society: Problematic pleasures of drugs and alcohol* (Basingstoke: Palgrave Macmillan, 2013), pp. 33–51.

Dade, P., *Drink Talking: 100 years of alcohol advertising* (London: Middlesex University Press, 2008).

Davison, L., 'Experiments in the social regulation of industry: Gin legislation, 1729–1751', in L. Davison, T. Hitchcock, T. Keirn and R. B. Shoemaker (eds), *Stilling the Grumbling Hive: The response to social and economic problems in England, 1689–1750* (Stroud: Alan Sutton, 1992), pp. 25–48.

Davison, L., Hitchcock, T. Keirn, T. and Shoemaker, R. B., *Stilling the Grumbling Hive: The Response to Social and Economic Problems in England, 1689–1750* (Stroud: Alan Sutton, 1992).

Dingle, A. E., *The Campaign for Prohibition in Victorian England: The United Kingdom Alliance 1872–1895* (London: Croom Helm, 1980).

Duncan, R., *Pubs and Patriots: The drink crisis in Britain during World War One* (Liverpool: Liverpool University Press, 2013).

Elliott, M., 'The Leicester Coffee-House and Cocoa-House Movement', *Transactions of the Leicestershire Archaeological and Historical Society*, 47 (1971–2), pp. 55–61.

Ensor, R. C. K., *England 1870–1914* (Oxford: Clarendon Press, 1936).

Fahey, D. M., 'Temperance and the Liberal Party – Lord Peel's Report, 1899', *Journal of British Studies*, 10:2 (1971), pp. 132–59.

—, 'Drink and the meaning of reform in late Victorian and Edwardian England', *Cithara*, 13:2 (1974), pp. 46–56.

Ferentzy, P., 'From sin to disease: Differences and similarities between past and current conceptions of chronic drunkenness', *Contemporary Drug Problems*, 28 (2001), pp. 363–90.

### Anti-drink

Finnish Foundation for Alcohol Studies, Addiction Research Foundation and WHO Regional Office for Europe. *Alcohol Control Policies in Public Health Perspective* (Helsinki: Finnish Foundation for Alcohol Studies, 1975).

Glover, B., *Brewing for Victory: Brewers, beer and pubs in World War II* (Cambridge: Lutterworth Press, 1995).

Green, S. J. D., *The Passing of Protestant England: Secularisation and social change c. 1920–1960* (Cambridge: Cambridge University Press, 2011).

Greenaway, J. R., 'The local option question and British Politics, 1864–1914' (PhD dissertation, University of Leeds, 1974).

—, *Drink and British Politics since 1830: A study in policy making* (Basingstoke: Palgrave Macmillan, 2003).

Gusfield, J. R., *Contested Meanings: The construction of alcohol problems* (Madison, WI: University of Wisconsin Press, 1996).

Gutzke, D. W., '"The cry of the children": The Edwardian medical campaign against maternal drinking', *British Journal of Addiction*, 79:1 (1984), pp. 71–84.

—, 'Gentrifying the British public house, 1896–1914', *International Labor and Working-Class History*, 45 (1994), pp. 29–43.

Harding, C. and Wilkin, L., '"The dream of a benevolent mind": The late Victorian response to the problem of inebriety', *Criminal Justice History* 9 (1988), pp. 189–207.

Hargreaves, J. A., '"Arresting the progress of this degrading and brutalising vice": Temperance, Methodism and Chartism in Halifax and its hinterland', *Transactions of the Halifax Antiquarian Society*, 20 (new series) 2012, pp. 130–60.

Harrison, B., 'The Sunday Trading Riots of 1855', *Historical Journal*, 8:2 (1965), pp. 219–45.

—, '"A world of which we had no conception." Liberalism and the English temperance press: 1830–1872', *Victorian Studies*, 13:2 (1969), pp. 125–58.

—, 'Teetotal Chartism', *History*, 58:193 (1973), pp. 193–217.

—, *Drink and the Victorians: The temperance question in England 1815–1872* (Keele: Keele University Press, 2nd ed., 1994).

Herring, J., Regan, C., Weinberg, D. and Withington, P. (eds) *Intoxication and Society: Problematic pleasures of drugs and alcohol* (Basingstoke: Palgrave Macmillan, 2013).

Hunt, A., *Governing Morals: A social history of moral regulation* (Cambridge: Cambridge University Press, 1991).

Hunt, G., Mellor, J. and Turner, J., 'Wretched, hatless and miserably clad: Women and the inebriate reformatories from 1900–1913', *British Journal of Sociology*, 40:2 (1989), pp. 244–70.

—, 'Women and the inebriate reformatories', in L. Jamieson and H. Corr (eds), *State, Private Life and Political Change* (Basingstoke: Macmillan, 1990), pp. 163–85.

Innes, J., 'Politics and morals: The Reformation of Manners Movement in later eighteenth-century England', in E. Hellmuth (ed.), *The Transformation of Political Culture in England and Germany in the Late Eighteenth Century* (Oxford: Oxford University Press, 1990), pp. 57–118.

Jellinek, E. M., *The Disease Concept of Alcoholism* (New Haven, CT: College and University Press, 1960).

Jennings, P., *The Public House in Bradford, 1770–1970* (Keele: Keele University Press, 1995).

Jones, S. G., *Workers at Play: A social and economic history of leisure 1918–1939* (London: Routledge & Kegan Paul, 1986).

—, 'Labour, society and the drink question in Britain, 1918–1939', *Historical Journal*, 30:1 (1987), pp. 105–22.

Lambert, W. R., *Drink and Sobriety in Victorian Wales c. 1820–c. 1895* (Cardiff: University of Wales Press, 1983).

Luckin, B., 'A never-ending passing of the buck? The failure of drink-driving reform in interwar Britain', *Contemporary British History*, 24:3 (2010), pp. 363–84.

—, 'A kind of consensus on the roads? Drink driving policy in Britain 1945–1970', *Twentieth Century British History*, 21:3 (2010), pp. 350–74.

McAllister, A., '"The lives and the souls of the children": the Band of Hope in the North West', *Manchester Region History Review*, 22 (2011), pp. 1–18.

—, 'Rational recreation and leisure for children: The Band of Hope in the twentieth century', in R. Snape, H. Pussard and M. Constantine (eds), *Recording Leisure Lives: Everyday leisure in 20th century Britain* (Eastbourne: Leisure Studies Association, 2012), pp. 113–29.

—, 'Picturing the demon drink: How children were shown temperance principles in the Band of Hope', *Visual Resources*, 28:4 (2012), pp. 309–23.

McCandless, P., '"Curses of civilization": Insanity and drunkenness in Victorian Britain', *British Journal of Addiction* 79:1 (1984), pp. 49–58.

McDonald, C. D., 'The temperance movement in Halifax: 1832–1966', *Transactions of the Halifax Antiquarian Society*, 20 (new series) 2012, pp. 117–29.

McGregor, J. E., *Drink and the City: Alcohol and alcohol problems in urban UK since the 1950s* (Nottingham: Nottingham University Press, 2012).

MacLeod, R. M., 'The edge of hope: Social policy and chronic alcoholism 1870–1900', *Journal of the History of Medicine and Allied Sciences*, 22:3 (1967), pp. 215–45.

Martin, A. L., 'The reform of popular drinking in late medieval and early modern Europe', in D. Kirkby and T. Luckins (eds), *Dining on Turtles: Food, feasts and drinking in history* (Basingstoke: Palgrave Macmillan, 2007), pp. 121–35.

Masterman, C. F. G., *The Heart of the Empire: Discussions of problems of modern city life in England* (London: T. Fisher Unwin, new and popular ed., 1902).

Measham, F., 'The new policy mix: Alcohol, harm minimisation, and determined drunkenness in contemporary society', *International Journal of Drug Policy*, 17:4 (2006), pp. 258–68.

Mellor, J., Hunt, G., Turner, J. and Rees, L., '"Prayers and piecework": Inebriate reformatories in England at the end of the nineteenth century', *Drogalkohol*, 3 (1986), pp. 92–206.

Mews, S., 'Urban problems and rural solutions: Drink and disestablishment in the First World War', in D. Baker (ed.), *The Church in Town and Countryside: Studies in church history*, vol. 16 (Oxford: Blackwell, 1979), pp. 449–76.

Morrison, B., 'Controlling the "hopeless": Re-visioning the history of female inebriate institutions c. 1870–1920', in H. Johnston (ed.), *Punishment and Control in Historical Perspective* (Basingstoke: Palgrave Macmillan, 2008), pp. 135–57.

Mutch, D., 'Intemperate narratives: Tory tipplers, Liberal abstainers and Victorian British Socialist fiction', *Victorian Literature and Culture*, 36:2 (2008), pp. 471–87.

Nicholls, J. C., 'Gin Lane revisited: Intoxication and society in the gin epidemic', *Journal for Cultural Research*, 7:2 (2003), pp. 125–46.

—, *The Politics of Alcohol: A history of the drink question in England* (Manchester: Manchester University Press, 2009).

Olsen, G. W., 'From parish to palace: Working-class influences on Anglican temperance movements, 1835–1914', *Journal of Ecclesiastical History*, 40:2 (1989), pp. 239–52.

—, '"Physician heal thyself": Drink, temperance and the medical question in the Victorian and Edwardian Church of England, 1830–1914', *Addiction*, 89:9 (1994), pp. 1167–76.

Porter, R., 'The drinking man's disease: The "pre-history of alcoholism" in Georgian Britain', *British Journal of Addiction*, 80:4 (1985), pp. 385–96.

Pruitt, A. A., 'Approaches to alcoholism in mid-Victorian England', *Clio Medica*, 9:2 (1974), pp. 93–101.

Radzinowicz, Sir L. and Hood, R., *A History of English Criminal Law and its Administration from 1750, vol.5, The Emergence of Penal Policy* (London: Stevens and Sons, 1986).

Rappaport, E., 'Sacred and useful pleasures: The temperance tea party and the creation of a sober consumer culture in early industrial Britain', *Journal of British Studies*, 52:4 (2013), pp. 990–1016.

Reid, D. A., 'The decline of Saint Monday 1766–1876', *Past and Present*, 71 (1976), pp. 76–101.

—, 'Weddings, weekdays, work and leisure in urban England 1791–1911', *Past and Present*, 153 (1996), pp. 135–63.

Roberts, J. S., *Drink, Temperance and the Working Class in Nineteenth-Century Germany* (London: George Allen & Unwin, 1984).

Rowntree, J. and Sherwell, A., *The Temperance Problem and Social Reform* (London: Hodder and Stoughton, 7th ed., 1900).

—, *British 'Gothenburg' Experiments and Public-House Trusts* (London: Hodder and Stoughton, 1901).

Russell, G. W. E., (ed.), *Sir Wilfrid Lawson. A Memoir* (London: Smith, Elder, 1909).

Scharlieb, M., 'Alcohol and the children of the nation', *British Journal of Inebriety*, 5:2 (1907), pp. 59–71.

Searle, G. R., *The Quest for National Efficiency: A study in British politics and political thought, 1899–1914* (London: Ashfield Press, 1990).

Shadwell, A., *Drink in 1914–1922: A lesson in control* (London: Longmans, Green, 1923).

Sharpe, J. A., 'Crime and delinquency in an Essex parish 1600–1640', in J. S. Cockburn (ed.), *Crime in England 1550–1800* (London: Methuen, 1977), pp. 90–109.

Shepard, A., '"Swil-bols and tos-pots"': Drink culture and male bonding in England, c. 1560–1640', in L. Gowing, M. Hunter and M. Rubin (eds), *Love, Friendship and Faith in Europe, 1300–1800* (Basingstoke: Palgrave Macmillan, 2005), pp. 110–30.

Shiman, L. L., 'The Church of England Temperance Society in the nineteenth century', *Historical Magazine of the Protestant Episcopal Church*, 41:2 (1972), pp. 179–95.

—, 'The Band of Hope Movement: Respectable recreation for working-class children', *Victorian Studies*, 17:1 (1973), pp. 49–74.

—, 'The Blue Ribbon Army: Gospel Temperance in England', *Historical Magazine of the Protestant Episcopal Church*, 50:4 (1981), pp. 391–408.

—, '"Changes are dangerous": Women and temperance in Victorian England', in G. Malmgreen (ed.), *Religion in the Lives of English Women, 1760–1930* (Beckenham: Croom Helm, 1986), pp. 193–215.

—, 'Temperance and class in Bradford 1830–1860', *Yorkshire Archaeological Journal*, 58 (1986), pp. 173–8.

—, *Crusade against Drink in Victorian England* (Basingstoke: Macmillan, 1988).

Shoemaker, R. B., 'Reforming the city: The Reformation of Manners Campaign in London, 1690–1738', in L. Davison, T. Hitchcock, T. Keirn and R. B. Shoemaker (eds), *Stilling the Grumbling Hive: The response to social and economic problems in England, 1689–1750* (Stroud: Alan Sutton, 1992), pp. 99–120.

Shrank, C., 'Beastly metamorphoses: Losing control in early modern literary culture', in Herring *et al.*, *Intoxication and Society*, pp. 193–209.

Smyth, A., '"It were far better be a *Toad*, or a *Serpent*, than a Drunkard": Writing about drunkenness', in A. Smyth (ed.), *A Pleasing Sinne: Drink and conviviality in seventeenth-century England* (Cambridge: D. S. Brewer, 2004), pp. 193–210.

Thom, B., *Dealing with Drink: Alcohol and social policy from treatment to management* (London: Free Association Books, 1999).
Thomas, K., 'Work and leisure in pre-industrial society', *Past and Present*, 29 (1964), pp. 50–66.
Thompson, E. P., 'Time, work-discipline, and industrial capitalism', *Past and Present*, 38 (1967), pp. 56–97.
Thorne, R., 'Places of refreshment in the nineteenth-century city', in A. D. King (ed), *Buildings and Society: Essays on the social development of the built environment* (London: Routledge & Kegan Paul, 1980), pp. 228–53.
Tracy, S. W., *Alcoholism in America: From Reconstruction to Prohibition* (London: Johns Hopkins University Press, 2005).
Turner, J., 'State purchase of the liquor trade in the First World War', *Historical Journal*, 23:3 (1980), pp. 589–615.
Valverde, M., *Diseases of the Will: Alcohol and the dilemmas of freedom* (Cambridge: Cambridge University Press, 1998).
Waller, P. J., *Town, City and Nation: England 1850–1914* (Oxford: Oxford University Press, 1983).
Warner, J., 'Before there was "alcoholism": Lessons from the medieval experience with alcohol', *Contemporary Drug Problems*, 19:3 (1992), pp. 409–29.
—, '"Resolv'd to drink no more": Addiction as a preindustrial construct', *Journal of Studies on Alcohol*, 55:6 (1994), pp. 685–81.
—, 'Shifting categories of the social harms associated with alcohol: Examples from late medieval and early modern England', *American Journal of Public Health*, 87:11 (1997), pp. 1788–97.
—, 'The sanctuary of sobriety: The emergence of temperance as a feminine virtue in Tudor and Stuart England', *Addiction*, 92:1 (1997), pp. 97–111,
White, J., 'The "slow but sure poyson": The representation of gin and its drinkers, 1736–1751', *Journal of British Studies*, 42:1 (2003), pp. 35–64.
Wright, D. and Chorniawry, C., 'Women and drink in Edwardian England', *Historical Papers/Communications historiques*, 20:1 (1985), pp. 117–31.
Wrightson, K., 'Two concepts of order: Justices, constables and jurymen in seventeenth-century England', in J. Brewer and J. Styles (eds), *An Ungovernable People?: The English and their law in the seventeenth and eighteenth centuries* (London: Hutchinson, 1980), pp. 21–46.
—, 'Alehouses, order and Reformation in rural England, 1590–1660', in E. and S. Yeo (eds), *Popular Culture and Class Conflict 1590–1914: Explorations in the history of labour and leisure* (Brighton: Harvester press, 1981), pp. 1–27.
—, *English Society 1580–1680* (London: Hutchinson, 1982).
Yeomans, H., *Alcohol and Moral Regulation: Public attitudes, spirited measures and Victorian hangovers* (Bristol: Policy Press, 2014).
Zanetti, F., 'Inebriety in women and its influence on child-life', *British Journal of Inebriety*, 1:2 (1903), pp. 47–57.

# 7  Regulation

**Regulation in context**

The consumption of drink has been subject to regulation for centuries. The result has been a regulatory regime, also generally known as the licensing, or liquor licensing, system, of great complexity. As one nineteenth-century Lord Chief Justice fittingly described it: 'a labyrinth of chaotic legislation'.[1] This has been a common observation, not least from those working in the drink trades. The *Licensed Victuallers' Official Annual* for 1908 placed the offences which a publican might commit into no fewer than sixty-three categories.[2] Towards the close of that century, in 1984, the laws were described by Conservative MP Rob Hayward, later chief executive of the Brewers' and Licensed Retailers' Association, as in 'a general mess' and 'anachronistic'.[3] Those twin criticisms were central to the reasoning behind New Labour's licensing-reform proposals at the turn of the millennium.[4] This chapter seeks to get to grips with that complexity in historical perspective, first by making some general observations on the context of regulation, second by setting out chronologically the key phases of its development and third by examining how those regulations were administered and policed.

What has been the purpose of regulation? Paramount at all times has been the preservation of public order and, allied to that, the maintenance of certain standards of individual behaviour. For Sidney and Beatrice Webb, introducing their historical survey of liquor licensing, published in 1903, the prevention of 'the social disorder and personal misconduct brought about by excessive drinking' was its 'primary aim'.[5] Almost a century later New Labour's reform proposals similarly identified its first purpose as the protection of the public from crime and disorder.[6] In an effective licensing system, therefore, certain types of behaviour had to be suppressed or controlled. But from the Webbs' temperance-minded perspective this was complicated and thwarted by two further considerations governing regulation: the state's revenue and the promotion of brewing and distilling.[7] In forming this view, they were no doubt aware from their detailed researches that the first parliamentary inquiry into licensing, which reported in 1817, had in fact placed 'the conservation of the public peace and morals' as a secondary purpose to 'the advance and security of the Revenue against the unlicensed vend of excisable liquors'.[8]

The state's financial interest in drink was always considerable. The fines levied under the thirteenth-century assize of ale, which regulated price, quality and measures, were a source of revenue and constituted, it has been argued, a de facto licensing system.[9] The first customs duties were the levies on imported wines.[10] To customs was added excise by the Long Parliament in 1643. The Excise became the largest department of government and in the eighteenth and nineteenth centuries generated an essential financial support to Britain's dominant position in the world.[11] At their highest level, during the Revolutionary and Napoleonic wars, taxes on drink made up over half the government's revenue and throughout the nineteenth century it continued to average around one third.[12] As the structure of taxation changed the proportion declined, such that by the mid 1930s it accounted for 14.2 per cent of revenue, which had fallen to 6 per cent by the 1970s.[13] But the total revenue was still significant. By the beginning of the twenty-first century the government's Alcohol Harm Reduction Strategy for England reported that excise duty contributed £7 billion to the national exchequer, in the context of a total budget in 2003–4 of over £439 billion, although this of course did not include revenues from VAT and central and local taxation. Whilst it may not have phrased it as the promotion of brewing and distilling, the Strategy nevertheless stressed the overall importance of the alcoholic drinks market as 'a substantial and valuable part of the UK economy and society', generating annually over £30 billion and providing around one million jobs.[14] On the other hand the economically harmful effects of alcohol have been stressed. The Strategy itself noted that the harms from alcohol misuse cost the economy up to £20 billion a year. But the social costs have been estimated much higher: a British Medical Association report of 2008 cited an annual overall cost to society of over £55 billion.[15]

The issues of economic benefit or economic and social harm historically have generated questions of what should be the proper role of regulation. At times the emphasis has been on supporting the drink and related industries. This was the case, for example, in the early eighteenth century with the promotion of distilling and in the mid nineteenth century with the creation of free trade in beer and the introduction of measures to promote the sale of wine, although the latter two were also presented as aids to moderation. Free trade was meant to benefit the consumer, too, as had the medieval assize of ale. At other times the emphasis has been on restriction for the greater economic and social good, as was the case with the efforts to curb gin-drinking in the mid eighteenth century, or to maintain national efficiency to aid the war effort in the First World War.

Still other objectives have been sought from regulation. New Labour's reform proposals of 2000 placed particular emphasis on the protection of children from early exposure to alcohol.[16] This particular concern, however, had not been present throughout most of the history of regulation. Consumption by children and their presence in drinking places were not thought to be problematic. Only in the nineteenth century, and then tentatively and slowly, were they brought within its compass, as attitudes towards childhood, as well as to drink, changed. But those attitudes shifted again towards the end of the twentieth century. Whilst legislation of 1908 had banned children under the age of fourteen altogether from public houses, that which followed New Labour's reform proposals in 2003, in deference to changed lifestyles, now permitted them if accompanied, although drink was still denied them.

As the specific example of children and drink and the general concerns of order, revenue and economy with which we began demonstrate, drink was never an isolated issue. Rather, it was one which interlinked with many others in the wider society and culture. This point is central to any attempt to understand the history of regulation.[17] All in turn were the subject of debate and contest. And since the state was ultimately responsible for regulation, they were accordingly political questions, at times intensely so. The complex politics of drink has been the subject of two important modern studies, offering perspectives which complement one another. The high politics of the question – 'how elite politicians and decision-makers reacted and wrestled with it' – has been examined by John Greenaway in the period from the Beer Act of 1830 to the 1970s. In avowed contrast, James Nicholls presented a view of 'drink as a political issue in the widest sense' that took account 'of the cultural anxieties and political attitudes' present over a longer period from the seventeenth century to the 2003 Licensing Act.[18] Both works are essential to augment the outline presented here and both underscore the complexity of the question.

Complexity is evident in the next point, too. The creation of a system of regulation is one thing; we must also examine its administration and enforcement. Two general observations will again give context to what follows. First, there is the ambiguous nature of alcohol. On the one hand drinking was seen by many people as productive of a variety of undesirable consequences, but on the other it was viewed, and experienced, by many others (and sometimes they were the same people) as necessary, enjoyable, legitimate and a source of profit. Thus large numbers of people had an interest in its ready availability, from individual consumers (always the majority of the population) to the drink industry, broadly defined, of producers and sellers and the many associated trades and their workers. The consequences for administration and enforcement can be seen throughout the history of regulation. Part-time parish constables of the sixteenth to nineteenth centuries had in the end to live amongst the neighbours whom they policed. This need to work with local communities, together with a range of bureaucratic and practical constraints, also shaped how their professional successors policed drunks and licensed premises. It is true, too, of much broader questions, as when, for example, from the later nineteenth century moves to reduce the number of public houses perceived to be superfluous raised the thorny question of financial compensation to those affected.

Second is the importance of local circumstances, for it was at this level that regulation was played out; it was the responsibility of local agents of the state, in the form of magistrates, police and local authorities. But regulation also utilized private individuals, as it has been argued, 'contracting out the governmental work of preventing disorder and monitoring risks to the private sector'.[19] In return for the right to trade the device of licensing placed upon drink sellers a range of supervisory functions, although these were underpinned by criminal sanctions: not to permit drunken behaviour on their premises, for example, or gambling or prostitution. At these local levels, whether benches of licensing magistrates, parish constables, urban police forces, or individual publicans, myriad other influences can be discerned in shaping how regulation worked out in practice. Local licensing magistrates administered centrally created laws, but they enjoyed for most of their 450 years of authority considerable discretion, which in turn might be shaped by their individual preferences, from rural justices mindful of drink's importance to agriculture to urban nonconformists keen to hold it in check. Publicans might be charged with supervisory responsibilities, but they had also to form good relations with their customers, and being overly strict over last orders or whether someone had taken too much drink were not necessarily conducive to that aim.

The foregoing certainly does not cover all the many questions raised by regulation. For example, they naturally encompass ideas about the proper role of the state and its relationship in turn to the individual, and of the balance to be drawn between freedom and restriction.[20] Nor, it must be said, does it claim to be exhaustive in the face of the system's complexity. The excise regulations in particular were, as Peter Mathias observed of those of the eighteenth century, 'a jungle into which few Englishmen penetrated very far'; and nor will I.[21] But it is hoped that enough has been said to provide some measure of coherence to the chronological survey which follows.

## The early development of regulation

The modern licensing system is generally viewed as dating from the mid sixteenth century. But there were many precedents for later regulation from the Anglo-Saxon period and through the medieval. As noted above, the revenue derived from fines under the assize of ale may be said to have constituted a de facto licensing system. But these were not designed solely to generate revenue: they sought to protect the consumer, as was also the case with that other staple, bread, by ensuring the availability of good drink at a fair price in specified measures. This in turn was aimed at maintaining order by preventing possible disturbances resulting from unscrupulous practices or pressure on incomes.[22] In addition to this national measure there was much local regulation, variously covering the right to trade, the number of drinking places, the location, designation and construction of premises, permitted opening hours, the character and conduct of the retailer and the behaviour of customers. Examples are a mid-fourteenth-century order to Bristol's ale-sellers to display a sign, or a Nottingham requirement of the mid fifteenth century that they close at 9 pm.[23]

At the local level evidence from manorial, borough and hundred courts shows mounting concern about behaviour over the course of the fifteenth century, with a gradual rise in the number of reports of disorderly alehouses.[24] By the close of that century parliament was taking action and a statute, significantly concerned with 'vagabonds and beggars', gave to local justices of the peace the power to suppress alehouses and to take surety of their proprietors for good behaviour.[25] Alongside this, local initiatives continued to be taken: in 1516, for example, the

188  *Regulation*

jurors of Basingstoke, Hampshire, issued an order to all alehouse keepers not to keep apprentices in their houses after 7 pm or servants after 9 pm, on pain of a substantial penalty of 20s.[26] Many other towns took similar steps, particularly from the 1540s.[27] But it is the statute of 1552 which is usually taken to be the first Licensing Act. This placed the right to trade as alehouse or tipling-house keeper under the authority of local justices of the peace and required them to enter into sureties for the good conduct of their premises.[28] In the following year, in part also aimed at ensuring good order, the sale of wine was to be licensed by local authorities and limited to specified numbers of taverns in London and other towns.[29]

This, however, was only the beginning of the development of licensing. The Acts were followed by several additional royal proclamations and orders of the privy council, but, overall, government efforts to promote more vigorous action by justices were 'at best spasmodic' before 1600 and local initiatives continued to be taken. The legislation on taverns does not appear to have been effective, as the survey of drinking places in 1577 listed more than the permitted number. Moreover, the Crown retained the power to grant wine licences, and freedom of the Vintners' Company of London also conferred the privilege of retailing wine.[30] With respect to alehouses, in the early seventeenth century there was a further round of statutory activity, with four acts and other government orders culminating in a detailed royal proclamation in 1619, which clarified a number of issues and codified law and practice. Licences were to be granted annually by local justices of the peace, who were to have discretion over whom they chose; forms of words for the licence and the recognizance were set out; and the various conditions as to closure during times of church service and their good conduct listed. This important proclamation was followed during the 1620s by further statutes tightening up aspects of this system.[31] Whilst all this was directed at alehouses, inns too, as retailers of beer, were brought within its remit.

This series of measures, which by the close of the 1620s had put in place a national framework of licensing, was driven by the concerns outlined in the previous chapter. It reflected, too, the Crown's determination to assert its authority in the localities and that of local country gentry similarly within their parishes. But although there was certainly hostility to them, alehouses were also deemed to have legitimate and essential purposes. The 1619 proclamation noted the requirements that they provide lodging for at least one person and ale and beer for labourers and travellers, and this proper purpose was recorded in statutes. It is also noteworthy that the 1552 Act provided for the sale of drink at fairs without magistrates' authority 'for the Relief of the King's Subjects'. The government's interest was financial, too. One way to raise cash was through the issue of royal patents, especially one of 1617 to Sir Giles Mompesson to license for a fee suitable victualling houses as inns, and one to Sir James Spence and others to recover money forfeited by tipplers for breaches of the conditions of their licence. Such was the 'avalanche of protest' about these patents that when parliament met in 1621 Mompesson was impeached and the two grants rescinded. The whole affair 'badly discredited' central involvement in licensing and served to underline for the localities the need to establish their own effective administration to safeguard against Crown intervention.[32] The Crown's authority over wine licences, however, remained a regular source of income until 1757, when their grant was transferred to the Stamp Office.

To see how this national framework of regulation worked it is at particular localities that we need to look. Certainly there are examples of apparently vigorous enforcement. One notable case was the Dorset county and market town of Dorchester, where, following a disastrous fire in 1613, the town's authorities waged a concerted campaign against all forms of sin in an attempt to create a godly, sober and disciplined town. Accordingly, of 1,386 cases recorded in the town's offenders book in the five years to Michaelmas 1637 over 35 per cent were drink-related, by far the largest category. Yet the campaign's historian concluded that these moves against excessive drinking were in fact its 'most conspicuous failure'. The justices had been unable to reduce the number of alehouses, and although unlicensed houses were constantly being suppressed, they nearly always managed to stay in business.[33] A detailed study of the Essex village of Terling showed how from the early seventeenth century, in a drive by village elites and officers to establish a more disciplined social order, behaviour and alehouses were targeted. But in this 'particularly closely governed county' the results were tempered by circumstances, as when those prosecuted were supported by friends and kin and other influential villagers. Hence it was usual to prosecute only the most notorious offenders or those who ignored warnings.[34] That elites could have conflicting views is shown in two further examples. In the East Riding of Yorkshire efforts to suppress unlicensed alehouses were hampered by the willingness of some magistrates to grant licences against the wishes of their colleagues.[35] In Southampton magistrates deliberately did not implement policies perceived as harmful to the local economy and community, since selling ale was a means of earning a living for the poor and helped the civic budget, too. This contrasted with the more determined efforts of local office holders, who mixed economic motives (some actually kept inns or taverns and wanted to reduce the competition) with status concerns as they sought to distance themselves from their poorer neighbours and show how well they could carry out their governmental duties.[36]

Clearly there was local variation in the degree of enforcement of regulations, but over the century the key elements of the administration of licensing were put in place across the country as a whole. Licences were issued by local justices of the peace for specific divisions within counties, thus putting a stop to the practice noted above in the East Riding. They were granted only at special annual licensing sessions, or brewster sessions as they were called, a custom put on a statutory footing finally in 1729.[37] Applicants had to enter into recognizances and provide surety for their good behaviour, and the licence set out conditions for the proper conduct of their premises. This system was rendered effective at the turn of the century by several interconnected developments.[38] First was the relaxation of the earlier criticism of the alehouse. Although there were still calls for the moral reform of the lower orders, their impact on drinking and alehouse regulation was limited, as we saw with the Reformation of Manners movement. The growth in numbers entering the alehouse trade slowed down. Economic growth lessened the importance of alehouses as a safety valve. But in other ways inns and more substantial public houses became more important to a growing economy. More alehouses then upgraded to perform such functions, as the trade overall became more respectable. This was encouraged by local magistrates and in this they received the support of commercial brewers (in those parts of the country where their presence was becoming significant) and the Excise, which wanted a network of easily monitored businesses. Here, too, the zealous justice might find his enthusiasm circumscribed. In Norwich in 1681 the mayor was forced to abandon a campaign against the growing number of alehouses when he was reported to the central government by the Excise as politically suspect.[39]

The sale of spirits was incorporated into this system by the 1740s, although the process was protracted. Having earlier opened up the distilling trade and retail sale, with the consequences we have seen, a repentant parliament now sought in a succession of laws to confine sale to suitable, licensed premises. Only two, however, passed in 1743 and 1744, appear finally to have had the desired effect, since statistics of the number of excise spirit licences commence in the latter year. These licences were only to be granted to licensed inns, taverns, alehouses, victualling houses or coffee houses; their proprietors could not also be distillers, grocers or chandlers; and it was not permitted to trade solely in spirits. In a further attempt to raise the status of the trade, in London at least, they were only to be granted to houses valued at over £10.[40] Finally, an Act of 1753 restated the whole licensing system, with some modifications to deal more effectively, as its preamble put it, with 'Abuses and Disorders' and unlicensed retailing.[41] This system remained largely unchanged, except for the transfer of the sale of wine to the justices' authority in 1792,[42] for some three quarters of a century. Indeed, in essentials it endured for a further 250 years.

## Licensing in practice 1753–1828

How did licensing work in practice in the eighteenth and early nineteenth centuries? All existing publicans, new applicants and their sureties had to attend the brewster sessions in person on specified days. Individual licensing districts varied enormously in their numbers of publicans, underscoring, as in so many ways, the local diversity of the system. At one end of the scale in London, the biggest division, the Tower, dealt in the second decade of the nineteenth century with well over 900 applicants at its sessions, whilst at the other, the little borough of Hedon in the East Riding of Yorkshire processed annually throughout this period just eight or nine individuals.[43] The sessions might be held at a public building, but it was common for an inn to provide the venue and they could accordingly be convivial affairs: the magistrates of the Holborn division of Middlesex, for example, deliberated in the 1820s at the Freemasons' Tavern in Great Queen Street, Lincoln's Inn Fields, where they were provided with refreshments of tea, coffee, wine and cold meat.[44] There might be preliminary inquiry into the conduct through the year of the applicants and scrutiny of new ones. In the Surrey division of Southwark and the East Half Hundred of Brixton, with well over 800 applicants each year in the early nineteenth century, ministers and churchwardens of the various parishes in the division were asked about complaints against publicans and an adjourned sessions investigated any submitted, together with new applications, all of which were personally inspected by the magistrates.[45] It is, however, not possible to say how usual this was, and in any case perhaps hardly necessary in small jurisdictions. Two justices were required for the sessions themselves, although more did attend. The licences and recognizances were signed and the details recorded by the justices' clerk. Once completed, the sessions afforded an opportunity for exchanging news and views and general socializing, in which also the good relations of regulators and those regulated is sometimes apparent. William Hardy, a late eighteenth-century Norfolk brewer who owned or leased a number of public houses, usually dined with the magistrates, whilst John Carrington, a Hertfordshire head constable, noted in his diary how after the 1798 sessions at St Albans, for example, he enjoyed dinner with three widows who kept inns in his jurisdiction.[46]

In their study of licensing the Webbs, on the evidence of contemporary complaints, charged eighteenth-century justices with 'extreme laxness' in their administration of the system, when any suppression of disorderly premises 'went entirely into desuetude'.[47] In fact the statistical picture of the number of public houses shows a large reduction over the course of the eighteenth century. How this was effected has not been fully explored. Some local magistrates and clergy were working to get rid of troublesome alehouses, as were landowners intent on the improvement of their estates. For example, in 1766 the Rector of Newport Pagnell intervened with the justices to refuse the licences of alehouses frequented by local youth.[48] Also at this time at Kirkleatham, on the Yorkshire coast, landowner and magistrate Charles Turner replaced 'a collection of little blackguard alehouses' with two 'handsome inns' in the village and at his new port and resort respectively.[49] Whilst the laxness which the Webbs described may thus have been illusory, the tightening up of regulation from the 1780s, which was linked in particular, as we saw, to the Royal Proclamation of 1787, was real. As they documented, there are plenty of examples, such as over closing times and Sunday opening. But, as they themselves admitted, it was only systematic for half a dozen years, if surviving for longer 'as an ideal, and to some extent as a governing principle' until 1830 – and in any case, in their view its effectiveness could not really be discerned from the available evidence.[50] Moreover, its impact in London in particular was limited and allegations of laxness continued to be made. This was certainly the key finding of a parliamentary inquiry into licensing in the capital which reported in 1817, with regulatory mechanisms like character certificates and recognizances judged to be dead letters in the context of 'a general indifference ... to the existence of disorderly houses'.[51]

This apparent magisterial indifference was in the context of alleged abuse of their discretion in the grant of licences. To these was added concern over the growth of brewers' control of public houses in the capital, which the licensing inquiry confirmed. At the same time, another inquiry, set up in response to petitions complaining of the high price and inferior quality of beer, deplored the trend towards monopoly in the growth of brewery control of public houses, although it exonerated the brewers of profiteering or adulteration.[52] Both, together with general Radical criticism of the magistracy, were linked in the agitation to free up the licensing system, which was connected in turn with the wider movement towards free trade. The Whig wit Sydney Smith brought them together in a review of an article critical of the arbitrary conduct of magistrates, concluding: 'If the trade in public houses were free, there would be precisely the number wanted; for no man would sell liquor to his ruin'.[53]

This movement of opinion did produce some rather meagre changes in the law towards a freer trade in beer, as we saw in Chapter 2, but more immediately important was a consolidating licensing measure in 1828, which introduced a degree of limitation on the discretion of magistrates and some measures to open up the trade of publican. The requirement to enter into recognizances and find sureties was now abolished, as was that for new applicants to obtain character certificates. Provision was made for special sessions for the transfer of licences, rather than at petty sessions, to ensure greater openness in the process, and a right of appeal was introduced from the local licensing justices to quarter sessions. The licence itself was to be granted for one year and was subject to the conditions listed on it, covering drunkenness and disorder, unlawful games, adulteration and illegal measures. Closing during church services was also specified. The Act repealed a mass of earlier legislation and remained the basis of licensing law until a further consolidating Licensing Act of 1910.[54]

## Free trade

The 1828 Act largely reproduced the existing system and made only modest changes. Of much greater significance was a further measure of free trade: the Beer Act of 1830. This removed the sale of beer from magistrates' authority, permitting it simply on payment of an annual fee to the Excise. But it did not represent complete deregulation: there were provisions as to the value of properties which could be used; the conditions on keeping order and so on were the same as for licensed public houses; opening hours were more restricted; and the new retailers had to provide surety for the good conduct of their houses. As we saw, thousands availed themselves of the business opportunity offered by the measure, but complaints were immediately vocal and widespread, such that the government was compelled to acknowledge that 'inconveniences ... had been felt, particularly in some of the agricultural districts', which went beyond what had been anticipated, and conceded that inquiry was necessary.[55] Two years later a parliamentary select committee did indeed conclude that 'considerable evils' had arisen from the management and conduct of beerhouses.[56] This was to be a constant refrain over subsequent decades. It did fairly quickly lead to some minor regulatory changes in 1834 and 1840, when the qualifying rateable value was raised, certificates of good character were introduced and a distinction was created between on- and off-sale.

Alongside this, as we saw, the trade in table beer had been completely deregulated and measures taken to open up the sale of wine, with overall limited results. There were also a small number of local benches of magistrates who pursued a free-licensing policy. Most important was that of Liverpool, which attracted attention due in large part to the city's sheer size. Familiar arguments were aired: of the vagaries of magisterial discretion, of the more satisfactory operation of the free market on the provision of drinking places and the undue influence of brewers on the licensing process. In the event, the policy was only adopted briefly between 1862 and 1865, when a total of 370 licences were granted, before a shift in the composition of the licensing bench halted it.[57]

## The primacy of restriction

It should be noted that in none of these instances of deregulation was the central question of public order lost sight of. The Beer Act had in some ways subjected the new beerhouses to stricter regulation than the existing public houses. Gladstone's 1860 legislation on refreshment houses similarly contained familiar provisions as to the value of premises to be so licensed, opening hours and their conduct. The Act also contained public-order measures relating to drinking places generally, including a penalty for drunks refusing or neglecting to quit licensed premises when asked to do so by the landlord or the police. In a series of measures, opening hours also were progressively restricted, although by later standards they remained generous. Statutory hours, first introduced for the new beerhouses, were adopted for all licensed premises, previously only required to close during the time of church services on Sundays (plus Good Friday and Christmas Day). In 1848 closure for the whole of Sunday morning was introduced nationally, but a measure of 1854, extending this to most of Sunday afternoon, proved so unpopular that it was reduced to just two hours, retaining thereby the principle of an afternoon pause. Closure in the small hours on weekdays was introduced in London in 1864 and adopted widely throughout the country.[58]

In the end, public order became of greater moment than questions of free licensing, free trade or the promotion of particular drinks. First, the forty-year existence of free trade in beer was terminated when an 'unresisting parliament' in 1869 endorsed a private member's bill returning them to magistrates' authority.[59] The Act in fact limited the justices' discretion to refuse licences to these ante-69 beerhouses, as they were termed, to just four reasons, but these did cover questions principally of public order. Justices were quick to exercise their new authority at the ensuing brewster sessions. Licences were refused to beerhouses amounting to just over 13 per cent of those in existence prior to the legislation, or some 6,540 premises. As the House of Lords inquiry into intemperance later concluded: 'The process of weeding out the most disorderly beerhouses has been carried on throughout the country'.[60] Second, its provisions were made permanent in the general Licensing Act of 1872, the most important measure between the consolidating statutes of 1828 and 1910. The sale of all alcoholic drink, including at special occasions, with the sole minor exception of off-sale by wine and spirit dealers, now required a justices' licence. Existing provisions on the conduct of premises and their hours of opening were restated, in some cases tightened up, and penalties increased. Convictions were to be recorded on the licence. It also made a number of administrative changes, notably in ending the requirement for all publicans to attend the brewster sessions in person (except for new applicants and those to whom objection had been made) and creating a cheaper six-day licence for those willing to close on the Sabbath.

The Act signalled a definite shift to a more restrictive licensing climate. This is to be seen both in the operation of the system and in the permitted uses of licensed premises, which will be examined in turn. Justices for the moment showed themselves willing to grant new licences, but this did not last. Over the country as a whole 3,699 were granted in the eight years from 1873 to 1881; in the ten years from 1887 to 1896 the figure was 1,930. But many of these were not, strictly speaking, new licences. Of that 3,699 15 per cent were upgrades to a full licence by existing beerhouses; some were removals from one location to another; whilst others were granted in return for the surrender of one or more (usually beer) licences.[61] The last strategy was adopted in a number of places, notably Birmingham, where the chairman of its licensing bench, Arthur Chamberlain, proposed in 1897 what came to be known as the 'Birmingham Surrender Scheme'. Under this arrangement bench and brewers cooperated to close selected city-centre pubs, with the brewers setting up a company to provide compensation. Although in the six years to 1904 222 were closed, this number fell short of Chamberlain's aspirations and brewers were disappointed in their hopes of new licences in suburban areas.[62] Another point was that many new licences were granted to hotels or restaurants rather than public houses. Finally, licensing benches were largely unwilling to allow the replacement of pubs demolished as a result of redevelopment or slum clearance. The overall result was a continuing fall in the number of public houses. On licensing, finally, we must note a requirement in the 1902 Licensing Act that all clubs which sold drink had to be registered; and magistrates were given power to strike them from the register on various grounds, including those relating to order.

By the later nineteenth century the licensing system was thus working to reduce the number of public houses. But, as we saw, the view was now gaining ground that this number should be reduced still further. Reduction in the ways outlined or, of course, if a licence were refused for misconduct, could be effected without too much contention. But moves to increase the pace of reduction raised the question of financial compensation. For the trade, and indeed for much mainstream opinion, compensation for the loss of a business was only right and proper, as for any compulsory purchase, such as for street improvements. But for many temperance supporters this meant giving money to an evil trade. Moves in the direction of compensation, by Gladstone in 1880 and more determinedly by the Conservatives in 1888 and 1890, thus foundered on the strength of feeling aroused.[63] At issue in the continuing controversy was the status of a licence. In law it was granted for one year at the discretion of licensing magistrates, a fact affirmed in a succession of cases, culminating in that of Sharpe v. Wakefield, which went all the way to the

House of Lords in 1891. In practice, however, the licence had come to be treated as a form of property, for tax or insurance purposes, for example, the grant of which was assumed to be automatic unless there was misconduct.[64] So long as this practice was followed, matters might go on as they had, but when some licensing benches, notably at Farnham in Surrey in 1901, instigated moves to get rid of what they perceived as superfluous licences, the trade was quick to implore the government to intervene. The prime minister, Arthur Balfour, personally addressed the issue, which, however well intentioned, was little short of 'unjust confiscation of property'. The resulting controversial Licensing Act of 1904 was presented by the government on the one hand as a temperance measure, responding to the widespread desire to see a reduction in the number of licences, and on the other as a just settlement for a lawful trade in which large sums had been invested. Licences could now be refused on grounds other than misconduct, but only on payment of compensation. That compensation in turn was to come from a levy on licensed premises payable by the trade itself. The result was indeed a reduction in the number of licences. In the ten years of its operation down to 1914 9,801 licences were extinguished, representing a little under 10 per cent of those in existence at the beginning of the century and a quickening of the pace of reduction over the previous 32 years since the 1869 measure. But it was fewer than had been predicted, chiefly due its cost, and the pace of reduction, having peaked in 1907, was already by then slowing down.[65]

Turning now from the licensing system to premises and their use, restriction is seen in several areas. One important exception was opening hours, which remained essentially unchanged until the First World War, apart from the introduction of Sunday closing in Wales in 1881.[66] There, however, the exception created by the 1874 Licensing Act for the bona fide traveller of at least three miles seeking refreshment was to prove a fruitful source of the law's flouting, as, for example, with the sixty-three 'breaks' – small trams for seven passengers – taking travellers the four miles between Porth and Pontypridd.[67] Control was sought over the structure of premises, in addition to the requirements for minimum value. Local licensing benches variously tried to prevent conversion to gin-palace-style, more-open-plan premises, with long bars and minimal seating, as well as any increase in drinking space and to bring about improvements to sanitary arrangements or general décor. Pubs which doubled as shops were also targeted, the latter reflected in particular worries about their use by women. This also fuelled concern over small drinking rooms like 'snugs', where immoral acts might occur, and back and side doors, into which women might enter pubs unseen. The particular spaces of pubs and the difficulties they were felt to present for the effective supervision of their patrons have been explored by historical geographers. These concerns, however, met with limited practical success, and it was not until the Licensing Act of 1902 that general control over the structure of licensed premises was given to magistrates.[68]

Some of the varied uses of public houses were also now the subject of restriction and regulation. In political life, although they continued to play a vital, sometimes scandalous, role in elections for much of the century, anti-corruption legislation in 1883 and 1884 included a ban on holding committee rooms there in parliamentary and municipal elections. Administrative meetings were prohibited (unless there was no suitable alternative accommodation) for borough justices' sessions in 1882, in local government or Poor Law administration in 1894 and for all justices' sessions and coroners' courts in 1902.[69] The pub's thriving musical life came under greater scrutiny. Londoners had been subject to legislation since 1752 for music, dancing and other entertainment, but now many local authorities obtained similar legal powers, and in 1890 model regulations were provided for them to adopt, covering the conduct of patrons and the content of performances.[70] The once common practice of paying wages in pubs was prohibited. Attempts to achieve this, in the case of the London coal heavers, who unloaded coal from ships on the Thames, dated back to the eighteenth century, but not until 1843 did Gladstone at the Board of Trade introduce an effective measure to protect them.[71] The previous year coal miners had been similarly legislated for, and in 1883, finally, a general prohibition was enacted on paying wages in public houses.[72]

Finally, there was the use of licensed premises by children. As in all the above instances of regulation measures were the result of wider social and cultural changes. As we saw, children drank small beer as part of their normal diet and well into the nineteenth century neither this nor their presence in public houses was seriously questioned. Only in 1839 was any kind of restriction placed on children and drinking, of spirits by those under sixteen in London. Similar measures were adopted in other towns, but it was only in 1872 that the provision was made general. Thereafter, growing concern for the welfare of children linked with generalized temperance sentiment and the concern for the future of the race progressively increased restriction. The prohibition of spirits was extended to all drinks in 1886, but the drinking age for alcohol other than spirits was to be thirteen. This was raised in 1901, in the so called Child Messenger Act, to fourteen for both on- and off-sale, and the common practice of children taking home beer for their parents was acknowledged by permitting it in 'corked' and 'sealed' vessels.[73] Finally, in 1908, following a sensationalistic journalistic campaign, a general Children Act contained a provision banning children under fourteen altogether from the bars of licensed premises.[74] It made it an offence, too, to give alcohol to children under five and provided a penalty for 'overlaying' – the suffocation of a child under three in bed by a drunken adult.

**Enforcing the law**

In these and other ways, then, were created those sixty-three categories of offence which the Edwardian publican might commit. But again we return to the question of enforcement. Regarding the serving of children, after an initial peak from 1902, when national records begin, annual proceedings declined to average a little over 150 a year down to 1913.[75] Local examples reinforce this picture of limited enforcement. In Southampton between 1903 and 1914 there was just one conviction of a publican for serving a child under fourteen, and the provision on children in bars was similarly sparsely invoked.[76] Of course, there are a number of ways of interpreting this. The police may have been unable or unwilling to enforce the legilsation or it may have had the desired result; certainly contemporary newspapers reported its dramatic effect.[77] But a more recent study found 'mixed' evidence of the success of the reform in the face of what had been a common enough practice, ignorance of the new law itself and the willingness of publicans to risk flouting it.[78] Or the practice may have already begun to decline, to which the new law made little difference. All of these variables will be explored now in a historical survey of the policing of drinking places.

We have already seen how in the early to mid seventeenth century, when concern over disorderly alehouses was particularly in evidence, there were definite limits to the success of enforcement. Under the licensing system which had developed by the close of that century there was little prosecution of offenders. In the summary courts of Essex, for example, in selected years between 1770 and 1813 there were just eight hearings of licensing offences, a mere 0.7 per cent of the total. In the North Riding of Yorkshire the whole period between May 1781 and February 1800 saw just eight related convictions. Selling without a licence was the most common offence to be prosecuted: all but one of those in the North Riding, for example.[79] This was of course an offence which involved a loss of revenue to the Excise. In general, law enforcement relied chiefly upon small numbers of part-time, unpaid (except for expenses) parish constables, who lacked the time and resources to enforce licensing laws. They were also subject to community pressures. As Isaac Archer, a Church of England minister at Chippenham in Cambridgeshire observed resignedly one summer in 1663, 'In harvest time I observed that men used to frequent the alehouse on the Lord's day: I asked the constable to assist mee, but he said he should get the ill will of his neighbours'.[80] And, not least, they had their own inclinations. Constables were not infrequently publicans themselves well into the nineteenth century, despite repeated efforts to stop the practice, and might not be averse to a drink, like constable Obediah Martin of South Cave in the East Riding of Yorkshire, who was on good terms with the local publicans there in the 1830s.[81]

As we saw with drunkenness, it was the progressive reform of the police which led to greater scrutiny. Police visits to public houses became routine in town and country alike. The result was that more publicans, as more drunks, came before the courts. By the 1860s around 8,000 beerhouse keepers and 4,000 fully licensed publicans were proceeded against for offences annually. But these were peak years. The removal of disorderly beerhouses after 1869 produced an immediate reduction in proceedings against licensees. We can explore this in a little more detail and try to say something about long-term trends by focusing on offences which related in particular to order in public houses – those of permitting drunkenness and serving a drunken person – for which it is possible to compile a run of national statistics for the years 1873 to 1913. These are interesting, as contemporaries liked to point out the contrast between the large numbers of drunks proceeded against with the much lower number of publicans for serving them. They show a decline over the whole period, with fluctuations from around 2,500 at its mid-1870 peak to fewer than 1,000 annually by its end. How do we explain this? For the police the offences presented a number of difficulties. They were not easy to prove, although this was mitigated by the development of case law and the placing in 1902 of the burden of proof on the licensee to show that all reasonable steps had been taken to prevent it. It was difficult to obtain witnesses, whereas landlord and customers were only too willing to testify. Publicans increasingly had legal representation, which often resulted in cases being dismissed on technicalities. The courts generally were not willing to convict where the police were felt to have been over zealous. Police discretion was crucial, but it was more usually towards leniency.[82] Charles Booth's survey of London at the close of the century acknowledged that they 'may shut their eyes to minor infringements of the licensing acts' and made the essential point that it was difficult to go beyond public opinion in enforcing the law and risk thereby 'disturbing the happy relations between police and people'. There was also some evidence of bribery by publicans, although the survey preferred to call it 'treating' and felt that the situation was better than formerly, and as regards venality the police came out 'fairly well'.[83]

The other side of the question is that customers were becoming less prone to drunken disorder and pubs were actually better run. The former was suggested in Chapter 5; the latter was argued by the Lords committee on intemperance at the close of the 1870s, which attributed it to the influence of public opinion on the police, the earlier closing times introduced in 1872 and the fear of losing the licence as convictions were recorded. The latter fear was all the more potent as the overall rising profitability of the trade at this time meant greater pressure from owners through enforcement of better management and the removal of errant tenants.[84] The further growth of the tied-house system of brewery control, together with the rising value of licences as their numbers fell, further increased such pressure.

## The First World War

By 1914 the public house had become subject to an elaborate system of regulation, but this was still tempered by the degree of strictness with which it was enforced. Nor should one exaggerate how much had changed. Some changes, like the use of pubs for administrative or judicial purposes, or for paying wages, probably came about largely for reasons other than the law's intervention. In other ways pub life was little altered: pubs could still open from early in the morning and throughout the day and young people could still frequent and drink in them. It was the coming of war which saw regulation taken much further. Ideas which we have noted, about the future of the race and national efficiency, coupled with the now widespread temperance sentiment, found expression in considerably enhanced restriction.

In fact it had begun as soon as war was declared. The armed forces obtained powers under the first Defence of the Realm Act, and subsequent extensions to it, over the supply of drink in military and naval areas. Nearly 500 hundred restrictive orders, covering pub opening hours, the treating of servicemen and the serving of women at certain times, were made in the first ten months of the war. Licensing magistrates were also given the power, which was also widely taken up, to suspend the sale of alcohol or close pubs early if the chief constable recommended it in the interests of order. In London, to combat the problem of provincial recruits enjoying later opening hours and lavish treating by civilians closing time was brought forward first from 12.30pm to 11pm, later to 10pm, and then to 9pm in dock and arsenal areas.[85] Then, in May 1915, the Central Control Board (Liquor Traffic) was created, comprising politicians, employer and labour representatives, civil servants and later brewing and temperance men, under the chairmanship of former financier, diplomat and politician Lord D'Abernon. This was given powers in areas where servicemen assembled or war work was in progress to increase the efficiency of labour and prevent its impairment by 'drunkenness, alcoholism or excess'. Within six months most ports, the industrial Midlands and Yorkshire and about two thirds of Scotland had been scheduled, and in the end most of the country, except for agricultural and sparsely populated areas, was subject to it.[86]

Under the Board's restrictions, hours of sale were dramatically reduced as early-morning, afternoon and late-evening drinking were prohibited. By restricting sale to meal times it was hoped that alcohol's effects would be diluted by food and by creating gaps in the drinking day that 'soaking' would be discouraged. Complete Sunday closing was extended to some areas felt to be too close to dry Wales. A number of pub customs were now banned: treating (except with a meal), giving credit and the 'long pull' (giving a larger measure to encourage trade). In three areas of especial significance for the war effort the Board took direct control of the drink trade. The most important, with its extensive munitions works, was the Carlisle and Gretna district, where eventually some 340 licensed premises were acquired. Here in particular the Board was able to carry out what it saw as its more constructive policies, which drew upon the ideas promoted before the war of disinterested management and improvement. The sale of food and lighter drinks was promoted. The old post office in Carlisle, for example, was converted to the Gretna Tavern, selling only wine and beer and with a separate restaurant. Six other similar taverns were established and they, and other pubs under the Board's control, were consciously designed to do away with what were seen as obnoxious features, like snugs and concealed entrances, and to do without the garish advertising common on pub exteriors.[87]

The enforcement of restrictions could be irksome. In Bradford one landlord was described as akin to a traitor for permitting consumption in prohibited hours by a member of the armed forces, whilst a landlady was fined for treating in the customary way the draymen who helped her tap the barrels. In this last case the magistrate acknowledged that the new regulations cut across long-established customs. And when another case went successfully to appeal the Recorder noted how 'every man's hand seems to be against the Control Board'. But the overall statistics for prosecutions in Bradford do not support a view of excessively rigorous enforcement. Proceedings for opening in prohibited hours were most common, as one might expect given the much reduced hours of sale, at four times the pre-war level. But prosecutions for gaming were halved and the combined total of proceedings for the three offences of treating, giving credit and the long pull was actually matched by those for contravention of wartime lighting restrictions.[88] As to their effect on public order and drunkenness, certainly prosecutions for the latter fell dramatically and chief constables everywhere reported favourably on the improvement in order, but it is difficult in the end to disentangle the Board's work from many other influences, including the actual availability of drink and the absence of tens of thousands of young men from the drinking scene.[89]

## Twentieth-century licensing: restriction and liberalization

The restrictive licensing system of the later nineteenth century and the war years persisted for almost a further half century. At war's end, although the Central Control Board itself was wound up, many of the restrictions were now made permanent in a Licensing Act of 1921. The unpopular no-treating order had already been revoked in 1919, but credit and the long pull were still prohibited. Limited opening was also retained, introducing permitted hours within overall parameters, which created some anomalies, like the extra evening hour on one side of London's Oxford Street. Two years later, in response to concerns over young people's drinking which had been voiced during the war, Lady Astor's private member's bill prohibited the sale of alcohol to anyone under eighteen.[90] Local licensing benches continued with their pre-war severity. This was extended to the massive growth of new housing in the inter-war years in a common reluctance to provide their inhabitants with pubs, even where these were on 'improved' lines, although in some places, notably Birmingham and London, licensing magistrates were supportive of that movement.[91] Local authorities with particular interests might also favour a more liberal approach: in the early 1930s, for example, several south-coast resorts extended opening hours at holiday time as worries over continental competition outweighed fears about behaviour.[92] The police continued their supervision of licensed premises, but it seems to have been with a light touch. A study of York pubs found that earlier friction between police and licensees gave way in the 1920s to an acceptance and even a welcoming of the regular visits of sergeant and constable. Prosecutions continued at the low level of the pre-war years, but the general level of order merited this.[93] This changed climate was reflected in the approach to drink and the pub taken in the Second World War, where both were seen as conducive to morale and no further restrictions were applied.

The licensing system, including minor changes made in the inter-war and immediate post-war years, was the subject of a consolidating statute in 1953, the year following a comprehensive Customs and Excise Act, which had brought together and simplified 150 years of legislation.[94] The next half century then saw major changes to the licensing system. Much of this was towards greater liberalization – of opening hours, for example, or in the availability of alcohol. But restriction was also an important element in the story of licensing in these years. This outline will seek to convey both aspects. They were rooted in economic, social and cultural changes which often produced contradictory or conflicting responses. Growing affluence and everything that flowed from that, a belief in the virtues of modernization, more liberal attitudes towards a range of social questions from sex to gambling, an emphasis on individual rights and aspirations and from the 1970s a shift towards a more free-market approach to the economy all pushed towards liberalization. At the same time, the growth of alcohol consumption itself, concerns over threats to public order from the intoxicated young and general unease amongst many about the pace of change and its perceived social consequences all pushed in the opposite direction.

A Licensing Act of 1961, 'the first major revision of licensing law for forty years', embodied some of those contrasting influences.[95] The objects of the measure were, in the words of the minister of state:

> to revise social legislation in the light of present-day conditions; secondly, to achieve a balance between the restraints necessary to prevent abuse and the need for freedom in a responsible society; and thirdly, to introduce an Act to suit the general interest, and have particular regard to the needs of the consumer'.[96]

On the one hand, then, it made provision for licences for restaurants, hotels and guest houses, and limited magistrates' discretion to refuse them; it slightly increased permitted opening hours, but in particular allowed off-licences to open throughout the day; it made provision for removal by local option of Sunday closing in Wales; and it extended to the rest of the country a 1949 London measure allowing late-night drinking in clubs and restaurants with music and dancing. On the other, the under-eighteen rule was extended to off-licences, thus ending the age-old practice of sending one's child to obtain beer; and registration of clubs was tightened up. On balance, although this was not necessarily the Act's intention, the measures together represented a large measure of liberalization, notably in the way they facilitated an increase in the number of places licensed to sell alcohol both for on- and off-consumption.

This was not immediately sustained, however. A departmental committee appointed by the government under Lord Erroll of Hale reported in 1972 and recommended a number of further measures of liberalization. These included longer opening hours, the reduction of the age limit for drinking to seventeen and permitting children under fourteen to be in bars under certain conditions. Unlike a similar report for Scotland, however, Erroll's proposals came to nothing in the face of opposition from the medical profession, publicans and temperance groups. Private member's measures seeking to further some of the committee's aims met the same fate.[97]

Nevertheless, and despite the deepening, as we saw, of public-health concerns surrounding alcohol consumption, the pressures for liberalization continued to grow, both from the social and cultural changes identified above and more directly from the drink and tourism industries. This now found echo in the Conservative government's free-market approach to the economy and its related push for deregulation. Accordingly, the afternoon break instituted during World War One was ended in pubs on weekdays in 1988 and finally on Sundays in 1995.[98] Deregulation was taken up by New Labour, too, notably towards further limiting the discretion of licensing magistrates. In fact a Home Office Working Group on Licence Transfers had recommended in 1996 against their using a so called judgement of need on whether a licence was required in a given district. Now, in 1998, the new government's Better Regulation Taskforce endorsed this and suggested the transfer of licensing to local authorities. Faced with this, the Justices' Clerks' Society published a good-practice guide effectively abandoning the judgement of need.[99] Market forces and planning law would together regulate the number of premises, echoing thereby the nineteenth-century free-licensing view that 'no man would sell liquor to his ruin'. This now facilitated a policy of both central and local governments to promote the leisure industries, notably in the regenerative night-time economies of towns and cities. The transfer of responsibility for licensing matters from the Home Office to the Department for Culture, Media and Sport in 2001, which dealt with tourism, emphasized this connection of licensing with the leisure industries.

All this now came together in New Labour's proposals, which became the 2003 Licensing Act. It was widely felt that the 1964 Licensing Act, a consolidating statute which had updated that of 1953, was in need of modernization. This chimed well with New Labour's progressive self-perception. Embracing deregulation was also welcomed by the drinks industry, which was campaigning for change. In the event, however, it was the issue of public order which proved critical in shaping the final outcome, although in reality it had never gone away. Alongside liberalization there had continued to be measures of restriction. This combination of a light-touch approach to regulating the market and the targeting of individuals when things go wrong has been termed neoliberalism.[100] In response to concern about football violence, legislation in 1985 made it illegal to have alcohol whilst travelling to a 'designated' sporting event or at the event itself. Drinking by young people was targeted by legislation in 1988, 1997, 2000 and 2001.[101] In 2003 concern over the binge drinking and associated disorder of young people on city streets and over the prospect of 24-hour opening for licensed premises, orchestrated luridly by sections of the press, shifted the emphasis in the new Act towards its aims to ensure public order – hence the government played up its role in shaping a more 'continental' drinking culture and actually reducing nighttime disorder.[102] The Act, which came into force in 2005, radically transformed the old licensing system. Responsibility was transferred from magistrates to local councils, ending an authority that dated back to the sixteenth century. The justices' licence was replaced by two licences, one for the person and one for the premises. Instead of permitted hours there were now agreed hours, thereby creating the potential for 24-hour opening. Premises' applications were to be granted unless objections were received. Licensing authorities were given a duty to promote public safety, the protection of children and the prevention of crime, disorder and public nuisance. Accompanied children under sixteen were now permitted, except where the nature of the premises –for example, in offering entertainment of a sexual nature – made it undesirable.

Regulation at the turn of the millennium, then, continued to illustrate the points outlined at the beginning of this chapter. Despite consolidation, the system remained extremely complex. The proper role of regulation continued to be the subject of tension and conflict between the demands of the state's revenue, the needs of the economy and the preservation of public order and crime prevention. To these had been added newer concerns like the welfare of children and the broader question of public health. As the 2003 Act's passage demonstrated, it was still a highly charged political issue. It was an issue, too, which could only be understood in its social and cultural context, as its parallel features of liberalization and restriction showed. And, as always, local contexts would continue to shape its practical administration and enforcement.

## Notes

1 Royal Commission on Liquor Licensing Laws, First Report; PP 1897 [C.8356], XXXIV.253, p. 138.
2 E. A. Pratt, *The Policy of Licensing Justices* (London: P.S. King & Son, 1909), pp. 151–5.
3 J. P. Lewis, *Freedom to Drink: A critical review of the development of the licensing laws and proposals for reform* (London: Institute of Economic Affairs, 1985), p. 11.
4 Time for Reform: Proposals for the modernisation of our licensing laws (Home Office, CM 4696, 1999/2000), pp. 2 and 9.
5 S. and B. Webb, *The History of Liquor Licensing in England Principally from 1700 to 1830* (London: Frank Cass & Co, 1963), p. 5.
6 Time for Reform, p. 7.
7 Webb, *The History of Liquor Licensing*, p. 5.
8 First Report from the Committee On the State of the Police of the Metropolis; PP 1817 (233), VII.I, p. 7.
9 J. M. Bennett, *Ale, Beer and Brewsters in England: Women's work in a changing world, 1300–1600* (Oxford: Oxford University Press, 1996), pp. 99–101.
10 G. B. Wilson, *Alcohol and the Nation: A contribution to the study of the liquor problem in the United Kingdom from 1800 to 1935* (London: Nicholson and Watson, 1940), p. 188 and pp. 188–201 for details of the revenue from drink to the early twentieth century.
11 J. Brewer, *The Sinews of Power: War, money and the English state, 1688–1783* (London: Unwin Hyman, 1989), pp. 102–14; for the Excise see P. Mathias, *The Brewing Industry in England 1700–1830* (Cambridge: Cambridge University Press, 1959), pp. 339–83; M. Ogborn, *Spaces of Modernity: London's geographies, 1680–1780* (London: Guilford Press, 1998), pp. 158–200.
12 M. Daunton, *Trusting Leviathan, The Politics of Taxation in Britain, 1799–1914* (Cambridge: Cambridge University Press, 2001), p. 35.
13 Wilson, *Alcohol and the Nation*, p. 197; B. Harrison, *Drink and the Victorians: The temperance question in England 1815–1872* (Keele: Keele University Press, 2nd ed., 1994), p. 333.
14 Alcohol Harm Reduction Strategy for England (Cabinet Office, Prime Minister's Strategy Unit, 2004), p. 68; Statistical Bulletin: Public Spending Statistics April 2013 (HM Treasury, 2013), p. 18 at https://www.gov.uk/government/publications/national-statistics-release-april-2013 [accessed 18 December 2013].
15 Alcohol Harm Reduction Strategy, p. 68; *Alcohol misuse: Tackling the UK epidemic* (London: BMA Board of Science, 2008), p. 45.
16 Time for Reform, p. 7.
17 It is made, for example, by J. Nicholls, *The Politics of Alcohol: A history of the drink question in England* (Manchester: Manchester University Press, 2009), pp. 2–3.
18 J. Greenaway, *Drink and British Politics since 1830: A study in policy-making* (Basingstoke: Palgrave Macmillan, 2003), p. 1; Nicholls, *The Politics of Alcohol*, p. 2.

19 M. Valverde, 'Police science, British style: Pub licensing and knowledges of urban disorder', *Economy and Society*, 32:2 (2003), pp. 234–52.
20 For these questions see in particular Nicholls, *The Politics of Alcohol*.
21 Mathias, *The Brewing Industry in England*, p. 350.
22 A. L. Martin, *Alcohol, Violence and Disorder in Traditional Europe* (Kirksville, MO: Truman State University Press, 2009), pp. 187–93.
23 Webb, *The History of Liquor Licensing*, p. 3; C. M. Iles, 'Early stages of English public house regulation', *Economic Journal*, 13 (1903), pp. 251–62; P. Clark, *The English Alehouse: A social history 1200–1830* (London: Longman, 1983), pp. 24 and 28.
24 M. McIntosh, *Controlling Misbehaviour in England, 1370–1600* (Cambridge: Cambridge University Press, 1998), pp. 31 and 74.
25 11 Henry VII, c. 2.
26 McIntosh, *Controlling Misbehaviour*, p. 76.
27 Clark, *The English Alehouse*, p. 169.
28 5 & 6 Edward VI, c. 25.
29 7 Edward VI, c. 5.
30 Webb, *The History of Liquor Licensing*, pp. 22–4;
31 For details see J. Hunter, 'English inns, taverns and alehouses: The legislative framework, 1495–1797' in B. Kümin and B. A. Tlusty (eds), *The World of the Tavern: Public houses in early modern Europe* (Aldershot: Ashgate, 2002), pp. 65–82; S. K. Roberts, 'Alehouses, brewing and government under the early Stuarts', *Southern History*, 2 (1980), pp. 45–71. For the 1619 Proclamation see J. F. Larkin and P. L. Hughes, *Stuart Royal Proclamations Volume 1 Royal Proclamations of King James I 1603–1625* (Oxford: Clarendon Press, 1973), pp. 409–13.
32 Clark, *The English Alehouse*, pp. 173–4.
33 D. Underdown, *Fire from Heaven: The life of an English town in the seventeenth century* (London: Harper Collins, 1992), particularly pp. 72 and 104.
34 K. Wrightson and D. Levine, *Poverty and Piety in an English Village: Terling, 1525–1700* (Oxford: Clarendon Press, 1995), pp. 134–9.
35 G. C. F. Forster, *The East Riding Justices of the Peace in the Seventeenth Century* (East Yorkshire Local History Society, 1973), pp. 59–60.
36 J. Brown, 'Alehouse licensing and state formation in early modern England' in J. Herring, C. Regan, D. Weinberg and P. Withington (eds), *Intoxication and Society: Problematic pleasures of drugs and alcohol* (Basingstoke: Palgrave Macmillan, 2013), pp. 110–32, on pp. 125–6. See also W. J. King, 'Regulation of alehouses in Stuart Lancashire: An example of discretionary administration of the law', *Transactions of the Historic Society of Lancashire and Cheshire*, 129 (1979), pp. 31–46.
37 2 George II, c.28.
38 This follows Clark, *The English Alehouse*, pp. 178–87.
39 P. Corfield, 'A provincial capital in the late seventeenth century: The case of Norwich', in P. Clark and P. Slack (eds), *Crisis and Order in English Towns 1500–1700* (London: Routledge & Kegan Paul, 1972), pp. 263–310, on p. 288.
40 16 George II, c. 8; 17 George II, c. 17; 24 George II, c.40
41 26 George II, c.31.
42 By 32 George III, c. 59.
43 Account of Number of Magistrates' Licenses for Victuallers in Metropolis 1817–21; PP 1822 (261), XXI.523; Innkeepers' Licences, Borough of Hedon, East Riding Archives, DDHE 16/64.
44 Select Committee of the House of Commons on Victualling-House Licences (Holborn Division); PP 1833 (585), XV.261, pp. 40 and 47.
45 Third Report from the Committee on the State of the Police of the Metropolis; PP 1818 (423), VIII.1, pp. 120–1.
46 B. Cozens-Hardy (ed.), *Mary Hardy's Diary*, (Norfolk: Norfolk Record Society, 1968), p. 76; W. B. Johnson (ed.) '*Memorandoms for ...' The Diary between 1798*

*and 1810 of John Carrington* (London and Chichester: Philimore, 1973), p. 33. For further details on the operation of the licensing system and the records it generated in this period see P. Jennings, 'Liquor licensing and the local historian: Inns and alehouses 1753–1828', *Local Historian* 40:2 (2010), pp. 136–50.
47 Webb, *The History of Liquor Licensing*, pp. 19–52.
48 F. G. Stokes (ed.), *The Blecheley Diary of the Rev. William Cole 1765–1767* (London: Constable, 1931), pp. 111–12.
49 A. Young, *A Six Months Tour through the North of England, vol. 2* (New York: Kelley, 1967), pp. 98–104.
50 Webb, *The History of Liquor Licensing*, pp. 55–90.
51 PP 1817 (233), pp. 7–22.
52 Select Committee of the House of Commons on Public Breweries; PP 1818 (399), III.295, pp. 1–5.
53 Anon, 'Licensing of alehouses', *Edinburgh Review*, 44 (1826), pp. 441–57; see also Harrison, *Drink and the Victorians*, pp. 63–72.
54 9 George IV, c. 61.
55 3 *Hansard*, vol. 4, cols 502–12 (30 June 1831).
56 Select Committee on the Sale of Beer; PP 1833 (416), XV.1, p. 3.
57 Report from the Select Committee on Public Houses; PP 1852–53 (855), XXXVII.1, pp. 42–8, 67–80 and 92; First Report from the Select Committee of the House of Lords on Intemperance; PP 1877 (171), XI.1, pp. 19, 21–3 and 41; A. Mutch, 'Magistrates and public house managers, 1840–1914: Another case of Liverpool exceptionalism?' *Northern History* 49:2 (2003), pp. 325–42.
58 The variations produced by all these statutes are usefully tabulated in Harrison, *Drink and the Victorians*, pp. 315–18.
59 Ibid., pp. 231–2.
60 Wilson, *Alcohol and the Nation*, p. 236; Select Committee of the House of Lords for inquiring into Prevalence of Habits of Intemperance, and Effects of Recent Legislation; PP 1878–79 (113), X.469, pp. xxx–xxxi; Return of Number of Licences for Sale of Beer and Cider in England and Wales granted or refused in each County and Borough at Brewster Sessions; PP 1870 (215 and 215–1), LXI.177 and 261 and a similar Return for Middlesex and Surrey; PP 1870 (434), LXI.277.
61 Return of the Number of new Licences granted by Justices in each County of England and Wales; PP 1881 (135), LXXXIII.387 and 1882 (33), LXIV.489; Royal Commission on Liquor Licensing Laws: Statistics Relating to Number of Licensed Premises in Great Britain and Ireland; PP 1898 [C.8696], XXXVII, pp. 33–6 and 43–91.
62 D. W. Gutzke, *Pubs and Progressives: Reinventing the public house in England 1896–1960* (De Kalb, IL: Northern Illinois University Press, 2006), pp. 75–6; P. Jennings, *The Local: A history of the English pub* (Stroud: The History Press, 2nd. ed., 2011), pp. 168–9.
63 Sir R. Ensor, *England 1870–1914* (Oxford: Oxford University Press, 1936), p. 360; Greenaway, *Drink and British Politics*, pp. 43–8; for the temperance view see J. Newton, *W. S. Caine, MP: A biography* (London: Nisbet & Co, 1907).
64 For a contemporary discussion of the issues see C. P. Sanger, *The Place of Compensation in Temperance Reform* (London: P. S. King & Son, 1901).
65 For the full background to the measure and its passage and implementation see P. Jennings, '"Grasping a nettle": The 1904 Licensing Act', in M. Hailwood and D. Toner (eds), *Biographies of Drink: A case study approach to our historical relationship with alcohol* (Newcastle upon Tyne: Cambridge Scholars, 2015), pp. 30–48 and 'Liquor licensing and the local historian: The 1904 Licensing Act and its administration', *The Local Historian*, 39:1 (2009), pp. 24–37.
66 Minor changes were made in a further Licensing Act of 1874.

67 W. R. Lambert, 'The Welsh Sunday Closing Act, 1881', *Welsh History Review* 6:2 (1972), pp. 161–89 on pp. 176–7. For the Sunday traveller generally see Jennings, *The Local*, pp. 160–1.
68 J. Kneale, '"A problem of supervision": Moral geographies of the nineteenth-century British public house', *Journal of Historical Geography*, 25:3 (1999), pp. 333–48 and 'Surveying pubs, cities and unfit lives: Governmentality, drink and space in nineteenth- and early twentieth century Britain', *Journal for the Study of British Cultures*, 19:1 (2012), pp. 45–60; D. Beckingham, 'Gender, space and drunkenness: Liverpool's licensed premises, 1860–1914', *Annals of the Association of American Geographers*, 102:3 (2012), pp. 647–66; and see P. Jennings, *The Public House in Bradford, 1770–1970* (Keele: Keele University Press, 1995), pp. 115–17 and 176–9.
69 Municipal Corporations Act 1882; Local Government Act 1894; Licensing Act 1902.
70 25 George II, c. 36; Public Health Acts Amendment Act 1890.
71 M. D. George, *London Life in the Eighteenth Century*, (London: London School of Economics and Political Science, 3rd ed. 1951), pp. 295–6; R. Shannon, *Gladstone vol. 1 1809–1865* (London: Methuen & Co, 1984), pp. 140 and 244.
72 Mines Act 1842; Payment of Wages in Public Houses Prohibition Act 1883.
73 Intoxicating Liquors (Sale to Children) Act 1886; Intoxicating Liquors (Sale to Children) Act 1901; G. P. Williams and G. T. Brake, *Drink in Great Britain 1900–1979* (London: Edsall, 1980), pp. 180–1.
74 G. R. Sims, *The Cry of the Children* (London: Tribune, 1907).
75 Judicial Statistics England and Wales, 1912; PP 1914 (Cd 7282), C.1, pp. 20–1 and 1913; PP 1914–16 (Cd 7767), LXXXII.1, p. 52.
76 Southampton Register of Licences 1903–1923, Southampton Archive Services, SC/MAG 3/2.
77 Williams and Brake, *Drink in Great Britain*, p. 181.
78 S. Moss, '"A grave question": The Children Act and public house regulation, c. 1908–1939', *Crimes and Misdemeanours*, 3:2 (2009), pp. 98–117, on p. 102.
79 P. King, 'The Summary Courts and social relations in eighteenth-century England', *Past and Present* 183 (2004), pp. 125–72; Registers of Convictions 1781–1815, North Yorkshire Record Office, Northallerton, QDX.
80 M. Storey (ed.) *Two East Anglian Diaries 1641–1729. Isaac Archer and William Coe* (Woodbridge: The Boydell Press and Suffolk Record Society, 1994, vol. XXXVI), p. 91; for the general point on policing see D. Phillips and R. D. Storch, *Policing Provincial England 1829–1856: The politics of reform* (Leicester: Leicester University Press, 1999), pp. 12–13 and 22–5.
81 L. Radzinowicz, *A History of English Criminal Law and Its Administration from 1750, vol.2, The Clash between Private Initiative and Public Interest in the Enforcement of the Law* (London: Stevens and Sons, 1956), pp. 272–3; Phillips and Storch, *Policing Provincial England*, p. 12; J. E. and P. E. Crowther, *The Diary of Robert Sharp of South Cave: Life in a Yorkshire village 1812–1837* (Oxford: Oxford University Press, 1997), p. 535.
82 P. Jennings, 'Policing public houses in Victorian England', *Law, Crime and History* 1 (2013), pp. 52–75, on pp. 54–5 and 67. See also on policing pubs S. Petrow, *Policing Morals: The Metropolitan Police and the Home Office 1870–1914* (Oxford: Clarendon Press, 1994), pp. 187–212
83 C. Booth, *Life and Labour of the People in London: Third series religious influences* (London: Macmillan, 1902), pp. 52–3 and *Life and Labour of the People in London: Final volume: notes on social influences and conclusion* (London: Macmillan, 1902), pp. 132–5 and 141–2.
84 Select Committee of the House of Lords for inquiring into Prevalence of Habits of Intemperance and effects of Recent Legislation; PP 1878–9 (113), p. 16.

85 H. Carter, *The Control of the Drink Trade in Britain: A contribution to national efficiency during the Great War 1915–1918* (London: Longmans, Green, 2nd ed. 1919), pp. 17–37.
86 For the Board's work, in addition to Carter see Greenaway, *Drink and British Politics*, 97–113; D. H. Aldcroft, 'Control of the liquor trade in Great Britain, 1914–21' in W. H. Chaloner, and B. M. Ratcliffe (eds), *Trade and Transport: Essays in economic history in honour of T. S. Williams* (Manchester: Manchester University Press, 1977), pp. 242–57; M. E. Rose, 'The success of social reform? The Central Control Board (Liquor Traffic) 1915–21' in M. R. D. Foot, (ed.) *War and Society: Historical essays in honour and memory of J. R. Western 1928–71* (London: Elek, 1973), pp. 71–84; R. Duncan, *Pubs and Patriots: The Drink Crisis in Britain during World War One* (Liverpool: Liverpool University Press, 2013).
87 Carter, *The Control of the Drink Trade*, 200–33; Greenaway, *Drink and British Politics*, pp. 102–7.
88 Jennings, *The Public House in Bradford*, pp. 232–3; there is, however, a need for more detailed local research for a fuller picture of the enforcement of wartime restrictions.
89 See Carter, *The Control of the Drink Trade*, pp. 237–81 for a detailed and generally favourable assessment of the Board's work.
90 Intoxicating Liquor (Sale to Persons under Eighteen) Act 1923; Greenaway, *Drink and British Politics*, pp. 117–25; Askwith, *British Taverns*, pp. 203–4.
91 Jennings, *The Local*, pp. 195–9.
92 J. K. Walton, *The British Seaside: Holidays and resorts in the twentieth century* (Manchester: Manchester University Press, 2000), p. 136.
93 M. Race, *Public Houses, Private Lives: An oral history of life in York pubs in the mid-twentieth century* (York: Voyager, 1999), pp. 31–7; Jennings, *The Local*, pp. 202–3.
94 There is not space to detail these here, but see J. N. Martin, *Paterson's Licensing Acts* (London: Butterworth & Co, 79th ed. 1971), pp. 15–24.
95 Williams and Brake, *Drink in Great Britain*, p. 131; for discussion of the Act and the point of liberalization and restriction see R. Baggott, 'Licensing law reform and the return of the drink question', *Parliamentary Affairs*, 40:4 (1987), pp. 501–16; J. Greenaway, 'Calling "time" on last orders: The rise and fall of public house closing hours in Britain', *Revue Francaise de Civilisation Britannique*, 14:2 (2007), pp. 181–96, on p. 189.
96 A. Samuels, 'Some reflections on the Licensing Act, 1961', *Modern Law Review*, 25:1 (1962), pp. 68–73, on p. 68.
97 Baggott, 'Licensing law reform', pp. 504–10.
98 Greenaway, 'Calling "time"', p. 192.
99 R. Light and S. Heenan, *Controlling Supply: The concept of 'need' in liquor licensing* (Bristol: Bristol Centre for Criminal Justice, University of the West of England, 1999).
100 W. Haydock, 'Understanding English alcohol policy as a neoliberal condemnation of the carnivalesque', *Drugs: Education, prevention, and policy*, 22:2 (2015), pp. 143–9.
101 Sporting Events (Control of Alcohol etc) Act 1985; Licensing Act 1988; Confiscation of Alcohol (Young Persons) Act 1997; Licensing (Young Persons) Act 2000; Criminal Justice and Police Act 2001.
102 J. Greenaway, 'How policy framing is as important as the policy content: The story of the English and Welsh Licensing Act 2003', *British Politics* 6:4 (2011), pp. 408–29; see also R. Light, 'The Licensing Act 2003: Liberal constraint?', *Modern Law Review*, 68:2 (2005), pp. 268–85.

## Bibliography

Aldcroft, D. H., 'Control of the liquor trade in Great Britain, 1914–21', in W. H. Chaloner, and B. M. Ratcliffe (eds), *Trade and Transport: Essays in economic history in honour of T. S. Williams* (Manchester: Manchester University Press, 1977), pp. 242–57.
Askwith, Lord., *British Taverns: Their history and laws* (London: Routledge, 1928).
Baggott, R., 'Licensing law reform and the return of the drink question', *Parliamentary Affairs*, 40:4 (1987), pp. 501–16.
Beckingham, D., 'Gender, space and drunkenness: Liverpool's licensed premises, 1860–1914', *Annals of the Association of American Geographers*, 102:3 (2012), pp. 647–66.
Bennett, J. M., *Ale, Beer and Brewsters in England: Women's work in a changing world, 1300–1600* (Oxford: Oxford University Press, 1996).
Brewer, J., *The Sinews of Power: War, money and the English state, 1688–1783* (London: Unwin Hyman, 1989).
Brown, J., 'Alehouse licensing and state formation in early modern England', in J. Herring, C. Regan, D. Weinberg and P. Withington (eds), *Intoxication and Society: Problematic pleasures of drugs and alcohol* (Basingstoke: Palgrave Macmillan, 2013), pp. 110–32.
Carter, H., *The Control of the Drink Trade in Britain: A contribution to national efficiency during the Great War 1915–1918* (London: Longmans, Green, 2nd ed. 1919).
Clark, P., *The English Alehouse: A social history 1200–1830* (London: Longman, 1983).
Corfield, P., 'A provincial capital in the late seventeenth century: The case of Norwich', in P. Clark and P. Slack (eds), *Crisis and Order in English Towns 1500–1700* (London: Routledge & Kegan Paul, 1972), pp. 263–310.
Daunton, M., *Trusting Leviathan, The Politics of Taxation in Britain, 1799–1914* (Cambridge: Cambridge University Press, 2001).
Duncan, R., *Pubs and Patriots: The drink crisis in Britain during World War One* (Liverpool: Liverpool University Press, 2013).
Ensor, Sir R., *England 1870–1914* (Oxford: Oxford University Press, 1936).
Forster, G. C. F., *The East Riding Justices of the Peace in the Seventeenth Century* (East Yorkshire Local History Society, 1973).
George, M. D., *London Life in the Eighteenth Century*, (London: London School of Economics and Political Science, 3rd ed. 1951).
Greenaway, J., *Drink and British Politics since 1830: A study in policy-making* (Basingstoke: Palgrave Macmillan, 2003).
—, 'Calling "time" on last orders: The rise and fall of public house closing hours in Britain', *Revue Francaise de Civilisation Britannique*, 14:2 (2007), pp. 181–96.
—, 'How policy framing is as important as the policy content: The story of the English and Welsh Licensing Act 2003', *British Politics*, 6:4 (2011), pp. 408–29.
Gutzke, D. W., *Pubs and Progressives: Reinventing the public house in England 1896–1960* (De Kalb, IL: Northern Illinois University Press, 2006).
Harrison, B., *Drink and the Victorians: The temperance question in England 1815–1872* (Keele: Keele University Press, 2nd ed., 1994).
Haydock, W., 'Understanding English alcohol policy as a neoliberal condemnation of the carnivalesque', *Drugs: Education, prevention, and policy*, 22:2 (2015), pp. 143–9.
Hunter, J., 'English inns, taverns and alehouses: The legislative framework, 1495–1797', in B. Kümin and B. A. Tlusty (eds), *The World of the Tavern: Public houses in early modern Europe* (Aldershot: Ashgate, 2002), pp. 65–82.
Iles, C. M., 'Early stages of English public house regulation', *Economic Journal*, 13 (1903), pp. 251–62.

Jennings, P., *The Public House in Bradford, 1770–1970* (Keele: Keele University Press, 1995).
—, 'Liquor licensing and the local historian: The 1904 Licensing Act and its administration', *The Local Historian*, 39:1 (2009), pp. 24–37.
—, 'Liquor licensing and the local historian: inns and alehouses 1753–1828', *The Local Historian* 40:2 (2010), pp. 136–50.
—, *The Local: A history of the English pub* (Stroud: The History Press, 2nd ed., 2011), pp. 168–9.
—, 'Policing public houses in Victorian England', *Law, Crime and History* 1 (2013), pp. 52–75.
—, '"Grasping a nettle": The 1904 Licensing Act', in M. Hailwood and D. Toner (eds), *Biographies of Drink: A case study approach to our historical relationship with alcohol* (Newcastle upon Tyne: Cambridge Scholars, 2015), pp. 30–48.
King, P., 'The Summary Courts and social relations in eighteenth-century England', *Past and Present*, 183 (2004), pp. 125–72.
King, W. J., 'Regulation of alehouses in Stuart Lancashire: An example of discretionary administration of the law', *Transactions of the Historic Society of Lancashire and Cheshire*, 129 (1979), pp. 31–46.
Kneale, J., '"A problem of supervision": Moral geographies of the nineteenth-century British public house', *Journal of Historical Geography*, 25:3 (1999), pp. 333–48.
—, 'Surveying pubs, cities and unfit lives: Governmentality, drink and space in nineteenth- and early twentieth century Britain', *Journal for the Study of British Cultures*, 19:1 (2012), pp. 45–60
Lambert, W. R., 'The Welsh Sunday Closing Act, 1881', *Welsh History Review* 6:2 (1972), pp. 161–89.
Lewis, J. P., *Freedom to Drink: A critical review of the development of the licensing laws and proposals for reform* (London: Institute of Economic Affairs, 1985).
Light, R., 'The Licensing Act 2003: Liberal constraint?', *Modern Law Review*, 68:2 (2005), pp. 268–85.
Light, R. and Heenan, S., *Controlling Supply: The concept of 'need' in liquor licensing* (Bristol: Bristol Centre for Criminal Justice, University of the West of England, 1999).
McIntosh, M., *Controlling Misbehaviour in England, 1370–1600* (Cambridge: Cambridge University Press, 1998).
Martin, A. L., *Alcohol, Violence and Disorder in Traditional Europe* (Kirksville, MO: Truman State University Press, 2009).
Mathias, P., *The Brewing Industry in England 1700–1830* (Cambridge: Cambridge University Press, 1959).
Moss, S., '"A grave question": The Children Act and public house regulation, c. 1908–1939', *Crimes and Misdemeanours*, 3:2 (2009), pp. 98–117.
Mutch, A., 'Magistrates and public house managers, 1840–1914: Another case of Liverpool exceptionalism?' *Northern History* 49:2 (2003), pp. 325–42.
Newton, J., *W. S. Caine, MP: A biography* (London: Nisbet & Co, 1907).
Nicholls, J., *The Politics of Alcohol: A history of the drink question in England* (Manchester: Manchester University Press, 2009).
Ogborn, M., *Spaces of Modernity: London's geographies, 1680–1780* (London: Guilford Press, 1998).
Petrow, S., *Policing Morals: The Metropolitan Police and the Home Office 1870–1914* (Oxford: Clarendon Press, 1994).

Phillips, D. and Storch, R. D., *Policing Provincial England 1829–1856: The politics of reform* (Leicester: Leicester University Press, 1999).

Race, M., *Public Houses, Private Lives: An oral history of life in York pubs in the mid-twentieth century* (York: Voyager, 1999).

Radzinowicz, L., *A History of English Criminal Law and its Administration from 1750, vol. 2, The Clash between Private Initiative and Public Interest in the Enforcement of the Law* (London: Stevens and Sons, 1956).

Roberts, S. K., 'Alehouses, brewing and government under the early Stuarts', *Southern History*, 2 (1980), pp. 45–71.

Rose, M. E., 'The success of social reform? The Central Control Board (Liquor Traffic) 1915–21', in M. R. D. Foot (ed.) *War and Society: Historical essays in honour and memory of J. R. Western 1928–71* (London: Elek, 1973), pp. 71–84.

Samuels, A., 'Some reflections on the Licensing Act, 1961', *Modern Law Review*, 25:1 (1962), pp. 68–73.

Shannon, R., *Gladstone vol. 1 1809–1865* (London: Methuen & Co, 1984).

Underdown, D., *Fire from Heaven: The life of an English town in the seventeenth century* (London: Harper Collins, 1992).

Valverde, M., 'Police science, British style: Pub licensing and knowledges of urban disorder', *Economy and Society*, 32:2 (2003), pp. 234–52.

Walton, J.K., *The British Seaside: Holidays and resorts in the twentieth century* (Manchester: Manchester University Press, 2000).

Webb, S. and B., *The History of Liquor Licensing in England Principally from 1700 to 1830* (London: Frank Cass & Co, 1963).

Williams, G. P. and Brake, G. T., *Drink in Great Britain 1900–1979* (London: Edsall, 1980).

Wilson, G. B., *Alcohol and the Nation: A contribution to the study of the liquor problem in the United Kingdom from 1800 to 1935* (London: Nicholson and Watson, 1940).

Wrightson, K. and Levine, D., *Poverty and Piety in an English Village: Terling, 1525–1700* (Oxford: Clarendon Press, 1995).

# Conclusions

This history of drink and the English has been based upon five key assertions, as I set out in the introduction. I will now return to them briefly in turn, reviewing each in the light of the evidence presented. The first was drink's central importance in human societies, which has been amply evident in this particular case. But it is possible to argue for a diminution in that importance over the five centuries surveyed. Most basically, and despite all the problems in measuring it, total and individual consumption in modern England is undoubtedly less than in previous centuries, particularly those before around 1700. But even the late twentieth century, with all its concerns, did not see the consumption levels even of the nineteenth. In late medieval England, indeed for much of this history, ale, and later beer, was an essential item of daily diet. The same was true of wine for the better off. Consumption then was part of everyday life. But from the eighteenth century, and more especially in the nineteenth, drinking came to be a more purely recreational activity. One might suggest that with gin this was always the case. We saw how drinking was gradually separated from the workplace, albeit that the process was protracted and uneven, surviving even into the twentieth century. Further, alcoholic drinks from the late seventeenth century onwards faced competition from an expanding range of alternatives, from tea, coffee and chocolate to soft drinks and safe drinking water. Another example is the way consumption ceased to be universal. For much of the period drinking by children, albeit mostly weaker small beer, was perfectly acceptable. Only in the mid nineteenth century were spirits denied them and beer not until its close. And only in the twentieth century was their access to public drinking places restricted. This has been modified more recently, but only to a limited degree, and although legally children and young people (five years of age and over, that is) may consume alcohol in private, this by no means meets with general approval.

Some of this history, then, has been concerned with ways in which drink did indeed become less central to English society. This was particularly the case from the late nineteenth and through the first half of the twentieth centuries. Conversely, one can suggest in several ways a reversal of that trend in modern times. This is most obvious in two ways. The first is the increased availability of alcohol in public places from the 1960s, after a century of decline, in particular of the pub. In restaurants, hotels, or even the smallest guest house, in the bars and clubs of the night-time economy, drink is widely available. In modern England no development in the regeneration of towns and cities, like Liverpool's Albert Dock, to take just one example, has been complete without its range of facilities for drinking, as Victorians would have called them. Not only that, but drink again became publically available throughout the day, including Sunday, and since 2005 potentially through the night, too. The second, linked crucially to drink's ready availability, indeed visibility, in supermarkets, is the growth of home consumption. Whilst this too was common historically, its resurgence from the 1960s, whether it be the beer in the fridge or the wine with the evening meal, has gone some way to restoring consumption as part of everyday life.

The second assertion was of alcohol's ambivalence, the way it has been viewed both positively and negatively. This also has been evident throughout this history. Of course, it has varied in different historical periods. In matters of health and medicine, for example, there has been a long decline of belief in alcohol's efficacy, although elements persisted in both the lay and scientific mind into modern times. In contrast, the pleasures of intoxication, whilst more widely sought in the past, have never ceased to exert an irresistible appeal. Of course, one person's pleasurable intoxication is another's drunkenness, and the concern, at times panic, over the negative aspects of drinking has also been a constant. It found expression in turn in the long and complex history of regulation. But, as we saw, regulation was never just about the prevention of the crime and disorder consequent on heavy drinking and drunkenness: it was also about the maintenance of the state's revenue and was always cognizant of what was seen as a legitimate business, one moreover which was of immense importance to the economy.

Evident in my first two assertions has been the third, that the history of drink is a product of interlinked economic, social, cultural and political developments. As these are constantly changing so this is reflected in the history of drink. Of course, one can see many examples of apparent continuity. The disapproval and condemnation of drinking by women is an obvious example. But the essential point is that this was different at different times, however much we may detect similarities. Both during the Gin Craze of the early eighteenth century and again in the late nineteenth century there was a widespread belief that women's drinking and drunkenness were increasing. And at both periods this was especially acute in concern over drinking by women as the mothers of the nation's future workers and soldiers. But the later concern was based in late-nineteenth-century racial and social-Darwinist discourses, which was not, and indeed could not be, the case with the earlier panic. Eighteenth-century legislators did not come up with an answer to the problem in the form of reformatories for inebriates, which was one response in the very different historical context of the end of the nineteenth century. Similarly, we can find in the nineteenth century echoes of the seventeenth-century anxiety that drinking was impairing the reliability and efficiency of labour. But industrialization by that point had sharpened that concern and a custom such as Saint Monday, which had endured for so long, finally now disappeared.

There were two further assertions: the importance of the global on the one hand and of the local and regional on the other. The global dimension to drinking has in many ways been a constant. We saw from the beginning of this history the scale of the medieval wine trade, for example, and the introduction into England of hopped beer and distilled spirits. But this global dimension has undoubtedly grown over the years covered by this history. It is evident, of course, in the globalized drinks industry of the modern world, but it has exerted an important influence on drinking habits. Without that influence it is impossible, for example, to explain the modern growth of lager or wine consumption in England. Conversely, the importance of local and regional diversity has diminished. Contrast the domination of brewing, first by a small number of domestic companies in the post-war years and later by global brewing giants, with the locally and regionally based industry of the Victorian period and much of the twentieth century. Or contrast the regional strength of the temperance movement in the country's industrial and nonconformist heartlands with the location of public-health advocacy in national pressure groups. As we saw in our examination of regulation, the discretion which local magistrates enjoyed in licensing matters ensured that national laws worked out differently in different localities. That function now rests with a local government whose power is but a shadow of what it was in the nineteenth century to give expression to purely local concerns. Of course, variation persists. As we saw, drinking is still, for example, important to a particularly north-east identity.

This history has taken the turn of the millennium as its end point. Rod Phillips, concluding his global history of alcohol, suggested that some regions of the world had entered a 'post-alcohol' era of historic lows of consumption.[1] Former major drinking nations, like France, Italy or Spain, for example, had seen significant declines in consumption. In the UK signs of a reduction were being noted in the first decade of the new millennium. Amongst the young there was a small but growing number of abstainers. This was partly a result of demographic change, as the number from Muslim backgrounds increased, but greater concern about its consequences for health was also cited.[2] Early indications were that consumption by the young and young adults had levelled off since the year 2000 and that amongst adults both immoderate consumption (above the daily guidelines) and binge drinking (twice the daily guidelines) had peaked in 2001 and then declined slightly. Fiona Measham, reporting these findings, commented regarding young people in particular that they 'could be characterised as the calm after the storm'. But she also cautioned that 'it is not yet clear whether the most recent figures represent the beginning of a significant downturn in consumption, nor why this might be occurring'.[3] Given what this book has sought to outline, we can indeed expect drink to continue to have a history, one which awaits the attention of future historians.

## Notes

1 R. Phillips, *Alcohol: A history* (Chapel Hill, NC: University of North Carolina Press, 2014), p. 319.
2 J. Aldridge, F. Measham and L. Williams, *Illegal Leisure Revisited: Changing patterns of alcohol and drug use in adolescents and young adults* (London: Routledge, 2011), pp. 81 and 91.
3 F. Measham, 'The turning tide of intoxication: Young people's drinking in Britain in the 2000s', *Health Education*, 108:3 (2008), pp. 207–22.

# Index

alcohol consumption: by children and young people 10, 14, 19, 25–6, 213; difficulties of estimating 8–9, 13; European 2, 213; long-term trends 9–11, 20–2, 24–6; in Muslim world 2; sources for estimates 8, 13; by students 26; by women 10, 14, 16, 19–20, 21–2, 25, 27
alcohol-control policies 170
alcoholic drinks: as antiseptic 101; as aphrodisiac 102–3; for courage 103; and health 100–2; and identity 107–9; as medicine 101–2; and rituals 103–4; and sociability 109–12; and special occasions 105; symbolic importance 103; and thirst 100; and workplace 106–7; *see also* individual drinks
Alcohol Harm Reduction Strategy for England 185
alcoholism 164
ale 10–15, 14
alehouses: customers 75–6, 126; functions 76; hostility directed at 149–50; keepers 40, 47; numbers 40; physical 75; sociability in 109; unlicensed 40; use of term 44
ales for celebrations 103–5
anthropology: contribution to drinking studies 2, 99, 123

Balfour, Arthur MP 162, 163, 195
Bamford, Samuel 72
Banbury, Oxfordshire 47, 136
Barclay 51
Barclay, Edwyn 85
Barclay Perkins 85
bars 56
Bass 23
beer 11–14, 18–19, 22, 24, 57, 107; Bass 22–3; bottled 19, 22, 25; Burton 14, 19, 44; in cans 25, 57; Guinness, 22–3, 101, 102; keg 24; lager 24; table 46; Whitbread 22; Worthington 107; *see also* porter
beerhouses: customers 78; keepers 47, 51–2; numbers 46, 48–9; physical 78, 79
Beer Orders 57
Beer Trade Protection Society 48
Berkeley, Elizabeth, Countess of Warwick 39
Better Regulation Task Force 202
binge drinking 1, 125, 128, 132, 135, 136, 202
Birmingham 44, 51, 53, 55, 80, 82, 84, 85–6, 194, 200
Bolton, Lancashire 23, 78, 81, 110, 112, 127
*bona fide* traveller 195
Booth, Charles 20, 21, 49, 81, 84, 106, 161, 198
Boswell, James 74
bottle parties 50
Bradford, West Yorkshire 21, 45, 80, 81, 104, 106, 130, 155, 156, 163, 199
branded outlets 56, 87
Brewers' Society 23
brewing: private 13, 18, 20, 38, 42
brewing: by publicans 13, 51–2
brewing industry 13, 14, 43, 46, 50–5, 57–8, 108; advertising 23; Big Six 57; micro breweries 58; and tied-house system 51–5, 57; towns noted for 14; *see also* individual firms
British and Foreign Temperance Society 155
British Beer and Pub Association 55
British Workman Movement 163
Brontë, Branwell, 102
Burton on Trent 14, 52–3

Campaign for Real Ale (CAMRA) 24
Cardiff, 50

Central Control Board (Liquor Traffic) 199–200
Central Public House Trust Association 164
Chamberlain, Arthur 194
Chamberlain, Joseph MP 163–4
Church of England Temperance Society 157, 158
chocolate 9, 16
cider 10, 14, 24, 107
clubs: bogus 49–50; Club and Institute Union 49, 163; night 50, 56; numbers 49, 56; private 49; working men's 49, 84, 86, 162
coffee 9, 16, 154
coffee houses 41, 74
coffee taverns 163
counter attractions to pub 163
Coventry 21, 107
Crewe 132

D'Abernon, Lord 199
Dalrymple, Donald MP 164
Davies, Reverend David 18
Defoe, Daniel 1, 14, 41, 43, 71
disinterested management 163–4, 167, 199
Disraeli, Benjamin MP 101
distillers 42
Distillers Company of London 16
Dobson, Frank MP 1
Dorchester, Dorset 189
Dostoevsky, Fyodor 129
drink driving 168–9
drinking: English reputation for 1; other national reputations for 1–2; and public health 169–70
drinking cultures: European 2; French 107, 108; Mexican 107; northern 108; north-east 108; Scottish 107
Drink Question 160; and Conservatives 162; and Labour 162, 167–8; and Liberals 157, 162; and socialists 161, 164
drunken comportment 123, 126
drunkenness 105–6; biblical references to 147; defining 122–5; as disease 151, 164–5; history of 127–36; as legal defence 123; policing 131–2; and Puritans 147–9; reasons for 125–7; as sin 147, 150; as social threat 149–50; vocabulary of 123–5
drunks: in army and navy 128–9; in comedy acts 122–3; in Dickens 122; servants 129; social class of 132–3; women 133, 136, 165; young 134–6; *see also* binge drinking
Dubonnet, Tonic Wine 102

Eden, Frederick 18
Engels, Friedrich 129, 161
Enterprise Inns 58
European School Survey Project on Alcohol and Other Drugs (ESPAD) 25–6
Excise 185, 187, 1909

Fielding, Sir John 74
First World War: effects of 22, 54–5, 112, 166–7, 198–200
Forbes, Henry 155
France 2, 107, 213
Franklin, Benjamin 14

Gales 50
Gilbey 50
gin palaces 44, 77–8, 80
gin shops (and other names for) 40, 44, 76–80
Gladstone, W. E. MP 17–18, 20, 47, 162, 193, 194, 196
Gothenburg 163
Greene King 57
Guinness 22–3

Hales, Stephen 151
Halifax, West Yorkshire 49, 55–6, 84, 156, 167
Harcourt, Sir William 157
Harrison, William 12–13, 14, 71
Harrogate, North Yorkshire 45, 73
Hayward, Rob, MP 184
Hogarth, William 151–2
Home Office Working Group on Licence Transfers 201–2
hotels 44, 49

Ilkley, West Yorkshire 127
illegal beer shops 45
illicit distilling 45
Ind Coope 24
inebriate reformatories 165
inns: customers 73, 78; functions 39, 72–3; keepers 39; numbers 39; physical 73–4
Italy 213

Jellinek, E. M. 99, 169
Jenkins, Roy, MP 109
Johnson, Samuel 74, 102
Joynson-Hicks, Sir William MP 50
Justices' Clerks Society 202

Keighley, West Yorkshire 112
Kerr, Norman 1, 165

King, Gregory 13
Kirby Lonsdale 132
Kirby Stephen 132

Lawson, Sir Wilfrid MP 157, 161, 163
Ledermann, Sully 169
Leeds, West Yorkshire 51, 77, 110, 127, 129, 135
Leeds Licensed Beersellers' Association 48
Legislation, general: 1495 Vagabonds 187; 1829 Metropolitan Police 131; 1835 Highways 168; 1839 Metropolitan Police 131; 1843 London Hackney Carriages 168; 1847 Town Police Clauses 131, 168; 1908 Children 185, 196; 1913 Mental Deficiency 165; 1914 Defence of the Realm (DORA) 198; 1967 Road Safety 169
legislation licensing: 1552 on alehouses 149, 188; 1553 on taverns 149, 188; 1606 on drunkenness 131, 149; 1830 Beer 46, 155, 192–3; 1860 Refreshment Houses and Wine Licences 18, 193; 1869 Wine and Beerhouse 48–9, 83, 193; 1879 Habitual Drunkards 164; 1881 Welsh Sunday Closing 195; 1898 Inebriates 165; 1901 Child Messenger 196; 1913 Temperance (Scotland) 157; 1952 Customs and Excise 200; children and young people 196, 200, 202; gin 190; local option 167; on opening hours 193, 195, 199, 201; permissive prohibition 157; on sporting events 202; on use of licensed premises 195–6; *see also* individual licensing acts
Licensing Acts: 1729 189; 1753 190; 1828 192; 1872 131, 132, 162, 165, 168, 193–5; 1874 195; 1902 49, 195; 1904 53, 163, 165, 195; 1910 192; 1921 165, 200; 1949 201; 1953 200; 1961 56, 201; 1964 202; 2003 2, 186, 202–3; *see also* off licences
liver-cirrhosis mortality 113
Liverpool 49, 52, 53, 77, 104, 131, 163, 193, 212
Livesey, Joseph 155, 156
Livingstone, Mary 102
Lloyd George, David MP, 166
London 21, 72, 83, 86, 87, 104, 105, 131, 200

Major, John, MP 108
Manchester 44, 45, 51, 52, 84, 104
Mathew, Father 156
mead 10

Methuen Treaty 1703 15
milk 10
Mitchells and Butlers 85–6
Mompesson, Sir Giles 188
More, Hannah 154
*Morning Advertiser* 48
music halls 83

national efficiency 160, 167, 198
need for judgement in licensing 201–2
Nevile, Sydney 85
Newcastle 26, 53, 55, 135, 163, 164
night-time economy 26, 87, 135–6
Norwich 40, 73, 81, 83, 190
Nottingham 135

off licences 22, 23, 25, 50, 56–7, 201; *see also* supermarkets
Oldham, Lancashire 49
Owen, Robert 161
Oxford 39, 43

parliamentary inquiries: 1816 Police of the Metropolis 130; 1817 Police of the Metropolis and Licensing 184, 191; 1818 Public Breweries 191; 1834 Drunkenness 130, 163; 1852 Wine Duties 17, 78; 1872 Habitual Drunkards 164; 1877–9 Intemperance 130, 133, 193; 1896–9 Licensing Laws 130, 162; 1929–31 Licensing 133–4, 168; 1972–3 Liquor Licensing (Erroll) 201; 1988–9 Supply of Beer (MMC) 57; and drunkenness 129
Peel, Lord 162
People's Refreshment House Association 164
Pepys, Samuel 15, 41, 73–4, 76, 109, 125–6
perry 10, 24
piment 10
Pitt, William MP 17
Place, Francis 130
porter 14, 16, 50–1
Portsmouth, Hampshire 74, 80
Portugal 15
'pot houses' 44
pub companies (pubcos) 58
public houses: numbers 44, 48–9, 51; publicans 47–8, 51–4, 84; tied 51–4; use of term 43–4; *see also* pubs
pubs: customers 81; and English identity 107–8; functions 82–3; improved 84–6, 199, 200; Irish themed 87; as local 86; meals at 56; numbers

55–6; order in 83–4; physical 78–80; sociability 110–11; tied 57; use of term 48; and women 81–2, 84–6, 88; and young people 87
punch houses 40
Punch Taverns 58

Rabelais, François 1
railway refreshment rooms 49
rational recreation 163
Redding, Cyrus 17
Reformation: effects of 103, 104–5, 128, 150
Reformation of Manners societies 150
regulation of drink: development of 187–92; medieval precedents 187; policing of 196–8; purposes of 184–6, 203; restrictive 193–6; of structure of premises 195; twentieth century 200–3
resale price maintenance abolition 56
residential licences 56
respectability 21, 47–8, 134
restaurant licences 56
Rowntree, Joseph and Sherwell, Arthur 19, 161, 164
Royal Proclamation 1787 153

Saint Monday 105
Scharlieb, Mary 161
Second World War: effects on drinking 23–4, 200; and women in pubs 86
shades (saloons) 49
Sharpe v. Wakefield 1891 194
Sheridan, Richard 17
Shrewsbury 40
Smith, Sydney 167, 192
social Darwinism 160, 198
Society for the Study and Cure of Inebriety 161, 165
soft drinks 9
Solly, Reverend Henry 110
Somerset, Lady Henry 158
Southampton 40, 43, 47
Spain 213
spas 73
spirits 15–17, 19, 22, 23–4, 45, 57; arrack 16; brandy 15, 16, 41; gin 15–16, 23, 24, 41, 101, 150–1; punch 15, 16, 41; rum 16; vodka 24; whisky 23, 45
state purchase of the liquor trade 167
Stocks 52
supermarkets 56–7

taverns: customers 73–4; losing distinctiveness 41, 74; numbers 40; physical 74; and sex 74
taxation of drink 185

Taylor, John 102
tea 9, 16, 18, 23, 154
temperance movement: activities 155–6; and Anglicanism 150; anti-spirits 154–5; Band of Hope 156, 158–9, 167; decline 167; effects 165–6; generalized sentiment of 158–60, 165; literature 159; and nonconformity 157, 167; origins 152–4; prohibition 157–8; societies 155–6; teetotal Chartists 161; total abstinence 155–6; and women 158
Terling, Essex 189
Tetley 50
Timothy Taylor 108
tipling (or tippling) houses 40, 149
tobacco 20, 22
Trotter, Thomas 151
Truman 51

United Kingdom Alliance for the Suppression of the Liquor Traffic 157
United States of America 3; anti-spirits movement 155; college students and drinking 126; Maine Law 157; prohibition 3

vermouth 101
Victoria Wine Company 50
Vintners' Company 49, 74, 188
viticulture in England 12

Walpole, Sir Robert MP 15
water 10, 100, 154
Waters Butler, William 85
Wellington, Duke of 46
Wesley, John 153
Wetherspoon, J. D. 56, 87, 88
Whitbread 24, 25, 157
Whitby, North Yorkshire 80
Whittaker, Thomas 130, 155
Wilberforce, William 153
Wilson, Thomas 151
wine: consumption 12–13, 14–15, 17, 23–5, 57; Australian 23, 24; claret 15, 109; Mediterranean 12; port 15, 17, 18, 23, 107, 108, 109; sherry 17, 18, 23; South African 23; sweets 23 (other types included under consumption)
Woodforde, Parson James 100, 101
Woolton, Lord 168
Wordsworth, Dorothy and William 72

York 39, 40, 41, 44, 55, 105, 200

Zouch, Reverend Henry 152–3